# FEMINISM
# AND
# PHILOSOPHY

# Feminism and Philosophy

*Edited by*

MARY VETTERLING-BRAGGIN

FREDERICK A. ELLISTON

JANE ENGLISH

1978

LITTLEFIELD, ADAMS & CO.

Totowa, New Jersey

Reprinted 1978

**Library of Congress Cataloging in Publication Data**
Main entry under title:

Feminism and philosophy.

(Littlefield, Adams quality paperback ; 335)
Bibliographies.

1.  Feminism—United States—Addresses, essays, lectures.   2.   Sex role—Addresses, essays, lectures. 3.   Sex discrimination against women—United States— Addresses, essays, lectures.   4.   Women's rights— United States—Addresses, essays, lectures.   I.   Vetter- ling-Braggin, Mary.   II.   Elliston, Frederick. III.   English, Jane, 1947–

HQ1426.F45        301.41′2′0973        77–24207
ISBN 0–8226–0335–7

PRINTED IN THE UNITED STATES OF AMERICA

# Contents

Preface     ix

General Introduction     xi


PART I:   FEMINISM

Introduction     1

Political Philosophies of Women's Liberation     5
    ALISON JAGGAR

Toward a Phenomenology of Feminist Consciousness     22
    SANDRA LEE BARTKY

*Further References*     35


PART II:   SEX ROLES AND GENDER

Introduction     39

Androgyny As an Ideal for Human Development     45
    ANN FERGUSON

Two Forms of Androgynism     70
    JOYCE TREBILCOT

The Feminine As a Universal                                    79
  ANNE DICKASON

*Further References*                                           101


PART III:    SEXISM IN ORDINARY LANGUAGE

Introduction                                                  105

Sexism and Semantics                                          109
  PATRICK GRIM

Traits and Genderization                                      117
  ELIZABETH L. BEARDSLEY

The Myth of the Neutral "Man"                                 124
  JANICE MOULTON

The Hidden Joke: Generic Uses of Masculine
Terminology                                                   138
  CAROLYN KORSMEYER

Linguistics and Feminism                                      154
  VIRGINIA VALIAN

*Further References*                                          167


PART IV:    EQUAL OPPORTUNITY AND
            PREFERENTIAL HIRING

Introduction                                                  171

How Do We Know When Opportunities Are Equal?                  177
  ONORA O'NEILL

Preferential Treatment                                        190
  LAWRENCE CROCKER

On Preferential Hiring                                        210
  ROBERT K. FULLINWIDER

Limits to the Justification of Reverse Discrimination         225
  ALAN H. GOLDMAN

*Further References*                                          242

PART V:   MARRIAGE

Introduction                                                   245

On the Nature and Value of Marriage                            249
    LYLA H. O'DRISCOLL

Liberalism and Marriage Law                                    264
    SARA ANN KETCHUM

The Myth of the Complete Person                                277
    JOSEPH E. BARNHART and MARY ANN BARNHART

The Separation of Marriage and Family                          291
    JOSEPH MARGOLIS and CLORINDA MARGOLIS

*Further References*                                           302


PART VI:   RAPE

Introduction                                                   309

Rape: The All-American Crime                                   313
    SUSAN GRIFFIN

Rape and Respect                                               333
    CAROLYN M. SHAFER and MARILYN FRYE

What's Wrong with Rape                                         347
    PAMELA FOA

Coercion and Rape: The State As a Male Protection
Racket                                                         360
    SUSAN RAE PETERSON

*Further References*                                           372


PART VII:   ABORTION

Introduction                                                   377

The Roman Catholic Doctrine of Therapeutic Abortion            385
    SUSAN T. NICHOLSON

One Step Forward, Two Steps Backward: Abortion
and Ethical Theory                                            408
    ELIZABETH RAPAPORT and PAUL SAGAL

Abortion and the Concept of a Person                          417
    JANE ENGLISH

Abortion and the Quality of Life                              429
    HOWARD COHEN

*Further References*                                          441

Notes on Contributors                                         447

# Preface

Ten years ago, the male editors of the *Saturday Evening Post*, then a flourishing magazine, asked me to find out whether there was any truth to the rumor that women are being kept down in business. I hadn't given the proposition much thought at the time. But I dutifully researched the idea and what I found out made me furious. The *Post* then refused to buy the resultant article because, they said, I had failed to learn that what women really wanted was home and family.

*Born Female*, the book I wrote about my research, appeared in 1968. Since then, there has been a massive national consciousness raising. In 1977, *Born Female* appears to be a middle-of-the-road statement about the female condition in America. But it grieves me to report that most of what I found then still holds true of the female condition today. Women still need enforcement of equal employment opportunity laws, laws that recognize the contribution homemakers make to a marriage, and special programs to help women who have missed opportunities because of past discrimination and family responsibilities. We still need an end to discrimination in education and training, health care, housing, credit, and insurance. And we still need more women in the media, and child care on the basis of the ability to pay.

It is, in short, still necessary to identify and re-identify the problems facing women in today's world. But we must also consider the means for solving these problems, both politically and morally. *Feminism and Philosophy* is an unusual book in its approach to the moral issues. Rather than espousing a given type or style of feminism, the purpose of the book is to examine the deep and controversial questions discussed by all feminists: preferential hiring, sexism, abortion, rape, and marriage.

*Feminism and Philosophy* is must reading for any person who would like not only to identify and clarify his or her position on these issues, but who would like to consider some justifications for (and pitfalls of) that position.

CAROLINE BIRD

# General Introduction

Since the reemergence of the women's liberation movement in the 1960s, interest in the nature, history, and resolution of women's oppression has rapidly expanded and intensified. Yet no single work published to date provides for a full discussion of both sides of the philosophical issues of particular interest to feminists and anti-feminists alike. These issues are: feminism as an ethical theory, preferential hiring and equal opportunity, marriage, abortion, rape, sex roles and gender, and sexism in ordinary language. Our aim in this book is to provide a collection of essays by contemporary philosophers which ranges over all the feminist issues and which is readily intelligible to professionals and nonprofessionals alike.

Part I introduces the reader to some of the basic tenets of feminist theory and its recent history. This is followed by a section on the masculine-feminine distinction examining and questioning the ways in which this distinction has become embodied in social practices and institutions. Part III raises the question of whether ordinary language is sexist and, if so, asks whether there is a simple way for determining when it is. It also discusses whether language ought to be purged of sexist connotations. Part IV assesses feminist demands for equal opportunity, focusing on educational and occupational benefits. It considers whether such demands entail preferential hiring and, if so, whether it is ever justified. Part V evaluates marriage as a viable option for the liberated woman, and considers alternative life styles if it is not. The last two sections deal with abortion and rape.

Appended to each section is a comprehensive list of further references which lists relevant primary and secondary materials. Those that are of special interest to philosophers are marked by an asterisk.

This collection is a response to the needs of philosophers in particular, academics in general, and various segments of the community at large. We hope that it will help to aid, abet, and document the growing interest in human sexuality in general, and feminist concerns in particular.

M. V. B.

F. E.

J. E.

# Part I
# Feminism

# Part I
# Feminism

## *Introduction*

The feminism of the late 19th and early 20th centuries focused on the acquisition of a few basic political rights and liberties for women, such as the right of married women to own property and enter into contracts, the right of defendants to have women on juries, and the crucial right to vote. A campaign lasting a century and involving violence culminated in the right for some women to vote in England in 1918 and for all women to vote in the United States in 1920. However, the decades that followed revealed that women had been suffering from more than these basic political inequalities.

The feminism of the 1960s and 1970s seeks to discover and change the more subtle and deep-seated causes of women's oppression. Some of these are still to be found in the legal system, such as unequal labor, marriage, and divorce laws.[1] More pervasive are the widespread attitudes about women's proper or natural duties and the proper or natural relations between the sexes. Feminists have turned to the task of discovering which attitudes and beliefs these are. Making people aware of them is the monumental effort of "raising the consciousness" of an entire culture.

From childhood on, we are all bombarded with beliefs and attitudes that proclaim and help perpetuate women's inferior status. Some of these are not hard to discover and document, such as sex-role stereotyping in textbooks, unequal pay for equal work, and the traditional division of labor within the family. Other attitudes are more subtle: for example, hoping that a couple's first child will be a boy, thinking of a wife's salary as going to buy "extras" rather than as supporting the family, and expecting men to take the initiative in dating.[2] Even the pronoun structure of English suggests that women are different, that they are "other," not fitting the paradigm of "man."[3]

It is easy to think of discrimination as something other people do and to call for them to change their attitudes. It is harder to recognize and change one's own beliefs. SANDRA BARTKY investigates the extent to which feminism entails that a woman change her actions, her attitudes about herself, and her relationships with both men and women. (Although she restricts her discussion to feminist women, a related account could be developed of the effect of feminism on men.) One dramatic difference between the feminism of the 1960s and 1970s and that of the suffragettes is that the battle now has an internal front line. Recognizing one's own self-worth and abilities and standing up for one's rights can be a profound and difficult change to make in one's life.[4]

On the external battlefront, there are conflicting views as to what needs to be changed. ALISON JAGGAR describes and compares six major positions on women's liberation. They disagree not merely about the means that should be used, but about what equality and justice call for. Radical feminists, following Shulamith Firestone, agree with the conservatives that the source of women's oppression is fundamentally biological. They claim that equality requires technological means to relieve women from the burden of childbearing. They also look forward to the end of exclusive heterosexual relationships. Classical Marxist feminists, in contrast, see capitalism rather than biology as the primary cause of women's oppression, and they contend that the end of capitalism will make true monogamous relationships possible for the first time. They see economic inequalities as the central problem. Liberals, on the other hand, believe that changing discriminatory laws and practices, along with the unequal division of household labor, can liberate women (and men) without necessarily changing either capitalism or the technology of reproduction. Equal opportunity for individuals within the existing system is their central goal.[5]

Thus there is no single view that can be labeled "feminism." But these varying positions do share several basic in-

sights. One is that profound changes in traditional social structures such as the family will be needed before women are in an
important sense equal. Another is that, whether as cause or as
effect, the economic role and power of women will change.
Finally, fundamental attitudes and personal relationships must
also be affected if the improvement is to be lasting.

J. E.

## NOTES

1. For a catalogue of legal differences, see Shana Alexander, *State
   by State Guide to Women's Legal Rights* (Los Angeles: Wollstonecraft, 1975). Legal inequalities in marriage are discussed
   by Sara Ann Ketchum in Part V.
2. These sex-role stereotypes are the subject of Part II.
3. Simone de Beauvoir has developed this concept of "other." See
   *The Second Sex*, trans. H. M. Parshley (New York: Knopf,
   1953), especially the Introduction. For a treatment of the uses of
   "he," "man," etc., see "Sexism in Ordinary Language," Part III.
4. For example, see Alix Nelson, "How I Learned to Stop Being
   Grateful and Stand Up for My Rights," *Ms.*, June 1973; Thomas
   E. Hill, Jr., "Servility and Self-Respect," *Monist* 57 (1973):
   87–104.
5. Articulating this ideal has led to a debate about what constitutes
   equal opportunity. See Part IV.

Alison Jaggar

# Political Philosophies of Women's Liberation

Feminists are united by a belief that the unequal and inferior social status of women is unjust and needs to be changed. But they are deeply divided about what changes are required. The deepest divisions are not differences about strategy or the kinds of tactics that will best serve women's interests; instead, they are differences about what *are* women's interests, what constitutes women's liberation.

Within the women's liberation movement, several distinct ideologies can be discerned. All[1] believe that justice requires freedom and equality for women, but they differ on such basic philosophical questions as the proper account of freedom and equality, the functions of the state, and the notion of what constitutes human, and especially female, nature. In what follows, I shall outline the feminist ideologies which are currently most influential and show how these give rise to differences on some particular issues. Doing this will indicate why specific debates over feminist questions cannot be settled in isolation but can only be resolved in the context of a theoretical framework derived from reflection on the fundamental issues of social and political philosophy.

© 1977 by Alison M. Jaggar. This paper is a revised version of my "Four Views of Women's Liberation," read at the American Philosophical Association meeting, Western Division, 4–6 May, 1972.

## THE CONSERVATIVE VIEW

This is the position against which all feminists are in reaction. In brief, it is the view that the differential treatment of women, as a group, is not unjust. Conservatives admit, of course, that some individual women do suffer hardships, but they do not see this suffering as part of the systematic social oppression of women. Instead, the clear differences between women's and men's social roles are rationalized in one of two ways. Conservatives either claim that the female role is not inferior to that of the male, or they argue that women are inherently better adapted than men to the traditional female sex role. The former claim advocates a kind of sexual apartheid, typically described by such phrases as "complementary but equal"; the latter postulates an inherent inequality between the sexes.[2]

All feminists reject the first claim, and most feminists, historically, have rejected the second. However, it is interesting to note that, as we shall see later, some modern feminists have revived the latter claim.

Conservative views come in different varieties, but they all have certain fundamentals in common. All claim that men and women should fulfill different social functions, that these differences should be enforced by law where opinion and custom are insufficient, and that such action may be justified by reference to innate differences between men and women. Thus all sexual conservatives presuppose that men and women are inherently unequal in abilities, that the alleged difference in ability implies a difference in social function and that one of the main tasks of the state is to ensure that the individual perform his or her proper social function. Thus, they argue, social differentiation between the sexes is not unjust, since justice not only allows but requires us to treat unequals unequally.

## LIBERAL FEMINISM

In speaking of liberal feminism, I am referring to that tradition which received its classic expression in J. S. Mill's *The Subjection of Women* and which is alive today in various "moderate" groups, such as the National Organization for Women, which agitate for legal reform to improve the status of women.

The main thrust of the liberal feminist's argument is that an individual woman should be able to determine her social role with as great freedom as does a man. Though women now have the vote, the liberal sees that we are still subject to many constraints, legal as well as customary, which hinder us from success in the public worlds of politics, business and the professions. Consequently the liberal views women's liberation as the elimination of those constraints and the achievement of equal civil rights.

Underlying the liberal argument is the belief that justice requires that the criteria for allocating individuals to perform a particular social function should be grounded in the individual's ability to perform the tasks in question. The use of criteria such as "race, sex, religion, national origin or ancestry"[3] will normally not be directly relevant to most tasks. Moreover, in conformity with the traditional liberal stress on individual rights, the liberal feminist insists that each person should be considered separately in order that an outstanding individual should not be penalized for deficiencies that her sex as a whole might possess.[4]

This argument is buttressed by the classic liberal belief that there should be a minimum of state intervention in the affairs of the individual. Such a belief entails rejection of the paternalistic view that women's weakness requires that we be specially protected.[5] Even if relevant differences between women and men in general could be demonstrated, the existence of those differences still would not constitute a sufficient reason for allowing legal restrictions on women as a group. Even apart from the possibility of penalizing an outstanding individual, the liberal holds that women's own good sense or, in the last resort, our incapacity to do the job will render legal prohibitions unnecessary.[6]

From this sketch it is clear that the liberal feminist interprets equality to mean that each individual, regardless of sex, should have an equal opportunity to seek whatever social position she or he wishes. Freedom is primarily the absence of legal constraints to hinder women in this enterprise. However, the modern liberal feminist recognizes that equality and freedom, construed in the liberal way, may not always be compatible. Hence, the modern liberal feminist differs from the traditional one in believing not only that laws should not discriminate against women, but that they should be used to make discrimination illegal. Thus she would outlaw unequal pay scales, prejudice in the admission of women to job-training programs and professional schools, and discrimination by employers in hiring practices. She would also outlaw such things as discrimination by finance companies in the granting of loans, mortgages, and insurance to women.

In certain areas, the modern liberal even appears to advocate laws which discriminate in favor of women. For instance, she may support the preferential hiring of women over men, or alimony for women unqualified to work outside the home. She is likely to justify her apparent inconsistency by claiming that such differential treatment is necessary to remedy past inequalities—but that it is only a temporary measure. With regard to (possibly paid) maternity leaves and the employer's obligation to reemploy a woman after such a leave, the liberal argues that the bearing of children has at least as good a claim to be regarded as a social service as does a man's military or jury obligation, and that childbearing should therefore carry corresponding rights to protection. The liberal also usually advocates the repeal of laws restricting contraception and abortion, and may demand measures to encourage the establishment of private day-care centers. However, she points out that none of these demands, nor the father's payment of child support, should really be regarded as discrimination in favor of women. It is only the customary assignment of responsibility for children to their mothers which it makes it possible to overlook the fact that fathers have an equal obligation to provide and care for their children. Women's traditional responsibility for child care is culturally determined, not biologically inevitable— except for breast-feeding, which is now optional. Thus the liberal argues that if women are to participate in the world outside the home on equal terms with men, not only must our reproductive capacity come under our own control but, if we have children, we must be able to share the responsibility for raising them. In return, as an extension of the same principle of equal responsibility, the modern liberal supports compulsory military service for women so long as it is obligatory for men.

Rather than assuming that every apparent difference in interests and abilities between the sexes is innate, the liberal recognizes that such differences, if they do not result entirely from our education, are at least greatly exaggerated by it. By giving both sexes the same education, whether it be cooking or carpentry, the liberal claims that she is providing the only environment in which individual potentialities (and, indeed, genuine sexual differences) can emerge. She gives little weight to the possible charge that in doing this she is not liberating women but only imposing a different kind of conditioning. At the root of the liberal tradition is a deep faith in the autonomy of the individual which is incapable of being challenged within that framework.

In summary, then, the liberal views liberation for women as the freedom to determine our own social role and to compete with men on terms that are as equal as possible. She sees every individual as being engaged in constant competition with every other in order to maximize her or his own self-interest, and she claims that the function of the state is to see that such competition is fair by enforcing "equality of opportunity." The liberal does not believe that it is necessary to change the whole existing social structure in order to achieve women's liberation. Nor does she see it as being achieved simultaneously for all women; she believes that individual women may liberate themselves long before their condition is attained by all. Finally, the liberal claims that her concept of women's liberation also involves liberation for men, since men are not only removed from a privileged position but they are also freed from having to accept the entire responsibility for such things as the support of their families and the defense of their country.

## CLASSICAL MARXIST FEMINISM

On the classical Marxist view, the oppression of women is, historically and currently, a direct result of the institution of private property; therefore, it can only be ended by the abolition of that institution. Consequently, feminism must be seen as part of a broader struggle to achieve a communist society. Feminism is one reason for communism. The long-term interests of women are those of the working class.

For Marxists, everyone is oppressed by living in a society where a small class of individuals owns the means of production and hence is enabled to dominate the lives of the majority who are forced to sell their labor power in order to survive. Women have an equal interest with men in eliminating such a class society. However, Marxists also recognize that women suffer special forms of oppression to which men are *not* subject, and hence, insofar as this oppression is rooted in capitalism, women have additional reasons for the overthrow of that economic system.

Classical Marxists believe that the special oppression of women results primarily from our traditional position in the family. This excludes women from participation in "public" production and relegates us to domestic work in the "private" world of the home. From its inception right up to the present day, monogamous marriage was designed to perpetuate the consolidation of wealth in the hands of a few. Those few are men. Thus, for Marxists, an analysis of the family brings out the inseparability of class society from male supremacy. From the very beginning of surplus production, "the sole exclusive aims of monogamous marriage were to make the man supreme in the family, and to propagate, as the future heirs to his wealth, children indisputably his own."[7] Such marriage is "founded on the open or concealed domestic slavery of the wife,"[8] and is characterized by the familiar double standard which requires sexual fidelity from the woman but not from the man.

Marxists do not claim, of course, that women's oppression is a creation of capitalism. But they do argue that the advent of capitalism intensified the degradation of women and that the continuation of capitalism requires the perpetuation of this degradation. Capitalism and male supremacy each reinforce the other. Among the ways in which sexism benefits the capitalist system are: by providing a supply of cheap labor for industry and hence exerting a downward pressure on all wages; by increasing the demand for the consumption goods on which women are conditioned to depend; and by allocating to women, for no direct pay, the performance of such socially necessary but unprofitable tasks as food preparation, domestic maintenance and the care of the children, the sick and the old.[9]

This analysis indicates the directions in which classical Marxists believe that women must move. "The first condition for the liberation of the wife is to bring the whole female sex back into public industry."[10] Only then will a wife cease to be economically dependent on her husband. But for woman's entry into public industry to be possible, fundamental social changes are necessary: all the work which women presently do—food preparation, child care, nursing, etc.—must come within the sphere of public production. Thus, whereas the liberal feminist advocates an egalitarian marriage, with each spouse shouldering equal responsibility for domestic work and economic support, the classical Marxist feminist believes that the liberation of women requires a more radical change in the family. Primarily, women's liberation requires that the economic functions performed by the family should be undertaken by the state. Thus the state should provide child care centers, public eating places, hospital facilities, etc. But all this, of course, could happen only under socialism. Hence it is only under socialism that married women will be able to participate fully in public life and end the situation where "within the family [the husband] is the bourgeois and the wife represents the proletariat."[11]

It should be noted that "the abolition of the monogamous family as the economic unit of society"[12] does not necessitate its disappearance as a social unit. Since "sexual love is by its nature exclusive,"[13] marriage will continue, but now it will no longer resemble an economic contract, as it has done hitherto in the property-owning classes. Instead, it will be based solely on "mutual inclination"[14] between a woman and a man who are now in reality, and not just formally, free and equal.

It is clear that classical Marxist feminism is based on very different philosophical presuppositions from those of liberal feminism. Freedom is viewed not just as the absence of discrimination against women but rather as freedom from the coercion of economic necessity. Similarly, equality demands not mere equality of opportunity to compete against other individuals but rather approximate equality in the satisfaction of material needs. Hence, the classical Marxist feminist's view of the function of the state is very different from the view of the liberal feminist. Ultimately, the Marxist pays at least lip service to the belief that the state is an instrument of class oppression which eventually will wither away. In the meantime, she believes that it should undertake far more than the minimal liberal function of setting up fair rules for the economic race. Instead, it should take over the means of production and also assume those economic responsibilities that capitalism assigned to the individual family and that placed that woman in a position of dependence on the man. This view of the state presupposes a very different account of human nature from that held by the liberal. Instead of seeing the individual as fundamentally concerned with the maximization of her or his own self-interest, the classical Marxist feminist believes that the selfish and competitive aspects of our natures are the result of their systematic perversion in an acquisitive society. Viewing human nature as flexible and as reflecting the economic organization of society, she argues that it is necessary for women (indeed for everybody) to be comprehensively reeducated, and to learn that ultimately individuals have common rather than competing goals and interests.

Since she sees women's oppression as a function of the larger socioeconomic system, the classical Marxist feminist denies the possibility, envisaged by the liberal, of liberation for a few women on an individual level. However, she does agree with the liberal that women's liberation would bring liberation for men, too. Men's liberation would now be enlarged to include freedom from class oppression and from the man's traditional responsibility to "provide" for his family, a burden that under liberalism the man merely lightens by sharing it with his wife.

## RADICAL FEMINISM

Radical feminism is a recent attempt to create a new conceptual model for understanding the many different forms of the social phenomenon of oppression in terms of the basic concept of sexual oppression. It is formulated by such writers as Ti-Grace Atkinson and Shulamith Firestone.[15]

Radical feminism denies the liberal claim that the basis of women's oppression consists in our lack of political or civil rights; similarly, it rejects the classical Marxist belief that basically women are oppressed because they live in a class society. Instead, in what seems to be a startling regression to conservatism, the radical feminist claims that the roots of women's oppression are biological. She believes that the origin of women's subjection lies in the fact that, as a result of the weakness caused by childbearing, we became dependent on men for physical survival. Thus she speaks of the origin of the family in apparently conservative terms as being primarily a biological rather than a social or economic organization.[16] The radical feminist believes that the physical subjection of women by men was historically the most basic form of oppression, prior rather than secondary to the institution of private property and its corollary, class oppression.[17] Moreover, she believes that the power relationships which develop within the biological family provide a model for understanding all other types of oppression such as racism and class society. Thus she reverses the emphasis of the classical Marxist feminist by explaining the development of class society in terms of the biological family rather than explaining the development of the family in terms of class society. She believes that the battles against capitalism and against racism are both subsidiary to the more fundamental struggle against sexism.

Since she believes that the oppression of women is basically biological, the radical feminist concludes that our liberation requires a biological revolution. She believes that only now, for the first time in history, is technology making it possible for women to be liberated from the "fundamental inequality of the bearing and raising of children." It is achieving this through the development of techniques of artificial reproduction and the consequent possibility of diffusing the childbearing and child-raising role throughout society as a whole. Such a biological revolution is basic to the achievement of those important but secondary changes in our political, social and economic systems which will make possible the other prerequisites for women's liberation. As the radical feminist sees them, those other prerequisites are: the full self-determination, including economic independence, of women (and children); the total integration of women (and children) into all aspects of the larger society; and the freedom of all women (and children) to do whatever they wish to do sexually.[18]

Not only will technology snap the link between sex and reproduction and thus liberate women from our childbearing and child-raising function; the radical feminist believes that ultimately technology will liberate both sexes from the necessity to work. Individual economic burdens and dependencies will thereby be eliminated, along with the justification for compelling children to attend school. So both the biological and economic bases of the family will be removed by technology. The family's consequent disappearance will abolish the prototype of the social "role system,"[19] the most basic form, both historically and conceptually, of oppressive and authoritarian relationships. Thus, the radical feminist does not claim that women should be free to determine their own social roles: she believes instead that the whole "role system" must be abolished, even in its biological aspects.

The end of the biological family will also eliminate the need for sexual repression. Male homosexuality, lesbianism, and extramarital sexual intercourse will no longer be viewed in the liberal way as alternative options, outside the range of state regulation, in which the individual may or may not choose to participate. Nor will they be viewed, in the classical Marxist way, as unnatural vices, perversions resulting from the degrading influence of capitalist society.[20] Instead, even the categories of homosexuality and heterosexuality will be abandoned; the very "institution of sexual intercourse", where male and female each play a well-defined role, will disappear.[21] "Humanity could finally revert to its natural 'polymorphously perverse' sexuality."[22]

For the radical feminist, as for other feminists, justice requires freedom and equality for women. But for the radical feminist "equality" means not just equality under the law nor even equality in satisfaction of basic needs: rather, it means that women, like men, should not have to bear children. Correspondingly, the radical feminist conception of freedom requires not just that women should be free to compete, nor even that we should be free from material want and economic dependence on men; rather, freedom for women means that any woman is free to have close relationships with children without having to give birth to them. Politically, the radical feminist envisions an eventual "communistic anarchy,"[23] an ultimate abolition of the state. This will be achieved gradually, through an intermediate state of "cybernetic socialism" with household licenses to raise children and a guaranteed income for all. Perhaps surprisingly, in view of Freud's reputation among many feminists, the radical feminist conception of human nature is neo-Freudian. Firestone believes, with Freud, that "the crucial problem of modern life [is] sexuality."[24] Individuals are psychologically formed through their experience in the family, a family whose power relationships reflect the underlying biological realities of female (and childhood) dependence. But technology will smash the universality of Freudian psychology. The destruction of the biological family, never envisioned by Freud, will allow the emergence of new women and men, different from any people who have previously existed.

The radical feminist theory contains many interesting claims. Some of these look almost factual in character: they include the belief that pregnancy and childbirth are painful and unpleasant experiences, that sexuality is not naturally genital and heterosexual, and that technology may be controlled by men and women without leading to totalitarianism. Other presuppositions are more clearly normative: among them are the beliefs that technology should be used to eliminate all kinds of pain, that hard work is not in itself a virtue, that sexuality ought not to be institutionalized and, perhaps most controversial of all, that children have the same rights to self-determination as adults.

Like the other theories we have considered, radical feminism believes that women's liberation will bring benefits for men. According to this concept of women's liberation, not only will men be freed from the role of provider, but they will also participate on a completely equal basis in childbearing as well as child-rearing. Radical feminism, however, is the only theory which argues explicitly that women's liberation also necessitates children's liberation. Firestone explains that this is because "The heart of woman's oppression is her childbearing and child-rearing roles. And in turn children are defined in relation to this role and are psychologically formed by it; what they become as adults and the sorts of relationships they are able to form determine the society they will ultimately build."[25]

## NEW DIRECTIONS

Although the wave of excitement about women's liberation which arose in the late '60's has now subsided, the theoretical activity of feminists has continued. Since about 1970, it has advanced in two main directions: lesbian separatism and socialist feminism.

*Lesbian separatism* is a less a coherent and developed ideology than an emerging movement, like the broader feminist movement, within which different ideological strains can be detected. All lesbian separatists believe that the present situation of male supremacy requires that women should refrain from heterosexual relationships. But for some lesbian separatists, this is just a temporary necessity, whereas for others, lesbianism will always be required.

Needless to say, all lesbian separatists reject the liberal and the classical Marxist beliefs about sexual preferences; but some accept the radical feminist contention that ultimately it is unimportant whether one's sexual partner be male or female.[26] However, in the immediate context of a male-supremacist society, the lesbian separatist believes that one's sexual choice attains tremendous political significance. Lesbianism becomes a way of combating the overwhelming heterosexual ideology that perpetuates male supremacy.

Women . . . become defined as appendages to men so that there is a coherent ideological framework which says it is natural for women to create the surplus to take care of men and that men will do other things. Reproduction itself did not have to determine that. The fact that male supremacy developed the way it has and was institutionalized is an ideological creation. The ideology of heterosexuality, not the simple act of intercourse, is the whole set of assumptions which maintains the ideological power of men over women.[27]

Although this writer favors an ultimate de-institutionalization of sexual activity, her rejection of the claim that reproduction as such does not determine the inferior status of women clearly places her outside the radical feminist framework; indeed, she would identify her methodological approach as broadly Marxist. Some lesbian separatists are more radical, however. They argue explicitly for a matriarchal society which is "an affirmation of the power of female consciousness of the Mother."[28] Such matriarchists talk longingly about ancient matriarchal societies where women were supposed to have been physically strong, adept at self-defense, and the originators of such cultural advances as: the wheel, pottery, industry, leather working, metal working, fire, agriculture, animal husbandry, architecture, cities, decorative art, music, weaving, medicine, communal child care, dance, poetry, song, etc.[29] They claim that men were virtually excluded from these societies. Women's culture is compared favorably with later patriarchal cultures as being peaceful, egalitarian, vegetarian, and intellectually advanced. Matriarchal lesbian separatists would like to re-create a similar culture which would probably imitate the earlier ones in its exclusion of men as full members. Matriarchal lesbian separatists do not claim unequivocally that "men are genetically predisposed towards destruction and dominance,"[30] but, especially given the present research on the behavioral effects of the male hormone testosterone,[31] they think it is a possibility that lesbians must keep in mind.

*Socialist feminists* believe that classical Marxism and radical feminism each have both insights and deficiencies. The task of socialist feminism is to construct a theory that avoids the weaknesses of each but incorporates its (and other) insights. There is space here for only a brief account of some of the main points of this developing theory.

Socialist feminists reject the basic radical feminist contention that liberation for women requires the abolition of childbirth.

Firestone's view is criticized as ahistorical, anti-dialectical, and utopian. Instead, socialist feminists accept the classical Marxist contention that socialism is the main precondition for women's liberation. But though socialism is necessary, socialist feminists do not believe that it is sufficient. Sexism can continue to exist despite public ownership of the means of production. The conclusion that socialist feminists draw is that it is necessary to resort to direct cultural action in order to develop a specifically feminist consciousness in addition to transforming the economic base. Thus their vision is totalistic, requiring "transformation of the entire fabric of social relationships."[32]

In rejecting the radical feminist view that the family is based on biological conditions, socialist feminists turn toward the classical Marxist account of monogamy as being based "not on natural but on economic conditions."[33] But they view the classical Marxist account as inadequate, overly simple. Juliet Mitchell[34] argues that the family should be analyzed in a more detailed, sophisticated, and historically specific way in terms of the separate, though interrelated, functions that women perform within it: production, reproduction, sexuality, and the socialization of the young.

Socialist feminists agree with classical Marxists that women's liberation requires the entry of women into public production. But this in itself is not sufficient. It is also necessary that women have access to the more prestigious and less deadening jobs and to supervisory and administrative positions. There should be no "women's work" within public industry.[35]

In classical Marxist theory, "productive labor" is viewed as the production of goods and services within the market economy. Some socialist feminists believe that this account of productiveness obscures the socially vital character of the labor that women perform in the home. They argue that, since it is clearly impossible under capitalism to bring all women into public production, individuals (at least as an interim measure) should be paid a wage for domestic work. This reform would dignify the position of housewives, reduce their dependence on their husbands and make plain their objective position, minimized by classical Marxists, as an integral part of the working class.[36] Not all socialist feminists accept this position, however, and the issue is extremely controversial at the time of this writing.

One of the main insights of the feminist movement has been

that "the personal is political." Socialist feminists are sensitive to the power relations involved in male/female interaction and believe that it is both possible and necessary to begin changing these, even before the occurrence of a revolution in the owner-ship of the means of production. Thus, socialist feminists rec-ognize the importance of a "subjective factor" in revolutionary change and reject the rigid economic determinism that has characterized many classical Marxists. They are sympathetic to attempts by individuals to change their life styles and to share responsibility for each other's lives, even though they recognize that such attempts can never be entirely successful within a capitalist context. They also reject the sexual puritanism in-herent in classical Marxism, moving closer to the radical femi-nist position in this regard.

Clearly there are sharp differences between socialist feminism and most forms of lesbian separatism. The two have been dealt with together in this section only because each is still a devel-oping theory and because it is not yet clear how far either represents the creation of a new ideology and how far it is simply an extension of an existing ideology. One suspects that at least the matriarchal version of lesbian separatism may be viewed as a new ideology: after all, the interpretation of "free-dom" to mean "freedom from men" is certainly new, as is the suggestion that women are innately superior to men. Socialist feminism, however, should probably be seen as an extension of classical Marxism, using essentially similar notions of human nature, of freedom and equality, and of the role of the state, but attempting to show that women's situation and the sphere of personal relations in general need more careful analysis by Marxists.[37]

This sketch of some new directions in feminism completes my outline of the main contemporary positions on women's liberation. I hope that I have made clearer the ideological pre-suppositions at the root of many feminist claims and also shed some light on the philosophical problems that one needs to resolve in order to formulate one's own position and decide on a basis for action. Many of these philosophical questions, such as the nature of the just society, the proper account of freedom and equality, the functions of the state and the relation between the individual and society, are traditional problems which now arise in a new context; others, such as the role of technology in human liberation, are of more recent origin. In either case, feminism adds a fresh dimension to our discussion of the issues and points to the need for the so-called philosophy of man to be transformed into a comprehensive philosophy of women and men and their social relations.

## NOTES

1. All except one: as we shall see later, Lesbian separatism is evasive on the question whether men should, even ultimately, be equal with women.
2. The inequalities between the sexes are said to be both physical and psychological. Alleged psychological differences between the sexes include women's emotional instability, greater tolerance for boring detail, incapacity for abstract thought, and less aggression. Writers who have made such claims range from Rousseau (*Émile, or Education* [1762; translation, London: J.M. Dent, 1911]; see especially Book 5 concerning the education of "Sophie, or Woman"), through Schopenhauer (*The World As Will and Idea* and his essay "On Women"), Fichte (*The Science of Rights*), Nietzsche (*Thus Spake Zarathustra*), and Freud down to, in our own times, Steven Goldberg with *The Inevitability of Patriarchy* (New York: William Morrow, 1973–74).
3. This is the language used by Title VII of the Civil Rights Act with Executive Order 11246, 1965, and Title IX.
4. J. S. Mill, *The Subjection of Women* (1869; reprint ed., London: J.M. Dent, 1965), p. 236.
5. Ibid., p. 243.
6. Ibid., p. 235.
7. Friedrich Engels, *The Origin of the Family, Private Property and the State* (1884; reprint ed., New York: International Publishers, 1942), pp. 57–58.
8. Ibid., p. 65.
9. This is, of course, very far from being a complete account of the ways in which Marxists believe that capitalism benefits from sexism.
10. Engels, op. cit., p. 66.
11. Ibid., pp. 65–66.
12. Ibid., p. 66.
13. Ibid., p. 72.
14. Ibid.
15. Ti-Grace Atkinson, "Radical Feminism" and "The Institution of Sexual Intercourse" in *Notes from the Second Year: Major Writings of the Radical Feminists*, ed. S. Firestone (N.Y., 1970);

and Shulamith Firestone, *The Dialectic of Sex: The Case for Feminist Revolution* (N.Y.: Bantam Books; 1970).

16. Engels recognizes that early forms of the family were based on what he calls "natural" conditions, which presumably included the biological, but he claims that monogamy "was the first form of the family to be based, not on natural, but on economic conditions—on the victory of private property over primitive, natural communal property." Engels, op. cit., p. 57.

17. Atkinson and Firestone do talk of women as a "political class," but not in Marx's classic sense where the criterion of an individual's class membership is her/his relationship to the means of production. Atkinson defines a class more broadly as a group treated in some special manner by other groups: in the case of women, the radical feminists believe that women are defined as a "class" in virtue of our childbearing capacity. "Radical Feminism," op. cit., p. 24.

18. These conditions are listed and explained in *The Dialectic of Sex*, pp. 206–9.

19. "Radical Feminism," op. cit., p. 36.

20. Engels often expresses an extreme sexual puritanism in *The Origin of the Family, Private Property and the State*. We have already seen his claim that "sexual love is by its nature exclusive." Elsewhere (p. 57) he talks about "the abominable practice of sodomy." Lenin is well known for the expression of similar views.

21. "The Institution of Sexual Intercourse," op. cit.

22. *The Dialectic of Sex*, p. 209.

23. Ibid., final chart, pp. 244–45.

24. Ibid., p. 43.

25. Ibid., p. 72.

26. "In a world devoid of male power and, therefore, sex roles, who you lived with, loved, slept with and were committed to would be irrelevant. All of us would be equal and have equal determination over the society and how it met our needs. Until this happens, how we use our sexuality and our bodies is just as relevant to our liberation as how we use our minds and time." Coletta Reid, "Coming Out in the Women's Movement," in *Lesbianism and the Women's Movement*, ed. Nancy Myron and Charlotte Buch (Baltimore: Diana Press, 1975), p. 103.

27. Margaret Small, "Lesbians and the Class Position of Women," in *Lesbianism and the Women's Movement*, p. 58.

28. Jane Alpert, "Mother Right: A New Feminist Theory," *Ms.*, August 1973, p. 94.

29. Alice, Gordon, Debbie, and Mary, *Lesbian Separatism: An Amazon Analysis*, typescript, 1973, p. 5. (To be published by Diana Press, Baltimore.)

30. Ibid., p. 23.
31. It is interesting that this is the same research on which Steven Goldberg grounds his thesis of "the inevitability of patriarchy"; see note 2 above.
32. Barbara Ehrenreich, "Socialist/Feminism and Revolution" (unpublished paper presented to the National Socialist-Feminist Conference, Antioch College, Ohio, July 1975), p. 1.
33. Engels, op. cit., p. 57.
34. Juliet Mitchell, *Woman's Estate* (New York: Random House, 1971). Lively discussion of Mitchell's work continues among socialist feminists.
35. For one socialist feminist account of women's work in public industry see Sheila Rowbotham, *Woman's Consciousness, Man's World* (Baltimore: Penguin Books, 1973), chap. 6, "Sitting Next to Nellie."
36. One influential exponent of wages for housework is Mariarosa Dalla Costa, *The Power of Women and the Subversion of Community* (Bristol, England: Falling Wall Press, 1973).
37. Since I wrote this section, I have learned of some recent work by socialist feminists which seems to provide an excitingly new theoretical underpinning for much socialist feminist practice. An excellent account of these ideas is given by Gayle Rubin in "The Traffic in Women: Notes on the 'Political Economy' of Sex." This paper appears in *Toward an Anthropology of Women*, ed. Rayna R. Reiter (New York: Monthly Review Press, 1975). If something like Rubin's account is accepted by socialist feminists, it will be a difficult and important question to work out just how far they have moved from traditional Marxism and how much they still share with it.

Sandra Lee Bartky

# Toward a Phenomenology of Feminist Consciousness

## I

Contemporary feminism has many faces. The best attempts so far to deal with the scope and complexity of the movement have divided feminists along ideological lines.[1] Thus, liberal, Marxist, neo-Marxist and "radical" feminists have differing sets of beliefs about the origin and nature of sexism and thus quite different prescriptions for the proper way of eliminating it. But this way of understanding the nature of the women's movement, however indispensable, is not the only way. While I would not hesitate to call someone a feminist who supported a program for the liberation of women and who held beliefs about the nature of contemporary society appropriate to such a political program, something crucial to an understanding of feminism is overlooked if its definition is so restricted.

To be a feminist, one has first to become one. For many

I would like to thank members of the Society for Women in Philosophy, to whom I read an earlier version of this paper, not only for many helpful critical comments but for their willingness to share experiences both of discrimination and of personal transformation. This paper is reprinted by permission from *Social Theory and Practice* 3, no. 4 (Fall 1975): 425–39.

feminists, this takes the form of a profound personal transformation, an experience which goes far beyond that sphere of human activity ordinarily regarded as "political." This transforming experience, which cuts across the ideological divisions within the women's movement, is complex and multi-faceted. In the course of undergoing the transformation to which I refer, the feminist changes her *behavior*: she makes new friends; she responds differently to people and events; her habits of consumption change; sometimes she alters her living arrangements or, more dramatically, her whole style of life. These changes in behavior go hand in hand with changes in *consciousness*:[2] to become a feminist is to develop a radically altered consciousness of oneself, of others, and of what for lack of a better term I shall call "social reality."[3] Feminists themselves have a name for the struggle to clarify and to hold fast to this way of apprehending things: they call it "consciousness-raising." A "raised" consciousness on the part of women is not only a causal factor in the emergence of the feminist movement itself but also an important part of its political program: many small discussion groups exist solely for the purpose of consciousness-raising. But what happens when one's consciousness is raised? What is a developed feminist consciousness *like*? In this paper, I would like to examine not the full global experience of liberation, involving as it does new ways of being as well as new ways of perceiving, but, more narrowly, those distinctive ways of perceiving which characterize feminist consciousness. What follows will be a highly tentative attempt at a morphology of feminist consciousness: without claiming to have discovered them all, I shall try to identify some structural features of that altered way of apprehending oneself and the world which is both product and content of a raised consciousness. But first, I would like to make some very general remarks about the nature of this consciousness and about the conditions under which it emerges.

Although the oppression of women is universal, feminist consciousness is not. While I am not sure that I could demonstrate the necessity of its appearance in this time and place and not in another, it is possible to identify two features of current social reality which, if not necessary and sufficient, are at least necessary conditions for its emergence. These features constitute, in addition, much of the *content* of this consciousness. I refer first to the existence of what Marxists call "contradictions" in our society and second, to the presence, due to these contradictions, of specific conditions which permit a significant alteration in the status of women.

In Marxist theory, the stage is set for social change when existing forms of social interaction—property relations as well as values, attitudes, and beliefs—come into conflict with new social relations which are generated by changes in the mode of production.

At a certain stage of their development, the material forces of production in society come in conflict with the existing relations of production or—what is but a legal expression for the same thing— with the property relations within which they had been at work before. From forms of development of the forces of production these relations turn into their fetters. Then comes the period of social revolution.[4]

To date, no one has offered a comprehensive analysis of those alterations in the socioeconomic structure of contemporary American society which have made possible the emergence of feminist consciousness.[5] This task is made doubly difficult by the fact that these changes are no convenient object for dispassionate historical investigation but part of the fluid set of circumstances in which each of us find our way from one day to another and whose ultimate direction is as yet unclear.

Nevertheless, certain changes in contemporary social life are too significant to escape notice: the development of cheap and efficient types of contraception; the reentry, beginning in the early fifties, of millions of women into the market economy; the growing and unprecedented participation of women in higher education during the same period; innovations in production (such as prepared foods) to ease the burden of housekeeping; a general undermining of traditional family life; and the social upheavals and mass movements of the 1960s. When the position of women within the social whole is altered, new conceptions of self and society come directly into conflict with older ideas about a woman's role, her destiny, and even her "nature."

Clearly, any adequate account of the "contradictions" of late capitalism—i.e., of the conflicts, the instabilities, the ways in which some parts of the social whole are out of phase with others—would be a complex and elaborate task. But even in the absence of a comprehensive analysis, it is essential to understand as concretely as possible how the contradictory factors we are able to identify are lived and suffered by particular people. The facts of economic development are crucial to an understanding of any phenomenon of social change, but they are not the phenomenon in its entirety. While only dogmatic Marxists have regarded consciousness as a mere reflection of material conditions and therefore uninteresting as an object for study in and of itself, even Marxist scholars of a more humane cast of mind have not paid sufficient attention to the ways in which the social and economic tensions they study are played out in the lives of concrete individuals. There is an anguished consciousness—an inner uncertainty and confusion which characterizes human subjectivity in periods of social change (and I shall contend that feminist consciousness, to some degree, is "anguished")—of whose existence Marxist scholars seem largely unaware. Indeed, the only sort of consciousness that is discussed with any frequency in the literature is "class consciousness," a somewhat unclear idea whose meaning Marxists themselves dispute. The incorporation of a phenomenological perspective into Marxist analysis is necessary if the proper dialectical relations between human consciousness and the material modes of production are ever to be grasped in their full concreteness.

Women have long lamented their condition, but a lament, pure and simple, need not be an expression of feminist consciousness. As long as their situation is apprehended as natural, inevitable, and inescapable, women's consciousness of themselves, no matter how alive to insult and inferiority, is not yet feminist consciousness. This consciousness, as I contended earlier, emerges only when the partial or total liberation of women is possible. This possibility is more than a mere accidental accompaniment of feminist consciousness: feminist consciousness *is* the apprehension of possibility. The very *meaning* of what the feminist apprehends is illuminated by the light of what ought to be: the given situation is first understood in terms of a state of affairs not yet actual and in this sense a possibility, a state of affairs in which what is given would be negated and radically transformed. To say that feminist consciousness is the experience in a certain way of certain specific contradictions in the social order is to say that the feminist apprehends certain features of social reality *as* intolerable, as to be rejected in behalf of a transforming project for the future. "It is on the day that we can conceive of a different state of affairs that a new light falls on our troubles and we *decide* that these are unbearable."[6] What Sartre would call her "transcendence," her project of negation and transformation, makes possible what are specifically feminist ways of apprehending contradictions in the social order. Women workers who are not feminists know that they receive unequal pay for equal work, but they may think that the arrangement is just; the feminist sees this situation as an instance of exploitation and an occasion for struggle. Feminists are not aware of different things than other people; they are aware of the same things differently. Feminist consciousness, it might be ventured, turns a "fact" into a "contradiction;" often, features of social reality are only apprehended *as* contradictory from the vantage point of a radical project of transformation.

Thus, we understand what we are and where we are in the light of what we are not yet. But the perspective from which I understand the world must be rooted in the world, too. That is, my comprehension of what I and my world can become must take account of what they *are*. The possibility of a transformed society that allows the feminist to grasp the significance of her current situation must somehow be contained in the way she apprehends her current situation: the contradictory situation in which she finds herself is perceived *as* unstable, as carrying within itself the seeds of its own dissolution. There is of course no way of telling, by a mere examination of some form of consciousness, whether the possibilities it incorporates are realizable or not; this depends on whether the situation is such as to contain within itself the sorts of material conditions that will bring to fruition a human expectation. To sum up, the relationship between consciousness and concrete circumstances can best be described as "dialectical." Feminist consciousness is more than a mere reflection of external material conditions, for the transforming and negating perspective which it incorporates first allows these conditions to be revealed as the conditions they *are*—that is, as contradictions. The mere apprehension of some state of affairs as intolerable does not, of course, transform it. This only power can do.

## II

Feminist consciousness is consciousness of *victimization*. To apprehend oneself as victim is to be aware of an alien and hostile force which is responsible for the blatantly unjust treatment of women and for a stifling and oppressive system of sex-roles; it is to be aware, too, that this victimization, in no way earned or deserved, is an *offense*. For some feminists, this hostile power is "society" or "the system"; for others, it is, simply, men. Victimization is impartial, even though its damage is done to each of us personally. One is victimized as a woman, as one among many, and in the realization that others are made to suffer in the same way that I am made to suffer lies the beginning of a sense of solidarity with other victims. To come to see oneself as victim is not to see things in the same old way while merely judging them differently or to superimpose new attitudes on things like frosting on a cake: the consciousness of victimization is immediate and revelatory; it allows us to discover what social reality really *is*.

The consciousness of victimization is a divided consciousness. To see myself as victim is to know that I have already sustained injury, that I live exposed to injury, that I have been at worst mutilated, at best diminished, in my being. But at the same time, feminist consciousness is a joyous consciousness of one's own power, of the possibility of unprecedented personal growth and of the release of energy long suppressed. Thus, feminist consciousness is consciousness both of weakness and of strength. But this division in the way we apprehend ourselves has a positive effect, for it leads to the search both for ways of overcoming those weaknesses in ourselves which support the system and for direct forms of struggle against the system itself.

But consciousness of victimization is a consciousness divided in still another way. This second division does not have the positive effect of the first, for its tendency is to produce confusion, guilt, and paralysis in the political sphere. The awareness I have of myself as victim rests uneasily alongside the awareness that I am at the same time more privileged than the overwhelming majority of the world's population. I enjoy both white-skin privilege and the advantage of comparative wealth.[7] I have some measure of control, however small, over my own productive and reproductive life. The implications of this split in consciousness for feminist political theory and the obstacles it presents to the formulation of a coherent feminist strategy are frequently mentioned in the literature of the women's movement. It is not my task in this paper to develop a conception of political praxis appropriate to a consciousness of oppression so divided; I only intend to identify this division. But two things follow upon consideration of the phenomenon of the "guilty victim:" first, that an analysis of "psychological" oppression is essential to feminist political theory; second, that any feminist analysis that ignores the guilty-victim phenomenon or else sees in it the expression of a low level of political awareness will fail to do justice to the disturbing complexity of feminist experience.

To apprehend myself as victim in a sexist society is to know that there are few places where I can hide, that I can be attacked anywhere, at any time, by virtually anyone. Innocent chatter—the currency of ordinary social life—or a compliment ("You don't think like a woman"), the well-intentioned advice of psychologists, the news item, the joke, the cosmetics advertisement—none of these is what it is or what it was. Each is revealed (depending on the circumstances in which it appears) as a threat, an insult, an affront—as a reminder, however subtle, that I belong to an inferior caste—in short, as an instrument of oppression or as the articulation of a sexist institution. Since many things are not what they seem to be, and since many apparently harmless sorts of things can suddenly exhibit a sinister dimension, social reality is revealed as *deceptive.*

Contemporary thinkers as diverse as Heidegger and Marcuse have written about the ambiguity and mystification which are so prominent a feature of contemporary social life. Feminists are alive to one certain dimension of a society which seems to specialize in duplicity—the sexist dimension. But the deceptive nature of this aspect of social reality itself makes the feminist's experience of life, her anger and sense of outrage, difficult to communicate to the insensitive or uninitiated: it increases her frustration and reinforces her isolation. There is nothing ambiguous about racial segregation or economic discrimination: it is far less difficult to point to these abuses than it is to show how, for example, the "tone" of a news story can transform it from a piece of reportage into a refusal to take women's political struggles seriously or even into a species of punishment. The male reporter for a large local daily paper who described the encounter of Betty Friedan and the Republican Women's Caucus at Miami never actually used the word "fishwife" nor did he say outright that the political struggles of women are worthy of ridicule; he merely chose to describe the actions of the individuals involved in such a way as to make them appear ridiculous. (Nor, it should be added, did he fail to describe Ms. Friedan as "petite.") It is difficult to characterize the tone of an article, the patronizing implications of a remark, the ramifications of some accepted practice, and it is even more difficult to describe what it is like to be bombarded ten or a hundred times daily with these only half-submerged weapons of a sexist system. This, no doubt, is one reason why, when trying to make a case for feminism, we find ourselves referring almost exclusively to the "hard data" of discrimination, like unequal pay, rather than to those pervasive intimations of inferiority which rankle at least as much.

Many people know that things are not what they seem to be. The feminist knows that the thing revealed in its truth at last will, likely as not, turn out to be a thing that threatens or demeans. But however unsettling it is to have to find one's way about in a world that dissimulates, it is worse to be unable to determine the nature of what is happening at all. Feminist consciousness is often afflicted with category confusion—an inability to know how to classify things. The timidity I display at departmental meetings, for instance—is it nothing more than a personal shortcoming, or is it a typically female trait, a shared inability to display aggression, even verbal aggression? And why is the suggestion I make ignored? Is it intrinsically unintelligent or is it because I am a woman and therefore not to be taken seriously? The persistent need I have to make myself "attractive," to fix my hair and put on lipstick—is it the false need of a chauvinized woman, encouraged since infancy to identify her value as a person with her attractiveness in the eyes of men? Or does it express a wholesome need to express love for one's own body by adoring it, a behavior common in primitive societies, allowed us but denied to men in our own still-puritan culture? Uncertainties such as these make it difficult to decide how to struggle and whom to struggle against, but the very possibility of understanding one's own motivations, character traits and impulses is also at stake. In sum, feminists suffer what might be called a "double ontological shock": first, the realization that what is really happening is quite different from what appears to be happening; and second, the frequent inability to tell what is really happening at all.

Since discriminatory sex-role differentiation is a major organizing principle of our society, the list of its carriers and modes of communication would be unending: the sorts of things already mentioned were chosen at random. Little political, professional, educational, or leisure-time activity is free of the blight of sexism. Few personal relationships are free of it. Feminist consciousness is something like paranoia, especially when the feminist first begins to apprehend the full extent of sex discrimination and the subtle and various ways in which it is enforced. The System and its agents are everywhere, even inside her own mind, since she can fall prey to self-doubt or to a temptation to compliance. In response to this, the feminist becomes vigilant and suspicious: her apprehension of things, especially of direct or indirect communication with other people, is characterized by what I shall call "wariness." Wariness is anticipation of the possibility of attack, of affront or insult, of disparagement, ridicule, or the hurting blindness of others; it is a mode of experience which anticipates experience in a certain way. While it is primarily the established order of things of which the feminist is wary, she is wary of herself, too. She must be always on the alert lest her pervasive sense of injury provoke in her without warning some public display of emotion, such as violent weeping. Many feminists are perpetually wary lest their own anger be transformed explosively into behavior too hostile to be prudently or safely displayed.

Some measure of wariness is a constant in feminist experience, but the degree to which it is present will be a function of other factors in a feminist's life—her level of political involvement, perhaps, the extent of her sensitivity to the social milieu, or the degree to which she allows resignation or humor to take away the sting. Characteristic of this kind of consciousness, too, is the alternation of a heightened awareness of the limitations placed on one's free development with a duller self-protecting sensibility without which it would be difficult to function in a society like ours.

The revelation of the deceptive character of social reality brings with it another transformation in the way the social milieu is present in feminist experience. Just as so many apparently innocent things are really devices to enforce compliance, so are many "ordinary" sorts of situations transformed into opportunities or *occasions* for struggle against the system. In a light-hearted mood, I embark upon a Christmas-shopping expedition, only to have it turn, as if independent of my will, into an occasion for striking a blow against sexism. On holiday from political struggle, I have abandoned myself to the richly sensuous atmosphere of Marshall Field's. I have been wandering about the toy department, looking at chemistry sets and miniature ironing boards. Then, unbidden, the following thought flashes into my head: what if, just this once, I send a doll to my nephew and an erector set to my niece? Will this confirm the growing suspicion in my family that I am a crank? What if the children themselves misunderstand my gesture and covet one another's gifts? Worse, what if the boy believes that I have somehow insulted him? The shopping trip turned occasion for resistance now becomes a *test*. I will have to answer for this, once it becomes clear that Marshall Field's has not unwittingly switched the labels. My husband will be embarrassed. A didactic role will be thrust upon me, even though I have determined earlier that the situation was not ripe for consciousness-raising. The special ridicule reserved for movement women will be heaped upon me at the next family party—all in good fun, of course.

Ordinary social life presents to the feminist an unending sequence of such occasions, and each occasion is a test. It is not easy to live under the strain of constant testing. Some tests we pass with honor, but often as not we fail, and the price of failure is self-reproach and the shame of having copped out. To complicate things further, much of the time it is not clear what criteria would allow us to distinguish the honorable outcome of an occasion from a dishonorable one. Must I seize every opportunity? May I never take the easy way out? Is what I call prudence and good sense merely cowardice? On the occasion in question, I compromised and sent both children musical instruments.

The transformation of day-to-day living into a series of invitations to struggle has the important consequence for the feminist that she finds herself, for a while at least, in an ethical and existential impasse. She no longer knows what sort of person she ought to be, and therefore she does not know what she ought to do. One moral paradigm is called into question by the laborious and often obscure emergence of another. The ethical issues involved in my shopping trip were relatively trivial, but this is not true of all occasions. One thinks of Nora's decision in *A Doll's House* to leave her husband and children and seek independence and self-fulfillment on her own. Ibsen, her creator, betrays a certain lack of sensitivity to feminist experience: Nora makes the decision too easily; a real-life Nora would have suffered more.

To whom will a woman in such a predicament turn for guidance? To choose a moral authority, as Sartre tells us, is already to anticipate what kind of advice we are prepared to take seriously. Having become aware of the self-serving way in which a male-dominated culture has defined goodness for the female, a woman may decide on principle that the person she wants to be will have little patience, meekness, complaisance, self-sacrifice, or any of the other "feminine" virtues. But will such a solution satisfy a reflective person? Must the duty I have to myself (if we have duties to ourselves) always win out over the duty I have to others? To develop feminist consciousness is to live a part of one's life in the sort of *ambiguous ethical situation* which existentialist writers have been most adept at describing. Here it might be objected that this feature of feminist experience is characteristic not of a fully emergent feminist consciousness but of periods of transition to such consciousness, that the feminist is a person who has chosen her moral paradigm and who no longer suffers the inner conflicts of those in ambiguous moral predicaments. I would deny this. Even the woman who has decided to be this new person and not that old one can be tormented by recurring doubts. Moreover, the pain inflicted on other persons in the course of finding one's way out of an existential impasse, one continues to inflict. The feminist is a person who, at the very least, has been marked by the experience of ethical ambiguity: she is a moral agent with a distinctive history.

Feminist consciousness, it was suggested earlier, can be understood as the negating and transcending awareness of one's own relationship to a society heavy with the weight of its own contradictions. The inner conflicts and divisions which make up so much of this experience are just the ways in which each of us, in the uniqueness of her own situation and personality, *lives* these contradictions. In sum, feminist consciousness is the consciousness of a being radically alienated from her world and often divided against herself, a being who sees herself as victim and whose victimization determines her being-in-the-world as resistance, wariness, and suspicion. Raw and exposed much of the time, she suffers from both ethical and ontological shock. Lacking a moral paradigm, sometimes unable to make sense of her own reactions and emotions, she is immersed in a social reality that exhibits to her an aspect of malevolent ambiguity. Many "ordinary" social situations and many human encounters organized for quite a different end she apprehends as occasions for struggle, as frequently exhausting tests of her will and resolve. She is an outsider to her society, to many of the people she loves, and to the still-unemancipated elements in her own personality.

But this picture is not as bleak as it appears; indeed, its "bleakness" would be seen in proper perspective had I described what things were like *before*. Coming to have a feminist consciousness is the experience of coming to know the truth about oneself and one's society. This experience, the acquiring of a "raised" consciousness, is an immeasurable advance over that false consciousness which it replaces. The scales fall from our eyes. We are no longer required to struggle against unreal enemies, to put others' interests ahead of our own, or to hate ourselves. We begin to see why it is that our images of ourselves are so depreciated and why so many of us are lacking any genuine conviction of personal worth. Understanding things makes it possible to change them. Coming to see things differently, we are able to make out possibilities for liberating collective action as well as unprecedented personal growth—possibilities that a deceptive sexist social reality has heretofore concealed. No longer do we have to practice upon ourselves that mutilation of intellect and personality required of individuals, caught up in an irrational and destructive system, who are nevertheless not permitted to regard it as anything but sane, progressive, and normal. Moreover, that feeling of alienation from established society which is so prominent a feature of feminist experience is counterbalanced by a new identification with women of all conditions and a growing sense of solidarity with other feminists. It is a fitting commentary on our society that the growth of feminist consciousness, in spite of its ambiguities, confusion, and trials, is apprehended by those in whom it develops as an experience of liberation.

## NOTES

1. "Four Views of Women's Liberation," read by Alison Jaggar at the American Philosophical Association meeting, Western Division, 4–6 May 1972.
2. In what follows, the consciousness I discuss is the consciousness of a feminist who is female. I do not discuss the modes of awareness, whatever they may be, of men who are feminists.
3. By "social reality" I mean the ensemble of formal and informal relationships with other people in which we are now enmeshed or in which we are likely to become enmeshed, together with the

attitudes, values, types of communication, and conventions which accompany such relationships. "Social reality" is the social life-world, the social environment as it is present to my consciousness.

4. Karl Marx, *A Contribution to the Critique of Political Economy* (Chicago: Charles H. Kerr & Co., 1904), pp. 11–12.

5. See, however, Margaret Benston, "The Political Economy of Women's Liberation," *Monthly Review*, vol. 21, no. 4; also Valerie K. Oppenheimer, *The Female Labor Force in the United States: Demographic and Economic Factors Governing Its Growth and Changing Composition* (Berkeley: University of California Press, 1970). Highly recommended, too, is the special issue, "The Political Economy of Women," *Review of Radical Political Economics*, vol. 4, no. 3 (July 1972), as well as Juliet Mitchell, *Woman's Estate* (New York: Vintage Books, 1973), pp. 19–39.

6. Jean-Paul Sartre, *Being and Nothingness* (New York: Philosophical Library, 1956), p. 531.

7. Clearly, this is not a description of any feminist consciousness whatsoever. Some feminists must contend with poverty, racism, and imperialism as part of their oppression as women.

# Feminism

# *Further References*

Starred items are those of philosophical interest.

Adilson, Joseph. "Is Women's Lib a Passing Fad?" *New York Times Magazine*, 19 March 1972.

Amundsen, Kristen. *The Silenced Majority*. Englewood Cliffs, N.J.: Prentice-Hall, 1971.

*Baker, Robert, and Elliston, Frederick. *Philosophy and Sex*. Buffalo, N.Y.: Prometheus Books, 1975.

Beauvoir, Simone de. *The Second Sex*. Translated by H. M. Parshley. New York: Knopf, 1953.

Bernard, Jessie. *Women and the Public Interest*. Chicago: Aldine-Atherton, 1971.

Boston Women's Health Book Collective. *Our Bodies, Ourselves*. New York: Simon & Schuster, 1973.

Calderwood, Ann; Eastwood, Mary; Frances-Myrna; Hackett, Amy; Jehlen, Myra; Ortner, Sherry; Walkowitz, Judith R.; and Zellner, Harriet; eds. *The Feminist Studies*. New York: Feminist Studies, Inc: Vol. 1 (1972) through the present.

Chesler, Phyllis. *Women and Madness*. Garden City, N.Y.: Doubleday, 1972.

Cott, Nancy F., ed. *The Roots of Bitterness*. New York: E. P. Dutton, 1972.

Davis, Elizabeth Gould. *The First Sex*. Baltimore: Penguin Books, 1971.

Diner, Helen. *Mothers and Amazons: The First Feminine History of Culture*. Edited and translated by John Philip Lendin. New York: Julian Press, 1965.

Duverger, Maurice. *The Political Role of Women.* Paris: UNESCO, 1955.

Edwards, Lee R.; Heath, Mary; and Baskin, Lisa; eds. *Women: An Issue.* Boston: Little, Brown, 1972.

Etzioni, Amitai. "The Women's Movement: Tokens vs. Objectives." *Saturday Review,* 20 May 1972, pp. 31–35.

Feldman, Sylvia. *The Rights of Women.* Rochelle Park, N.J.: Hayden Book Co., 1974.

Firestone, Shulamith. *The Dialectic of Sex: The Case for Feminist Revolution.* New York: William Morrow, 1970.

Freeman, Jo, ed. *Women: A Feminist Perspective.* Palo Alto, Calif.: Mayfield Publishing Co., 1975.

Friedan, Betty. *The Feminine Mystique.* New York: Dell, 1963.

Gager, Nancy, ed. *Women's Rights Almanac.* New York: Harper & Row, 1975.

Glazer-Malbin, Nona, and Waehrer, Helen Youngelson, eds. *Woman in a Man-Made World.* Chicago: Rand McNally, 1972.

Gornick, Vivian, and Moran, Barbara K., eds. *Woman in Sexist Society: Studies in Power and Powerlessness.* New York: Basic Books, 1971.

Greer, Germaine. *The Female Eunuch.* New York: Bantam Books, 1971.

Hole, Judith, and Levine, Ellen, eds. *Rebirth of Feminism.* New York: Quadrangle Books, 1971.

Ibsen, Henrik. *A Doll's House.* In *Four Great Plays by Ibsen.* Translated by R. Farquharsen Sharp. New York: Bantam Books, 1959.

Janeway, Elizabeth. *Man's World, Woman's Place: A Study in Social Mythology.* New York: William Morrow, 1971.

Kanowitz, Leo. *Women and the Law.* Albuquerque: University of New Mexico Press, 1968.

Koedt, Anne; Levine, Ellen; and Rapone, Anita; eds. *Radical Feminism.* New York: Quadrangle Books, 1973.

Lamson, Peggy. *Few Are Chosen.* Boston: Houghton Mifflin, 1969.

Lenin, V. I. *The Emancipation of Women.* New York: International Publishers, 1969.

*Mill, John Stuart. *The Subjection of Women.* 1869. Reprint. Cambridge, Mass.: MIT Press, 1970.

Millett, Kate. *Sexual Politics.* Garden City, N.Y.: Doubleday, 1970.

*Monist.* Vol. 57, no. 1 (January 1973).

Morgan, Elaine. *The Descent of Woman.* New York: Bantam Books, 1972.

Morgan, Robin, ed. *Sisterhood Is Powerful.* New York: Random House, 1970.

O'Neill, William. *Everyone Was Brave: The Rise and Fall of Feminism in America.* New York: Quadrangle Books, 1969.

──────. *The Woman Movement*. New York: Quadrangle Books, 1971.

*\*Philosophical Forum*. Vol. 5, nos. 1–2. (Fall-Winter 1973–74).

Reed, Evelyn. *Problems of Women's Liberation: A Marxist Approach*. New York: Pathfinder Press, 1971.

──────. *Woman's Evolution*. New York: Pathfinder Press, 1975.

Reeves, Nancy. *Womankind*. Chicago: Aldine-Atherton, 1971.

Rosaldo, Michelle Zimbalist, and Lamphere, Louise. *Woman, Culture, and Society*. Stanford, Calif.: Stanford University Press, 1974.

Rossi, Alice S., ed. *The Feminist Papers: From Adams to de Beauvoir*. New York: Bantam Books, 1973.

Roszak, Betty, and Roszak, Theodore, eds. *Masculine/Feminine*. New York: Harper & Row, 1969.

Rowbotham, Sheila. *Woman's Consciousness, Man's World*. Baltimore: Penguin Books, 1973.

──────. *Women, Resistance and Revolution: A History of Women and Revolution in the Modern World*. New York: Random House, Vintage Books, 1974.

Safilios-Rothschild, Constantina, ed. *Toward a Sociology of Women*. Lexington, Mass.: Xerox College Publishing, 1972.

──────, ed. *Women and Social Policy*. Englewood Cliffs, N.J.: Prentice-Hall, 1974.

Salper de Tortella, Roberta. *Female Liberation: History and Current Politics*. New York: Knopf, 1972.

Schneir, Miriam, ed. *Feminism: The Essential Historical Writings*. New York: Random House, 1972.

Shepard, Don, ed. *Women in History*. Los Angeles: Manland Publishing Co., 1973.

Tanner, Leslie B., ed. *Voices from Women's Liberation*. New York: New American Library, Signet, 1971.

Tarbell, Ida Minerva. *The Business of Being a Woman*. New York: Macmillan, 1912.

Thomson, Mary Lou, ed. *Voices of the New Feminism*. Boston: Beacon Press, 1970.

Tremain, Rose. *The Fight for Freedom for Women*. New York: Ballantine Books, 1973.

Welter, Barbara, ed. *The Woman Question in American History*. Hinsdale, Ill.: Dryden Press, 1973.

Wortes, Helen, and Rabinowitz, Clara, eds. *The Woman's Movement*. New York: Halsted Press, 1972.

# Part II
# Sex Roles and Gender

# Part II

# Sex Roles and Gender

## Introduction

"Sex roles" and "gender traits" refer to the patterns of behavior which the two sexes are socialized, encouraged, or coerced into adopting, ranging from "sex-appropriate" personalities to interests and professions. Boys are rewarded for developing the accepted "masculine" characteristics; girls are trained to be "feminine."

Psychologists and anthropologists are investigating such scientific questions as to what extent sex differences are biologically based rather than taught, what characteristics develop at what ages, how widely sex roles vary from society to society, and what happens when we try to change them. They use the current stereotypes of our society to define the terms "masculine" and "feminine," but without assuming that females are (or must be) feminine, or males masculine. According to recent studies, a typical feminine individual is sympathetic, warm, soft-spoken, tender, gullible, childlike, loyal, and cheerful. It is masculine to be self-reliant, independent, athletic, dominant, decisive, aggressive, and ambitious.[1] Of course, sex is not entirely correlated with gender, so males often score "feminine" and females "masculine" on this scale. Individuals who show a balance or mixture of the two types are called "androgynous." Social scientists are studying the prevalence, the causes, and the effects of these gender differences.

Philosophers, on the other hand, are more interested in

analyzing and evaluating than in describing sex-role differences. For moral philosophers, the central question is, "Is sex-role stereotyping wrong?" Or should we believe, with Mrs. Norman Vincent Peale,

If the good Lord chose to divide the human race into two distinctive sexes, I don't see why anyone should try to blur the distinction. It seems to me that a man should possess—and occasionally display— the basic characteristics of the male animal: aggressiveness, combativeness, a drive to be dominant in most areas, including marriage. I also think that unless a woman is willing to look and act and be feminine, she's never going to be a success as a wife or a mother or even as a person.[2]

Other philosophers are scrutinizing scientific research for built-in bias, cultural assumptions, and unsupported conclusions. Some philosophers are also attempting to develop alternative possibilities such as an androgynous model, and to show why this would be preferable to sex-role stereotyping.

Is there anything wrong with sex stereotyping? For one thing, it limits personal *freedom* to develop any personality and interests one chooses. This alone is a serious moral objection to sex-role assignment. To justify stereotyping, one would at least have to show not only that it serves some social purpose (such as producing happiness, efficiency, or stability), but also that this good result is more valuable than the freedom lost.[3] This general method of measuring and comparing the costs and benefits of the various alternatives is the *utilitarian* method. On this approach, sex roles are wrong unless the happiness produced by them outweighs the happiness lost.

Other philosophers, such as John Rawls, reject even this possible justification for sex roles. On Rawls' theory, no amount of happiness or efficiency, however large, can compensate for a loss in basic liberty or equal opportunity.[4] If we follow his view, sex-role assignment cannot be justified by citing gains in happiness or efficiency, however large, because liberty and equal opportunity are always more important.

Of course it may be true that there are some personality differences between the sexes in any case, regardless of social pressures on children to conform. With the present evidence, however, since there is no stereotype-free society available to observe, we cannot establish scientifically whether such biological or innate differences exist. Some evidence from sex-assignment of ambiguous or hermaphroditic children suggests that sex characteristics are more largely a product of social conditioning than many authors have assumed.[5] But as John Stuart Mill observed, whatever differences between the sexes are natural or inevitable will exist in any case, and a worry that they will not develop without enforcement or encouragement is "an altogether unnecessary solicitude."[6]

Sex stereotyping extends beyond personality factors to include job assignment by sex. The ways in which television and textbooks encourage girls in early childhood to become stewardesses rather than pilots, secretaries rather than executives, and so forth, have received wide publicity in recent years.[7] In high school, guidance counseling channels individuals into sex-appropriate careers. For example, career-interest tests are designed to be evaluated differently depending upon the sex of the responder. A girl giving the same answers as a boy is told that she shows interest in being a dietitian or dental assistant, whereas he is told that he shows interest in being an optometrist, dentist, or pharmacist.[8] In adult life, a woman still receives less pay than a man with the same training. She may receive disapproval for "neglecting" her husband and children, if any, by working—or she may be assumed to be miserable or a failure as a woman if she has no job. These are all pressures which enforce sex stereotyping of jobs and thus inhibit equal opportunity by providing women with lower incentives and rewards than men in the traditionally male occupations. If equal opportunity is required as a matter of justice, then these pressures are morally wrong. Thus these questions are intimately related to the discussion of equal opportunity in Part IV.

Another aspect of sex stereotyping is that it prescribes special interests for the two sexes. Women are supposed to be interested in fashion, movie stars, and cooking; men in sports, cars, and fishing. Subtle disapproval awaits a man who wants to crochet or a woman who chooses to lift weights. In addition to being a totally unnecessary infringement on personal freedom, these stereotypes decrease the contact and understanding between the sexes. One often finds the women at a party talking together about sewing or dates, men about the latest baseball scores. A couple may even find that they have few topics or activities in common. This is a sad and unnecessary loss of opportunities for human understanding, communication, and happiness.

Role differentiation is most obvious within the family, where the woman is expected to handle cleaning, cooking, and child-rearing, while the man provides the larger paycheck, takes care of the car, and fixes things. Similarly, boys are expected to take out the garbage and mow the lawn, girls to wash dishes and set the table. Whether this stereotyped division of labor is unfair and should be changed has been a controversial subject, tending to raise strong emotions. This is not surprising, since it is primarily a question of dividing up the tasks that everyone would rather not have to do. Since every household requires some division of labor, the question seems rather to be whether the division should be dictated by society or left as a matter of personal choice. Presumably, rational household members free from stereotypes would never choose a division that did not divide the amount of work approximately equally and base the assignment of tasks on abilities and interests. This does not imply that no one should specialize, of course. But in a just society, we would expect to see some households where the wife earns a living and the husband cooks, some that reverse this arrangement, some where husband and wife alternate, and others where they share both tasks. We certainly would not expect to find any couples in which the wife both earns a living and shoulders the entire burden of housekeeping and child-rearing.[9]

Androgyny is a third personality type different from traditional masculinity and femininity and combining some elements of each. An androgynous person is both self-reliant and supportive, neither overly aggressive nor overly dependent, and so forth. ANN FERGUSON articulates the undesirability of the present sex-stereotyped model and develops androgyny as a superior alternative. On this view we would present children of both sexes with the ideal of what a good person is like, rather than with the goal of becoming either a masculine man or a feminine woman. Ferguson argues that this change is needed to free women from the confines of the home and the consequences of being overly dependent and lacking in self-confidence. Ultimately, she foresees a society in which the sex of an individual is not so noticeable nor felt to be so important as it is today. Sex would be unnoticed in the choice of business associates or friends—ultimately even in the choice of sexual partners, she hopes.

JOYCE TREBILCOT notes two opposing tendencies in the androgynists' position. On the one hand, androgynism calls for greater liberty to develop any kind of personality and interests, rather than the restriction of conventional stereotypes. On the other hand, it advocates the androgynous type as a single ideal to which all are to be encouraged to conform; we simply would have one ideal for both sexes rather than two different ones. But these two views seem to conflict: one calls for freedom, while the other calls simply for changing the number of ideals to which children are taught to conform. Trebilcot examines the arguments for both forms of the view, and concludes that the first, which she dubs "polyandrogynism," with its emphasis on freedom, is superior.

A fully androgynous society will be impossible, however, if many personality traits are genetically sex-linked. Most feminists hold what ANNE DICKASON calls "accidentalism" about the psychological characteristics of the sexes. That is, they hold that psychological differences are the product of social conditioning rather than being natural or genetically determined. The opposite view, "essentialism," has been held by the majority of psychological theorists. Dickason recounts six major psychological/anthropological theories. Except for Margaret Mead's, all are essentialist. Then she points out a background assumption that would tend to explain this agreement on essentialism despite their divergence on other matters: they all assume that in primitive sexual encounters, the male forced himself on the female. This sets up the primary aggressive/active versus passive/receptive dichotomy from which the other "essential" sex differences are derived. But this assumption is not documented, and without it the essentialists' conclusions would not follow. Dickason concludes that scientific agreement on essentialism, being an artifact of this assumption, does not tend to refute the feminists' accidentalist position.

In sum, it is not known whether sex-stereotyped personalities and preferences are partly natural or entirely a result of social conditioning. Differences between societies tend to show that they are at least not entirely dictated by biology. But even to the extent that sex-stereotyping is biologically determined, freedom and equal opportunity are important enough to indicate that sex roles need not be enforced and should not be extended by differential treatment of men and women.

J. E.

# NOTES

1. These characteristics are taken from the Bem Sex Roles Inventory. See Sandra Bem, "The Measurement of Psychological Androgyny," *Journal of Consulting and Clinical Psychology* 42 (1974). These lists only apply to our society, and considerably different ones would apply to other cultures. Compare Margaret Mead, *Sex and Temperament* (New York: William Morrow, 1963).

2. Mrs. Norman Vincent Peale, *The Adventure of Being a Wife* (Englewood Cliffs, N.J.: Prentice-Hall, 1971), pp. 234–35.

3. See Joyce Trebilcot, "Sex Roles: The Argument from Nature," *Ethics* 85 (1975): 249–55.

4. John Rawls, *A Theory of Justice* (Cambridge, Mass.: Harvard University Press, 1971).

5. John Money and Anke Ehrhardt, *Man and Woman, Boy and Girl* (Baltimore: Johns Hopkins University Press, 1972).

6. John Stuart Mill, *The Subjection of Women* (1869).

7. See Judith Stacey, Susan Béreaud, and Joan Daniels, eds., *And Jill Came Tumbling After: Sexism in American Education* (New York: Dell, 1974).

8. On the Kuder DD Occupational Interest Survey. See Carol Tittle, "The Use and Abuse of Vocational Tests," in Stacey, Béreaud, and Daniels, op. cit., pp. 242–43.

9. See Madelon Bedell, "Supermom!" *Ms.*, May 1973.

Ann Ferguson

# Androgyny As an Ideal for Human Development

In this paper I shall defend androgyny as an ideal for human development. To do this I shall argue that male/female sex roles are neither inevitable results of "natural" biological differences between the sexes, nor socially desirable ways of socializing children in contemporary societies. In fact, the elimination of sex roles and the development of androgynous human beings is the most rational way to allow for the possibility of, on the one hand, love relations among equals, and on the other, development of the widest possible range of intense and satisfying social relationships between men and women.

## I. ANDROGYNY: THE IDEAL DEFINED

The term "androgyny" has Greek roots: *andros* means man and *gynē*, woman. An androgynous person would combine some of each of the characteristic traits, skills, and interests that we now

I'd like to acknowledge the help and encouragement of the socialist and feminist intellectual communities at the University of Massachusetts in Amherst, particularly the help of Sam Bowles, Jean Elshtain, and Dennis Delap, who read and commented extensively on earlier drafts of this paper. John Brentlinger and Susan Cayleff also provided feedback and comments. Many students who read the paper were helpful and supportive. A first version of this paper was read in the fall of 1974 at Bentley College, Boston, Massachusetts.

associate with the stereotypes of masculinity and femininity. It is not accurate to say that the ideal androgynous person would be both masculine and feminine, for there are negative and distorted personality characteristics associated in our minds with these ideas.[1] Furthermore, as we presently understand these stereotypes, they exclude each other. A masculine person is active, independent, aggressive (demanding), more self-interested than altruistic, competent and interested in physical activities, rational, emotionally controlled, and self-disciplined. A feminine person, on the other hand, is passive, dependent, non-assertive, more altruistic than self-interested (supportive of others), neither physically competent nor interested in becoming so, intuitive but not rational, emotionally open, and impulsive rather than self-disciplined. Since our present conceptions of masculinity and femininity thus defined exclude each other, we must think of an ideal androgynous person as one to whom these categories do not apply—one who is neither masculine nor feminine, but human: who transcends those old categories in such a way as to be able to develop positive human potentialities denied or only realized in an alienated fashion in the current stereotypes.

The ideal androgynous being, because of his or her combination of general traits, skills, and interests, would have no internal blocks to attaining self-esteem. He or she would have the desire and ability to do socially meaningful productive activity (work), as well as the desire and ability to be autonomous and to relate lovingly to other human beings. Of course, whether or not such an individual would be able to *achieve* a sense of autonomy, self-worth, and group contribution will depend importantly on the way the society in which he/she lives is structured. For example, in a classist society characterized by commodity production, none of these goals is attainable by anyone, no matter how androgynous, who comes from a class lacking the material resources to acquire (relatively) non-alienating work. In a racist and sexist society there are social roles and expectations placed upon the individual which present him/her with a conflict situation: either express this trait (skill, interest) and be considered a social deviant or outcast, or repress the trait and be socially accepted. The point, however, is that the androgynous person has the requisite skills and interests to be able to achieve these goals if only the society is organized appropriately.

## II. LIMITS TO HUMAN DEVELOPMENT:
## THE NATURAL COMPLEMENT THEORY

There are two lines of objection that can be raised against the view that androgyny is an ideal for human development: first, that it is not possible, given the facts we know about human nature; and second, that even if it is possible, there is no reason to think it particularly desirable that people be socialized to develop the potential for androgyny. In this section I shall present and discuss Natural Complement theories of male/female human nature and the normative conclusions about sex roles.

There are two general facts about men and women and their roles in human societies that must be taken into account by any theory of what is possible in social organization of sex roles: first, the biological differences between men and women—in the biological reproduction of children, in relative physical strength, and in biological potential for aggressive (dominant, demanding) behavior; and second, the fact that all known human societies have had a sexual division of labor.

According to the Natural Complement theory, there are traits, capacities, and interests which inhere in men and women simply because of their biological differences, and which thus define what is normal "masculine" and normal "feminine" behavior. Since men are stronger than women, have bodies better adapted for running and throwing, and have higher amounts of the male hormone androgen, which is linked to aggressive behavior,[2] men have a greater capacity for heavy physical labor and for aggressive behavior (such as war). Thus it is natural that men are the breadwinners and play the active role in the production of commodities in society and in defending what the society sees as its interests in war. Since women bear children, it is natural that they have a maternal, nurturing instinct which enables them to be supportive of the needs of children, perceptive and sensitive to their needs, and intuitive in general in their understanding of the needs of people.

The Natural Complement theory about what men and women should do (their moral and spiritual duties, ideal love relations, etc.) is based on this conception of what are the fundamental biologically based differences between men and women. The universal human sexual division of labor is not only natural, but also desirable: men should work, provide for their families, and when necessary, make war; women should stay home, raise their children, and, with their greater emotionality and sensitivity, administer to the emotional needs of their men and children.

The ideal love relationship in the Natural Complement view is a heterosexual relationship in which man and woman complement each other. On this theory, woman needs man, and man, woman; they need each other essentially because together they form a whole being. Each of them is incomplete without the other; neither could meet all their survival and emotional needs alone. The woman needs the man as the active agent, rationally and bravely confronting nature and competitive social life; while the man needs the woman as his emotional guide, ministering to the needs he doesn't know he has himself, performing the same function for the children, and being the emotional nucleus of the family to harmonize all relationship. Love between man and woman is the attraction of complements, each being equally powerful and competent in his or her own sphere —man in the world, woman in the home—but each incompetent in the sphere of the other and therefore incomplete without the other.

The validity of the Natural Complement theory rests on the claim that there are some natural instincts (drives and abilities) inherent in men and women that are so powerful that they will determine the norm of masculine and feminine behavior for men and women under any conceivable cultural and economic conditions. That is, these natural instincts will determine not only what men and women can do well, but also what will be the most desirable (individually satisfying and socially productive) for them.

Even strong proponents of the Natural Complement theory have been uneasy with the evidence that in spite of "natural" differences between men and women, male and female sex roles are not inevitable. Not only are there always individual men and women whose abilities and inclinations make them exceptions to the sexual stereotypes in any particular society, but there is also a wide cross-cultural variation in just what work is considered masculine or feminine. Thus, although all known societies indeed do have a sexual division of labor, the evidence is that what behavior is considered masculine and what feminine is *learned* through socialization rather than mandated through biological instincts. So, for example, child care is said by the proponents of the Natural Complement theory to be women's work, supposedly on the grounds that women have a natural maternal instinct that men lack, due to women's biological role in reproduction. And it is true that in the vast majority of societies in the sexual division of labor women do bear a prime responsibility for child care. However, there are some societies where that is not so. The Arapesh have both mother and father play an equally strong nurturant role.[3] A case of sex-role reversal in child care would be the fabled Amazons, in whose society those few men allowed to survive past infancy reared the children. In the case of the Amazons, whose historical existence may never be conclusively proved, what is important for the purposes of our argument is not the question of whether such a culture actually existed. Rather, insofar as it indicated that an alternative sexual division of labor was possible, the existence of the myth of the Amazon culture in early Western civilizations was an ongoing challenge to the Natural Complement theory.

It is not only the sexual division of labor in child care that varies from society to society, but also other social tasks. Natural Complement theorists are fond of arguing that because men are physically stronger than women and more aggressive, it is a natural division of labor for men to do the heavy physical work of society as well as that of defense and war. However, in practice, societies have varied immensely in the ways in which heavy physical work is parceled out. In some African societies, women do all the heavy work of carrying wood and water, and in most South American countries Indian men and women share these physical chores. In Russia, women do the heavy manual labor involved in construction jobs, while men do the comparatively light (but higher-status) jobs of running the machinery.[4] In predominantly agricultural societies, women's work overlaps men's. From early American colonial times, farm women had to be prepared to fight native American Indians and work the land in cooperation with men. Israeli women make as aggressive and dedicated soldiers as Israeli men. Furthermore, if we pick any *one* of the traits supposed to be primarily masculine (e.g., competitiveness, aggressiveness, egotism), we will find not only whole societies of both men *and* women who seem to lack these traits, but also whole societies that exhibit them.[5]

Further evidence that general sex-linked personality traits are learned social roles rather than inevitable biological developments is found in studies done on hermaphrodites.[6] When chil-

dren who are biological girls, but because of vestigial penises
are mistaken for boys, are trained into male sex roles, they
develop the cultural traits associated with males in their society
and seem to be well adjusted to their roles.

Faced with the variability of the sexual division of labor and
the evidence that human beings as social animals develop their
self-concept and their sense of values from imitating models in
their community rather than from innate biological urges, the
Natural Complement theorists fall back on the thesis that complementary roles for men and women, while not inevitable, are
desirable. Two examples of this approach are found in the writings of Jean-Jacques Rousseau (in *Émile*) and in the contemporary writer George Gilder (in *Sexual Suicide*).[7] Both of these
men are clearly male supremacists in that they feel women
ought to be taught to serve, nurture, and support men.[8] What is
ironic about their arguments is their belief in the biological
inferiority of men, stated explicitly in Gilder and implicitly in
Rousseau. Rousseau's train of reasoning suggests that men can't
be nurturant and emotionally sensitive the way women can, so if
we train women to be capable of abstract reasoning, to be self-
interested and assertive, women will be able to do both male
and female roles, and what will be left, then, for men to excel
at? Gilder feels that men need to be socialized to be the breadwinners for children and a nurturant wife, because otherwise
men's aggressive and competitive tendencies would make it
impossible for them to cooperate in productive social work.

The desirability of complementary sex roles is maintained
from a somewhat different set of premises in Lionel Tiger's
book *Men in Groups*.[9] Tiger argues that the earliest sexual
division of labor in hunting and gathering societies required
men to develop a cooperative division of tasks in order to
achieve success in hunting. Therefore, men evolved a biological
predisposition toward "male bonding" (banding together into
all-male cohort groups) that women lack (presumably because
activities like gathering and child care didn't require a cooperative division of tasks that would develop female bonding). Because of this lack of bonding, women are doomed to subjection
by men, for this biological asset of men is a trait necessary for
achieving political and social power.

It is hard to take these arguments seriously. Obviously, they
are biased toward what would promote male interests, and give
little consideration to female interests. Also, they reject an

androgynous ideal for human development, male and female, merely on the presumption that biological lacks in either men or women make it an unattainable ideal. It simply flies in the face of counter-evidence (for example, single fathers in our society) to argue as Gilder does that men will not be providers and relate to family duties of socializing children unless women center their life around the nurturing of men. And to argue as Tiger does that women cannot bond ignores not only the present example of the autonomous women's movement, but also ethnographic examples of women acting as a solidarity group in opposing men. The women of the Ba-Ila in southern Africa may collectively refuse to work if one has a grievance against a man.[10] A more likely theory of bonding seems to be that it is not biologically based, but learned through the organization of productive and reproductive work.

## III. HISTORICAL MATERIALIST EXPLANATIONS OF SEX ROLES

Even if we reject the Natural Complement theory's claims that sex roles are either inevitable or desirable, we still have to explain the persistence, through most known societies, of a sexual division of labor and related sexual stereotypes of masculine and feminine behavior. This is due, I shall maintain, to patriarchal power relations between men and women based initially on men's biological advantages in two areas: that women are the biological reproducers of children, and that men as a biological caste are, by and large, physically stronger than women.[11] As Shulamith Firestone argues in *The Dialectic of Sex* and Simone de Beauvoir suggests in *The Second Sex,* the fact that women bear children from their bodies subjects them to the physical weaknesses and constraints that pregnancy and childbirth involve. Being incapacitated for periods of time makes them dependent on men (or at least the community) for physical survival in a way not reciprocated by men. Breast-feeding children, which in early societies continued until the children were five or six years old, meant that women could not hunt or engage in war. Men have both physical and social advantages over women because of their biological reproductive role and the fact that allocating child-rearing to women is the most socially efficient division of reproductive labor in societies with scarce material resources. Thus, in social situations in which men come to perceive their interests to lie in making women subservient to them, men have the edge in a power struggle based on sexual caste.

It is important to note at this point, however, that these biological differences between men and women are only *conditions* which may be *used* against women by men in certain economic and political organizations of society and in social roles. They are like *tools* rather than mandates. A tool is only justified if you agree with both the tool's efficiency and the worth of the task that it is being used for, given other available options in achieving the task. In a society with few material resources and no available means of birth control, the most efficient way of ensuring the reproduction of the next generation may be the sexual division of labor in which women, constantly subject to pregnancies, do the reproductive work of breast-feeding and raising the children, while the men engage in hunting, trading, and defense. In a society like ours, on the other hand, where we have the technology and means to control births, feed babies on formula food, and combat physical strength with weapons, the continuation of the sexual division of labor can no longer be justified as the most efficient mode for organizing reproductive work.

It seems that we should look for a social explanation for the continued underdevelopment and unavailability of the material resources for easing women's reproductive burden. This lack is due, I maintain, to a social organization of the forces of reproduction that perpetuates the sexual division of labor at home and in the job market, and thus benefits the perceived interests of men, not women.

The two biological disadvantages of women, relative male strength and the female role in biological reproduction, explain the persistence of the sexual division of labor and the sexual stereotypes based on this. Variations in the stereotypes seem to relate fairly directly to the power women have relative to men in the particular society. This, in turn, depends on the mode of production of the society and whether or not women's reproductive work of raising children is in conflict with their gaining any power in the social relations of production.

There are disagreements between anthropological theorists as to whether early human history contained matriarchal societies, in which bloodlines and property were traced through the maternal side and in which women had the edge over men in political and economic power. Early theorists like Engels and Morgan[12] argue that the social organization of the family and women's power in society is directly related to women's role in production. In primitive hunting-and-gathering and agricultural societies, organization of production is communal and tribal. Women have a central role in production and reproduction, there is no separation of productive work from home and re-productive work, and bloodlines are matrilineal. Moreover, Engels uses examples like the Iroquois Indians, and Bachofen, myths of powerful goddesses, to argue that these societies were not just matrilineal but also matriarchal. According to Engels' theory, the "world-historical defeat of the female sex" came when the mode of production changed to an animal-herding economy, and the sexual division of labor thus gave men control over production and over any surplus. Men thus gained political and economic power over women, whose productive and reproductive work was concentrated on production for use in the home rather than for exchange.

Engels' theory is somewhat too simple. It doesn't sufficiently account for the fact that in *any* non-communal mode of production, the ability to control biological reproduction (progeny, future labor power) is a material power to be struggled for, and that there will be a dialectical struggle to control both production and reproduction in all but the most simple tribal societies.[13] It also doesn't take into account the possibility that even in communal modes of production there may be patriarchal power relations between men and women caused by male fear of women's biological ability to reproduce. This may result in "womb-envy," and in male attempts to compensate for women's reproductive power by setting up male-dominated areas in economic, political, and religious relations.[14]

Whatever the origin of the power struggle between men and women to control reproduction, the fact seems to be that the degree of a woman's oppression in a society is related to the amount of power she has at any particular historical period in the relations of reproduction in the family as well as the relations of production in society. Her oppression is thus relative to her class position as well as to her power in relation to men in her family.

There is no easy formula by which to determine the amount of power women have by simply looking at how much productive work and child care they do relative to men in a certain historical period. What is important is not the *amount* of work done, but the control a woman has over her work and the kind of independence this control offers her in the case of actual or potential conflicts with men over how the work should be done. Thus, although American slave women did as much productive work as slave men, and were almost totally responsible for the child care not only for their own children but for those of the plantation owner as well, slave women had no control over this work. Their children could be sold away from them, and they could be brutally punished if they refused to do the work assigned them by their masters. The lady of the plantation, on the other hand, did little productive work. She was more in a managerial position, usually responsible for managing the health care, clothing, and food of the slaves. She usually had little say in economic decisions about the plantation, since she was not considered a joint owner. On the other hand, the Victorian sexual division of labor and the Cult of True Womanhood gave the wealthy white woman almost total control over her children in decisions about child-rearing. Relative to her husband, all in all, she had less power; relative to her female slave she had more; and her female slave in turn had more power than the male slave because of her central role in child-rearing and the greater likelihood that fathers rather than mothers would be sold away from children.

## IV. THE SOCIAL ARTICULATION OF THE NATURAL COMPLEMENT THEORY

If we look at the beliefs of different societies about the proper roles for men and women, we note that these beliefs vary widely. We also see that societies always tend to appeal to the Natural Complement theory to back up their socially relative allocations of sex roles. The question arises, then: why, in the light of this obvious social variation, do people *persist* in clinging to the belief that there are inherent natural roles for men and women?

It would be simplistic to maintain that the ideology of sex roles directly reflects the degree of women's power in relation to men at a given historical period in a society. The Medieval religious view of women was extremely low,[15] yet there is evidence that women had more power than the simple reflective view of ideology would lead us to believe. In fact, there were women who were sheriffs, innkeepers, and managers of large households. The elevation of the Virgin Mary as the ideal woman on a pedestal seems to contradict the other elements in the Medieval religious view of women, and, indeed, it should make us wary of assuming a one-to-one correlation between ideology and reality. So, for example, 19th-century Americans placed women on a pedestal where they were considered morally superior to men; but this, ironically, was in an economic, legal, and political context where they had less power than their Puritan ancestors.[16] Middle-class women had no role in commodity production, which had become the dominant mode of production in the 19th century. Women could not own property if they were married, nor receive an education, nor hold political office, nor vote. Their husbands had complete legal control over children in case of divorce.

There is a more plausible way to understand how the ideology of sex roles is connected to the actual social and historical roles of men and women. Sex-role ideologies mystify the existing power relations between men and women and economic classes. This mystification justifies the social and economic roles of two dominant groups: men as a caste, on the one hand, and the dominant economic class on the other.

If we look at 19th-century America, we see the prevailing ideology, which held that women are too frail, "moral," and emotional to take part in commodity production (the amoral, competitive world of business). This ideology ignored the reality of black slave women, treated the same as male slaves and forced to do field work under brutal conditions. It ignored immigrant women, who worked long hours in crowded factories under conditions that caused many sicknesses and deaths. And it ignored farm women, who continued production for use on the farm. These working women made up the majority of the female population, yet the reality of their productive role was overlooked.

Why? A number of factors seem to be at work here. All end by supporting the interests and maintaining the status-quo power relations of the white male bourgeoisie. The first factor was the need to pacify bourgeois wives, whose role in production had evaporated but who were crucial to maintaining the system by lending emotional support and being subservient to their husbands, and by training their children, the future owners and controllers of capital. There was also a need for the bour-

geois male to justify his position of dominance over his wife in
legal, political, and financial matters. Second, the hierarchical
control that the bourgeois male enjoyed over men of the lower
classes was seen as inevitable (after all, it is masculine nature to
be competitive and avaricious, and may the best man win!)
Third, lower-class working women were thought to be fallen
women, degraded and unnatural because of their role in produc
tion, and this conveniently made them free targets for bourgeoi
men (with their "natural" sexual appetites) to lure into prosti
tution. Finally, as production became more alienating, hierarch
ical, and competitive, working-class men as well needed th
haven of women's emotional support and also the male domi
nance that being the breadwinner allowed them. As a result
both the men and the women of the working class struggled
to achieve the ideal complementary sex-role relationships o
woman-at-home/man-as-breadwinner that the Cult of Tru
Womanhood assumed.

## V. CONCLUSIONS ABOUT THE
## NATURAL COMPLEMENT THEORY

We have discussed several different views of the "natural" se
differences between men and women prevalent in different his
torical periods. When we observe the shift in ideology as to
what constitutes "true" female and male nature, we note that
the shift has nothing to do with the further scientific discover
of biological differences between men and women. It seem
rather to correlate to changes in the relation between men's an
women's roles in production and reproduction, and to wha
serves the interests of the dominant male economic class. Give
this fact of its ideological role, the Natural Complement theory
and any other static universal theory of what the "natural rela
tionship" of man to woman should be, loses credibility.

Instead, it seems more plausible to assume that human natur
is plastic and moldable, and that women and men develop thei
sexual identities, their sense of self, and their motivation
through responding to the social expectations placed upo
them. They develop the skills and personality traits necessary t
carry out the productive and reproductive roles available t
them in their sociohistorical context, given their sex, race
ethnic identity, and class background.

If we wish to develop a realistic ideal for human develop

ient, then, we cannot take the existing traits that differentiate
ien from women in this society as norms for behavior. Neither
an we expect to find an ideal in some biological male and
emale substratum, after we strip away all the socialization pro-
esses we go through to develop our egos. Rather, with the
resent-day women's movement, we should ask: what traits are
esirable and possible to teach people in order for them to
each their full individual human potential? And how would our
ociety have to restructure its productive and reproductive rela-
ons in order to allow people to develop in this way?

## VI. AN IDEAL LOVE RELATIONSHIP

One argument for the development of androgynous personalities
and the accompanying destruction of the sexual division of
abor in production and reproduction) is that without such a
adical change in male and female roles an ideal love relation-
nip between the sexes is not possible. The argument goes like
nis. An ideal love between two mature people would be love
etween equals. I assume that such an ideal is the only concept
f love that is historically compatible with our other developed
leals of political and social equality. But, as Shulamith Fire-
one argues,[17] an equal love relationship requires the vulner-
 bility of each partner to the other. There is today, however, an
nequal balance of power in male-female relationships. Con-
ary to the claims of the Natural Complement theory, it is not
ossible for men and women to be equal while playing the
omplementary sex roles taught in our society. The feminine
ole makes a woman less equal, less powerful, and less free than
ne masculine role makes men. In fact, it is the emotional
nderstanding of this lack of equality in love relations between
en and women which increasingly influences feminists to
noose lesbian love relationships.

Let us consider the vulnerabilities of women in a heterosex-
al love relationship under the four classifications Juliet
itchell gives for women's roles:[18] production, reproduction,
ocialization of children, and sexuality.

1. *Women's role in production.* In the United States today,
? percent of women work, and about 33 percent of married
omen work in the wage-labor force. This is much higher than
ie 6 percent of women in the wage-labor force around the turn
the century, and higher than in other industrialized countries.

Nonetheless, sex-role socialization affects women's power in two important ways. First, because of job segregation by sex into part-time and low-paying jobs, women, whether single or married, are at an economic disadvantage in comparison with men when it comes to supporting themselves. If they leave their husbands or lovers, they drop to a lower economic class, and many have to go on welfare. Second, women who have children and who also work in the wage-labor force have two jobs, not one: the responsibility for the major part of child-raising and housework, as well as the outside job. This keeps many house-wives from seeking outside jobs, and makes them economically dependent on their husbands. Those who do work outside the home expend twice as much energy as the man and are less secure. Many women who try to combine career and mother-hood find that the demands of both undermine their egos be-cause they don't feel that they can do both jobs adequately.[1]

2. *Women's role in reproduction.* Although women currently monopolize the means of biological reproduction, they are at a disadvantage because of the absence of free contraceptives, adequate health care, and free legal abortions. A man can enjoy sex without having to worry about the consequences the way a woman does if a mistake occurs and she becomes preg-nant. Women have some compensation in the fact that in the United States today they are favored legally over the father in their right to control of the children in case of separation or divorce. But this legal advantage (a victory won by women in the early 20th century in the ongoing power struggle between the sexes for control of children, i.e. control over social repro-duction) does not adequately compensate for the disadvantage to which motherhood subjects one in this society.

3. *Women's role in socialization: as wife and mother.* The social status of women, and hence their self-esteem, is measured primarily in terms of how successful they are in their relation-ships as lovers, wives, and mothers. Unlike men, who learn that their major social definition is success in work, women are taught from childhood that their ultimate goal is love and mar-riage. Women thus have more invested in a love relationship than men, and more to lose if it fails. The "old maid" or the "divorcee" is still an inferior status to be pitied, while the "swinging bachelor" is rather envied.

The fact that men achieve self- and social definition from their work means that they can feel a lesser commitment to working out problems in a relationship. Furthermore, men have more options for new relationships than do women. The double standard in sexuality allows a man to have affairs more readily than his wife. Ageism is a further limitation on women: an older man is considered a possible lover by both younger and older women, but an older woman, because she is no longer the "ideal" sex object, is not usually considered a desirable lover by either male peers or by younger men.

A woman's role as mother places her in a more vulnerable position than the man. Taking care of children and being attentive to their emotional needs is very demanding work. Many times it involves conflicts between the woman's own needs and the needs of the child. Often it involves conflict and jealousy between husband and children for her attention and emotional energy. It is the woman's role to harmonize this conflict, which she often does at the expense of herself, sacrificing her private time and interests in order to provide support for the projects of her husband and children.

No matter how devoted a parent a father is, he tends to see his time with the children as play time, not as work time. His job interests and hobbies take precedence over directing his energy to children. Thus he is more independent than the woman, who sees her job as making husband and children happy. This is the sort of job that is never completed, for there are always more ways to make people happy. Because a woman sees her job to be supporting her husband and mothering her children, the woman sees the family as her main "product." This makes her dependent on their activities, lives, and successes for her own success, and she lives vicariously through their activities. But as her "product" is human beings, when the children leave, as they must, to live independent lives, middle age brings an end to her main social function. The woman who has a career has other problems, for she has had to support her husband's career over hers wherever there was a conflict, because she knows male egos are tied up with success and "making it" in this competitive society. Women's egos, on the other hand, are primed for failure. Successful women, especially successful women with unsuccessful husbands, are considered not "true" women, but rather as deviants, "castrating bitches," "ball-busters," and "masculine women." For all these reasons, a woman in a love relationship with a man is geared by the Natural Complement view of herself as a woman to put her interests last, to define herself in terms of husband and children, and therefore to be more dependent on them than they are on her.

A woman is also vulnerable in her role as mother because there are limited alternatives if, for example, she wishes to break off her relationship with the father of her children. As a mother, her social role in bringing up children is defined as more important, more essential for the well-being of the children than the man's. Therefore, she is expected to take the children to live with her, or else she is considered a failure as a mother. But the life of a divorced or single mother with children in a nuclear-family-oriented society is lonely and hard: she must now either do two jobs without the companionship of another adult, in a society where jobs for women are inadequate, or she must survive on welfare or alimony with a reduced standard of living. When this is the alternative, is it any wonder that mothers are more dependent on maintaining a relationship —even when it is not satisfying—than the man is?

4. *Women's role in sexuality.* A woman's sexual role is one in which she is both elevated by erotic romanticism and deflated to being a mere "cunt"—good for release of male sexual passions but interchangeable with other women. Because women play a subordinate role in society and are not seen as equal agents or as equally productive, men must justify a relationship with a particular woman by making her something special, mystifying her, making her better than other women. In fact, this idealization doesn't deal with her as a real *individual*; it treats her as either a beautiful object or as a mothering, supportive figure.

This idealization of women which occurs in the first stages of infatuation wears off as the couple settles into a relationship of some duration. What is left is the idea of woman as passive sex object whom one possesses and whose job as wife is to give the husband pleasure in bed. Since the woman is not seen as (and doesn't usually see herself as) active in sex, she tends to see sex as a duty rather than as a pleasure. She is not socially expected to take the active kind of initiative (even to the extent of asking for a certain kind of sex play) that would give her a sense of control over her sex life. The idea of herself as a body to be dressed and clothed in the latest media-advertised fashions "to please men" keeps her a slave to fashion and forces her to change her ego-ideal with every change in fashion. She can't see herself as an individual.

# VII. ANDROGYNY AS A PROGRESSIVE IDEAL

It is the sexual division of labor in the home and at work that perpetuates complementary sex roles for men and women. In underdeveloped societies with scarce material resources such an arrangement may indeed be the most rational way to allow for the most efficient raising of children and production of goods. But this is no longer true for developed societies. In this age of advanced technology, men's relative strength compared to women's is no longer important, either in war or in the production of goods. The gun and the spinning jenny have equalized the potential role of men and women in both repression and production. And the diaphragm, the pill, and other advances in the technology of reproduction have equalized the potential power of women and men to control their bodies and to reproduce themselves.[20] (The development of cloning would mean that men and women could reproduce without the participation of the opposite sex.)

We have seen how complementary sex roles and their extension to job segregation in wage labor make an ideal love relationship between equals impossible for men and women in our society. The questions that remain are: would the development of androgynous human beings through androgynous sex-role training be possible? If possible, would it allow for the development of equal love relationships? What other human potentials would androgyny allow to develop? And how would society have to be restructured in order to allow for androgynous human beings and equal love relationships?

There is good evidence that human babies are bisexual, and only *learn* a specific male or female identity by imitating and identifying with adult models. This evidence comes from the discovery that all human beings possess both male and female hormones (androgen and estrogen respectively), and also from concepts first developed at length by Freud. Freud argued that heterosexual identity is not achieved until the third stage of the child's sexual development. Sex identity is developed through the resolution of the Oedipus complex, in which the child has to give up a primary attachment to the mother and learn either to identify with, or love, the father. But Shulamith Firestone suggests that this process is not an inevitable one, as Freud presents it to be. Rather, it is due to the power dynamics of the patriarchal nuclear family.[21] Note that, on this analysis, if the sexual division of labor were destroyed, the mechanism that trains boys and girls to develop heterosexual sexual identities would also be destroyed. If fathers and mothers played equal nurturant roles in child-rearing and had equal social, economic, and political power outside the home, there would be no reason for the boy to have to reject his emotional side in order to gain the power associated with the male role. Neither would the girl have to assume a female role in rejecting her assertive, independent side in order to attain power indirectly through manipulation of males. As a sexual identity, bisexuality would then be the norm rather than the exception.

If bisexuality were the norm rather than the exception for the sexual identities that children develop,[22] androgynous sex roles would certainly be a consequence. For, as discussed above, the primary mechanism whereby complementary rather than androgynous sex roles are maintained is through heterosexual training, and through the socialization of needs for love and sexual gratification to the search for a love partner of the opposite sex. Such a partner is sought to complement one in the traits that one has repressed or not developed because in one's own sex such traits were not socially accepted.

## VIII. THE ANDROGYNOUS MODEL

I believe that only androgynous people can attain the full human potential possible given our present level of material and social resources (and this only if society is radically restructured). Only such people can have ideal love relationships; and without such relationships, I maintain that none can develop to the fullest potential. Since human beings are social animals and develop through interaction and productive activity with others, such relationships are necessary.

Furthermore, recent studies have shown that the human brain has two distinct functions: one associated with analytic, logical, sequential thinking (the left brain), and the other associated with holistic, metaphorical, intuitive thought (the right brain). Only a person capable of tapping both these sides of him/herself will have developed to full potential. We might call this characteristic of the human brain "psychic bisexuality,"[23] since it has been shown that women in fact have developed skills which allow them to tap the abilities of the right side of the brain more than men, who on the contrary excel in the analytic, logical thought characteristic of the left side. The point is that men and women have the potential for using both these functions, and yet our socialization at present tends to cut off from one or the other of these parts of ourselves.[24]

What would an androgynous personality be like? My model for the ideal androgynous person comes from the concept of human potential developed by Marx in *Economic and Philosophical Manuscripts*. Marx's idea is that human beings have a need (or a potential) for free, creative, productive activity which allows them to control their lives in a situation of co-operation with others. Both men and women need to be equally active and independent; with an equal sense of control over their lives; equal opportunity for creative, productive activity; and a sense of meaningful involvement in the community.

Androgynous women would be just as assertive as men about their own needs in a love relationship: productive activity outside the home, the right to private time, and the freedom to form other intimate personal and sexual relationships. I maintain that being active and assertive—traits now associated with being "masculine"—are positive traits that all people need to develop. Many feminists are suspicious of the idea of self-assertion because it is associated with the traits of aggression and competitiveness. However, there is no inevitability to this connection: it results from the structural features of competitive, hierarchical economic systems, of which our own (monopoly capitalism) is one example. In principle, given the appropriate social structure, there is no reason why a self-assertive person cannot also be nurturant and cooperative.

Androgynous men would be more sensitive and aware of emotions than sex-role stereotyped "masculine" men are today. They would be more concerned with the feelings of all people, including women and children, and aware of conflicts of interests. Being sensitive to human emotions is necessary to an effective care and concern for others. Such sensitivity is now thought of as a "motherly," "feminine," or "maternal" instinct, but in fact is is a role and skill learned by women, and it can equally well be learned by men. Men need to get in touch with their own feelings in order to empathize with others, and, indeed, to understand themselves better so as to be more in control of their actions.

We have already discussed the fact that women are more

vulnerable in a love relationship than men because many men consider a concern with feelings and emotions to be part of the woman's role. Women, then, are required to be more aware of everyone's feelings (if children and third parties are involved) than men, and they are under more pressure to harmonize the conflicts by sacrificing their own interests.

Another important problem with a non-androgynous love relationship is that it limits the development of mutual understanding. In general, it seems true that the more levels people can relate on, the deeper and more intimate their relationship is. The more experiences and activities they share, the greater their companionship and meaning to each other. And this is true for emotional experiences. Without mutual understanding of the complex of emotions involved in an ongoing love relationship, communication and growth on that level are blocked for both people. This means that, for both people, self-development of the sort that could come from the shared activity of understanding and struggling to deal with conflicts will not be possible.

In our society as presently structured, there are few possibilities for men and women to develop themselves through shared activities. Men and women share more activities with members of their own sex than with each other. Most women can't get jobs in our sexist, job-segregated society which allow them to share productive work with men. Most men just don't have the skills (or the time, given the demands of their wage-labor jobs) to understand the emotional needs of children and to share the activity of child-rearing equally with their wives.

How must our society be restructured to allow for the development of androgynous personalities? How can it be made to provide for self-development through the shared activities of productive and reproductive work? I maintain that this will not be possible (except for a small privileged elite) without the development of a democratic socialist society. In such a society no one would benefit from cheap labor (presently provided to the capitalist class by a part-time reserve army of women). Nor would anyone benefit from hierarchical power relationships (which encourage competition among the working class and reinforce male sex-role stereotypes as necessary to "making it" in society).

As society is presently constituted, the patriarchal nuclear family and women's reproductive work therein serve several crucial roles in maintaining the capitalist system. In the family, women do the unpaid work of social reproduction of the labor force (child-rearing). They also pacify and support the male breadwinner in an alienating society where men who are not in the capitalist class have little control of their product or work conditions. Men even come to envy their wives' relatively non-alienated labor in child-rearing rather than dealing with those with the real privilege, the capitalist class. Since those in power relations never give them up without a struggle, it is utopian to think that the capitalist class will allow for the elimination of the sexual division of labor without a socialist revolution with feminist priorities. Furthermore, men in the professional and working classes must be challenged by women with both a class and feminist consciousness to begin the process of change.

In order to eliminate the subordination of women in the patriarchal nuclear family and the perpetuation of sex-role stereotypes therein, there will need to be a radical reorganization of child-rearing. Father and mother must have an equal commitment to raising children. More of the reproductive work must be socialized—for example, by community child care, perhaps with parent cooperatives. Communal living is one obvious alternative which would de-emphasize biological parenthood and allow homosexuals and bisexuals the opportunity to have an equal part in relating to children. The increased socialization of child care would allow parents who are incompatible the freedom to dissolve their relationships without denying their children the secure, permanent loving relationships they need with both men and women. A community responsibility for child-rearing would provide children with male and female models other than their biological parent—models that they would be able to see and relate to emotionally.

Not only would men and women feel an equal responsibility to do reproductive work, they would also expect to do rewarding, productive work in a situation where they had equal opportunity. Such a situation would of course require reduced work-weeks for parents, maternity and paternity leaves, and the development of a technology of reproduction which would allow women complete control over their bodies.

As for love relationships, with the elimination of sex roles and the disappearance, in an overpopulated world, of any biological need for sex to be associated with procreation, there would be no reason why such a society could not transcend sexual gender. It would no longer matter what biological sex

66 FEMINISM AND PHILOSOPHY

individuals had. Love relationships, and the sexual relationships developing out of them, would be based on the individual meshing-together of androgynous human beings.

## NOTES

1. I owe these thoughts to Jean Elshtain and members of the Valley Women's Union in Northampton, Massachusetts, from discussions on androgyny.
2. See Roger Brown, *Social Psychology* (New York: Free Press, 1965).
3. For information on the Arapesh and variations in male/female roles in primitive societies, see Margaret Mead, *Sex and Temperament* (New York: William Morrow, 1963).
4. See "The Political Economy of Women," *Review of Radical Political Economics*, Summer 1973.
5. Contrast the Stone Age tribe recently discovered in the Philippines, where competition is unknown, with the competitive male and female Dobus from Melanesia. See Ruth Benedict, *Patterns of Culture* (Boston: Houghton Mifflin, 1934).
6. See Eleanor E. Maccoby, ed., *The Development of Sex Differences* (Stanford, Calif.: Stanford University Press, 1966).
7. George Gilder, *Sexual Suicide* (New York: Bantam Books, 1973).
8. Rousseau says, in a typical passage from *Émile*, "When once it is proved that men and women are and ought to be unlike in constitution and in temperament, it follows that their education should be different." And on a succeeding page he concludes, "A woman's education must therefore be planned in relation to man. To be pleasing in his sight, to win his respect and love, to train him in childhood, to tend him in manhood, to counsel and console, to make his life pleasant and happy, these are the duties of woman for all time, and this is what she should be taught while she is young. The further we depart from this principle, the further we shall be from our own good, and all our precepts will fail to secure her happiness or our own" (trans. Barbara Foxley [New York: E. P. Dutton, 1911] pp. 326, 328).

Gilder's conclusion is as follows: "But at a profounder level the women are tragically wrong. For they fail to understand their own sexual power; and they fail to perceive the sexual constitution of our society, or if they see it, they underestimate its importance to our civilization and to their own interest in order and stability. In general across the whole range of the society, marriage and careers—and thus social order—will be best served if most men have a position of economic superiority over the relevant women in his [*sic*] community and if in most jobs in which colleagues must work together, the sexes tend to be segregated either by level or function." *Sexual Suicide*, p. 108.

9. Lionel Tiger, *Men in Groups* (New York: Random House, 1969).

10. Edwin W. Smith and Andrew M. Dale, *The Ila-Speaking Peoples of Northern Rhodesia* (London: Macmillan, 1920).

11. It is not simply the fact that men are physically stronger than women which gives them the edge in sexual power relations. It is also women's lesser psychological capacity for violence and aggressiveness. However, this has as much to do with socialization into passive roles from early childhood as it does with any inequality in the amount of the male hormone androgen, which is correlated to aggressive behavior in higher primates. As Simone de Beauvoir points out in *The Second Sex* (New York: Knopf, 1953), male children develop training in aggressive behavior from an early age, while female children are kept from the psychological hardening process involved in physical fights. Feeling that one is by nature submissive will cause one to be submissive; so even women who are equal in strength to men will appear to themselves and to men not to be so.

12. See Friedrich Engels, *The Origin of the Family, Private Property and the State* (New York: International Publishers, 1942); also Lewis Morgan, *Ancient Society*, ed. Eleanor Leacock (New York: World Publishing Co., 1963).

13. Perhaps part of the reason for the solidarity in these societies is due to the meager resources to be struggled for.

14. Karen Horney develops this theory in her book *Feminine Psychology* (New York: W. W. Norton, 1967); as does Eva Figes in *Patriarchal Attitudes* (New York: Stein & Day, 1970). Note the striking difference between Horney's and Tiger's (op. cit.) explanations of the phenomenon of male bonding.

15. Catholic Church doctrine maintains a dualism between soul and body. The soul is thought to be rational and spiritual, the valuable part of the self that loves God; while the body is sinful, animal, given to sexual lusts and passions. Women are identified with the body because of their childbearing function, hence with sexuality, evil, and the devil. (The story of Eve in Genesis was used ,to support this view.) It is women who lead men away from the pure spiritual life and into the evils of sexuality: they are thus inferior beings whose only positive function is the reproduction of children. Even in this role they are merely receptacles, for the theory of reproduction is that woman is the lowly, unclean vessel into which man puts the seed of life.

16. In the Cult of True Womanhood prevalent in America and England in the 19th century, women are thought to be passive and

emotional but *not* sexual or tied to the body. Rather, the woman is the moral and spiritual guardian of the male, who is thought to be more naturally sinful than she—avaricious, competitive, self-interested, and imbued with sexual passions. The one sphere, then, in which woman is thought to be naturally skilled is the home and the spiritual education of children and husband.

17. Shulamith Firestone, *The Dialectic of Sex* (New York: William Morrow, 1970), chap. 6.

18. Juliet Mitchell, *Woman's Estate* (New York: Random House, 1971).

19. Socialization into complementary sex roles is responsible not only for job segregation practices' keeping women in low-paid service jobs which are extensions of the supportive work women do in the home as mothers, but also for making it difficult for women to feel confident in their ability to excel at competitive "male-defined" jobs.

20. Thanks to Sam Bowles for this point.

21. Firestone, op. cit. The boy and girl both realize that the father has power in the relationship between him and the mother, and that his role, and not the mother's, represents the possibility of achieving economic and social power in the world and over one's life. The mother, in contrast, represents nurturing and emotionality. Both boy and girl, then, in order to get power for themselves, have to reject the mother as a love object—the boy, because he is afraid of the father as rival and potential castrator; and the girl, because the only way as a girl she can attain power is through manipulating the father. So she becomes a rival to her mother for her father's love. The girl comes to identify with her mother and to choose her father and, later, other men for love objects; while the boy identifies with his father, sublimates his sexual attraction to his mother into superego (will power), and chooses mother substitutes, other women, for his love objects.

22. It should be understood here that no claim is being made that bisexuality is more desirable than homo- or heterosexuality. The point is that with the removal of the social mechanisms in the family that channel children into heterosexuality, there is no reason to suppose that most of them will develop in that direction. It would be more likely that humans with androgynous personalities would be bisexual, the assumption here being that there are no innate biological preferences in people for sexual objects of the same or opposite sex. Rather, this comes to be developed because of emotional connections of certain sorts of personality characteristics with the male and female body, characteristics which develop because of complementary sex-role training, and which would not be present without it.

The other mechanism which influences people to develop a heterosexual identity is the desire to reproduce. As long as the social institution for raising children is the heterosexual nuclear family, and as long as society continues to place social value on biological parenthood, most children will develop a heterosexual identity. Not, perhaps, in early childhood, but certainly after puberty, when the question of reproduction becomes viable. Radical socialization and collectivization of child-rearing would thus have to characterize a society before bisexuality would be the norm not only in early childhood, but in adulthood as well. For the purposes of developing androgynous individuals, however, full social bisexuality of this sort is not necessary. All that is needed is the restructuring of the sex roles of father and mother in the nuclear family so as to eliminate the sexual division of labor there.

23. Charlotte Painter, Afterword to C. Painter and M. J. Moffet, eds., *Revelations: Diaries of Women* (New York: Random House, 1975).

24. It is notable that writers, painters, and other intellectuals, who presumably would need skills of both sorts, have often been misfits in the prevalent complementary sex stereotyping. In fact, thinkers as diverse as Plato (in the *Symposium*) and Virginia Woolf (in *A Room of One's Own*) have suggested that writers and thinkers need to be androgynous to tap all the skills necessary for successful insight.

Joyce Trebilcot

# Two Forms of Androgynism

Traditional concepts of women and men, of what we are and should be as females and males, of the implications of sex for our relationships to one another and for our places in society, are not acceptable. But what models, if any, should we adopt to replace them? In this paper I consider just two of the alternatives discussed in recent literature—two versions of androgynism.

In discussing these two views I follow the convention of distinguishing between sex (female and male) and gender (feminine and masculine). Sex is biological, whereas gender is psychosocial. Thus, for example, a person who is biologically female may be—in terms of psychological characteristics or social roles—feminine or masculine, or both.

Although what counts as feminine and masculine varies among societies and over time, I use these terms here to refer to the gender concepts traditionally dominant in our own society. Femininity, on this traditional view, has nurturing as its core: it centers on the image of woman as mother, as provider of food,

Reprinted by permission of the *Journal of Social Philosophy*. An earlier version of this paper was read for the Society for Women in Philosophy at the American Philosophical Association meeting, Pacific Division, San Diego, California, March 1975. My thanks to Professors Jane English and Mary Anne Warren of SWIP and especially to Professor Kathryn Guberman of the Women's Studies Program at Washington University for discussions of this topic.

warmth, and emotional sustenance. Masculinity focuses on mastery: it comprises the notion of man struggling to overcome obstacles, to control nature, and also the notion of man as patriarch or leader in society and the family.

The first form of androgynism to be discussed here takes the word "androgyny" literally, so to speak. In this word the Greek roots for man (*andros*) and woman (*gynē*) exist side by side. According to the first form of androgynism, both feminine and masculine characteristics should exist "side by side" in every individual: each woman and man should develop personality traits and engage in activities traditionally assigned to only one sex. Because this view postulates a single ideal for everyone, I call it monoandrogynism, or, for brevity, *M*.

Monoandrogynism, insofar as it advocates shared roles, is now official policy in a number of countries. For example, the Swedish government presented a report to the United Nations in 1968 specifying that in Sweden, "every individual, regardless of sex, shall have the same practical opportunities not only for education and employment but also fundamentally the same responsibility for his or her own financial support as well as shared responsibility for child upbringing and housework."[1]

Closer to home, Jessie Bernard, in her discussion of women's roles, distinguishes the one-role view, according to which woman's place is in the home; the two-role pattern, which prescribes a combination of the traditional housewife-mother functions and work outside the home; and what she calls the "shared-role ideology" which holds "that children should have the care of both parents, that all who benefit from the services supplied in the household should contribute to them, and that both partners should share in supporting the household."[2]

Caroline Bird in her chapter "The Androgynous Life" writes with approval of role-sharing. She also suggests that the ideal person "combines characteristics usually attributed to men with characteristics usually attributed to women."[3]

The psychological dimension of *M* is stressed by Judith M. Bardwick. In her essay "Androgyny and Humanistic Goals, or Goodbye, Cardboard People," she discusses a view according to which the ideal or "healthy" person would have traits of both genders. "We would then expect," she says, "both nurturance and competence, openness and objectivity, compassion and competitiveness from both women and men, as individuals, according to what they were doing."[4]

The work of these and other writers provides the basis for a normative theory, $M$, which prescribes a single ideal for everyone: the person who is, in both psychological characteristics and social roles, both feminine and masculine.

The second form of androgynism shares with the first the principle that biological sex should not be a basis for judgments about the appropriateness of gender characteristics. It differs from the first, however, in that it advocates not a single ideal but rather a variety of options including "pure" femininity and masculinity as well as any combination of the two. According to this view, all alternatives with respect to gender should be equally available to and equally approved for everyone, regardless of sex. Thus, for example, a female might acceptably develop as a completely feminine sort of person, as both feminine and masculine in any proportion, or as wholly masculine. Because this view prescribes a variety of acceptable models, I call it polyandrogynism, or $P$.[5]

Constantina Safilios-Rothschild supports $P$ in her recent book *Women and Social Policy*. In this work she makes a variety of policy recommendations aimed at bringing about the liberation of both sexes. Liberation requires, she says, that individuals live "according to their wishes, inclinations, potentials, abilities, and needs rather than according to the prevailing stereotypes about sex roles and sex-appropriate modes of thought and behavior." Some persons, she adds, "might *choose* to behave according to their sex's stereotypic . . . patterns. But some women and some men may *choose*, if they are so inclined, to take options in some or all of the life sectors now limited to the opposite sex."[6]

Carolyn Heilbrun's work also suggests $P$. In *Toward a Recognition of Androgyny* she writes, "The ideal toward which I believe we should move is best described by the term 'androgyny.' This ancient Greek word . . . defines a condition under which the characteristics of the sexes, and the human impulses expressed by men and women, are not rigidly assigned. Androgyny seeks to liberate the individual from the confines of the appropriate." Androgyny suggests, Heilbrun says, "a full range of experience open to individuals who may, as women, be aggressive, as men, tender; it suggests a spectrum upon which human beings choose their places without regard to propriety or custom."[7]

This second form of androgynism focuses on a variety of options rather than on the single model of the part-woman/part-man (that is, of the androgyne in the classic sense). It is appropriate, however, to extend the term "androgynism" to apply to it; for, like *M*, it seeks to break the connection between sex and gender.

For both forms of androgynism, the postulated ideals are best construed so as to exclude aspects of traditional gender concepts which are morally objectionable. Femininity should not be taken to include, for example, weakness, foolishness, or incompetence. Similarly, tendencies such as those to authoritarianism and violence should be eliminated from the concept of masculinity. Most importantly, aspects of the gender concepts which prescribe female submissiveness and male domination (over women and over other men) must, on moral grounds, be excluded from both the single ideal advocated by *M* and the range of options recommended by *P*.

Either form of androgyny may, in the long run, lead to major changes in human attributes. It is often suggested that the androgyne is a person who is feminine part of the time and masculine part of the time. But such compartmentalization might be expected to break down, so that the feminine and masculine qualities would influence one another and be modified. Imagine a person who is at the same time and in the same respect both nurturant and mastery-oriented, emotional and rational, cooperative and competitive, and so on. I shall not undertake here to speculate on whether this is possible, or, if it is, on how such qualities might combine. The point is just that androgyny in the long run may lead to an integrating of femininity and masculinity that will yield new attributes, new kinds of personalities. The androgyne at this extreme would perhaps be not part feminine and part masculine, but neither feminine nor masculine, a person in whom the genders disappear.

I turn now to the question of which of these two forms of androgynism is more acceptable. I am not concerned here to evaluate these positions in relation to other alternatives (for example, to the traditional sexual constitution of society or to matriarchy).[8] For the sake of this discussion, I assume that either *M* or *P* is preferable to any alternative, and that the problem is only to decide between them. Let us first consider this problem not as abstract speculation, and not as a problem for some distant society, but rather as an immediate issue for our own society. The question is then: Which form of androgynism is preferable as a guide to action for us here and now?

Suppose we adopt $M$. Our task then is to provide opportunities, encouragement, and perhaps even incentives for those who are now feminine to be also masculine, and conversely. Suppose, on the other hand, that we adopt $P$. Our task is to create an environment in which, without reference to sex, people choose among all (moral) gender alternatives. How can this best be accomplished? What is required, clearly, is that the deeply-entrenched normative connection between sex and gender be severed. Virtually everyone now, in formulating preferences for the self and in judging the appropriateness of gender characteristics for others, at least on some occasions takes it, consciously or otherwise, that the sex of the individual in question is a relevant consideration: that one is female tends to count in favor of a feminine trait and against a masculine one, and conversely. In order to break this connection, it must be shown that masculinity is acceptable for females and femininity for males. There must, then, be opportunities, encouragement, and perhaps even incentives for gender-crossing. But this is what is required by $M$. Hence, under present conditions, the two forms of androgynism prescribe the same course of action—that is, the promotion of gender-crossing.

The question "Which form of androgynism is preferable here and now?" then, is misconstrued. If one is an androgynist of either sort, what one must do now is seek to break the normative connection between sex and gender by bringing about gender-crossing. However, once the habit of taking sex as a reason for gender evaluation is overcome, or is at least much weaker and less widespread than it is today, then the two forms of androgynism do prescribe different courses of action. In particular, on $M$ "pure" gender is condemned, but on $P$ it is accepted. Let us consider, then, which version of androgynism is preferable for a hypothetical future society in which femininity and masculinity are no longer normatively associated with sex.

The major argument in favor of $P$ is, of course, that because it stipulates a variety of acceptable gender alternatives it provides greater gender freedom than $M$. Now, freedom is a very high priority value, so arguments for $M$ must be strong indeed. Let us consider, then, two arguments used to support $M$ over $P$—one psychological, one ethical.

The psychological argument holds that in a society which is open with respect to gender, many people are likely to experience anxiety when faced with the need, or opportunity, to choose among different but equally acceptable gender models. Consider the words of Judith M. Bardwick:

People need guidelines, directions that are agreed upon because they help each individual to know where one ought to go, how one can get there, and how far one is from one's goal. It is easier to sustain frustration that comes from knowing how far you are from your objective or what barriers are in your way than it is to sustain the anxiety that comes from not being sure about what you want to do or what others want you to do. It will be necessary, then, to develop new formulations by which people will guide their lives.[9]

Bardwick says that anxiety "comes from not being sure about what you want to do or what others want you to do." But in a society of the sort proposed by $P$, the notion that one should seek to please others in deciding among gender models would be rejected; ideally "what others want you to do" in such a society is to make your own decisions. Of course there is still the problem of not being sure about what *you* want to do. Presumably, under $P$, people would provide one another with help and support in finding suitable life styles. Nevertheless, it could be that for some, choosing among alternatives would be anxiety-producing. On the other hand, under $M$, the lack of approved alternatives could produce frustration. Hence, the argument from anxiety should be paired with an argument from frustration. In $M$, socialization is designed to make everyone androgynous (in ways similar, perhaps, to those which have traditionally produced exclusive femininity and masculinity in our own society), and frustration is part of the cost. In $P$, socialization is directed toward enabling people to perceive, evaluate, and choose among alternatives, and there is a risk of anxiety. We are not now in a position to decide whether the frustration or the anxiety is worse, for there are no data on the numbers of people likely to suffer these emotions nor on the extent of the harm that they are likely to do. Hence, neither the argument from anxiety nor the argument from frustration is of any help in deciding between the two forms of androgynism.

I turn now to a more persuasive argument for $M$, one which claims that androgyny has universal value. This argument supports $M$ not, as the argument from anxiety does, because $M$ prescribes some norm or other, but rather because of the content of the norm. The argument holds that both traditional genders include qualities that have human value, qualities that it would be good for everyone to have. Among the elements of femininity, candidates for universal value are openness and responsiveness to needs and feelings, and being gentle, tender, intuitive, sensitive, expressive, considerate, cooperative, compassionate. Masculine qualities appealed to in this connection include being logical, rational, objective, efficient, responsible, independent, courageous. It is claimed, then, that there are some aspects of both genders (not necessarily all or only the ones I have mentioned) which are desirable for everyone, which we should value both in ourselves and in one another. But if there are aspects of femininity and masculinity which are valuable in this way—which are, as we might call them, virtues—they are *human* virtues, and are desirable for everyone. If Smith is a better person for being compassionate or courageous, then so is Jones, and never mind the sex of Smith or Jones. Hence, the argument concludes, the world envisioned by *M*, in which everyone or nearly everyone is both feminine and masculine, is one in which life for everyone is more rewarding than the world advocated by *P*, in which some people are of only one gender; therefore we should undertake to bring about *M*.

The argument claims, then, that both genders embody traits that it would be valuable for everyone to have. But how is this claim to be tested? Let us adopt the view that to say that something is valuable for everyone is, roughly, to say that if everyone were unbiased, well-informed, and thinking and feeling clearly, everyone would, in fact, value it. As things are now, it is difficult or impossible to predict what everyone would value under such conditions. But there is an alternative. We can seek to establish conditions in which people do make unbiased, informed, etc., choices, and see whether they then value both feminine and masculine traits.

But this reminds us, of course, of the program of *P*. *P* does not guarantee clear thought and emotional sensitivity, but it does propose an environment in which people are informed about all gender options and are unbiased with respect to them. If, in this context, all or most people, when they are thinking clearly, etc., tend to prefer, for themselves and others, both feminine and masculine virtues, we will have evidence to support the claim that androgyny has universal value. (In this case, *P* is likely to change into *M*.) On the other hand, if "pure" gender is preferred by many, we should be skeptical of the claim that androgyny has universal value. (In this case we should probably seek to preserve *P*.) It appears, then, that in order to discover whether $M$ is preferable to $P$, we should seek to bring about $P$.

In summary, we have noted the argument from freedom, which supports $P$; arguments from anxiety and frustration, which are indecisive; and the argument from universal value, whose analysis suggests the provisional adoption of $P$. As far as I know, there are no additional major arguments which can plausibly be presented now for either side of the issue. Given, then, the problem of deciding between $M$ and $P$ without reference to other alternatives, my tentative conclusion is that because of the great value of freedom, and because in an atmosphere of gender-freedom we will be in a good position to evaluate the major argument for $M$ (that is, the argument from the universal value of androgyny), $P$ is preferable to $M$.

Of course all we have assumed about the specific nature of the hypothetical society for which we are making this judgment is that the connection between sex and gender would be absent, as would be the unacceptable components of traditional gender concepts, particularly dominance and submission. It might be, then, that particular social conditions would constitute grounds for supporting $M$ rather than $P$. For example, if the society in question were hierarchical with leadership roles tightly held by the predominantly masculine individuals, and if leaders with feminine characteristics were more likely to bring about changes of significant value (for example, eliminating war or oppression), it could reasonably be argued that $M$, in which everyone, including leaders, has both feminine and masculine characteristics, would be preferable to $P$. But such considerations are only speculative now.

## NOTES

1. Official Report to the United Nations on the Status of Women in Sweden, 1968. Quoted in Rita Liljeström, "The Swedish Model," in *Sex Roles in Changing Society*, ed. Georgene H. Seward and Robert C. Williamson (New York: Random House, 1970), p. 200.
2. Jessie Bernard, *Women and the Public Interest* (Chicago: Aldine, 1971); and idem, *The Future of Marriage* (New York: Bantam Books, 1972). The quotation is from the latter book, p. 279.
3. Caroline Bird, *Born Female* (New York: Pocket Books, 1968), p. xi.

4. Judith M. Bardwick, "Androgyny and Humanistic Goals, or Goodbye, Cardboard People," in *The American Woman: Who Will She Be?* ed. Mary Louise McBee and Kathryn A. Blake (Beverly Hills, Calif.: Glencoe Press, 1974), p. 61.

5. "Monoandrogynism" and "polyandrogynism" are perhaps not very happy terms, but I have been unable to find alternatives which are both descriptive and non-question-begging. In an earlier version of this paper I used "$A_1$" and "$A_2$" but these labels are not as perspicuous as "$M$" and "$P$". Mary Anne Warren, in "The Ideal of Androgyny" (unpublished) refers to "the strong thesis" and "the weak thesis," but this terminology tends to prejudice judgment as to which view is preferable. Hence, I use "$M$" and "$P$."

6. Constantina Safilios-Rothschild, *Women and Social Policy* (Englewood Cliffs, N.J.: Prentice-Hall, 1974), p. 7; emphasis hers.

7. Carolyn Heilbrun, *Toward a Recognition of Androgyny* (New York: Harper & Row, 1973), pp. 7–8.

8. My current view is that we should work for the universal realization of women's values; but that is another paper. (For some arguments against the use of the term "androgyny" in feminist theory, see, for example, Mary Daly, "The Qualitative Leap beyond Patriarchal Religion," *Quest: A Feminist Quarterly*, vol. 1, no. 4 [Spring 1975], pp. 29ff.; and Janice Raymond, "The Illusion of Androgyny," *Quest*, vol. 2, no. 1 [Summer 1975].)

9. Bardwick, op. cit., p. 50.

Anne Dickason

# The Feminine As a Universal

Throughout the history of ideas, few concepts have been so influential, yet so elusive, as that known as "the feminine." The concept appears well defined as early as the third century B.C. in both Western and Eastern thought; the Pythagorean Table of Opposites and the dualisms of Yin-Yang express similar divisions of nature clustered around "masculine" and "feminine" characteristics.[1] Recent scholarship has widely investigated the legal, economic, and religious status of women in various societies; and current research is exploring the biological and psychological characteristics of women and men in order to see if there are any innately feminine and masculine traits. But it is obvious from the level of current debate that final answers are not yet available on this question. There is, in fact, much contradictory evidence.

"Accidentalists" believe that all masculine and feminine qualities are nonessential properties of what it means to be a man or a woman. They argue that both men and women are primarily shaped by the surrounding culture, and that neither sex is born with any sex-linked psychological characteristics. Studies that show upbringing rather than gender as the molder of identity in hermaphrodite individuals are cited to support this position,[2] which is further upheld by sociological data on the enormous variety of sex-role assignments found among different cultures.[3] Many feminists are in sympathy with the accidentalists' position, thinking that they must abandon traditional conceptions of masculine and feminine behavior and attitudes if equality is to be achieved.

"Essentialists" take the counter position, and believe in definite, universal masculine and feminine characteristics. They cite studies that link the presence of male sex hormones to increased aggressive behavior,[4] and they emphasize the agreement among cultures on feminine and masculine identification.[5] According to this theory, psychosexual neutrality at birth is a misconception; the concepts of feminine and masculine contain specific qualities that are independent of cultural differences. The essentialist position varies greatly in interpretation from outright misogynism ("feminine is inferior") to more willing acceptance ("separate but equal"). Relatively few feminists support this position, though some feel forced into it by what they see as the weight of the arguments. Others accept it more easily, claiming that the traditional evidence has been unfairly interpreted; they believe that the natural superiority of women rather than second-class status is indicated by the research involved.

In the midst of the controversy generated by this problem lies the fact that there has been no thorough consideration of the concept of "feminine" itself. There are many modern theories regarding the masculine and the feminine. These vary from the biological explanation of Charles Darwin to the sociological thesis of J. J. Bachofen; from the economic analysis of Robert Briffault to the psychological theories of Sigmund Freud; from the mythic interpretations of C. G. Jung and Erich Neumann to the anthropological research of Margaret Mead. Basically, Darwin, Bachofen, Freud, Jung, and Neumann provide arguments often used by essentialists, while Briffault and Mead give foundations for the accidentalists. When we examine all of these views we find little agreement on the origins of the concept of the feminine, yet a surprising consistency on what the feminine is. We also find that although ideas about feminine characteristics are not universal enough to be considered necessary, they do occur often enough to seem more than coincidental. This paper is concerned with whether the disclosed commonality can be explained without reverting to the necessity of essentialism. It is my thesis that such an explanation is possible, if we look at the logical foundations of the theories themselves. To do this, I will first give a brief presentation of each view, and then analyze them all.

# I. DARWIN

The first modern theory of the feminine and masculine appears in Charles Darwin's discussion of evolution. Darwin thought that in addition to the primary influence of natural selection (the survival of the fittest) there is another influence on the development of a species, that of sexual selection. Less rigorous than natural selection, since the result is not death for the individual but the production of fewer offspring, sexual selection depends not on external conditions, but on the struggle of (usually) males for females.[6] Such small advantages as better weapons for driving away other males, more attractive ornaments, and more appealing odors will attract the most vigorous females, who breed earliest; and these traits will be transmitted to the young.[7]

If such variations are of no service to either sex, they will not be accumulated and increased by sexual or natural selection. Nevertheless, they may become permanent if the exciting cause acts permanently; and in accordance with a frequent form of inheritance they may be transmitted to that sex alone in which they first appeared. In this case the two sexes will come to present permanent, yet unimportant, differences of character.[8]

An example of this is different colors worn by males and females of the same species; the differences are unimportant in the sense that they are not necessary for survival, since females without brilliant plumage survive as well as males who possess it. In this way masculine and feminine traits could become sex-linked.

This theory, combined with careful observation of the animal world, led Darwin to draw analogous conclusions about men and women. "Man is more courageous, pugnacious and energetic than woman, and has more inventive genius."[9] The greater size and courage of men "are all due in chief part to inheritance from his half-human male ancestors."[10] Even with regard to the differences in mental powers between men and women, he says, "it is probable that sexual selection has played a highly important part."[11] Presumably, women chose to mate with men who were braver and more intelligent, thus perpetuating those qualities. And males developed these traits both through competing with other males for a female and through fighting females of equal dominance that they could overpower.

Gradually the human male gained the power of selection, unlike the lower animals where the female chooses her mate. When this transition occurred, males then chose females who possessed more submissive qualities.[12] Darwin notes that it is fortunate that there is some equality in the transmission of traits, "otherwise it is probable that man would have become as superior in mental endowment to women, as the peacock is in ornamental plumage to the peahen."[13]

Darwin unabashedly draws many of his conclusions about innate temperament from nonhuman life; he concludes that some difference is "at least probable from the analogy of the lower animals which present other secondary sexual characteristics."[14]

> No one disputes that the bull differs in disposition from the cow, the wild-boar from the sow, the stallion from the mare, and, as is well known to the keepers of menageries, the males of the larger apes from the females. Woman seems to differ from man in mental disposition, chiefly in her greater tenderness and less selfishness. . . . Woman, owing to her maternal instincts, displays these qualities towards her infants in an eminent degree; therefore it is likely that she would often extend them towards her fellow creatures. Man is the rival of other men; he delights in competition, and this leads to ambition which passes too easily into selfishness. These latter qualities seem to be his natural and unfortunate birthright. It is generally admitted that with women the powers of intuition, of rapid perception, and perhaps of imitation, are more strongly marked than in man; but some, at least, of these faculties are characteristic of the lower races, and therefore of a past and lower state of civilization.[15]

Darwin thus believes in the traditional attributes of masculine and feminine, and explains their origin in terms of biological development; these traits were considered more attractive by the opposite sex and so were preserved through the process of evolution. Since the power of selection eventually settled on the human male, his choice of feminine traits was reflected in the offspring.

## II. BACHOFEN

During the time that Darwin was developing his theory of biological evolution, J. J. Bachofen formulated his theory of cultural evolution through the doctrine of mother-right. After careful examination of myths, mortuary symbolism, and primitive societies, Bachofen concluded that each human society without exception passes through three stages. The first, the tellurian, is characterized by motherhood without marriage, the absence of agriculture, and abusive sexual treatment of women. In this primary phase women are important because of their maternal role; they establish kinship, and the feminine powers of fruitfulness and nourishment are called forth in religious rites. But, Bachofen believes, during the tellurian phase women are subject to man's uncontained lust. Eventually women revolt, demanding a more settled, monogamous life. This second stage is the lunar, and brings with it marriage and agriculture; as women insist upon a more gentle life, societies discover more peaceful occupations. It is at this time that men begin to recognize their biological relationship to children. This comprises the second, higher stage of mother-right. As fathers acquire almost exclusive rights over their children, society moves into the solar period of human development; this is the third and final phase, that of father-right. Here, division of labor arises and individual ownership of property gains importance. Bachofen considers father-right the highest stage of culture, and views mother-right as an essential prelude.

Mother-right is an important stage for several reasons:

> The relationship which stands at the origin of all culture, of every virtue, of every nobler aspect of existence, is that between mother and child; it operates in a world of violence as the divine principle of love, of union, of peace. Raising her young, the woman learns earlier than the man to extend her loving care beyond the limits of ego to another creature, and to direct whatever gift of invention she possesses to the preservation and improvement of this other's existence. Woman at this stage is the repository of all culture, of all benevolence, of all devotion, of all concern for the living and grief for the dead.[16]

The matriarchal principle, the feminine, is thus inherently universal; it provides the idea of inclusiveness in a broad family. "It is the basis of the universal freedom and equality so frequent among matriarchal peoples, of their hospitality, and of their aversion to restrictions of all sorts."[17] Bachofen believes that this comes because of the lack of an idea of paternity; if no one recognizes the biological connection between men and their children, then everyone sees all others as brothers and sisters. The maternal principle is subject to matter and the phenomena of natural life; it feels harmony with the universe and is keenly aware of pain and death. Because it was women who demanded an end to the primary stage, women were first drawn to a purer ethical view. But father-right overcomes this because "the triumph of paternity brings with it the liberation of the spirit from the manifestations of nature, a sublimation of human existence over the laws of material life."[18]

Bachofen, like Darwin, believes that the characteristics we term feminine and masculine are imbedded in our human nature; to Bachofen, the feminine begins with the maternal relationship and develops by influencing the cultural growth of society along a particular, universal path. Women are more inclusive, passive, and nurturing as a result of their role as mother; these qualities influence society for a while, bringing it to a more advanced stage, but eventually these qualities give way to the narrower but more successful concepts coming from patriarchy.

## III. BRIFFAULT

Robert Briffault was influenced by Bachofen, but provided a more neutral explanation for the prominent occurrence of patriarchy. Like Darwin, Briffault looks first to the animal world for explanatory models. But what Briffault finds is that instead of the male being smarter and braver, "the female is the more cautious, wary, ingenious, and sagacious; while the male is reckless, incautious, and often stupid in comparison."[19] To Briffault, it is the female, not the male, who forms the nucleus of the animal family; the mother and her offspring are the family. "The male, instead of being the head and supporter of the group, is not an essential member of it, and more often than not is altogether absent from it."[20] Thus, Briffault feels that animal life can provide us with valuable clues about the innate characteristics of male and female, but that the traits we find are often nearly opposite from those cited by Darwin. Further, when Briffault looks to primitive societies, he finds:

> There is not among primitive men and women the disparity in physical power, resourcefulness, enterprise, courage, capacity for endurance, which are observed in civilized societies and are often regarded as organic sexual differences. To a very large extent those differences in physical and mental capacity are the effect, rather than the cause, of that divergence in the avocations of men and women which has taken place in the course of cultural and social development.[21]

The reason for this divergence is economic, Briffault believes, and does not rest on physical advantages. He discovers that in primitive societies there is nothing corresponding to the domination of one sex by the other which characterizes later, patriarchal societies. But, unlike Bachofen, he does not see the transition from matriarchy to patriarchy as a universal, necessary pattern. Whereas Bachofen sees this transition as a result of the development of human nature toward the spiritual, Briffault ties it to economic changes which are frequent, but not necessary. So long as men are hunters, women remain gatherers; men may contribute the raw materials, but women actually make the products of household industry, for example, pottery and baskets. Women are in charge of administration as well. In such societies women remain important for the economy, contributing independently to the society, and are not subject to the rule of men. But when men cease to be hunters and develop domesticated cattle, society becomes patriarchal due to the concentration of wealth in the hands of the men. Here women's economic importance drastically declines. Pastoral society is "without exception . . . stringently patriarchal and moreover extensively polygamous."[22]

When agriculture is introduced at this later stage, rather than directly after the hunting and gathering mode, the importance of women continues to decrease. Briffault said that "the loss of woman's economic value as a worker abolished the purpose for which the association of individual marriage such as it is found in primitive societies, originally arose."[23] This results in an inversion of the original, biological sex roles and makes women compete for men, for example, through beauty. Primitive woman has little need to cultivate charm and attraction; but in pastoral life "her value is as an attractive sexual asset."[24] According to Briffault, those characteristics we call masculine and feminine are not found in the corresponding sexes in the animal world. Females, not males, possess courage and intelligence and ward off danger. And he finds that as long as primitive societies remain hunting-gathering groups, it is the women who are considered wise, and often strong and courageous as well. The "feminine" attributes in women develop only when males acquire superior economic power, usually through their prior association as hunters with animals. No longer having economic importance, women must cultivate other qualities if they are to survive in the society.

But any society, our own included, would at once lose its patriarchal character founded upon masculine economic dominance, were
the forms of industry and wealth-production to revert to the dimensions of household industry.[25]

To Briffault, our image of the feminine comes from economic
dominance, not biological or psychological characteristics, and
would disappear if the economic structure were to change, giving women more power.

## IV. FREUD

With Sigmund Freud, the discussion of masculine and feminine
moves to a new, internal plane. Freud's discussion of women
has long been scathed by feminists, for reasons easily seen, but
it should be pointed out that Freud himself asserted that "it is
not always easy to distinguish between what is due to the influence of the sexual function and what to social training."[26] Like
Darwin and Briffault, Freud sees some clues to the nature of
feminine and masculine in the animal world, though he is not
certain this carries enough force.

In an early writing Freud states that autoerotic sexuality in
young girls might be said to be "of a wholly masculine character."[27]

Indeed, if we were able to give a more definite connotation to the
concepts of 'masculine' and 'feminine,' it would even be possible
to maintain that libido is invariably and necessarily of a masculine
nature, whether it occurs in men or in women and irrespectively of
whether its object is a man or a woman.[28]

He explains the reason for this in a footnote added later:

'Masculine' and 'feminine' are used sometimes in the sense of activity and passivity, sometimes in a biological, and sometimes, again,
in a sociological sense. The first of these three meanings is the essential one and the most serviceable in psychoanalysis. When, for instance, libido was described in the text above as being 'masculine,'
the word was being used in this sense, for an instinct is always active
even when it has a passive aim in view. The second, or biological,
meaning of 'masculine' and 'feminine' is the one whose applicability
can be determined most easily. Here 'masculine' and 'feminine' are
characterized by the presence of spermatozoa or ova respectively
and by the functions proceeding from them. Activity and its concomitant phenomena (more powerful muscular development, aggressiveness, greater intensity of libido) are as a rule linked with

biological masculinity; but they are not necessarily so, for there are animal species in which these qualities are on the contrary assigned to the female. The third, or sociological, meaning receives its connotation from the observation of actually existing masculine and feminine individuals. Such observation shows that in human beings pure masculinity or femininity is not to be found either in a psychological or a biological sense. Every individual on the contrary displays a mixture of the character-traits belonging to his own and the opposite sex; and he shows a combination of activity and passivity whether or not these last character-traits tally with his biological ones.[29]

Here Freud reveals his ambiguity; on the one hand, the identification of male as active and female as passive seems verified by observation of animal or cellular life; on the other hand, Freud recognizes that this is far from a universal identification. Freud writes later, "even in the sphere of human sexual life, one soon notices how unsatisfactory it is to identify masculine behavior with activity and feminine with passivity."[30] But if Freud was not able to discover the origins of our behavior, if he could not find a clear biological basis for our characterizations of feminine and masculine, he was nonetheless able to describe the nature of these images which he thought we possess. Although the origin of the feminine might have been unknown to Freud, its essence was not.

He believed that women, unlike men, must make two important transformations in order to achieve adult sexuality; the erogenous zone must change from the clitoris to the vagina, and the love object must change from the mother to the father. These difficulties mean that it is harder for a girl to become a woman than it is for a boy to become a man; the female faces a sterner, more indirect task. But even in the child the feminine reveals itself:

The little girl is as a rule less aggressive, less defiant, and less self-sufficient; she seems to have a greater need for affection to be shown her, and therefore to be more dependent and docile. . . . One gets the impression, too, that the little girl is more intelligent and more lively than the boy of the same age; she is more inclined to meet the external world halfway, and, at the same time, she makes stronger object-cathexes.[31]

And in mature women we find additional characteristics:

We attribute to women a greater amount of narcissism (and this influences their object-choice) so that for them to be loved is a stronger need than to love. Their vanity is partly a further effect of penis-envy, for they are driven to rate their physical charms more highly as a belated compensation for their original sexual inferiority.[32]

It must be admitted that women have but little sense of justice, and this no doubt connected with the preponderance of envy in their mental life; for the demands of justice are a modification of envy. . . . We say also of women that their social interests are weaker than those of men, and that their capacity for the sublimation of their instincts is less.[33]

Freud notes that while a man of age thirty in analysis is usually relatively young, a woman of the same age "frequently staggers us by her psychological rigidity and unchangeability"; it is "as though, in fact, the difficult development which leads to femininity had exhausted all the possibilities of the individual."[34]

Freud does assert that "the anatomical distinction between the sexes, must, after all, leave its mark in mental life";[35] and in this way it seems that he would like his theory of what is masculine and feminine to carry some universality. He is often criticized as if he were writing about human nature itself, about how men and women are innately, rather than about how the masculine and feminine are currently expressed. But careful reading of his works does not support this view. For he also believes that psychology cannot solve the "riddle of femininity" until biology can explain how sexual division came about in life itself; since this has not been done, the full nature and importance of the feminine and masculine cannot be known. It is at least possible, to Freud, that cultural influences might someday be seen as more important than he thinks.

## V. JUNG AND NEUMANN

C. G. Jung, once a student of Freud, developed his own theory of the masculine and feminine. Whereas Freud was interested in personal conflicts and in the desires people acquire while very young, Jung formulated the concept of a collective unconscious, which each of us possesses and which contains the constant images or archetypes of a universal psychic life. Jung believed that we have access to this collective unconscious through myths, dreams, and art. When we examine these for repetitive features, we find portrayals of the feminine and masculine which clarify the meaning of these concepts. Jung does not look to the animal world for an explanatory model, and he does not discuss why these differences of masculine and feminine arose; like Freud, he is interested in describing what content the concepts have, and how they are expressed in human life. He states that

> Every man carries within him the eternal image of woman, not the image of this or that particular woman, but a definite feminine image. This image is fundamentally unconscious, an hereditary factor of primordial origin engraved in the living organic system of the man, an imprint or 'archetype' of all the ancestral experiences of the female, a deposit, as it were, of all impressions ever made by woman—in short, an inherited system of psychic adaptation. Even if no woman existed, it would still be possible, at any given time, to deduce from this unconscious image exactly how a woman would have to be constituted psychically. The same is true of the woman: she too has her inborn image of man.[36]

In man this archetype is the anima; in woman, the animus. Lovers project this image upon their beloved, and this often keeps them from seeing the beloved's true nature. It is a general human characteristic to do this, "but in woman it is given a particularly dangerous twist because in this respect she is not naive and it is only too often her *intention* to let herself be convinced by [the man's projected feelings]."[37] This is because of her feminine qualities. Jung believes that consciousness and activity are masculine attributes, while unconsciousness and passivity are feminine; but through the anima or animus each person contains something of the opposite sex. It is possible to "live out the opposite sex in oneself," for a man to live in his feminine part and a woman to live in her masculine part, but if this is done, "one's real individuality suffers."[38] This happens because people try to negate their true male or female nature, and want to pretend that such an essence does not exist.

The basic difference Jung sees between feminine and masculine is that "woman's psychology is founded on the principle of Eros, the great binder and loosener, whereas from ancient times the ruling principle ascribed to man is Logos."[39] Women are interested in feelings, psychic relatedness, and completeness, while men are drawn to logic, objectivity, and perfection. "To a woman it is generally more important to know how a man feels about a thing than to know the thing itself."[40] But while these characteristics are true of outer attitudes, "in the soul it is the other way round: inwardly it is the man who feels, and the woman who reflects."[41] "Hence a man's greater liability to total despair, while a woman can always find comfort and hope; accordingly, a man is more likely to put an end to himself than a woman."[42]

What Jung has done is to concretize and universalize particular attitudes toward the world as "feminine" and "masculine," yet offer an explanation of individual variations within each sex. For example, it is possible for a woman to be only feminine, but she is likely to seem shallow and to be only a mirror for men's projections onto her; once she attains some consciousness, she cannot return to this state. From then on she must accept the masculine element within her, integrating it into her feminine personality; she must accept her own rationality and assertiveness, and not try to bury them in the guise of only wanting to be a "man's woman." Only then will she be able to achieve relatedness, to be a feminine woman in the fullest sense.

Erich Neumann took many of these ideas from Jung, and discussed them in more literary, less psychoanalytic terms. He carries Jung's theory about masculine and feminine personal identification even further:

> It is in this sense that we use the terms 'masculine' and 'feminine' throughout the book, not as personal sex-linked characteristics, but as symbolic expressions. When we say masculine or feminine dominants obtrude themselves at certain stages, or in certain cultures or types of person, this is a psychological statement which must not be reduced to biological or sociological terms. The symbolism of 'masculine' and 'feminine' is archetypal and therefore transpersonal; in the various cultures concerned, it is erroneously projected upon persons as though they carried its qualities. In reality every individual is a psychological hybrid. Even sexual symbolism cannot be derived from the person, because it is prior to the person. Conversely, it is one of the complications of individual psychology that in all cultures the integrity of the personality is violated when it is identified with either the masculine or the feminine side of the symbolic principle of opposites.[43]

Neumann retains Jung's identification of the feminine with "unconsciousness—darkness—night" and the masculine with "consciousness—light—day." This holds true regardless of sex: that is, unconsciousness is feminine in men or women. Neumann believes, like Bachofen and Briffault, that society has moved from the matriarchal to the patriarchal with its increasing reach toward the conscious phase of objective, rational thought. The masculine is concerned with the ego, with "the qualities of volition, decision, and activity as contrasted with the determinism and blind 'drives' of the preconscious, egoless state."[44]

Neumann then considers the path the feminine follows in its emergence from this preconscious state. Unlike Freud, who emphasizes genital sexuality and feelings toward the parents, Neumann sees the journey in strikingly different terms. The myth of Amor and Psyche provides him with an ideal model. Psyche, a beautiful mortal, is given in marriage to a husband she never sees and does not know; he is, in fact, the god Eros. Psyche takes a lamp one night, and tries to glimpse him; but a drop of oil spills from the lamp, waking Eros, who flies away. Psyche then must accomplish several tasks in order to be united with Eros again. Neumann states:

The fundamental situation of the feminine, as we have elsewhere shown, is the primordial relation of identity between daughter and mother. For this reason the approach of the male always and in every case means separation. Marriage is always a mystery, but also a mystery of death. For the male—and this is inherent in the essential opposition between masculine and the feminine—marriage, as the matriarchate recognized, is primarily an abduction, an acquisition—a rape. When we concern ourselves with this profound mythological and psychological stratum, we must forget cultural development and the cultural forms taken by the relationship between man and woman and go back to the primordial phenomenon of the sexual encounter between them. It is not hard to see that the significance of this encounter is and must be very different for the masculine and the feminine. What for the masculine is aggression, victory, rape, and the satisfaction of desire—we need only take a look at the animal world and have the courage to recognize this stratum for man as well—is for the feminine destiny, transformation, and the profoundest mystery of life.[45]

Neumann describes what it is about the sexual encounter that provides such meaning for the feminine. Both women and men seek ego-stability, or personal identity.

Among men this stability is manifested as endurance of pain, hunger, thirst, and so forth; but in the feminine sphere it characteristically takes the form of resistance to pity. This firmness of the strong-willed ego, concentrated on its goal, is expressed in countless other myths and fairy tales, with their injunctions not to turn around, not to answer, and the like. . . . The feminine is threatened in its ego stability by the danger of distraction through 'relatedness,' through Eros.[46]

Psyche in her tasks comes to a donkey-driver, a corpse, and elderly weaving-women, all of whom ask for her help. But she has been instructed, "be thou not moved with pity . . . for it is not lawful."[47] The feminine must always keep in mind the distant goal and not give way to the close-at-hand. Like Jung, who believes that the feminine aims at completion, Neumann states that "the conception of the archetypal feminine as a unity is one of woman's fundamental experiences."[48] It is the collective, the group, the bringing together that characterizes the feminine; the masculine is tied to the individual, the self. But in order to attain this unity, "the feminine must develop toward and beyond the masculine, which represents consciousness over against the unconscious."[49] For either man or woman to become whole, both masculine and feminine elements must be accepted. And when this is done, love is possible. It is the experience of love that makes sexual union a "transformation" for the feminine, and, through the feminine, for the masculine as well. Psyche has, in effect, taught Eros to love, and this makes her divine.

## VI. MEAD

We can see now that all of these writers, with the exception of Briffault, agree that there is some unified concept to which "the feminine" refers, even if they do not agree on its origins. It was not until Margaret Mead's anthropological research that this idea was seriously undermined. In *Sex and Temperament* Mead describes three societies: the Arapesh, whose ideal is mild, responsive men and women; the Mundugumor, whose ideal prescribes violent, aggressive men and women; and the Tchambuli, whose ideal is dominant women and dependent men. Her conclusion is:

If those temperamental attitudes which we have traditionally regarded as feminine—such as passivity, responsiveness, and a willingness to cherish children—can so easily be set up as the masculine pattern in one tribe, and in another be outlawed for the majority of women as well as for the majority of men, we no longer have any basis for regarding such aspects of behavior as sex-linked.[50]

The history of the social definition of sex differences is filled with such arbitrary arrangements in the intellectual and artistic field, but because of the assumed congruence between physiological sex and emotional endowment we have been less able to recognize that a similar arbitrary selection is being made among emotional traits also. We have assumed that because it is convenient for a mother to wish to care for her child, this is a trait with which women have been more generously endowed by a carefully teleological process of evolution. We have assumed that because men have hunted, an activity requiring enterprise, bravery, and initiative, they have been endowed with these useful attitudes as part of their sex-temperament.[51]

Mead thus believes that cultural definitions of masculine and feminine vary considerably. Her explanation for this is that among all societies there are some disparities in individual temperament; some people are more aggressive, while others are restrained, and some people are brave, while others are more cautious. For various reasons, often relating to economic and geographic circumstances, societies come to value these temperaments differently. They educate the children accordingly, encouraging some behavior and not other. To Mead, there might be both "aggressive" and "passive" human dispositions, but assigning these universally as "masculine" and "feminine" is an illegitimate step. She believes that "we are forced to conclude that human nature is almost unbelievably malleable."[52] "Standardized personality differences between the sexes are of this order, cultural creations to which each generation, male and female, is trained to conform."[53] Our concept of the feminine had origins in specific cultural conditions, and we must not assume that other images of the feminine are identical or even similar; in fact, they may be nearly opposite.

## VII. ANALYSIS

Having seen these basic theories on the origin and nature of the feminine, we can take up the first basic question of this paper: Is the feminine a universal? Philosophy from the time of the Greeks has been interested in whether general objects of thought exist, and if they do, whether they have real existence independent of the mind. When Plato asked "What is virtue?" and "What is beauty?" he was asking for "a single and essential form common to all things of the same kind, by virtue of which they are things of the same kind."[54] Debate on the nature of the feminine has polarized around two common theories of universals  essentialists believe that there is one essence, or universal property, which characterizes every concept of the feminine, and accidentalists deny this, asserting that there is no one concept of the feminine, but rather that there are many varying images. It has become increasingly clear through research such as Mead's that the answer to the question of whether the feminine is a Platonic universal must be "no." It seems, as a matter of fact, that there is enormous variety throughout the world on what is masculine and what is feminine.

But, returning to the second question of this paper: Is there some general agreement on the nature of the feminine, even if the feminine is not a universal? Judging from the major theories we have considered, the answer must be "yes"; most of the writers agree that there is some essence of the feminine, and they also usually agree with each other on the qualities that this essence contains.

This raises our third major question: Is some explanation of this general agreement possible without reverting to essentialism? And here again, I believe, the answer must be "yes." When we recall the positions presented above, it seems more than coincidental that so many of them find a universal feminine and can agree almost completely on its nature (if not on its origins).

Before proceeding, we must separate two issues which are easily confused.[55] The historical problem of the origin and nature of concepts of the feminine is one question; the logical problem of the basis of theories about the feminine is another. The former problem is being considered by the writers we have presented; they examine various types of evidence and present diverse speculations on, for example, the biological purpose of sexual differentiation, or what notions the Greeks had of masculine and feminine. But one facet of their arguments on the historical problem intrigues me here. Darwin, Bachofen, Freud, Jung, and Neumann each occasionally admit, as we have seen, that there are some counter-examples that their theories cannot explain. Often this is an example in the animal world or a primitive society that does not comply with what the theory requires—for example, an instance where the male is passive and the female is aggressive. Why, I wonder, were such skilled scientists and scholars so drawn to universality, given the problem of exceptions? Why did they not settle for a claim of generality, and leave their conclusions more open-ended? Why did they believe so strongly that this is the way the feminine must be (Darwin and Bachofen), or, at any rate, always is (Freud, Jung, and Neumann)?

I believe that if we look at Briffault and Mead we can find at least a clue for answering these questions. Briffault is at times ambivalent on the conclusions we can draw from the examples of animal life, and portions of his position can be given an essentialist slant. But the area where he is the most convincing on the importance of nonhuman behavior is in his analysis of sexual encounters. He states, "Nowhere do we know of the male using compulsion towards the female. The family group of animals is the manifestation of a correlation of instincts, not of a process of physical domination."[56] The model of sexual activity among animals is one of female receptivity; she decides with whom she will mate. Briffault believes that this mode is maintained in primitive societies where women still have economic power; it is not until patriarchy that the bride-price is instituted. The rise of patriarchy brings with it an "inversion of the biological and primitive relations between the sexes";[57] through this inversion the rule of female receptivity is abandoned, and male dominance takes over. Thus Briffault does not consider the male-dominance model as having any basis in either animal life or primitive society.

Margaret Mead also analyzes the sexual relationship, and comes to a similar conclusion:

Many writers on the sexes and the human family lay great emphasis upon the fact that the human male is capable of rape. This is an abrupt and startling way of putting something that is actually much subtler. In the human species the male is capable of copulating with a relatively unaroused and uninterested female. We have no evidence that suggests that rape within the meaning of the act—that is, rape of a totally unwilling female—has ever become recognized social practice.[58]

There is, she believes, a shift from female to male readiness between the primates and humans; but rape itself "is a very different act from any behavior that can be postulated for the small groups of creatures who at the dawn of our history were just inventing social patterns."[59] I think this is a telling point; the two more liberal theories believe it is not correct to construe the sexual relationship as one where the male "has his way" with the female, for either animals or primitive human society.

But in Darwin, Bachofen, Freud, Jung, and Neumann, this is not true. Each of these writers assumes a picture of primitive sexuality where man forces himself on woman. They do not offer arguments on why they think this is true, and yet I feel that they use it as the basis for much broader conclusions. This assumption presupposes the very point the theories are designed to prove: that men are aggressive and women are passive. By accepting without justification the male-dominance model for primitive human relationships, each of these theories then claims on the basis of this model that men are by nature assertive and independent, while women by nature are passive and dependent. This unjustified model is used to attribute these qualities to the whole personality. The model assumes, by extension, that "man defines, woman conforms," that the masculine structures the feminine in a non-reciprocal way.

In Darwin, this presupposition of male dominance in primitive human life is seen in the theory of sexual selection:

> Man is more powerful in body and mind than woman, and in the savage state he keeps her in a far more abject state of bondage than does the male of any other animal; therefore it is not surprising that he should have gained the power of selection.[60]

The competition of women for men through beauty and feminine charms is not the result of recent economic or social conditions to Darwin, but has ancient biological origins. Because of his superior strength, man could choose any woman; the traits in her he favored were passed on to female offspring and are those we now call feminine. This process of selection was not two-way because a man could mate with any woman he wanted and did not need to be willingly accepted by her.

In Bachofen, the assumption is expressed in the idea that during the first stage women were "defenseless against abuse by men"[61] and only in the second level of mother-right did their position improve. Bachofen brings back this image of male force in the third, patriarchal stage. When patriarchy succeeds, it is because the spiritual, self-oriented male aspect rises over the material, group-oriented female existence. In the highest phase of civilization, masculine force takes on a more psychological character, as man acts as a restrictive foil to woman's universality. The masculine provides the human species with its highest goal and final direction, and so limits the power of the feminine. It shapes the feminine, yet finds itself when it is unfettered by feminine limits.

Freud expresses the presupposition of primitive male dominance when he discusses sex in this way:

> The male sexual cell is active and mobile; it seeks out the female one, while the latter, the ovum, is stationary, and waits passively.

This behavior of the elementary organisms of sex is more or less a model of the behavior of the individuals of each sex in sexual intercourse. The male pursues the female for the purpose of sexual union, seizes her and pushes his way into her.[62]

Woman's passivity is passive in relation to something, and this something is the activity found in the male; this activity can be observed in human behavior, in animal groups, in the sexual act, and even microscopically in the sexual cells themselves. Because of this, Freud feels that men find their adult sexuality more directly. A woman needs to transfer her erogenous zone and the love-object, and she is consequently more easily influenced by external factors. Women, as passive, are more receptive and malleable. They are more influenced by men, more defined by men, than men are by women.

In Jung and Neumann the assumption occurs again. Erich Neumann's interpretation of primitive sexual encounters has been given above. Because Jung and Neumann identify the feminine with unconsciousness and the masculine with consciousness, the masculine gives form and structure to the feminine but receives a subjective loosening in return. Both the masculine and the feminine are considered equally valuable, but the model of male definition of the female is still held. The masculine limits the feminine by providing objectivity and rationality; it tries to contain the darkness of the unconscious. Yet the masculine is itself only liberated, not confined, by what the feminine brings to it.

In conclusion, our investigation of the concept of the feminine has revealed several things. There does not seem to be any one quality which all images of the feminine must have; in this way we found that the feminine is not a Platonic universal. But there has been much traditional agreement among theories of the feminine on what characteristics are included in the concept. We found that this agreement can be explained without appealing to essentialism if we examine how the theories of the feminine themselves were constructed. Those writers (Darwin, Bachofen, Freud, Jung, and Neumann) who assume male dominance as the model of primitive human sexual relations seem to carry this model, by analogy, into all other personality traits of men and women; these authors accept or imply essentialist conclusions. But those writers (Briffault and Mead) who deny this model more easily accept wide cultural variations in concepts of the feminine. "The Eternal Feminine draws us on," judging from our analysis of these theories, only when we presuppose that early sexual encounters were the result of male force and female unwillingness, and when we then use this as a model for all female and male traits.

## NOTES

1. Aristotle, in the *Metaphysics* (986a 25–30), states that the Pythagoreans organized the ten principles in this way: in the Monad were male, limit, odd, one, right, resting, straight, light, good, and square; in the Dyad were female, unlimited, even, plurality, left, moving, curved, darkness, bad, and oblong. The Chinese constructed the characteristics according to Yin: female, negative, passive, weak, destructive, earth, completion; and Yang: male, positive, active, strong, constructive, heaven, beginning (Wing-tsit Chan, *A Source Book in Chinese Philosophy* [Princeton: Princeton University Press, 1963], pp. 244–48).
2. John Money, "Psychosexual Differentiation," in *Sex Research: New Developments*, ed. John Money (New York: Holt, Rinehart & Winston, 1965), pp. 10–11.
3. Margaret Mead, *Sex and Temperament* (New York: William Morrow, 1935), pp. 279–80.
4. Corine Hutt, *Males and Females* (Harmondsworth, England: Penguin, 1972), pp. 118–19.
5. C. G. Jung, *Civilization in Transition* (New York: Pantheon, 1964), pp. 117–18.
6. Charles Darwin, *The Origin of Species* (1859; New York: Mentor Books, 1958), p. 94.
7. Charles Darwin, *The Descent of Man* (1871; New York: D. Appleton, 1895), pp. 210–14.
8. Ibid., p. 224.
9. Ibid., p. 557.
10. Ibid., p. 563.
11. Ibid.
12. Ibid., p. 597.
13. Ibid., p. 565.
14. Ibid., p. 563.
15. Ibid., pp. 563–64.
16. J. J. Bachofen, *Myth, Religion, and Mother Right* (Princeton: Princeton University Press, 1967), p. 79.
17. Ibid., p. 80.
18. Ibid., p. 109.

19. Robert Briffault, *The Mothers* (New York: Macmillan, 1931), p. 21.
20. Ibid., p. 23.
21. Ibid., p. 159.
22. Ibid., p. 245.
23. Ibid., p. 249.
24. Ibid., p. 253.
25. Ibid., p. 176.
26. Sigmund Freud, "The Psychology of Women," in *New Introductory Lectures on Psychoanalysis* (New York: W.W. Norton, 1933), p. 180.
27. Sigmund Freud, "Three Essays on the Theory of Sexuality," in *The Complete Psychological Works*, vol. 7 (London: Hogarth, 1953), p. 219.
28. Ibid.
29. Ibid., pp. 219–20.
30. Freud, "Psychology of Women," p. 157.
31. Ibid., p. 160.
32. Ibid., p. 180.
33. Ibid., p. 183.
34. Ibid., p. 184.
35. Ibid., p. 170.
36. C. G. Jung, *The Development of Personality* (New York: Pantheon, 1954), p. 198.
37. Jung, *Civilization in Transition*, p. 117.
38. Ibid., p. 118.
39. Ibid., p. 123.
40. Ibid., p. 125.
41. C. G. Jung, *Psychological Reflections*, ed. Jolande Jacobi (Princeton: Princeton University Press, 1970), p. 110.
42. Ibid.
43. Erich Neumann, *The Origins and History of Consciousness* (New York: Pantheon, 1954), p. xxii.
44. Ibid., p. 125.
45. Erich Neumann, *Amor and Psyche* (New York: Pantheon, 1956), pp. 62–63.
46. Ibid., pp. 112–13.
47. Ibid., p. 48.
48. Ibid., p. 129.
49. Ibid., p. 130.
50. Mead, *Sex and Temperament*, p. 279.
51. Ibid., p. 286.
52. Ibid., p. 280.
53. Ibid.

54. *The Encyclopedia of Philosophy*, ed. Paul Edwards (New York: Macmillan, 1967), vol. 8, p. 195.
55. I am indebted to Dr. Jann Benson for valuable discussion on this point.
56. Briffault (above, n. 19), p. 20.
57. Ibid., p. 249.
58. Margaret Mead, *Male and Female* (New York: William Morrow, 1949), p. 203.
59. Ibid., p. 204.
60. Darwin, *Descent of Man*, p. 597.
61. Bachofen (above, n. 16), p. 94.
62. Freud, "Psychology of Women," p. 156.

# Sex Roles and Gender

# Further References

Starred items are those of philosophical interest.

Bardwick, Judith. *Psychology of Women*. New York: Harper & Row, 1971.

————, ed. *Readings on the Psychology of Women*. New York: Harper & Row, 1972.

Bardwick, Judith, and Douvan, Elizabeth. "Ambivalence: the Socialization of Women." In Gornick and Moran, eds., *Woman in Sexist Society*.

Bedell, Madelon. "Supermom!" *Ms.*, May 1973, pp. 84–87, 99–100.

Bem, Sandra. "Androgyny, vs. the Tight Little Lives of Fluffy Women and Chesty Men." *Psychology Today*, September 1975, pp. 58–62.

————. "The Measurement of Psychological Androgyny." *Journal of Consulting and Clinical Psychology* 42 (1974): 155–62.

Bem, Sandra, and Bem, D. J. "Training the Woman to Know Her Place." In *Beliefs, Attitudes and Human Affairs*, edited by D. J. Bem. Belmont, Calif.: Brooks/Cole, 1970.

Bernard, Jessie. *Women, Wives, Mothers*. Chicago: Aldine, 1975.

Bird, Caroline, with Briller, Sarah Welles. *Born Female: The High Cost of Keeping Women Down*. Rev. ed. New York: David McKay, 1970.

*Blackstone, William T. "Freedom and Women." *Ethics* 85 (1975): 243–48. [See Jaggar.]

Blum, L.; Homiak, M.; Housman, J.; and Scheman, N. "Altruism and Women's Oppression." *Philosophical Forum* 5 (1973–74): 222–47.

Broverman, Inge K., et al. "Sex-Role Stereotypes and Clinical Judgments of Mental Health." *Journal of Consulting and Clinical Psychology* 34 (1970): 1–7.

Campbell, Margaret. *"Why Would a Girl Go into Medicine?"* Old Westbury, N.Y.: Feminist Press, 1975.

Chafetz, Janet. *Masculine/Feminine or Human.* Itasca, Ill.: F.E. Peacock Publishers, 1974.

Chodorow, Nancy. "Being and Doing: A Cross-Cultural Examination of the Socialization of Males and Females." In Gornick and Moran, eds., *Woman in Sexist Society.*

*Cooper, W. E. "What Is Sexual Equality and Why Does Tey Want It?" *Ethics* 85 (1975): 256–57. [See Jaggar.]

Dahlstrom, Edmund, ed. *The Changing Roles of Men and Women.* Translated by Gunilla Anderson and Steven Anderson. Boston: Beacon Press, 1967.

*Dickason, Anne. "Anatomy and Destiny: The Role of Biology in Plato's Views of Women." *Philosophical Forum* 5 (1973–74): 45–53.

*English, Jane, ed. *Sex Equality.* Englewood Cliffs, N.J.: Prentice-Hall, 1977.

Firestone, Shulamith. *The Dialectic of Sex.* New York: William Morrow, 1970.

Freud, Sigmund. *The Psychology of Women.* New York: W.W. Norton, 1933.

Friedan, Betty. *The Feminine Mystique.* New York: Dell, 1963.

Friedl, Ernestine. *Woman and Man.* New York: Holt, Rinehart & Winston, 1975.

Galbraith, John Kenneth. "The Economics of the American Housewife." *Atlantic Monthly*, August 1973, pp. 78–83.

Gilder, George. *Sexual Suicide.* New York: Quadrangle, 1973.

Goldberg, Steven. *The Inevitability of Patriarchy.* New York: William Morrow, 1973.

Gornick, Vivian, and Moran, Barbara K., eds. *Woman in Sexist Society: Studies in Power and Powerlessness.* New York: Basic Books, 1971.

*Govier, Trudy. "Woman's Place." *Philosophy* 49 (1974): 305–9. [See Lucas.]

Graham, Patricia. "Women in Academe." *Science* 169 (1970): 1284–90.

*Haack, Susan. "On the Moral Relevance of Sex." *Philosophy* 49 (1974): 90–95. [See Lucas.]

Hall, Diana Long. "Biology, Sex Hormones, and Sexism in the 1920's." *Philosophical Forum* 5 (1973–74): 81–96.

Harrison, Barbara G. *Unlearning the Lie.* New York: Random House, 1973.

Heilbrun, Carolyn. *Toward a Recognition of Androgyny.* New York: Harper & Row, 1973.

*Hill, Thomas E., Jr. "Servility and Self-Respect." *Monist* 57 (1973): 87–104.

Horner, Matina. "Fail: Bright Women." *Psychology Today*, November 1969, p. 36.

———. "Toward an Understanding of Achievement-Related Conflicts in Women." In Stacey, et al., eds., *And Jill Came Tumbling After*.

*Jaggar, Alison. "On Sexual Equality." *Ethics* 84 (1974): 275–92. [See Blackstone, Cooper.]

Janeway, Elizabeth. *Man's World, Woman's Place*. New York: William Morrow, 1971.

Levy, Betty. "The School's Role in the Sex-Role Stereotyping of Girls." *Feminist Studies* 1 (1972): 5–23.

*Lucas, J. R. " 'Because You Are a Woman.' " *Philosophy* 48 (1973): 161–71. [See Govier, Haack.]

Lynn, David. *Parental and Sex-Role Identification*. Berkeley, Calif.: McCutchan Publishing Corp., 1969.

———. "The Process of Learning Parental and Sex-Role Identification." *Journal of Marriage and the Family* 28 (1966): 446–70.

Maccoby, Eleanor, ed. *The Development of Sex Differences*. Stanford, Calif.: Stanford University Press, 1966.

Maccoby, Eleanor, and Jacklin, Carol. *The Psychology of Sex Differences*. Stanford, Calif.: Stanford University Press, 1974.

Martin, M. Kay, and Voorhies, Barbara. *The Female of the Species*. New York: Columbia University Press, 1975.

Mead, Margaret. *Male and Female*. New York: William Morrow, 1949.

———. *Sex and Temperament*. New York: William Morrow, 1935.

Mednick, Martha; Tangri, S.; and Hoffman, L. *Women and Achievement*. Washington, D.C.: Hemisphere Publishers, 1975.

Mitchell, Juliet. *Woman's Estate*. New York: Pantheon, 1972.

Money, John, and Ehrhardt, Anke. *Man and Woman, Boy and Girl*. Baltimore: Johns Hopkins University Press, 1972.

Montagu, Ashley. *The Natural Superiority of Women*. New York: Macmillan, 1968.

Morgan, Robin, ed. *Sisterhood Is Powerful*. New York: Random House, 1970.

Oakley, Ann. *Sex, Gender and Society*. London: Temple Smith, 1972.

———. *The Sociology of Housework*. New York: Pantheon, 1974.

*Pierce, Christine. "Natural Law Language and Women." In Gornick and Moran, eds., *Woman in Sexist Society*.

Pleck, Joseph, and Sawyer, Jack, eds. *Men and Masculinity*. Englewood Cliffs, N.J.: Prentice-Hall, 1974.

Rousseau, Jean Jacques. *Émile*. 1762. Chapter 5, "Sophie, or Woman."

Rowbotham, Sheila. *Woman's Consciousness, Man's World*. Baltimore: Penguin Books, 1973.

Sherman, Julia. *On the Psychology of Women*. Springfield, Ill.: Charles C. Thomas, 1971.

Stacey, Judith; Béreaud, Susan; and Daniels, Joan, eds. *And Jill Came Tumbling After: Sexism in American Education*. New York: Dell, 1974.

Terman, L. M., and Miles, Catherine. *Sex and Personality*. New York: McGraw-Hill, 1936.

Terman, L. M., and Tyler, Leona. "Psychological Sex Differences." In *A Manual of Child Psychology*, edited by L. Carmichael. 2d ed. New York: Wiley, 1954.

Thomas, A. H., and Stewart, N. R. "Counselor Response to Female Clients with Deviate and Conforming Career Goals." *Journal of Counseling Psychology* 18 (1971): 352–57.

Tiger, Lionel. *Men in Groups*. New York: Random House, 1969.

*Trebilcot, Joyce. "Sex Roles: The Argument from Nature." *Ethics* 85 (1975): 249–55.

U'ren, Marjorie. "The Image of Women in Textbooks." In Gornick and Moran, eds., *Woman in Sexist Society*.

Vaughn, Gladys Gary, ed. *Women's Roles and Education: Changing Traditions in Population Planning*. New York: International Family Planning Project, 1975.

*Weisstein, Naomi. "Psychology Constructs the Female." In Gornick and Moran, eds., *Woman in Sexist Society*.

*Whitbeck, Caroline. "Theories of Sex Difference." *Philosophical Forum* 5 (1973–74): 54–80.

Women on Words and Images (A New Jersey N.O.W. Taskforce). "Look Jane Look. See Sex Stereotypes." In Stacey, et al., eds., *And Jill Came Tumbling After*.

Part III

# Sexism in Ordinary Language

# Part III

# Sexism in Ordinary Language

## *Introduction*

Sensitivity to the way in which women are talked about is not new with the advent of modern-day feminism. In as early as 1895, Elizabeth Cady Stanton dramatized what she saw as the unjust way in which women are written and spoken about by rewriting the Bible so as to eliminate its sexism.[1] With the resurgence of the feminist movement, we have found a renewed interest in ordinary language about women. Not until recently, however, have philosophers begun to take a serious look at the claim that ordinary language is sexist, or at the presuppositions of such a claim.

A large class of language-users appears to be able to tell, given any set of sentences about women, which of the sentences are, and which are not, sexist. Although certain sentences about men are also claimed to be sexist, we shall focus our attention here on those sentences about women which are claimed to be sexist. For example, from the set of sentences:

(1) Women make terrible drivers.
(2) She is a foxy chick.
(3) Some women drive poorly.
(4) She is an attractive woman.

it is likely that most of us would select (1) and (2) as sexist sentences about women, and (3) and (4) as non-sexist sentences about women.

Why is the distinction between sexist and non-sexist forms of discourse an important one, and why should philosophers be intrigued by it? If Wittgenstein is correct in his belief that the way we talk reflects our conception of things,[2] then the importance of the distinction becomes clear. For, if the way we talk reflects the way we think, and if the way we think reflects the way we act, then sexism in ordinary language has serious practical implications.

The claim that the way we talk reflects the way we think is not an unreasonable one. For example, few people have trouble identifying a person as a "racist," that is, as one who thinks about black persons in a discriminatory way, when that person consistently uses sentences such as:

(5) That nigger sure is dumb.
(6) Blacks love watermelons.
(7) He is a darn coon.

In turn, we expect that person to engage in certain activities as a result of his or her way of thinking. For instance, we expect that person not to advance black persons into his or her firm, not to invite black persons into his or her home, and, for that matter, not to have any black friends. In fact, we would probably be shocked to find that person engaging in any of these activities. Likewise, it is reasonable to suppose that people who talk about women in a sexist way are likely to engage in activities that discriminate against women.

But not all are willing to accept this view. Some, for example, argue that the analogy between blacks and women does not hold: even if talking about blacks in a discriminatory way is causally related to a tendency to treat blacks unfairly, the analogous claim will not hold for the way we talk about women. As CAROLYN KORSMEYER points out, many believe that talking about women in a sexist way is merely a humorous pastime, and implies no further negative consequences. Others, such as Michael Levin,[3] appear to hold that using sexist terminology actually has beneficial effects, such as facilitating heterosexual encounters.

Even if the thesis that sexist language reinforces sexist behavior is accepted, a difficult philosophical problem arises in the attempt to isolate sexist from non-sexist talk about women in an unambiguous way. If a rule or set of rules that captures our intuitions about sexist sentences cannot be found, the task of differentiating sexist from non-sexist thinkers becomes impossible.

At present, there is no workable set of necessary and sufficient conditions for distinguishing sexist from non-sexist sentences about women. As PATRICK GRIM shows, the view that all sexist sentences about women are false will not work, since there are many trivially true sentences about women ("If broads deserve what they get, then broads deserve what they get") that are clearly sexist. Nor can we presuppose that a sentence about women is sexist if and only if it is uncomplimentary to women, for many complimentary sentences about women ("It's nice to see a pretty woman lawyer like you in the courtroom") are sexist. Likewise, it cannot be claimed that a sentence about women is sexist if and only if it entails a false general claim about women. For, "All women have red hair" entails a false general claim about women, and yet it is not sexist.

For the most part we find philosophers giving up the search for a set of necessary and sufficient conditions that capture our intuitions about sexism in language. Instead, they seem to be taking a new route, one that first distinguishes between types of sentences about women commonly used in the English language, and then attempts to locate a rule that separates the sexist from the non-sexist sentences within that type. Robert Baker,[4] for example, examines sexual talk about women and calls much of it sexist insofar as for certain verbs (like "screwed"), names for males are subjects of sentences with active constructions, whereas names for females require passive constructions, where the passive constructions carry the implication of being hurt.

In what follows, ELIZABETH L. BEARDSLEY tries to show that in the English language there are many examples of what she calls "characterizing genderization," or the linguistic requirement of a sex distinction when human beings are characterized by many words standing for personality traits. Both CAROLYN KORSMEYER and JANICE MOULTON argue that generic uses of masculine terminology (for example, the uses of "he" and "man" to refer to all human beings) are sexist and perpetuate sexist attitudes.

If readers find themselves convinced that various parts of

language are sexist, they may wish to ponder a further question raised by this issue: will the elimination of sexist talk about women do away with unfair actions toward women, or vice versa? Robert Baker[5] offers an affirmative response to this question. Consider, he says, the case of the civil-rights movement of the 1960s. There, he says, a change in terminology from the use of the word "colored" to the use of the word "black" helped bring about an increased sensitivity to the plight of black persons. Likewise, he suggests, an elimination of sexist talk about women would have positive consequences for women. VIRGINIA VALIAN, on the other hand, disagrees. "Linguistic oppression," she says, "is not a symptom that will disappear when more fundamental social inequalities are removed."

M.V.B.

## NOTES

1. Elizabeth Cady Stanton, ed., *The Woman's Bible* (New York: European Publishing Co., 1895).
2. Ludwig Wittgenstein, *Philosophical Investigations*, trans. G. E. M. Anscombe (New York: Macmillan, 1958).
3. Michael Levin, "Vs. Ms.," unpublished (City University of New York, Department of Philosophy, 1975).
4. Robert Baker, " 'Pricks' and 'Chicks': A Plea for 'Persons,' " in *Philosophy and Sex*, ed. Robert Baker and Frederick Elliston (Buffalo, N.Y.: Prometheus Books, 1975), pp. 48–54.
5. Ibid., pp. 46–48.

Patrick Grim

# Sexism and Semantics

Sexism is of course not merely a matter of semantics; in various forms it pervades our lives. It shows up in the way we educate our young and plan our futures and befriend our friends and love our lovers.

It also shows up in the way we talk, in what we say and how we say it. I don't want to claim that this is the most important area in which sexism appears, but I'm not willing to claim that it's the least important, either. The sexism that appears in what we say and how we say it is often tied to the sexism that appears in other ways. It is also often the hardest form of sexism to get rid of. It may linger on the lips of the most honest converts and the most self-righteously liberated.

It is a particular issue concerning sexism and things people say, however, that I want to examine here. It is sometimes claimed that sexist statements are allowable or unavoidable in that some sexist statements are simply *true*. If we have an obligation to speak the truth, we may sometimes be stuck with sexist statements whether we like them or not. I think the appeal to truth is a particularly weak defense of the sexism that appears in what we say and how we say it; and I hope to show

---

As might be expected, the impetus for this essay was practical rather than philosophical. Jennifer Todd pointed out to me the sexism of a sentence which appears here as the rosé example, and I am grateful for seminal conversations on the topic with Ms. Todd and Jack Sanders. David Boyer was of invaluable assistance in carefully going over an earlier draft of the paper.

why. I don't think that the condemnation of what someone says as sexist can be adequately met with a rhetorical "So what? It's true, isn't it?"

A word of warning, however, must be added. In what follows I will be forced to appeal to particular examples of sexist statements. They are included despite their offensiveness, and precisely because they forcefully illustrate the issue at hand. I hope that their use as examples is justified in an attempt to understand why they are what they are and perhaps how to avoid them.

# I

Are all sexist statements false? If not, we may be the victims of conflicting ethical principles. We should speak the truth, and we should avoid sexism. But if some sexist statements are true, it seems that we can't do both, and thus one principle must take precedence. If speaking the truth takes precedence, we are left with an uncomfortable though partial vindication of chauvinism. It starts to look as if people who say "Sexist? So what? It's true, isn't it?" might sometimes be right.

Not everything sexist is false, for the simple reason that not everything that is sexist is the type of thing that can be either true or false. Hiring practices and medical plans are often sexist, but never false. Nor is it the case that every sexist thing said is false. Kinky Friedman's offensive "Get your biscuits in the oven and your buns in bed"[1] escapes falsehood simply because it's a command, and commands are neither true nor false.

In the classical philosophical tradition, then, the question calls for careful formulation and examination. Are all sexist statements false? Consider the statements, "If broads deserve what they get, then broads deserve what they get," and "She's either just like all the other lazy, stupid women in this world or she's not." In neither case can we deny the truth of the statement, because both of these are logically true. Sentences that use "if . . . then" and "either . . . or not" in the way that these do are true regardless of their subject matter. Yet both are blatantly sexist.

This might not be too worrisome, however, if it turns out that the only true sexist statements are like our examples above. The only true sexist statements might be those true because of their general grammatical form, regardless of their subject matter:

sexist statements might be true only when empty. Are there any substantive (non-logical) sexist truths? We can obviously get some by joining the examples above to claims that are both non-sexist and substantive. Consider the statements, "Smoking causes cancer, and if broads deserve what they get, then broads deserve what they get" and "If it hadn't been for Louise I wouldn't be doing this, and she's either just like all the other lazy, stupid women in this world or she's not." Both of these appear to be true, though not simply logically true, and both are sexist.

Once again, however, this simply forces us to delimit our problem more carefully. We can ask whether there are any purely substantive and true sexist statements. But by now we should be familiar enough with the ways in which statements can be sexist to expect an affirmative answer. The following statement is substantive in the desired sense, sexist, and true: "Louise, just like all the other lazy, stupid women in this world, will benefit from improvements in medicine."

## II

So far, it appears that our original question must be answered in the negative. There are true sexist statements, and thus we seem trapped by conflicting ethical norms. It appears that speaking the truth can force us to be sexist, and that being non-sexist may involve violation of the more traditional ethical principle of speaking the truth. It looks like people who say "Sexist? So what? It's true, isn't it?" might sometimes be right.

Moreover, the difficulty remains whether it is the statements themselves, or their assertion and use, that is sexist: speaking the truth involves the assertion and use of true sentences or statements. I think that there is a way out of this difficulty, but that it's a fairly complex way out.

What makes a statement sexist? Two well-worn candidates here are one or another of its (literal) truth conditions or one or another of its (non-formal) implications. Despite the literal truth of a particular statement, it can carry false or misleading implications in a number of ways. What is said can imply certain things, the way it is said can do so, the use of particular terms or phrases can be at fault, and to say it can be to imply certain things.[2] Since speaking the truth may involve what is said, ways of saying it, and the use of particular terms or phrases, each of these forms of implication seems very much at issue.

We might thus maintain that some sexist statements are true, but that their sexism is due not to their (literal) truth conditions but to their implications. If that is the case, we are faced with a dilemma as to speaking the truth while at the same time avoiding sexism only if there are true sexist statements that cannot be restated in a form that avoids particular implications. If that is the case, "It's true, isn't it?" is an insufficient justification for sexist statements.

Unfortunately, however, implication is as yet little understood. Even if we confine ourselves to the types of implication mentioned above, and thus put aside all sorts of context-dependent implications and implications people can make without saying anything,[3] a proof that either all implications or all sexist implications are avoidable would seem to require an exhaustive grasp of types of non-formal implication that is yet beyond our reach. What we can do is review some familiar types of implication with an eye to the possibilities of avoiding them.

Statements either sexist or racist in virtue of particular referential tokens can obviously be restated in a non-sexist or non-racist form. Thus consider the statements, "Broads will benefit from improvements in medicine" and "Niggers will benefit from improvements in medicine." In each case we may hold out for literal truth. But both statements involve untoward implications: at least that women are properly spoken of as "broads" and that blacks are properly spoken of as "niggers." (A hidden suggestion here is that one implication of calling $x$'s $y$'s may be that it is proper to speak of them as $y$'s.) But both implications are false, and both seem wholly eliminable. If anything is improperly spoken of as such-and-such, it seems that it must properly be spoken of as something else. If this is so, at least one type of sexist implication is always avoidable: we need simply replace an improper referential token with its alternative.

A second type of implication is as evident in the examples of the previous section as is implication by way of referential tokens. To say "She's either like all the other lazy, stupid women in this world or she's not" is to imply, I think, that all women are lazy and stupid or that they generally are.

I'm not sure, however, why such an implication is present. It may rely on the ambiguity of the phrase "lazy, stupid women" in that adjectival phrases can be used either to delimit or to describe. Thus "lazy, stupid women" may be used either to delimit a particular sub-class of the class of women (the set of those who are lazy and stupid) or to descriptively predicate laziness and stupidity as attributes of the entire class.[4] The latter use here would be explicitly sexist, and to use the phrase ambiguously could be sexist simply because one of its possible meanings is explicitly sexist.

Another possibility is that the glib use of a string of derogatory adjectives implies their usual propriety when conjoined with the noun in question. On this reading, "lazy, stupid women" differs from "broads" only in being an improper catchphrase instead of an improper catch-term.

On either interpretation, however, the implications can be easily removed. If it is a catch-phrase that is responsible for sexist suggestions, it can be treated in the same way that "broads" was treated above. If it's an ambiguous use that is at fault, we can clarify it by making it obvious that delimitation and not description is at stake: "lazy, stupid women" can be replaced with something like "those women who are lazy and stupid."

Statements sexist in virtue of selective mention follow a similar pattern. Consider the statements, "When it comes to business matters, women are stupid and ignorant" and "Rosé is an ignorant woman's choice." Each of these might be true simply if it's true that when it comes to business matters, *people* are stupid and ignorant, and rosé is an ignorant *person's* choice. The former statements are sexist and the latter are not because of an implication that there is something particularly stupid and ignorant about women. This appears to tie in with what the philosopher H. P. Grice considers an implication carried "in the operation of some general principle as that giving preference to the making of a stronger rather than a weaker statement in the absence of a reason for not so doing."[5]

But if it is in virtue of something like the fact that rosé is an ignorant person's choice that "Rosé is an ignorant woman's choice" is true, the sexist implications carried by the selective mention of women in such an example can be avoided by simply substituting "people" instead.

What have been called "presuppositions" form a further class of important non-formal implications. They, too, can be sexist. Thus, consider "Women have become a bit less stupid than they used to be." If this is purged of whatever implications it carries by way of other types of implication such as selective mention, it still presupposes that women used to be stupid. If it follows the pattern of "Smith has left off beating his wife," moreover, its implication appears to be unavoidable. Let us insert a "though" between the original statement and a denial of either the implication that women used to be stupid or its contrary. By doing so we get the following: "Women have become a bit less stupid than they used to be, though it's not being implied that they either were or were not stupid." This appears to be simply an eating of words; the speaker uses the right hand to remove a foot put in the mouth with the left. "Women used to be stupid" thus appears to be an unavoidable implication of "Women have become a bit less stupid than they used to be." One can't construct a statement that asserts just what the second asserts without the presupposition that it brings with it.

Presuppositions of this type, however, are not false implications of true statements. They seem rather to require their own truth before that by which they are presupposed can be either true or false. Thus, despite the fact that we have statements with unavoidable implications, we aren't faced with true statements that are sexist by virtue of an unavoidable implication.

A further class of implications is a bit more tricky. Consider "Jeannine is a woman, but she's quiet bright" and "Char does good work despite her sex." The implication carried in the first example is roughly that there is something at odds in being female and being bright. The second example carries a similar implication that doing good work is at odds with being female.

If we simply couple these with the denials of their proposed implications, we once again end up with what appears to be an eating of words: "Jeannine is a woman, but she's quite bright; though it's not being implied that the two are at odds" and "Char does good work despite her sex; though it's not being implied that the two are at odds." At best, these are peculiarly roundabout ways of saying that Jeannine is a woman *and* she's quite bright, and that Char does good work *and* she's female. To this extent, then, false and sexist implications are still avoidable.

A final and quite controversial form of implication deserves mention. Consider the statements, "Women seem capable enough" and "It looks like women deserve equal opportunity." Some philosophers have thought that "appear" words such as "looks" and "seems" carry what H. P. Grice has termed "doubt or denial" implications. It has been maintained that in asserting that something looks red, for example, "it is implied either that the object referred to is known or believed by the speaker not to *be* red, *or* that it has been denied by someone else to be red, *or* that the speaker is doubtful whether it is red, *or* that someone else has expressed doubt whether it is red, *or* that the situation is such that though no doubt has actually been expressed and no denial has actually been made, some person or other might feel inclined towards doubt or denial if he [*sic*] were to address himself [*sic*] to the question whether the object is actually red."[6] H. P. Grice has argued that such implications can be eliminated, but his position is controversial and the question seems to remain open.

There are a number of possibilities here. We can deny that the two examples and their ilk are true, we can maintain (following Grice) that they're true but that their implications can be avoided, or we can insist on both their truth and the unavoidability of their implications. For present purposes, the first two options are harmless: neither gives support to the claim that sexist statements are allowable or unavoidable because they may be true. If the third is correct, however, and in circumstances which don't satisfy the "denial" clauses of the "doubt or denial" implication, the examples above would seem likely candidates for purely substantive true sexist statements which can't be replaced by non-sexist alternatives. One moral of *that* story is that philosophical positions in areas as apparently diverse as sexism and sense-data can hang together in peculiar and unsuspected ways.

## III

It is clear from the first section above that not all substantive sexist statements are false. On the basis of work done in the second section, however, it is at least arguable that all substantive sexist statements are either false or carry implications that are false. If that is the case, the answer to "Sexist? So what? They're true, aren't they?" is simply that all sexist statements are either false or carry implications that are false. That does not mean, however, that the fact that they are false or carry false implications is *all* that is wrong with sexist statements.

The attempt to excuse sexist statements on the basis of truth, or on the basis of an appeal for speaking the truth, has been weakened considerably. Such an argument now seems to rest on the controversial thesis that certain statements concerning how things look or seem, though they may be literally true, carry unalterable sexist implications.

Sexism is not simply a matter of semantics, but it involves semantics as it involves just about everything else in our lives. I hope to have indicated some of the ways in which what we say and how we say it can be sexist, as a means to both understanding sexism and avoiding it.

## NOTES

1. Kinky Friedman, "Get Your Biscuits in the Oven and Your Buns in Bed." The song appears on the album *Sold American* by Kinky Friedman (Vanguard Records, 1973), and is copyright by Kinky Friedman, Glaser Publications, Inc., BMI.
2. J. L. Austin started all this. See especially "The Meaning of a Word" and "Performative Utterances" in his *Philosophical Papers* (New York: Oxford University Press, 1970).
3. I am obliged to David Boyer for constantly giving me trouble on this kind of thing.
4. The fact that these two functions of adjectival phrases are syntactically differentiated in languages other than English supports the validity of the distinction.
5. H. P. Grice, "The Causal Theory of Perception," *Proceedings of the Aristotelian Society*, supp. vol. 35 (1961), pp. 121–168.
6. Ibid.

Elizabeth L. Beardsley

# Traits and Genderization

By the term "genderization" I mean the linguistic practice of requiring a sex distinction in discourse about human beings, in such a way that to disregard the sex distinction produces a locution which is incorrect (where genderization is formal) or inappropriate (where genderization is informal). Genderization may occur in either of two modes: in *referring* to human beings ("referential genderization" or "RG"), or in *characterizing* human beings ("characterizing genderization" or "CG").[1]

In this paper I shall discuss CG, seeking to show how extensive it is and how it may have arisen.

## I

I shall say that genderization is *universal in scope* in a mode $M$ of a language $L$ if in $M$ of $L$ it is impossible to speak of a human being in a sex-neutral way, i.e., without specifying his or her sex. English exhibits, within its referential mode, genderization that is fully universal in scope with respect to definite personal pronouns and nearly universal in scope with respect to proper names. With respect to class nouns, however, it is possible to refer to a human being (as "a human being" or "a person") in a sex-neutral way.[2]

What features would a language need to have in order for it to exhibit CG of universal scope? If in a language $L$ no characterizing expression could be used in a sex-neutral way, then $L$ would exhibit CG of fully universal scope. This is the case for those highly inflected languages that require any adjective used of a human being to show by its syntactical form whether it is used of a male or a female. Here, however, CG is dependent on RG. The speaker must first know whether he or she is characterizing a male or a female before being able to give the adjective its appropriate form. I shall term this linguistic pattern "secondary CG." For "primary CG," a speaker must first know whether a trait is "masculine" or "feminine" before he or she can apply the corresponding adjective to a male or female human being.

That English does not exhibit primary CG of universal scope is clear. There are many adjectives in our language that are applied to human beings in a sex-neutral way. But it does not follow that there is no primary CG at all. In the following section I shall examine two examples of primary CG. Both will concern traits of personality, or "P-traits." It is unnecessary for my present purposes to provide precise definitions of the psychological terms to be used here. I take "trait" to refer to a disposition to perform certain kinds of act or to experience certain kinds of feeling or to do both. Personality traits (P-traits) are subject to non-moral appraisal, but only character traits (C-traits) are subject to moral appraisal. A P-trait may be desirable or undesirable, but only a C-trait may be morally good or morally bad, a virtue or a vice.

## II

Let us now consider the P-trait of liveliness in social behavior, manifested chiefly, though not exclusively, in conversation. I shall try to show that some primary CG is found among expressions attributing this trait to human beings. But it is important not to overstate this thesis. Both males and females can be described as "lively": there is evidently no belief regarding the nature of this trait that has given rise to wholesale genderization here. "John is animated" and "Jane is a lively conversationalist" are equally acceptable locutions.

Yet it is impossible to deny that the P-trait in question is differentially evaluated in males and females; and in this differential evaluation lies a potential source of CG. A term that denotes liveliness and at the same time carries an explicit normative force is very likely to be genderized, for it will be deemed appropriate to apply it to one sex but not to the other. A term of just this kind is the adjective "vivacious." The expression "vivacious man" is incongruous; "vivacious woman" is not. To discern such subtle 'incongruities requires prolonged linguistic and social conditioning. Here is a dictionary definition of "vivacity" which both reflects and reinforces the conditioning process:

**vivacity** . . . Animation; liveliness; sprightliness; as, the *vivacity* of a discourse; a lady of great *vivacity*.[3]

A second P-trait that has given rise to some measure of CG is the trait of aggressiveness, understood as a disposition to pursue forcefully what one takes to be one's own interests (which may include an interest in being noticed). The term "aggressive" has undergone some change in its general normative force. Within the memory of many speakers of English, a general negative normative force has been replaced by a general positive normative force, or at least by a normative force which can be made positive if suitable contents are supplied. Since aggressiveness is differentially evaluated in males and females, it is more difficult to provide a context in which "aggressive" will have a clearly laudatory force when applied to a female. Still, this can be done. For genderization to occur, there must be an expression which, like "vivacious," is appropriately used of one sex but not of the other. In highly colloquial language, such an expression is easily found: the word "pushy." "A pushy man" is as incongruous as "a vivacious man." The former phrase attributes a trait presented as undesirable to a member of a group in whom it is not undesirable. The second phrase attributes a trait presented as desirable to a member of a group in whom it is not desirable. In each case the differential appraisal of the trait in question is the basis for CG. The genderization here is informal, prescribing what we may appropriately say rather than what we may correctly say. Still, it is undeniably present.

## III

It seems that the differential appraisal of the traits considered in the preceding section has two sources. First, there is a differential allocation of tasks and responsibilities. Females are typically charged with the major responsibility for seeing that certain kinds of social intercourse are conducted smoothly and agreeably, and, in discharging this responsibility, liveliness is an asset. Second, there is a differential assessment of the capacities and abilities of males and females. Some kinds of social intercourse—like exchanging information, harmonizing interests, solving problems cooperatively—are carried on for ends other than relaxation or entertainment. In the attainment of such ends, liveliness is not an asset, and may in fact be a distracting liability. What is called for, among other things, is a capacity for clear, consecutive, cogent discourse, and a capacity to attend to such discourse. It is beyond dispute that these capacities are widely believed to characterize males more typically than females. Liveliness is a desirable trait in those who cannot realistically be expected to deal effectively with the serious ends of social intercourse. In those who can, liveliness may be actually unattractive, and is at best of negligible value. Hence the usefulness of a genderized term like "vivacious," which those suitably conditioned will know how to apply.

The differential appraisal of aggressiveness seems to have the same two sources. First, there is a differential allocation of tasks and responsibilities. A male is typically charged with primary responsibility for the well-being of "his" dependents (spouses and offspring). Aggressiveness is a valuable trait in the competition of the marketplace. It takes on the status of being an occupational virtue for a "breadwinner," just as liveliness or animation is an occupational virtue for a "hostess."[4] To be a breadwinner, one must be a go-getter. Second, there is a differential assessment of the capacities and abilities of males and females. In persons with the strength and independence to pursue their own interests effectively, aggressiveness is desirable, an attractive trait. In those who lack such strength and independence, it is not. Hence the usefulness of "pushy." A comparison here with the *racialized* word "uppity"—an ugly word from another time and social milieu—might prove to be of considerable interest.

## IV

It is more difficult to find examples of primary CG with respect to traits of character than to find examples of primary CG with respect to traits of personality. This curious state of affairs can be explained in more than one way, as I shall try to show below. But first I should make a few general observations concerning CG for C-traits.

First, it seems likely that those traits that depend essentially on *acting* rather than *reacting* (the "active" rather than the "passive" virtues) would, being differentially appraised in males and females, give rise to primary CG. Despite this consideration, CG does not seem to have developed. Taking courage as an example of an "active" virtue, and patience as an example of a "passive" virtue, we might expect to find expressions which, like "vivacious" and "pushy," exhibit incongruity when applied to members of the "wrong" sex. For courage there seems to be no such expression, though if the concept of courage had not been broadened to include moral courage as well as physical courage a genderized expression would have been more likely to develop. For an excessive degree of patience there are colloquial expressions that verge on genderized status. A woman can presumably be called a "doormat," but can she be called a "milksop"? Could there have been a female version of the comic-strip figure Caspar Milquetoast?[5]

The differential appraisal of C-traits is chiefly manifested in the use of differential standards of application, so that it takes less for a woman to be judged brave or self-reliant than for a man to be so judged. Similarly, it takes less for a man to be judged gentle or compassionate than for a woman to be so judged. And we typically look to males for paradigms, actually or imaginary, of certain virtues, to females for others.[6] There is considerable evidence of a differential appraisal of certain C-traits, but this has evidently not shaped our vocabulary in any clear fashion.

My claim that primary CG has occurred more frequently for P-traits than for C-traits calls for support by empirical data that I cannot supply. One may, however, speculate about the causes of the phenomenon, should my claim be well-founded. Let us consider two hypotheses.

*Hypothesis 1:* A recognition that C-traits are conceptually linked to a concept of personhood has served to impede the development of CG for C-traits.

*Hypothesis 2:* A failure to accord to females the full status of persons has fostered a tendency to see *personality*, rather than *character*, as the domain of distinctively "feminine" traits. Thus the tendency is to find an appropriate basis for CG in P-traits rather than C-traits.

To put these complex matters in a markedly oversimplified but useful way, we may say that Hypothesis 1 states essentially that character traits are too important to have been genderized, whereas Hypothesis 2 states essentially that women are too unimportant for character traits to have been genderized.

Hypothesis 1 depends centrally on the claim that a shared sex-neutral concept of personhood has been available to influence the development of language. This claim seems to me ill-founded. An examination of genderization in its referential mode yields the conclusion that concepts of personhood thus far available have been unable to counteract the deep-rooted urge toward linguistic genderization.[7] I conclude that Hypothesis 1, as an explanation of linguistic developments prior to the present time, must be rejected.

Hypothesis 2 seems to me much more acceptable. At first glance it may seem that the more extensive genderization of P-traits reflects a respect for women as persons, in that language has (largely) stopped short of developing a bifurcated vocabulary for the most significant human characteristics, C-traits. Further reflection, however, supports a more depressing interpretation: that C-traits have not led to CG because they were seen from the outset as belonging to one sex, and hence were not perceived to have "masculine" and "feminine" forms. A powerful linguistic aid here has been the use of "man" and "he" in a purportedly sex-neutral way.[8] In the characterizing mode of our language, the term "manly" carries a dual force: both sex-specific and sex-neutral. The bearers of C-traits being assumed to be males, there is no need for a word such as "humanly," and, by the same token, no need for genderization in speaking of C-traits. Females as bearers of C-traits have simply not been present to be observed.

We live in a time when females are at last recognizably present. This fact has great potential for linguistic-ethical progress. It could foster a genuine concept of personhood capable of obstructing genderization in both its modes and ultimately rendering it archaic in our language. Genderization would then be present only as a survival from the past.

## NOTES

1. I have examined RG in "Referential Genderization," *Philosophical Forum* 5 (1973–74): 285–93.
2. In "Referential Genderization" I argue that these sex-neutral class nouns have entered into colloquial use to a very limited extent.

3. *Webster's New International Dictionary*, 2d ed.
4. The genderization of terms for occupational roles provides a bridge between RG and CG.
5. The word "sissy" is of interest here. A child who is insufficiently brave and excessively patient is colloquially branded a "sissy." Can a little girl be a sissy?
6. It is worth noting that J. O. Urmson, in his influential paper "Saints and Heroes," offers one (hypothetical) exemplar of saintliness who is female, but only male exemplars of heroism. See A. I. Melden, ed., *Essays in Moral Philosophy* (Seattle: University of Washington Press, 1968), pp. 198–216.
7. See "Referential Genderization," op. cit.
8. In "Referential Genderization" I argue that this linguistic practice is self-defeating. The point is also argued, on different grounds, by Janice Moulton in "The Myth of the Neutral 'Man' " in this volume.

Janice Moulton

# The Myth of the
# Neutral "Man"

## I

Here are two riddles:

(1) A man is walking down the street one day when he suddenly recognizes an old friend whom he has not seen in years walking in his direction with a little girl. They greet each other warmly and the friend says, "I married since I last saw you, to someone you never met, and this is my daughter, Ellen." The man says to Ellen, "You look just like your mother." How did he know that?

(2) A boy and his father were driving when suddenly a large truck careened around a corner and hit their car head-on. The car was crushed, and when their bodies were removed from the wreck the father was already dead. The son, badly injured but still alive, was rushed to the hospital, where hasty preparations were made for immediate surgery. As the boy was brought in

This paper owes a special thanks to G. M. Robinson and Cherin Elias for their comments and encouragement. Many other people at the Society for Women in Philosophy, the American Philosophical Association meetings, and the University of Maryland philosophy department gave me valuable comments. I would particularly like to thank Mary Vetterling-Braggin, Virginia Valian, Larry Stern, Christine Pierce, Susan Rae Peterson, Stan Munsat, Susan Moore, W. G. Lycan, Ron Laymon, Adele Laslie, Gale Justin, Carl Ginet, Alan Donagan, Richard Brandt, and H. D. Block.

for the operation, the surgeon saw him and said, "I can't operate, that's my son." How is that possible?

If you have not heard these riddles before and they puzzle
you, that's an important datum for this paper.

## II

Recently it has been argued that the words "he," "man," etc.
should not be used as gender-neutral terms because it is unfair
to women; anyone who looks for the best *man* for the job or
tells an applicant to send *his* credentials is less likely or less able
to consider a female candidate fairly.

Two claims should be distinguished here. The first accepts
that there is a gender-neutral meaning for terms like "he,"
"man," etc. Adherents of this view consider the gender-neutral
uses of these terms an *effect* of, and an unpleasant reminder of,
the lower status of women, and urge that the gender-neutral use
be eliminated as a sign of good will and for symptomatic relief.

The second claim denies that terms such as "he" and "man"
have gender-neutral uses. It argues that using these terms as if
they were neutral terms *causes* unfairness. This is because not
really being gender-neutral, the use of such terms leads one to
apply the context to males, and makes it difficult to apply it to
females.

The first claim is sometimes followed up with a shift to the
second claim: once the first claim has been articulated, the
second claim is thought to become true. Refusing to adopt this
sign of good will indicates a lack of good will—that is, sexism.
Continued use of "he" and "man" as neutral terms indicates
that the attitude of the speaker is not gender-neutral. It will be
recognized on some level of awareness that the speaker intends
men to be preferred to women, and intends terms such as "he"
or "man," although hitherto neutral, to apply primarily to men.
Only people who have these intentions will continue to use these
terms as if they were neutral. Such an argument defends and
reinforces the first claim by appeal to the second claim.

The first claim, that there *are* neutral uses but they are symptoms of unfairness and should be eliminated, has greater initial
plausibility than the second. Using "he" and "man" as neutral
terms may well be the result of the greater prominence of men
in our culture. But once this use has been established, it appears
that it can be both intended and understood neutrally. There is

no initial reason to suppose that these terms are less likely to be applied to women than men, *if* used neutrally.

I am going to defend the second claim, but I would like to do so without appealing to any connection with the first claim. I believe that the second claim can be defended on its own, without appeal to sexist attitudes of the speakers. I shall try to show that however innocently and neutrally they are intended, the words "he," "man," etc. may not function as genuine gender-neutral terms; that their use is unavoidably somewhat gender-specific; and that male gender-specific descriptions make it difficult to recognize that descriptions in that context could apply to a female.

### III

Let us first consider the criticism of the use of "he," "man," etc. as gender-neutral terms which, while allowing that the uses may be neutral, nevertheless requests relief from these symptoms of other injustices. This criticism reminds us that there are other neutral terms: One can look for the best *person* for the job, tell *applicants* to send their credentials to one, etc. It continues: If we change our language, we will increase awareness of past unfair treatment of women and save women from being constantly reminded of the male priority and domination that the neutral uses of "he" and "man" indicate. Although some of the suggested changes will be awkward at first, they will be signs of a spirit of sympathy and cooperation with the criticism and therefore with efforts of women to attain equal human status.

Once this request has been made, the continued use of "he" and "man" as gender-neutral terms does not *make* a person less likely to consider a woman for the job. Nevertheless it may be an indication that the person is not especially sympathetic to the problems of being automatically assigned a lower status, and therefore that the person may be less likely to consider a woman for the job. On this view, the gender-neutral use of "he," etc., is a consequence, or a symbol, not a cause, of existing unjust attitudes.

This request seems to be asking very little, just that a few words be changed, but it is actually asking more than that. The change in language might also publicize a political position, or challenge friends and colleagues. In our language where a lower socioeconomic class is detectable by dialect variants such as the use of "gutter," "nylons," and "light bill," instead of "street" or "road," "stockings," and "electric bill," and a graduate education turns a "resume" into a "vita," a "convention" into "meetings," and "manuscripts" into "stuff" (as in "send me your stuff"), the change of few words is likely to announce a life style, broadcast a political position, or misdirect attention to the wrong issue.

If, after their relation to male status has been pointed out, "he" and "man" continue to be used in place of other neutral terms, it does not necessarily follow that the user lacks good will toward females. Small variations in language may have great social significance. It may not be a lack of good will, but a desire to concentrate on more significant issues or a shyness about taking poliitcal stands in casual conversations, that leaves the request unfulfilled.

## IV

Perhaps you've recognized by now that the above riddles are intended to illustrate that assuming that a description (a surgeon, the friend of a man) applies to a male makes it difficult to recognize that the description could also apply to a female.

The second riddle is frequently presented as an illustration of our sexist presuppositions. We automatically assume that the surgeon has to be a man. But the first riddle has a similar effect without the presence of a professional description to receive the blame. I do not believe that the surgeon riddle does show sexism. What it shows is that once the assumption is made that a description is of a man, it is very, very hard to change that assumption. In the first riddle the assumption is probably made merely because an old friend of a man is somewhat more likely to be a man than a woman. (The assumption about gender need not have any empirical basis. There appears to be a tendency to assume that "my cousin," if spoken by a woman, refers to a female, and if spoken by a man, refers to a male.) Yet however weak the basis for the assumption, the perplexity caused by the riddles shows that it is still very hard to change one's assumptions about gender.

Note that these riddles do not show that the use of "he" or "man" in their alleged neutral sense makes it difficult to realize that a description in that context could be of a female. The only thing the riddles show is that if one assumes that a description applies to a male, it is hard to realize that the description could apply to a female. But genuine gender-neutral terms should not foster such an assumption. Therefore I still have to show that the alleged gender-neutral uses of these terms are, in fact, somewhat gender-specific.

## V

It is not legitimate to assume that any use of "he" makes people think of a male instead of a female. Language has an influence on thought, but there are many other influences, too. Consider another example: "being doctored" has worse connotations than "being nursed." Things that have been doctored are in a worse condition than if left alone, whereas things that have been nursed are frequently in a better condition as a result. However, such linguistic usage does not prevent people from seeking doctors rather than nurses for serious illnesses. It seems very likely that these verb forms are derived from the functions of doctors and nurses. Yet there is no reason to suppose that use of these expressions causes discrimination against doctors in favor of nurses.

So even though the use of "he" as a gender-neutral pronoun is related to the position of males as compared with that of females in this culture,[1] and even though women are in a position inferior to men, it still has to be shown that gender-neutral uses of "he," "man," etc. affect people's thinking by preventing them from applying the context in question to women.[2]

The claim that there is no really neutral use might not need defense if there were no other terms that had both a neutral and non-neutral use. But such is not the case. Many adjectives that refer to one of a pair of opposite qualities can be used neutrally to indicate the dimension whose extremes are the opposites. One can ask "How tall is she?" of a short person, and "How wide is that?" of a narrow object. "Tall" and "wide" are used not only as the opposites of "short" and "narrow," but as neutral terms to describe the quality or dimension of which the opposites are extremes. One *can* ask "How short is she?" or "How narrow is that?" but doing so expresses the expectation that the answer will lie on one end of the range of possible answers. In contrast, any tendency to suppose that anyone of whom it is asked how tall they are is in fact a tall person, is certainly very slight. Such uses of "short," "narrow," as well as "young," "impure," "bad," and "small" are called *marked* while similar uses of the opposite terms, "tall" and "long," "wide," "old," "pure," "good," and "big" are termed *unmarked*.[3]

In this respect, unmarked and marked adjectives behave very much like the he-she, man-woman, his-her pairs. The use of "he" or "man" may be either gendered or neutral. However, if one uses "she" or "woman," one conveys the expectation that a person who fits the description will be female, not male.[4] If one is going to argue that "he" and "man" cannot function as gender-neutral terms, it cannot be merely because such terms also have gender-specific meanings.

# VI

It might be argued that, given that there are other neutral terms ("they," "one," "human," "person"), perpetuation of a neutral use of one of a pair of opposites gives that quality a priority or superiority over the opposite quality. There is some evidence that the unmarked term of a pair of opposites has higher positive associations. The use of a marked term often has a pejorative tone.[5] It is not an accident that "good" and "pure" are unmarked, "bad" and "impure" marked. If by perpetuating the neutral uses of "he" and "man" one encouraged the continuation of the unfair priority of males, then there would be a sense in which such uses were not really neutral.

Granted that people usually do have higher positive associations for the term with the neutral use than with its opposite.[6] And people have higher positive associations for "he" than "she." But it is far from clear that the positive association is a *result* of the neutral use; it may well be the other way around. The neutral uses of "tall," "wide," "high," "long," "big," etc. tell us that, in general, the larger size is better, or standard, or ideal. I suspect the reason for this is that children, during the time of first language learning, are expected to increase in size and are often praised for doing so and worried over when they do not. Thus at the outset they learn the term for the extreme that is their goal, and then come to use it to stand for the whole dimension.[7] (This would explain why "old" is unmarked even though youth is so much admired and valued. The post-adolescent youth that is valued is many years older than the language-learning child.) When one uses an adjective that can stand for one end of a dimension neutrally to name the dimension, one presents that end of the dimension as expected or standard. For example: "How cold is it?" vs. "How hot is it?"; "How hard is it?" vs. "How soft is it?". If one end of a dimension is a standard independently of a particular context, the term for that end would acquire a neutral use. If this explanation of the origin of unmarked adjectives is correct, the similarity to unmarked adjectives is no reason to suppose that the more positive evaluation of "he" is the *result* of its neutral use. It indicates, instead, that men's being more highly regarded than women promotes the neutral uses of male terms.

In any case, the higher positive associations of adjectives with neutral uses do not affect evaluations in particular cases. Although "wide" has a higher positive association for people than "narrow," wider objects are not necessarily valued more than narrower objects. For example, pocket calculators are touted for their narrow dimensions (although in advertisements one is more likely to hear the term "slim" than "narrow"). And so there is no reason to suppose that using "he" and "man" as unmarked neutral terms affects evaluations of females in particular cases. If one is going to argue that such uses are not really neutral, one has to show something more about these terms— something other than that they have the properties of other unmarked terms.

## VII

There are important differences between unmarked adjectives and words like "he" and "man." The neutral use of adjectives is quite unambiguous, restricted to contexts in which a quantity or amount of that dimension is the topic (i.e., three inches *high*, 99 & 44/100% *pure*). The neutral uses of "he" and "man" have no restricted contexts to disambiguate them. Moreover, uses of these terms are frequently in need of disambiguation. We might be inclined to say that "man" in "The Neanderthal man was a hunter" was being used neutrally to mean "human." But this sentence could be used to describe just males. One might say, "The Neanderthal man was a hunter. The Neanderthal woman raised crops." In this context "man" is clearly intended to mean "male human." In an example from an introductory philosophy text, an apparently neutral use of "he" turns out to be intentionally gender-specific. This ambiguity is resolved only by the last word:

Consider, firstly, two comparatively simple situations in which a cyberneticist might find himself. He has a servomechanism, or a computing machine, with no randomising element, and he also has a wife.[8]

Although "he" and "man" behave like unmarked adjectives in some respects, their double roles as both gender-specific and gender-neutral terms permit ambiguity in ways that the double roles of unmarked adjectives do not.

The ambiguity in the beginning of these examples allows an intended gender-specific "he" or "man" to be interpreted as a neutral term so that a context may be inadvertently applied to women. And ambiguity may also allow an intended neutral "he" to be interpreted as a gender-specific term so that the context is accidentally not applied to women. But if this is so, the culprit is ambiguity, which could be resolved without forsaking the neutral uses of male terms. Add that you are an equal-opportunity employer and there should be no gender-specific interpretation of "man" in "the best man for the job." One need not eliminate the neutral use of "he" and "man" in order to eliminate ambiguity. There will be other ways of resolving the ambiguity besides using other neutral terms that are not ambiguous.

## VIII

Here's the problem: However the use of a term gets started, it would seem that if it was intended a certain way when used, and understood that way by others, then, on any available theory of meaning, that's what it means. If "man" or "he" are intended neutrally, as they often are, and if people know that, as they do, then it would seem that "man" and "he" do refer to the members of the human species, and that they are as neutral as "human" and "they."

In order to show that "man" and "he" and like terms are not really neutral, I have to show that even though speakers may intend to use these terms in a gender-neutral way, they can fail to do so.

Let's compare "he" and "man" with other terms whose gender neutrality is not in dispute, such as "one," "they," "human," and "person." One striking difference is the inability to use "he" and "man" to refer to a female human. It would be a rare person who could say without irony "She's the best *man* for the job" or say of a female, "He's the best." Yet the undisputed gender-neutral terms can indeed be used this way: "She's the best person"; "That one is the best" (of a female). If "he" and "man" are genuinely gender-neutral, then they ought to be applicable to any person regardless of gender.

One might argue that one does not say "he's the best" of a female for the same reason one does not merely say "I believe" when one knows. On Grice's account of the latter, it is not that believing *implies* not knowing, but that one does not usually convey less information than one can.[9] Therefore if one says one believes, people may assume one does not actually know. Similarly, one might argue, if it is clear in some context that the gender of a referent is known to the speaker, then the speaker is expected to specify that gender. It is not that uses of "he" and "man" *imply* that the referent is male, but simply that one does not convey less information than one can. If one uses "he" or "man," people may assume that either a male is being referred to or that the gender is not known.

This explanation, however, does not account for all the facts. It offers no explanation for why "She's the best man" is not permissible since gender *has* been specified. Moreover, it would predict that undisputed neutral terms could not be used if the gender were known. If the problem were only that speakers are expected to specify gender when known, the sentence "That's the best person" would be as inappropriate to say of either a male or a female as "That's the best man" is to say of a female.

On some theories of meaning, the meaning of a term is a function of its use. I have already pointed out that "he" and "man" do not have the same uses as undisputed gender-neutral terms. Recent theories of meaning have analyzed meaning as a function of the intentions of the speaker. Yet failures of gender-neutrality of "he" and "man" occur even though the speaker may intend a gender-neutral use. For example, Bertrand Russell in his classic paper "On Denoting" says:

Suppose now we wish to interpret the proposition, "I met a man." If this is true, I met some definite man; but that is not what I affirm. What I affirm is, according to the theory I advocate:—" 'I met *x*, and *x* is human' is not always false."[10]

If Russell were correct, then parents familiar with his theory would have no cause for anxiety if their young female child, on arriving home several hours late from kindergarten, said, "I met a man." Russell did not notice that "man" is not used neutrally in his context. This example shows that it is not enough that one *intend* a term to have a particular meaning for it to have that meaning. One cannot account entirely for the meaning of a term by the intentions of the speaker on a particular occasion. The meaning of a term involves, among other things, its expected interpretation, the way it functions with other terms, and its use in linguistic enterprises such as reasoning. This is important for the next point.

"He" and "man" cannot be used in some contexts where undisputedly gender-neutral terms can. But what about other contexts? Suppose it can be shown that a familiar and paradigmatic example of a gender-neutral use of "man" or "men" is not really neutral at all? Then I think it can be argued that there is no real gender-neutral meaning of these terms. Consider the first line of the familiar syllogism:

All men are mortal.

Most people would agree that the occurrence of "men" is intended to be neutral; this is a statement about the whole human species. But if it is a neutral use, then this syllogism, that paradigm of valid syllogisms, is invalid, for the second line usually reads

Socrates is a man.

The occurrence of "man" in this sentence is *not* a neutral use. If it were a neutral use, then replacing "Socrates" with the name of a female human being or a child would not affect the syllogism. Yet the usual interpretation of

Sophia is a man.

makes it false, or insulting. It is not taken to mean that Sophia is a member of the human species.[11]

Thus the reference from "All men are mortal" and "Socrates is a man" to "Socrates is mortal" is invalid if the occurrence of "men" is intended to be gender-neutral in the first premise. Instead of a paradigm of valid inference we would have an equivocation, because the meaning of the terms has changed. It would be just like the argument:

All banks are closed on Sunday.
The Outer Banks are banks.
Therefore, the Outer Banks are closed on Sunday.

That the occurrence of "men" in the first premise is believed to be gender-neutral, and that the syllogism is believed to be neither enthymematic nor invalid, is evidence either that we are confused about neutral uses or that we are confused about validity even in the simplest cases. There is further evidence that it is the former. Consider another example:

Man is a mammal.

This use of "man" is neutral if any use is. But if this is conjoined with the dictionary definition of "mammalia":

the highest class of Vertebrata comprising man and all other animals that nourish their young with milk, that have the skin usu. more or less covered with hair, that have mammary glands. . . .[12]

it should be legitimate to conclude:

Man has mammary glands.

But this conclusion is less acceptable than:

Humans have mammary glands.

because "man" does not function in the same gender-neutral way as "human" in this context. A statement that members of the human species have mammary glands is not peculiar, but a statement that males have mammary glands is. Although both men and women have mammary glands, only the mature glands of women are ordinarily likely to be topics of conversation. If "man" could be used gender-neutrally, its occurrence in a context that applies to both male and female humans, particularly to female humans, would be given a gender-neutral interpretation. Instead, its occurrence in such a context is plainly gender-specific.

Alleged neutral uses of "he" are not as frequently found in syllogisms. But *if* it sounds strange to ask an applicant about the interests of his husband or wife, to instruct a child on the cleaning of his vagina or penis, or to compliment a guest on his gown or tuxedo, then something is less than neutral about "he" and "his" as well. Note that there is no ambiguity about these uses. The contexts make it clear that "man" and "his" are supposed to be understood to be gender-neutral, if possible. Other obvious failures of gender neutrality are:

> Man has two sexes
> Some men are female.

## IX

There are undoubtedly many more contexts in which attempts to use terms such as "he" and "man" gender-neutrally produce false, funny, or insulting statements, even though the gender-neutrality was clearly intended. How can this obvious failure of gender-neutrality be accounted for when people think they are using "he," "man," etc. in a gender-neutral sense? Rather than attribute the failure to peculiar properties of each context in an ad hoc fashion, I believe it is the result of a broader linguistic phenomenon: Parasitic Reference. Tissues are called Kleenex; petroleum jelly, Vaseline; bleach, Clorox; etc. to the economic benefit of the specific brands referred to and to the economic detriment of those brands that are ignored by this terminology. The alleged gender-neutral uses of "he," "man," etc. are just further examples of this common phenomenon. A gender-specific term, one that refers to a high-status subset of the whole class, is used *in place of* a neutral generic term. Many of us who deplore the efforts of drug companies to get us to use the brand name rather than the generic name of a product have failed to recognize that the use of "he," "man," etc. in place of "they," "one," "person," or "human" is a similar phenomenon with similar effects. Manufacturers realize that someone sent to buy "the cheapest Clorox" is less likely to return with the equal-strength half-price store brand than someone sent to buy the cheapest bleach. And this is true even when the term "Clorox" is intended and understood to be synonymous with "bleach." The failure of "Clorox" to be brand-neutral and the failure of "he" and "man" to be gender-neutral appear to be instances of the same phenomenon.[13]

Regardless of the intentions of the speakers and hearers, and regardless of their beliefs about the meanings of the terms, if the terms refer parasitically, substitutivity can fail, inferences may not go through, and equivocations will be produced. This is true not merely for brand names but for other terms, such as "he" and "man," whose neutral performances have been advertised by lexicographers but which break down easily even under normal speaking conditions. The existence of Parasitic Reference requires that theories of reference and meaning recognize that the functioning of terms in one context may be affected by their uses in other contexts that are not explicitly present.

# NOTES

1. Many people believe this claim, but Robin Lakoff in "Language and Woman's Place," *Language in Society* 2 (1973): 45–80, supports it with an impressive number of gender asymmetries in language whose best explanation appears to be the superior position of one gender in the culture. See also Mary Ritchie Key, *Male/Female Language* (Metuchen, N.J.: Scarecrow Press, 1975); and Casey Miller and Kate Swift, *Words and Women* (Garden City, N.Y.: Anchor Press/Doubleday, 1976).

2. Even if the gender-neutral uses of "he," etc., prevent people from considering women in those contexts, there are some contexts where one does not want to be considered (for example, as a murder suspect). So one has also to show that the disadvantages of not being considered for jobs, awards, and consultation outweigh the advantages of not being considered for criminal activities, punishment, and obligations. Women who oppose the Equal Rights Amendment seem to disagree with other women not on the actual unequal status of women but rather on whether the advantages of this status outweigh the disadvantages.

3. Although this terminology was originally applied to phonological distinctions (e.g., the third-person singular of regular verbs is *marked* with an "s"), it has been extended to the use I cite. See John Lyons, *Introduction to Theoretical Linguistics* (Cambridge: Cambridge University Press, 1971), p. 79.

4. Porter G. Perrin and Karl W. Dykema, in *Writer's Guide and Index to English*, 3d ed. (Glenview, Ill.: Scott, Foresman, 1959), pp. 538–39, 551–52, say: "As we must often refer to nouns that name either or both male and female, the language has developed . . . ways of making up for the lack of an accurate pronoun: The usual way is to use *he* or *his* alone even when some of the persons are female. . . . Sometimes when the typical individuals or the majority of the group referred to would be women, *her* is used in in the same way."

5. According to Lyons, *Theoretical Linguistics*, p. 467.

6. Evidence for this is to be found in C. E. Osgood, Suci, and Tannenbaum, *The Measurement of Meaning* (Urbana: University of Illinois Press, 1957), especially pp. 36–62. Unmarked

terms tend to be scored more positively by subjects on the semantic differential evaluative scale. But this is not always the case. It is worth remarking that "feminine" receives a higher positive evaluation than "masculine."

7. Eve V. Clark in "What's in a Word? On the Child's Acquisition of Semantics in his First Language," in *Cognitive Development and the Acquisition of Language*, ed. T. E. Moore (New York: Academic Press, 1973), pp. 65–110, points out that children learn to use the unmarked term of a pair before they learn the marked term.

8. L. Jonathan Cohen, "Can There Be Artificial Minds?" in *Reason and Responsibility*, 2d ed., ed. Joel Feinberg (Encino, Calif.: Dickenson Publishing Co., 1971), p. 288.

9. H. Paul Grice, "Logic and Conversation," in *Syntax and Semantics*, vol. 3, ed. Peter Cole and Jerry L. Morgan (New York: Academic Press, 1975).

10. Bertrand Russell, "On Denoting," *Mind* 13 (1905): 479.

11. Let me add two explanations here. (1) The meaning of a term is not determined by the interpretation of one person alone. How others will understand it must be considered as well. Although some people might argue that in this context the syllogism "Sophia is a man" can be read as "Sophia is a human being," they will recognize that many other people will not take it this way (this is due in part to our inability to use "man" to refer to a female in other contexts). Although *some* people might be able to *read* "man" neutrally in this context, it does not follow that this is what it means. Further examples where "man" and "his" fail to be gender-neutral are offered to convince those who can make a gender-neutral reading in one case. (2) It might be argued that I have changed the meaning of "man" in the syllogism by substituting "Sophia" for "Socrates." The original syllogism might have had a neutral occurrence of "man" which changed with the substitution. For example, if I substituted "The Outer Banks" for "Savings and loan institutions" in "——— are banks," I would change the meaning of "banks." However, if "man" has a gender-neutral use, it should retain that use regardless of the gender of the referent. There is no reason to claim that it has a gender-neutral meaning unless it has a use that can be applicable to females as well as males. Gender-neutral terms such as "human" and "person" are not affected by the substitution of a female name in their context.

12. *Webster's Third New International Dictionary*.

13. Elizabeth Lane Beardsley, in "Referential Genderization," *Philosophical Forum* 5 (1973–74): 285–93, calls this phenomenon "linguistic imperialism."

Carolyn Korsmeyer

# The Hidden Joke: Generic Uses of Masculine Terminology

*Vir* is male and *Femina* is female: but *Homo* is male and female.

This is the equality claimed and the fact that is persistently evaded and denied. No matter what arguments are used, the discussion is vitiated from the start, because Man is always dealt with as both *Homo* and *Vir*, but Woman only as *Femina*.[1]

The terms *masculine* and *feminine* are used symmetrically only as a matter of form, as on legal papers. In actuality the relation of the two sexes is not quite like that of two electrical poles, for man represents both the positive and the neutral, as is indicated by the common use of *man* to designate human beings in general; whereas woman represents only the negative, defined by limiting criteria, without reciprocity. . . . It amounts to this: just as for the ancients there was an absolute vertical with reference to which the oblique was defined, so there is an absolute human type, the masculine.[2]

## I

From the time that the women's rights movement began to emerge in the late 18th century to the present "second wave" of feminism in the 1960s and 1970s, women dissatisfied with conventional roles have confronted the argument that certain aspects of female nature determine to at least a degree their position in society.[3] According to hoary custom, a woman's biologically proper place is with children and in homes, and so the assumption of other kinds of jobs and activities can actually be viewed as "unnatural." In the United States this stereotype is fading now: women are gradually entering lines of work that used to be occupied solely by males, and the traditional view of women is espoused only by the most conservative. Despite significant changes over recent years, however, we are far from a state of sexual equality, and ideas of the limits of woman's "proper place" still persist.

One indicator of lingering stereotyes is language. The common usage of idioms and colloquial expressions concerning women reflects both the past and present social conditions of their referents. The sex discrimination that is endemic to certain grammatical conventions is a subject fairly familiar to 20th-century feminists, who often point out, for example, the confusion and distortion that result from the fact that "man" is used both generically to denote all human beings and specifically to differentiate one half of those human beings from the other. So pervasive is this convention that from many descriptions of human life one might conclude that we are a single-sexed race. Not only can "man" be used to mean "men and women," but "he" can mean "he and/or she." Grammar requires that the pronoun accompanying the neutral "one" be "he," and that where women are not explicitly specified, "he" is also the proper pronoun. Until recently, business letters to unknown heads of companies and offices usually used the greeting "Dear Sirs" or "Gentlemen." Again until recently, any woman objecting that she was left out or unaccounted for by such expressions was greeted with the reply that "of course," "he" in such contexts meant her, too. For several years now, feminists have fought and gained against the consistent generic use of masculine terms to designate persons of both sexes.[4]

In a study assessing the extent of the generic use of masculine terms in colloquial speech, Elizabeth Lane Beardsley calls the colloquial or grammatical necessity of sexing a referring term "referential genderization."[5] Although English does contain sex-neutral terms like "person," grammar and colloquial usage make consistent use of neutral terms awkward if not impossible, and when a generic term is needed, it is the masculine that is proper. Beardsley argues that such linguistic conventions have a significant influence on concept formation—both general concepts about what it means to be a person, and the self-concepts of individuals.[6] Because of this influence, she argues, we should strive to develop and use sex-neutral terms to take the place of the expressions that are now current.

Beardsley concludes her essay with a comment from which I would like to begin my own analysis. She is responding to the possible objection that referential genderization is *not* sexist or detrimental because it is *parallel*—for every "he" there is a balancing "she"; for every masculine, a reciprocal feminine:

This latter suggestion about RG [referential genderization] shows an egregious failure to recognize the overpowering inclination of human beings to make a differential appraisal wherever they have made a distinction. RG, though it admittedly does not directly prescribe the subordination of one sex to the other or specify which sex should occupy the subordinate position, makes it more likely that some subordination and discriminatory treatment will take place. And, by incorporating sex-distinctions in language, RG helps to provide a conceptual framework useful for rationalizing sex-based discriminatory treatment if (and for whatever complex nonlinguistic reasons) this treatment should develop.[7]

In this paper I would like to consider several aspects of sexist conventions in language as they relate to the "differential appraisal" that occurs with sex-distinguishing terms. I am hesitant to rely on the speculation that there is a "human inclination" to make such appraisals; nor indeed is such a hypothesis necessary, for the roots of this phenomenon can be seen by further extending the analysis of sex-distinguishing expressions. If we search for parallelism or symmetry between masculine and feminine expressions in a variety of contexts, we find that in a significant number of instances, the feminine counterpart of a masculine expression carries a different connotation. Under certain conditions, female-designating terms connote something humorous or cute, trivial or ridiculous, where male-designating terms do not; and I shall appeal to a theory of comedy to help illuminate the significance of these situations. My interest is not only to point out that language reveals sexist practices—the customary discriminatory treatment of women. It is also to explore the extent to which linguistic conventions—particularly the generic use of masculine terminology—can be a perpetuator of sexist distinctions, regardless of the intent of the speaker.

## II

A woman preaching is like a dog's walking on his hind legs. It is not done well; but you are surprised to find it done at all.[8]

The woman's movement has the distinction of being the only social movement in the history of the United States that is regarded by its opponents as a joke.[9]

Political activity on the part of women and on behalf of women seems to have received a notably regular reaction of smiles and ridicule. Perhaps the most succinct linguistic indication of the lack of seriousness accorded feminism today is summed up in that infamous diminutive, "women's lib." ("Suffragette" for a time served the same function during the woman suffrage movement, though it later came to be accepted by feminists themselves.)

Of course, humor is by no means reserved for politically charged situations. It is such a ubiquitous feature of much of women's relations with society that it is preserved in ever-repeated stock expressions: "Don't bother your pretty head about it" (indulgent smile); "The ladies, God bless them!" (hearty laugh); "Thank heaven for little girls, for without them what would little boys do?" (smile and wink). But what is playful and affectionate in one context takes on a tougher character in another, and laughter is a formidable weapon. It may not be quite fair to quote such a notorious misogynist on this score, but Nietzsche's reaction to successful women is illustrative of laughter in its more acid form:

It betrays a corruption of the instincts—quite apart from the fact that it betrays bad taste—when a woman adduces Madame Roland or Madame de Staël or Monsieur George Sand, of all people, as if they proved anything in *favor* or "woman as such." Among men these three are the three *comical* women as such—nothing more!— and precisely the best involuntary *counterarguments* against emancipation and feminine vainglory.[10]

Extremes of sentiment such as those expressed by Dr. Johnson and Nietzsche are comparatively rare, but we should not quickly conclude that the phenomenon displayed is rare. If we look for other than outright derision, if we examine situations where no misogynistic intent exists, if we extend our investigation of the "comical" to include any circumstances that induce a less serious atmosphere than might be expected to accompany a man in the same circumstances—then we have ample evidence of situations that become shaded with comedy when a woman is introduced into the picture. Furthermore, consider the ease with which the epithet "male chauvinist" has made its way into public banter. The term was coined to apply to someone who exhibited condemnable prejudice and social practice, but now it is not uncommon to hear men being called "male chauvinist pigs" as a joke. (Compare the sobering effect of "racist.")

The various ridiculing or bantering reactions to women are more than an annoyance. They serve to show us how indeed there is little parallelism, little symmetry, between the concepts of male and female. If the pronouns "he" and "she" (and related sex-distinguishing terms and the contexts in which they occur) were really parallel, serving only to designate persons of different sex and not to carry significantly different connotations, then one should be able to say the same kinds of things about a "he" as about a "she." We should expect statements not directly related to sex and biology to have parallel colloquial usage, such that the sorts of things regularly said about males and about females would be interchangeable, and such that no shift in connotation would be evident.

This sort of test obviously relies on common, expected usage and not on actual grammatical rules, on what "sounds right" and what "sounds funny," and on an intuitive assessment of the connotations of various terms and idioms. Consequently, conclusions drawn on this subject are likely to be open to some degree of argument, and, for that matter, to a certain amount of historical relativism. Language analysis of this sort is rather like scanning an aerial photograph for evidence of ruined cities beneath, and occasionally one may mistake a ditch for a canal. Despite these conditions, however, it is not hard to demonstrate that in a significant number of contexts there is little or no parallel connotation between male-denoting and female-denoting terminology.

Some of the most obvious instances illustrating this point are a result of the contemporary social position of women—or, more accurately, the contemporary popular stereotype of that position. Since women in that major occupation called "housewife" devote a great deal of their energies to a home and a family, we are accustomed to descriptions of the following sort:

*Mrs. George Hollander has recently been elected president of the tri-city chapter of the PTA. The wife of one of the community's most respected bankers, Mrs. Hollander's wide smile and fashionable figure are familiar to many residents of Belledowns who are regular attendants at the bi-annual Community Council picnics. She will devote her first energies this fall to investigating the recent violence at two junior high schools.*

These sorts of things, of course, *could* be said about Mr. Hollander, for he is also married, has distinctive physical characteristics, and wears clothes. But it is unlikely that these features would be singled out for special mention; certainly they would not be stressed. Dorothy Sayers wittily inverts the situation and demonstrates how odd it sounds when descriptions of men are cast in the same mold as descriptions that are common of women. For example:

Professor Bract, although a distinguished botanist, is not in any way an unmanly man. He has, in fact, a wife and seven children. Tall and burly, the hands with which he handles his delicate specimens are as gnarled and powerful as those of a Canadian lumberjack, and when I swilled beer with him in his laboratory, he bawled his conclusions at me in a strong, gruff voice that implemented the promise of his swaggering moustache.[11]

The parody is evident, but the point is well made: We regularly think of women in contexts that stress directly or indirectly their sexual nature, and this custom underscores the fact that a large part of their social relations involve what are ultimately sex-related functions. Their family connections and marital status, their appearance and dress, the "femininity of their manner" are all accepted aspects of descriptions of women in newspapers and magazines. These aspects are clearly not evenly paralleled in contexts involving men, for if they were, we would hardly laugh at the tables Sayers has turned.

We do not laugh at similar descriptions of women, for we have grown accustomed to them. But is it the case that they connote nothing humorous at all, or nothing akin to humor? I would argue that in fact this common way of speaking about women contains the germs of humor, and that it helps explain the full significance of referential genderization and similar sex-based modes of expression. It also helps explain, I think, why ridicule and humor remain prime weapons in the battle against women's equality.

Let us expand our check for parallel connotations between masculine and feminine terms by gathering a sample of expressions used to refer to men and women engaged in the same or similar activities:

| Male Term | Female Term in Common Usage | Neutral Term |
|---|---|---|
| I. singer | singer | singer |
| teacher | teacher | teacher |
| II. actor | actress | |
| launderer | laundress | |
| III. chairman | chairwoman, Madam chairman | chairperson |
| Congressman | Congresswoman | Representative |
| policeman | policewoman | officer |
| IV. fisherman | | |
| V. driver | woman driver | driver |
| wrestler | lady/woman wrestler | wrestler |
| professor | female/woman professor | professor |
| doctor | lady/woman doctor | doctor |
| cop | lady cop | cop |
| VI. bachelor | spinster, bachelorette | |
| traffic cop | meter maid | |
| riveter | Rosie the riveter | riveter |
| suffragist | suffragette | suffragist |
| (airplane race | powder puff derby | airplane race) |
| VII. male prostitute | prostitute | prostitute |
| male nurse | nurse | nurse |
| male secretary | secretary | secretary |
| househusband | housewife | |
| VIII. welfare recipient | welfare mother | welfare recipient |
| worker | working mother | worker |
| janitor | maid, cleaning lady | |

Clearly there are a number of different ways that we speak of persons engaged in various activities. Some do and some do not specify the sex of the person, and of those that do, some do and some do not specify it in a way that seems particularly important. Though there may well be more, I have isolated eight groups of expressions. The first three either do not specify the sex of the referent or do so without any significant difference in connotation between terms used for males and terms used for females. (Not surprisingly, those terms that either make no distinction or indicate it in the suffix all pertain to occupations in which women are customary participants.) Terms in group III must add an adjunct like "-woman" or "-person" in order to accommodate female participants, and although some tongue-tied awkwardness may be encountered with the first use of a newly minted term, still no (lasting) difference in connotation exists. Group IV can contain no such differences because terms like this have only one form, but they seem peripheral to this study and are of interest only in passing.

It is the last four groups that are of special interest. Group V, it seems to me, contains terms that really need no specification of sex either according to grammar or by reason of idiomatic ease, though they frequently do receive such specification. Although the neutral term is also the one used for males, females are denoted equally well by the same term without any discomfort or confusion of expression. The fact that frequently their sex is also mentioned no doubt has to do with the fact that women are a minority in those occupations, but the important feature of the combination expression is the subtle shift in connotation that can occur with the addition of the feminizing adjunct "-woman" or "-lady." This shift is not always immediately noticeable, but it is clearly present in cases like "woman driver" or "lady cop," and "lady (or female) wrestler." An expression so formed connotes something slightly comical, lighthearted, or cute in a way that those in the male column do not. (In almost every case, adding the adjunct "-lady" to a term, as opposed to "-woman," is a sign of an added humorous dimension. The same holds true of the suffix "-ette" as opposed to "-ess," I would imagine because "-ette" is used to form a diminutive as well as a feminized term.) Because almost any noun denoting an occupation can take a qualifying adjunct, group V no doubt could contain the largest collection of terms in this list.

With the terms in group VI, the shift in connotation is quite obvious. They are similar to those in group V, but the female designation is established more descriptively. Once again, in a number of those cases where the masculine and the neutral terms are identical ("riveter," "suffragist"), the same term could be used to denote a woman in the same occupation. The feminized expressions in common use are humorous-sounding, cartoonish, or cute. Probably the most dramatic difference in connotation—though it is by no means a uniformly humorous

one—exists between "bachelor" and "spinster." Although
"bachelor" can be used in contexts where its connotation is
grim or lonely or sad, it can also be used to connote someone
free, debonair, independent, and enviable. "Spinster" has invariably the former connotation, hence the coining of the coy
"bachelorette" (not "bacheloress," note) to connote the independent, sexually desirable female.

With the exception of sex-neutral terms, in groups I–VI the
standard term designating a person in a particular occupation
has been male. "Chairwoman" (or "Madam Chairman," which
is actually a contradiction) and "actress" are variations or
standard forms. With the terms in group VII, however, the
female-designating term (at least in the United States in this
generation) is the standard one, with the male-specifying term
being the departure from the norm. If a shift in connotation
occurs only because a term is used in a way that deviates from
the standard expression or context, then we would expect a
similar shift in connotation to be noticeable with the male-
designating terms in this group. But with the exception of
"househusband," which is used invariably in a jocular way,
none of the male variations on the standard themes connote
anything odd or cute. (In fact, some may even carry more
dignity than the standard female forms.) Therefore, it seems
that more than just unusual usage is responsible for the comical
connotations evident in groups V and VI.

Group VIII contains terms that are humorous in neither
form, but which are similar to the others in that the term used
for the female specifies sex in a way that the term for the male
does not. I shall return to these terms later.

In summary, although there is a trend toward using neutral
terms more and more ("chairperson" and "firefighter," for
example), such changes are far from universal. It is still true
that colloquial practices very often trivialize the terms used to
refer to women by connoting something slightly cute or funny,
thus underscoring the fact that "he" and "she" in various contexts are in fact not parallel.

## III

It is clear that the humor that frequently awaits women, particularly those engaged in non-traditional occupations, is of some
significance to the full achievement of sexual equality. What

more can we make of it? Why is comedy a ready attendant to expressions involving women? Do these expressions have anything in common with other circumstances that cause laughter? What *are* the circumstances that cause laughter? This last question of course opens up an avenue of inquiry that reaches far beyond the scope of this paper, but we can at least begin here to make some fair guesses about the comical nature of certain female-designating expressions.

Perhaps the immediate explanation that comes to mind is that it is our experience that is at fault. Our limited associations regarding the tasks women usually perform are rather narrow, and so we are surprised into a smile when we think of a woman in the ranks of wrestlers or hockey players. Expressions indicating out-of-the-ordinary circumstances subtly startle one. Therefore, it would stand to reason that as women in fact broaden their scope of activity, language will catch up with social and political change, and feminized expressions will no longer be humorous.

This probably is the case with some of the expressions discussed above. It seems likely to be true in particular of those in group III, and it is probably responsible for the fact that any peculiarity of connotation that may arise with the initial use of "chairperson" or "Congresswoman" is short-lived. However, militating against this as a total explanation is the fact that the terms in group VII (in which the male form is a deviation from the standard female form for an occupation customarily associated with women) suffer no connotation shift.

Is there, then, more to the story? Is language only a passive partner in the asymmetry between expressions concerning men and women? I suggest not only that we customarily associate women with particular activities, thereby mentally restricting their scope, but that the notion of what it is to be a woman is limited as well. As this limitation is reflected in language, "woman" and "she" have a more limited connotation than "man" and "he."

Proceeding on this hypothesis, can we continue speculation about the comic and the source of the laughter that is directed at women? At this point it is helpful to enlist the aid of a classic theory of laughter, that of Henri Bergson. Some elements of his extensive theory suggest a way of understanding the full significance of referential genderization and the generic use of the masculine. Admittedly, Bergson is concerned primarily with

comedy as a literary and theatrical genre, and it is arguable that
he has exhausted all the sources and types of the comic or has
noted all the causes of laughter.[12] However, it is by no means
necessary to accept all of a theory in order to profit by it, and
quite apart from his larger philosophy, some of Bergson's observations have an intuitive correctness and are particularly
congenial to our analysis.

Bergson's remarks about the context in which laughter occurs
are relevant to an understanding of the political effect of ridicule as a weapon. Laughter, he claims, occurs in situations
where the spectators are relatively uninvolved, at least temporarily, with the subject of their mirth. In his words, the comic
demands "something like a momentary anaesthesia of the
heart."[13] Whether or not all instances of laughter follow this
design, certainly this is a component of the ridicule that serves a
political purpose in the chivalrous resistance to "women's lib."
It keeps sympathy at a distance and allows one to dismiss the
subject of laughter as not deserving serious consideration.

The conditions that foster laughter in response to women are
illuminated by two related Bergsonian concepts: rigidity and
inversion. Bergson is particularly famous for his vitalism, his
anti-materialistic theory of human nature. His notion that the
laughable is the appearance of the purely physical or mechanical, of the not-quite-human, is intimately connected to this idea.
Whereas the fully human is flexible and elastic and vital, that
which is laughable exhibits a mechanical inflexibility, a *rigidity*.
The simplest example of this is the banana peel of slapstick
comedy: the human body does not accommodate itself to the
unexpected, and, like a machine running amuck, it involuntarily
flounders, causing laughter. Such situations direct attention to
clumsy physicality, allowing spectators to regard the unfortunate subject as a thing, an object.[14] Our emotions are temporarily suspended, and we are preoccupied with the ridiculous
physical situation. "Any incident is comic that calls our attention to the physical in a person, when it is the moral side that is
concerned."[15]

Slapstick exploits a physical kind of rigidity, but there are
also forms of character rigidity in comic situations. Bergson
terms one such form "inversion." Here, laughter arises in reaction to the kind of circumstance that we might call by the more
modern term "role-reversal." Whenever a character is cast in a
role with built-in limitations, the violation of those limits and

ie adoption of an opposite role creates a situation in which we
iugh.

icture to yourself certain characters in a certain situation: if you
everse the situation and invert the *roles*, you obtain a comic scene.
. . Thus, we laugh at the prisoner at the bar lecturing the magis-
ate; at a child presuming to teach its parents; in a word, at every-
iing that comes under the heading of 'topsyturvydom.'[16]

The idea that laughter can be stimulated when an inherent
gidity is exposed in its object, that the assumption of a non-
aditional role can be perceived as comically "inverted," sug-
ests a way of understanding the humorous connotations sur-
ounding women. It is clear that our concept of woman carries
ith it implicit limitations, such that it does not wholly belong
i contexts that are not regarded as "feminine." Consequently,
hen a woman acts contrary to "rigid" stereotype, the results
in be seen as laughable, especially by an audience so predis-
osed. Moreover, linguistic convention itself, not merely cus-
imary associations, helps perpetuate this state of affairs. What
etter way to ensure such limitation than to reserve female-
esignating terms, as a grammatical convention, only for people
hose sex is specifically noted? ("Where sex is not specified,
e 'he.' ") The extension of the masculine in its generic use to
over general situations involving all of humanity, and the res-
vation of feminine terms only for situations where sex is spe-
fied, would seem to guarantee the perpetuation of non-parallel
innotations for "he" and "she," "man" and "woman," and
lated expressions. The use of "she" always remains the tacit
ception to the rule—the specifically mentioned, deviating
ise.

It stands to reason that this convention also guarantees that
hen feminized terms are used, a disproportionate attention will
e directed to the sexual character of the referent. A term that
so has generic usage connotes "person"; one that is used to
ecify persons according to sex connotes "person who is re-
arkable for a physical feature." "He" is bound to be more
exible, more natural in a multitude of contexts, than "she."[17]
iis is surely at least a partial explanation for the shift in
innotation, slight though it may be, that occurs when one
ialifies a person engaged in a particular occupation with the
junct "woman" or "lady" (group V). Nothing the person
ies changes, nor is there an accompanying mocking descrip-

tion (as there may be in group VI). But specifying the subject in this way calls attention to her physical character, diverting attention from the occupation or activity itself. As Simone de Beauvoir says, "The term 'female' is derogatory not because it emphasizes woman's animality but because it imprisons her in her sex."[18]

In this regard, of course, expressions connoting the comic are only the tip of the iceberg. Perhaps they are the most noticeable linguistic indicators of the asymmetry between masculine and feminine expressions, but they are by no means the only ones, nor are they the most pernicious.

A consideration of group VIII makes this evident. Two of the most common terms in current usage are "welfare mother" and "working mother"—expressions which not only call attention to the sex of their referents, but define them in relation to their offspring as well. The tendency to think of women who work as "working wives" or "working mothers" should make one skeptical about the ultimate reforming effect of recent encouragements to "get women out of the house." Such endeavors, while they may alleviate the problems of individuals, are unlikely to do much toward eliminating the traditional stereotype. As long as the stereotype of woman is formed in relation to the stereotype of man, extending the activities of people who remain "working mothers" will do little to repair the asymmetry that now exists between "woman" and "man." Let us look at language again: Would a man say "I have a career and a family, too"? This statement might well be true of him, but only his wife is likely to express the situation in that way. So it is with the well-intentioned husband who "helps with the housework." Does his wife help with the housework too? No, she simply does it. She is a "working wife and mother," whose very name indicates that this is her job, not as part of the supporting crew, but in the starring role.

Whether or not it is blatantly sexist, our way of talking about women continues to promote a notion of female nature that is quite out of balance with that of the male, for it continues to identify a woman primarily in terms of her sex. Sexist conventions in language may be all the more tenacious because their effects are not conscious. If you accuse someone of being sexist when he or she is just speaking the King's English, that person is likely to respond with understandable indignation. But the situation is discriminatory nonetheless. So long as this disparity xists in language, equality is still distant, and since in Bergson's :rms this situation continues to be one in which "the physical vershadows the moral," it is to be expected that humor and dicule will be waiting in the wings.

Insofar as generic usage of masculine terms perpetuates our mited or "rigid" concept of woman (and, by extension, of erson), the increasing use of neutral expressions mentioning oth males and females where "persons in general" are con- :rned should have more than a cosmetic effect. It is clear by ow that in some ways language is not always the intransigent e that one might have thought, for new usage can supplant the ld with comparative ease. Certainly the battle for sexual equal- y neither begins nor ends with language, but it is encouraging at there is one barrier that can be scaled with relative ease. owever, to conclude on a cautionary note, perhaps the ease ith which this barrier falls should make us a little suspicious.

## NOTES

. Dorothy Sayers, "The Human Not-Quite-Human," in *Mascu-line/Feminine*, ed. Betty Roszak and Theodore Roszak (New York: Harper & Row, 1969), p. 117.

. Simone de Beauvoir, *The Second Sex*, trans. H. M. Parshley (New York: Knopf, 1953), p. xv.

. For views at both ends of the chronological spectrum, see Rous-seau, *Émile* (1762), and Steven Goldberg, *The Inevitability of Patriarchy* (New York: William Morrow, 1973).

. Accompanying this argument against the generic use of mascu-line terminology has been a campaign to rid textbooks and children's reading matter of material reflecting only stereotypic occupations for men and women. These efforts have had a no-ticeable effect: McGraw-Hill, Inc. has issued extensive guidelines requiring elimination of sexist language from their publications, and many states now have anti-sex-discrimination rules for school materials.

. Elizabeth Lane Beardsley, "Referential Genderization," *Philoso-phical Forum* 5 (1973–74): 285–93; reprinted in *Women and Philosophy*, ed. C. Gould and M. Wartofsky (New York: Put-nam's, 1976). I have also made use of some of Beardsley's other terminology, such as "sex-neutral" and "sex-distinguishing" to refer to terms which respectively do not and do indicate the sex of a referent.

Occasionally, I use "masculine expressions" and "feminine

expressions" as shorthand for "expressions which indicate tha their subject is male" and "expressions which indicate that the subject is female."

6. Throughout this paper I am sharing Beardsley's assumption tha language—what one can and cannot say—is an important fac tor in concept formation and transmission. (Cf. Beardsley, pp 287, 291.)

7. Beardsley, p. 291.

8. Samuel Johnson, 31 July 1763, in James Boswell, *Life of John son.*

9. Roberta Salper, introduction to *Female Liberation* (New York Knopf, 1972), p. 3. Ridicule is not reserved for political move ments involving only women (witness the effect of political ca toons), but the woman's movement and women in gener receive a disproportionate share of jokes and jibes.

10. Friedrich Nietzsche, "Woman De-Feminized," in Roszak an Roszak, p. 5.

11. Sayers, p. 118.

12. See Wylie Sypher, editor's introduction to *Comedy* (Garde City, N.Y.: Doubleday, 1956).

13. Henri Bergson, "Laughter" in *Comedy*, ed. Sypher, p. 64. A though Bergson did not intend to extend his comments to in clude the view that laughter can be an ally of reaction an tradition, some of his observations are amenable to this exter sion: "Laughter is, above all, a corrective. Being intended t humiliate, it must make a painful impression on the perso against whom it is directed. By laughter, society avenges itse for the liberties taken with it. It would fail in its object if bore the stamp of sympathy or kindness" (p. 187; cf. p. 148 We might compare George Meredith's essay on comedy, writ ten shortly before Bergson's, in which he asserts that gre comedy—that is, comedy that does not rely on prejudice exploitative human relations for its effect—cannot develop in society where there is "a state of marked inequality betwee the sexes" ("An Essay On Comedy" in *Comedy*, ed. Syphe p. 3; cf. p. 31).

14. Bergson, p. 97.

15. Bergson, p. 93.

16. Bergson, p. 121.

17. An explicit affirmation that "she" and "woman" have on specific usage occurred in 1974 during the chartering procee ings for the Woman's Studies College at the State University New York, Buffalo. The chartering committee, concerned abo possible sex discrimination on the part of the College, inquir about the consistent use of "woman" and "she" to refer to Co lege participants. It was explained that both terms were bei

used generically to include both men and women, which was appreciated by the audience but was deemed unacceptable by the administration, despite attempts to specify clearly when the generic use was to obtain.

18. Beauvoir, p. 3.

Virginia Valian

# Linguistics and Feminism

At least three important issues arise from a reading of Robin Lakoff's articles "Language and Woman's Place" and "Why Women Are Ladies".[1] One issue is methodological: it is concerned with how to evaluate data about language use in making claims about the utility of men's and women's speech. The second issue is linguistic: it concerns the definition of language and the nature of the domain that linguists study. The third issue is political: it concerns the relation between language and other areas of oppression. It also concerns the proper advisory role of linguistic "experts" who are exploring how language can be used to oppress women.

This paper explores three questions related to these issues: (1) With respect to the first issue, is women's speech inferior to men's? (2) Do men and women speak different languages? (3) What is the relationship between linguistic and social change? It concludes that:

First, some of the alleged differences between men's and women's speech argue for the superiority of women's speech. Lakoff notes that women make finer color distinctions, use more adjectives, and are more courteous. If this is indeed so,

I dedicate this paper to J. J. Katz and T. G. Bever. I would also like to thank M. Garrett of M.I.T., M. Parlee of Wellesley College (now at Barnard College), and T.G. Bever of Columbia University for making available the subjects who served in the experiment reported in the text.

the first two characteristics would enable one to make more true statements than would be possible with a leaner vocabulary. The stereotyped male view that such refinements are trivial reflects sexist values rather than a scientific assessment.

Second, criteria such as those Lakoff offers are not sufficient to establish the claim that men and women speak different languages. It is necessary to draw a distinction between speech and language in order to avoid the reductio that people speak a different language from one minute to the next, and that everyone is a polyglot. The distinction between speech and language is politically important as well: women should not erroneously think that in order to overcome their oppression they must learn another "language."

Third, the paper concludes that linguistic oppression is not a symptom that will disappear when more fundamental social inequalities are removed.

# I

Lakoff claims that, compared to men, women make finer color distinctions, use more adjectives, use tag questions more, and are more courteous. The claims have been questioned by Dubois and Crouch,[2] but the argument here depends not upon the truth of the claims but on what conclusions can be drawn from them, assuming that they are true. Lakoff concludes that such differences are evidence for "triviality in subject-matter and uncertainty about it." The conclusion does not follow. If a color is mauve or ecru or crimson, being able to say so is an advantage rather than a liability: there are more true statements that can be made with such a vocabulary than without it. There is nothing trivial about this ability.

Lakoff's treatment of non-color adjectives also leads to erroneous conclusions. Lakoff claims that women use more "women's" adjectives than do men, who use "neutral" adjectives. Examples of "women's" adjectives are words like "lovely," "adorable," and "divine." "Neutral" adjectives include words like "terrific" and "great." There are actually two separate issues here: one has to do with what adjectives can modify what nouns, independent of the speaker's sex; the other has to do with what adjectives speakers commonly use as a function of their sex.

Lakoff confuses the two issues. For example, she finds the

sentence "What a lovely steel mill" to be unacceptable if uttered by a man, and acceptable if uttered by a woman. A steel mill, however, normally cannot properly be termed lovely, regardless of the speaker's sex, since a steel mill is normally not an aesthetic object, and to judge something as "lovely" is to judge it favorably as an aesthetic object. If a chair is described as "lovely," it is the chair's aesthetic, rather than functional, qualities that are being praised.[3]

If this analysis is correct, what could it mean for Lakoff to claim that the sentence "What a lovely steel mill" is unacceptable only if a man utters it? Are women ignorant of the meaning of "lovely?" Even if they are, that would seem to be a matter independent of the language. It would only reflect women's knowledge and use of the language. Or is the unacceptability to be interpreted not relative to the sentence, but relative to the speaker? That is, perhaps Lakoff is claiming that a semantically deviant sentence is socially unacceptable if a man utters it, but acceptable if a woman utters it. If this is so, the use of a double standard needs to be justified.

Lakoff's discussion indicates that she has something slightly different in mind. She suggests that even women can only use "women's" adjectives if "the concepts to which they are applied are not relevant to the real world of (male) influence and power."[4] That is, the use of such adjectives automatically connotes triviality, and women will use them only if they are willing to be trivial. Again, there seems to be confusion between adjective appropriateness independent of the speaker and speakers' usage. The confusion is accompanied by a negative value-judgment of women's usage.

Let us consider adjectives in more detail. The adjectives Lakoff categorizes as "neutral" are multi-purpose and have a broad usage of application, e.g., "terrific." The "women's adjectives" have a narrow usage of application, e.g., "divine." There is a parallel here with words like "small," which can be used to describe any extent, whereas words like "short" are limited to things having vertical extension. Compared to men, do women also use more specific words like "short" just as they use more specific color adjectives? This hypothesis is not considered, although its verification would challenge an image of women as trivia-mongers and substitute an image in which women are more precise and have larger vocabularies than men.

Lakoff narrows the range of possible explanations for women's adjective use in another way. Returning again to the analogy of "short," there is a counterpart term, namely "tall." Similarly, there are counterparts to the "trivial" adjectives Lakoff lists for women, such as "magnificent," "dynamic," "brilliant," "powerful," "hideous," "forceful," etc. Do women also use words like "forceful" more than men? Lakoff fails to consider the possibility that her selection is biased, that there exists a counterpart category that is also more frequently used by women than men, because women have larger vocabularies than men. In almost all of her comparisons between men's and women's usage, Lakoff assumes that the women's usage is somehow inferior.[5] That assumption seems unwarranted.

## II

Lakoff distinguishes between "women's language" and "men's language" and discusses the implications of the distinction for women's role. There are two principal criticisms of her view: first, that Lakoff fails to distinguish language and speech and only argues for sex differences in speech; second, that she erroneously complicates the task of women by implying that we will have to learn another "language." What is the criterion by which people are held to speak different languages? This is never discussed. It is assumed that because women may use different vocabulary items from men, and may use some linguistic constructions more than men, women and men speak different languages.

There are two separate, though related, problems here. One is how to determine what are the criteria for languagehood; the other is how to distinguish between speech and language. By confusing speech and language, Lakoff accepts the evidence that men and women have different speech habits as also being evidence that men and women speak two different languages.

Let us first explore what the criteria for languagehood are. If vocabulary and favored use of one construction over another are sufficient, then no two people speak the same language: no two people use just the same vocabulary and linguistic constructions. One is also led to the conclusion that the language I am speaking today is different from the one I spoke yesterday and the one I will speak tomorrow, since I will use different words and constructions on each of these occasions. Even if individual differences are somehow exempted from the criterion, there is still the problem of differences between groups. If men and women speak different "languages" by virtue of using different vocabulary items and different constructions, then many groups could be distinguished on the basis of the vocabulary items and constructions they use. In fact, there is no a priori reason to limit the number of such groups: there are skiers vs. non-skiers, parents vs. the childless, students vs. non-students, etc.

Lakoff claims that some women become "bilingual" in men's and women's language and that this may be a strain on them, reducing their performance. (Presumably it is also a strain on male intellectuals, clergy, and upper-class Britons who, according to Lakoff, have speech more similar to women than to other men.) By this argument, if I were a student mother who skis I would speak at least four "languages" and add another for each new classification I fall under. Therefore, by this argument, all of us are extraordinary polyglots, and under extraordinary strain, since each of us falls into an extremely large number of such categories. Are we also to conclude that each of these "languages" has the same status as genuine languages like French and Russian? If Lakoff is satisfied with the conclusion that everyone speaks a different language from everyone else (or the alternate conclusion that everyone speaks indefinitely many languages) then we must understand her to be using "language" in a metaphorical rather than technical sense. If she is not satisfied with the conclusion, she must provide and justify alternate criteria so that only men and women will end up speaking different "languages."

The reductio ad absurdum occurs because Lakoff confuses speech with language. An analogy with another field may clarify matters. Perhaps men and women add and multiply differently. That is not evidence for "women's mathematics" and "men's mathematics," but for different computational styles. The structure of mathematics is the same, no matter who uses it. Similarly, there is a difference between the English language and how people use that language, and nothing is served by obscuring that difference, except to make it seem as if linguists have "discovered" that women and men speak English I and English II and that linguists therefore have some special competence in discussing sex differences in this realm. Lakoff maintains the confusion when she says "my feeling is that language use by any other name is still linguistics." In saying this, Lakoff denies the linguistic distinction between competence and performance.

Competence refers to the speaker's knowledge of the language, and is described by a rule system called a grammar; performance refers to the speaker's use of language, and is described by a model of processing.[6]

The confusion between speech and language is also maintained in Lakoff's discussion of women's inability to express themselves strongly. She argues that women do not have the linguistic means to express themselves strongly, rather than saying that they lack the social will to use the available forms. Assume that it is true that women find it difficult to express strong emotion, that they find it difficult to swear. Is this due to speaking a different language or to an upbringing that demands that women not be assertive, not argue, not fight? We can accept as fact that women have difficulty being assertive and angry, and that the difficulty is reflected in our manner of speaking (as well as in other ways). There can be no quarrel with this; it is a truism from the women's movement. The quarrel is with dressing the understanding up in linguistic clothes and drawing conclusions such as that some women learn to be "bilingual" in both men's and women's language and that this is a strain.[7] Such conclusions are based on premises that have never been proved in the first place (i.e., that there really are different languages).

The failure to make a speech/language distinction is finally seen in Lakoff's discussion of what information a grammar should include. She argues that significant generalizations will not be captured in a grammar that ignores the social causes for differential word meanings. For example, she points out that "a professional" has two different meanings depending on whether it is applied to a man or a woman. When applied to a man it means that he is a doctor, lawyer, or has some other profession. When applied to a woman it means that she is a prostitute. There are also word pairs that have similarly non-parallel meanings, such as "bachelor" and "spinster." Unless the grammar contains information about social and political conditions, the generalization that all these cases reflect the oppression of women cannot be made by the grammar.

The claim may be true, but it does not constitute an argument for including such information in the grammar. Lakoff's reasoning is an argument for making appropriate generalizations; a separate argument is needed to support the claim that an appropriate place to make such generalizations is in the grammar

of a language, rather than in ancillary fields such as sociolin-
guistics. She does not supply such an argument.

There is one further point in this connection: Lakoff never
states what the generalization is. She offers no hypothesis that
would account for the non-parallels that exist. The oppression
of women is not a sufficient hypothesis, because there are cases
of parallel usage. In fact, the non-parallelisms are a small minority compared to the number of words that apply equally to
men and women, including explicitly sexual or gender terms,
such as "horny" and "man/woman" (where the two forms have
equivalent connotations).

In summary, Lakoff incorrectly identifies the differences between men's and women's speech as differences between men's
and women's language. The problem occurs because she fails to
distinguish between speech and language. Two unfortunate consequences are her suggestions that women need to overcome
their linguistic background by learning "men's language," and
that the grammar should include social and political information.

# III

In the final sections of "Language and Women's Place" Lakoff
analyzes the relation between social change and linguistic
change; she also considers which changes in linguistic usage, on
the part of both men and women, are desirable. Her position is
that linguistic change follows from social change, and that some
changes in usage will be impossible to effect even under conditions of social equality. Let us examine in detail Lakoff's position on the relation between social and linguistic change. Lakoff
writes that:

The presence of the words is a signal that something is wrong, rather
than (as too often interpreted by well-meaning reformers) the problem itself.[8]

Linguistic imbalances are worthy of study because they bring into
sharper focus real-world imbalances and inequities. They are clues
that some external situation needs changing, rather than items that
one *should* seek to change directly. A competent doctor tries to eliminate the germs that cause measles, rather than trying to bleach the
red out with peroxide. I emphasize this point because it seems to be
currently fashionable to try, first, to attack the disease by attempting
to obliterate the external symptoms; and, secondly, to attack *every*

instance of linguistic sexual inequity, rather than selecting those that reflect a real disparity in social treatment, not mere grammatical nonparallelism; we should be attempting to single out those linguistic uses that, by implication and innuendo, demean the members of one group or another, and should be seeking to make speakers of English aware of the psychological damage such forms do. The problem, of course, lies in deciding which forms are really damaging to the ego, and then in determining what to put in their stead.[9]

It should be recognized that social change creates language change, not the reverse; or at best, language change influences changes in attitudes slowly and indirectly, and these changes in attitudes will not be reflected in social change unless society is receptive already. Further, the linguist can suggest which linguistic disparities reflect real and serious social inequalities; which are changeable, which will resist change; and can thus help the workers in the real world to channel their energies most constructively and avoid ridicule.[10]

The only substantive claim in these discussions is an inconsistent one that linguistic change follows social change and not vice versa. The thesis seems to be that linguistic oppression is a symptom of the disease of social inequality, rather than the disease itself. Thus there is no point in trying to eliminate the symptoms alone; the disease itself must be attacked. But Lakoff is not consistent on this point. Shifting ground somewhat, she says that we should not try to eliminate all linguistic inequality at once; this implies that it does make sense to try to change some of the external symptoms. She also says that we should try to make people realize the psychological harm that oppressive usage inflicts—again as if to say that the symptom can have its own ill effects on top of the disease. In another place, she vacillates between saying that social change creates linguistic change and saying that linguistic change is slow and can only create social change if social change has already been in the wind. Lakoff nowhere defines social change or tells us what the disease is of which oppressive language is one of the symptoms.

There are three different arguments against the point she wants to make about linguistic change, and each accepts the disease analogy as valid. First, while we are curing the disease —no overnight affair—we can use a little relief from the symptoms. Second, not only is reduction of suffering a good in itself, it often gives the patient the strength necessary to fight the disease more effectively.

The third argument is more basic and more complex. It requires a definition of social inequality and the nature of the disease. Are the two identical? Social inequality could refer to salary, the distribution of women in different kinds of jobs, the number of women with paying jobs, or educational level; Lakoff is not specific. Is changing the socioeconomic status of women attacking the disease rather than the symptoms? By all socio-economic criteria, Jews do very well. Yet there is prejudice against Jews, and no lack of epithets to refer to them. If the disease has been cured in the case of Jews, why do the linguistic symptoms remain? The point of the example is that social change does not guarantee linguistic change: we can imagine women being socioeconomically equal but still linguistically oppressed. It could be argued that the linguistic oppression was formerly much worse, or at least more widely practiced; but my point is that linguistic oppression can exist in a socioeconomic vacuum.

That argument, however, only proves that social change is not sufficient to guarantee linguistic change. But even if it is insufficient, it could still be necessary. If we look at the early years of the recent women's movement, there is evidence from the radical movement as a whole that linguistic change can occur before social change. Before there were any tangible changes in women's education or jobs, feminists changed the way they themselves spoke, and also changed the speech habits of non-feminist radical women and men.

One counter-argument Lakoff could make is that I have in-correctly defined social inequality: that I am incorrectly using it as synonymous with economic and educational inequality. She might propose a more abstract definition, such as a lack of self-determination or power over one's own life. Having asserted such power, women became an important influence on the radical movement. The linguistic effect of feminists on the radical movement was then a consequence of their having more political power. The problem changes, however, if put in these terms. Now the chain of events is not properly described as first social change and then linguistic change, but rather as first self-determination and then choices about what changes are desirable. The disease is therefore not social inequality but lack of power over one's own life; all forms of oppression—be they economic, psychological, social, or linguistic—are merely symptoms of it.

On my analysis, feminists have already developed the correct strategy with respect to oppressive linguistic usage: eliminate it wherever it exists. On Lakoff's analysis, the feminist strategy is incorrect. On the acceptance of "Ms." as a title for women, she says:

One must distinguish between acceptance in official use and documents (where Ms. is already used to some extent) and acceptance in colloquial conversation, where I have never heard it. . . . it would seem that trying to legislate a change in a lexical item is fruitless.[11]

The change to Ms. will not be generally adopted until women's status in society changes to assure her an identity based on her own accomplishments.[12]

On the desire of many women to do away with forms of "he" being used as the generic pronoun:

I think one should force oneself to be realistic: certain aspects of language are available to the native speakers' conscious analysis, and others are too common, too thoroughly mixed throughout the language, for the speaker to be aware each time he uses them. It is realistic to hope to change only those linguistic uses of which speakers themselves can be made aware, as they use them. One chooses, in speaking or writing, more or less consciously and purposefully among nouns, adjectives, and verbs; one does not choose among pronouns in the same way. My feeling is that this area of pronominal neutralization is both less in need of changing, and less open to change, than many of the other disparities that have been discussed earlier.[13]

Many speakers, feeling this is awkward and perhaps even discriminatory, attempt a neutralization with *their*, a usage frowned upon by most authorities as inconsistent or illogical.[14]

With respect to changing the use of "he" as the generic pronoun, Lakoff says that she does not think it is important, and that in any event it is not possible to stop using "he" as the generic. That is, even if women suddenly stopped being discriminated against, "he" would continue, because speakers do not have control over this aspect of their speech. No evidence is offered for the claim.

Lakoff acknowledges that many women object to the use of "he" as the generic, but asserts that an attempt to change the use is futile. But the women who object to "he" have presumably been able to control their speech. Perhaps Lakoff is arguing that these women may have been able to, but that other people cannot or will not. There does not, however, seem to be anything in the way except lack of motivation or lack of a suitable alternative. Lakoff's pessimism seems to be a personal statement rather than a scientific judgment. This is also apparent in her remarks on the use of "Ms." as a title. The danger is that her assertions could have a pernicious effect on feminists: a linguist, who apparently should know, is stating that a certain change is not possible. But the linguist does not know and presents neither argument nor evidence.

Lakoff's willingness to use an appeal to authority as an argument is apparent in the brief remark she makes about the suggestion that "they" be used instead of "he." "Most authorities" frown upon it as "inconsistent or illogical." Who are these "authorities?" What is their evidence? Inconsistent or illogical in what way? "They" in fact seems an admirable substitute, since it already freely occurs in speech. Bodine demonstrates that "they" was commonly used until the end of the 18th century, when social and political pressures were responsible for its demise.[15]

There has been little research on the frequency with which "they" is used as the generic. In an experiment Carla Fink and I ran to see what pronoun male and female college students would use to fill in the blank of a generic sentence like "Everybody should wipe ———— feet before entering," we found that subjects used the appropriate form of the generic pronoun "they" about 45 percent of the time. Further, many subjects who used the masculine third-person singular reported remembering being taught not to use the third-person plural in grammar school. The evidence is scanty, but does suggest that "they" is a useful substitute for "he."

If women think "he" should be eliminated, the role of linguists should not be to tell us either that they do not think it is important or that they do not feel it is possible. Rather, they should help supply a substitute. For example, the creation of new pronouns will be less useful than the resurrection of "they," because in general it is easier to increase the frequency of a behavior that already exists than to create a new behavior.

In her discussion of the neologisms "herstory" and "himicanes," I think Lakoff misses the point. (Since she does not quote any sources, however, I cannot be sure.) Women do not necessarily believe that these words are etymologically sexist. By using "herstory" they believe that they can point out that women are ignored in most historical accounts and that they themselves are involved in doing history from a feminist viewpoint. It is a play on words to make a point. With hurricanes, it is politically and sociologically interesting that they are all named after women, and calling them "himicanes" could be a play on words in which only this fact is intended to be brought out. Surely even non-linguists are entitled to have a little fun with words. Lakoff's concern over these suggestions is shown by her statement that:

If this sort of stuff appears in print and in the popular media as often as it does, it becomes increasingly more difficult to persuade men that women are really rational beings.[16]

Even if the "himicane" suggestion were dead serious, who are these unworthy creatures who generalize that all women are irrational on the basis of the irrationality of a few? Their sexism should be attacked rather than catered to.

To sum up, Lakoff's views on the value of attacking oppressive linguistic usage have been criticized here on two grounds. First, her analysis of the relation between linguistic and social change is faulty. Second, her claim that some usage is unalterable is supported by neither logic nor evidence. The feminist strategy of trying to eliminate all oppressive usage is preferrable.

To return to one of the issues posed at the beginning of this paper: How can linguists (as linguists) contribute to the feminist strategy? The answer is, by helping to implement it, rather than by using a presumed linguistic expertise to answer a political question. No linguist can properly tell us to learn to live with a certain amount of oppression, or to try not to think of it as oppression, because our decisions about what we will tolerate are not linguistic decisions but political ones.

## NOTES

1. Robin Lakoff, "Language and Woman's Place," *Language in Society* 2 (1973): 45–80; reprinted in Robin Lakoff, ed., *Language and Woman's Place* (New York: Harper & Row, 1975); and idem, "Why Women Are Ladies," in *Language and Woman's Place*.
2. B. L. Dubois and I. Crouch, "The Question of Tag Questions in Women's Speech: They Don't Really Use More of Them, Do They?" *Language in Society* 4 (1975): 289–94.

3. When "lovely" modifies nouns that are not physical objects, the analysis is more complicated. For example, in "What a lovely day for a picnic" the adjective "lovely" is not simply making an aesthetic evaluation, but a functional one as well. It can be seen, however, that the functional evaluation only carries because of the implicit aesthetic evaluation: if "What a lovely day to stay indoors" is uttered because it is raining outside, there is still something odd about the sentence. One can properly say "What a good day to stay indoors" in such a situation because "good" has no independent aesthetic meaning.

4. Lakoff, *Language and Woman's Place*, p. 13.

5. The one exception is in her discussion of women's tendency to speak indirectly, where she suggests that both direct and indirect styles of talking are of value. See *Language and Woman's Place*, p. 74.

6. See Noam Chomsky, *Aspects of the Theory of Syntax* (New York: Harper & Row, 1965); and my "The Relation between Competence and Performance: A Theoretical Review," *CUNY Forum in Linguistics* 1 (1976).

7. Lakoff, *Language and Woman's Place*, p. 6, n. 2.

8. Ibid., p. 21.

9. Ibid., p. 43.

10. Ibid., p. 47.

11. Ibid., p. 36.

12. Ibid., p. 41.

13. Ibid., p. 45.

14. Ibid., p. 44.

15. A. Bodine, "Androcentrism in Prescriptive Grammar: Singular 'They,' Sex-Indefinite 'He,' and 'He or She,' " *Language in Society* 4 (1975): 129–46.

16. Lakoff, *Language and Woman's Place*, p. 46.

# Sexism in Ordinary Language

# *Further References*

Starred items are those of philosophical interest.

Ackerman, Louise M. " 'Lady' As a Synonym for 'Woman.' " *American Speech* 37:4 (December 1962): 284–85.

*Baker, Robert. " 'Pricks' and 'Chicks': A Plea For 'Persons.' " In *Philosophy and Sex*, edited by Robert Baker and Frederick Elliston. Buffalo, N.Y.: Prometheus Books, 1975.

Baron, Naomi. "A Reanalysis of English Grammatical Gender." *Lingua* 27 (August 1971): 113–40.

Barron, Nancy. "Sex-Typed Language: The Production of Grammatical Cases." *Acta Sociologica* 14:2 (1971): 24–42.

Bosmajian, Haig A. "The Language of Sexism." *Etc.* 29:3 (September 1972): 305–13.

Burr, Elizabeth; Dunn, Susan; and Farquhar, Norma. *Guidelines for Equal Treatment of the Sexes in Social Studies Textbooks*. Westside Women's Committee, P.O. Box 24 D 20, Los Angeles, California 90024.

Chamberlain, Alexander F. "Women's Languages." *American Anthropologist* 14 (1912): 579–81.

Conklin, Nancy F. "Toward a Feminist Analysis of Linguistic Behavior." *University of Michigan Papers in Women's Studies* 1:1 (February 1974): 51–73.

Converse, Charles C. "That Desired Impersonal Pronoun." *The Writer* 3 (1889): 247–48.

Ellis, Albert, and Abarbanel, Albert, eds. "Language and Sex." In *The Encyclopedia of Sexual Behavior*. Vol. 2, pp. 585–98.

Ervin, Susan M. "The Connotations of Gender." *Word* 18 (1962): 249–61.

Faust, Jean. "Word That Oppress." In *Women Speaking*. Reprint. KNOW, Inc., P.O. Box 10197, Pittsburgh, Pa. 15232.

Feminist Writers Workshop. *An Intelligent Woman's Guide to Dirty Words: English Words and Phrases Reflecting Sexist Attitudes toward Women in Patriarchal Society*. Chicago: YWCA, Loop Center, 1973.

Frazer, Sir James George. "A Suggestion As To the Origin of Gender in Language." *Fortnightly* 73 (January 1900): 79–90.

*Frye, Marilyn. "Male Chauvinism: A Conceptual Analysis." In *Philosophy and Sex*, edited by Robert Baker and Frederick Elliston. Buffalo, N.Y.: Prometheus Books, 1975.

Furfey, Paul Hanley. "Men's and Women's Language." *American Catholic Sociological Review* 5 (1944): 218–23.

*Garry, Ann. "Pornography, Sex Roles and Morality." Unpublished. Fullerton, Calif.: California State University, Department of Philosophy, 1976.

Gary, Sandra. "What Are We Talking About?" *Ms.*, December 1972, pp. 72–73.

George, Mary Lee. "Alternatives to Sexist Language." In *Sexism in Education*. Available from Emma Willard Task Force on Education, University Station, Box No. 14229, Minneapolis, Minn. 55414.

Graham, Alma. "The Making of a Nonsexist Dictionary." *Ms.*, December 1973, pp. 12–14.

Hall, Robert A., Jr. "Sex Reference and Grammatical Gender in English." *American Speech* 26:3 (October 1951): 170–72.

Hancock, Cecily Raysor. " 'Lady' and 'Woman.' " *American Speech* 38 (October 1963): 234–35.

*Harding, Sandra. "Against Common Sense." Unpublished. Newark, Del.: University of Delaware, Department of Philosophy, 1975.

*Hayakawa, S. I. "Semantics and Sexuality." *Etc.* 25 (June 1968): 135–53.

Hole, Judith, and Levine, Ellen. "The Politics of Language." In *Rebirth of Feminism*. New York: Quadrangle Books, 1971.

Howard, Pamela. "Watch Your Language, Men." *More: A Journalism Review* 2 (February 1972): 3–4.

Jespersen, Otto. "Sex and Gender." In *The Philosophy of Grammar*. New York: W.W. Norton, 1924.

Kelly, Edward Hanford. "A 'Bitch' by Any Other Name Is Less Poetic." *Word Study* 45:1 (October 1969): 1–4.

Key, Mary Ritchie. *Male/Female Language*. Metuchen, N.J.: Scarecrow Press, 1975.

Komisar, Lucy. "The Image of Woman in Advertising." In *Woman in Sexist Society: Studies in Power and Powerlessness*, edited by

Vivian Gornick and Barbara Moran. New York: Basic Books, 1971.

Kramer, Cheris. "Women's Speech: Separate but Unequal?" *Quarterly Journal of Speech* 60:1 (February 1974): 14–22.

*Lakoff, Robin. *Language and Woman's Place.* New York: Harper & Row, 1975.

*———. "You Are What You Say." *Ms.*, July 1974, pp. 65–67.

Langenfelt, Gösta. "*She* and *Her* Instead of *It* and *Its.*" *Anglia* 70:1 (1951): 90–101.

*Lawrence, Barbara. "Four-Letter Words *Can* Hurt You." In *Philosophy and Sex*, edited by Robert Baker and Frederick Elliston. Buffalo, N.Y.: Prometheus Books, 1975.

Lennert, Midge, and Wilson, Norma. *A Woman's New World Dictionary.* Available from 51% Publications, Box 371, Lomita, Calif. 90717.

*Levin, Michael. "Vs. Ms." Unpublished. New York: City University of New York, Department of Philosophy, 1975.

McKissick, Dorothy. "Language, Sex Roles and Women's Self-Concept." Unpublished. Los Angeles: University of California, Department of Sociology, 1973.

Meredith, Mamie. " 'Doctoresses,' 'Authoresses,' and Others." *American Speech* 26:3 (October 1953): 231–32.

Miller, Kate, and Swift, Casey. "De-sexing the English Language." *Ms.*, preview issue, Spring 1972.

Millett, Kate. "Instances of Sexual Polities." In *Sexual Politics.* Garden City, N.Y.: Doubleday, 1970.

Moe, Albert F. " 'Lady' and 'Woman': The Terms' Use in the 1880's." *American Speech* 38:4 (December 1963): 295.

Morgan, Robin. "Know Your Enemy: A Sampling of Sexist Quotes." In *Sisterhood Is Powerful*, edited by Robin Morgan. New York: Random House, 1970.

*Moulton, Janice. "Sex and Reference." In *Philosophy and Sex*, edited by Robert Baker and Frederick Elliston. Buffalo, N.Y.: Prometheus Books, 1975.

Nilsen, Aileen P. "Sexism in English: A Feminist View." In *Female Studies*, vol. 6. Available from Feminist Press, Old Westbury, New York.

*Pierce, Christine. "Natural Law Language and Women." In *Woman in Sexist Society: Studies in Power and Powerlessness*, edited by Vivian Gornick and Barbara Moran. New York: Basic Books, 1971.

Reik, Theodore. "Men and Women Speak Different Languages." *Psychoanalysis* 1–2 (1954): 3–15.

Stanton, Elizabeth Cady, ed. *The Woman's Bible.* New York: European Publishing Co., 1895.

Steadman, J. M., Jr. "Affected and Effeminate Words." *American Speech* 13:1 (February 1938): 13–18.

Strainchamps, Ethel. "Our Sexist Language." In *Woman In Sexist Society: Studies in Power and Powerlessness*, edited by Vivian Gornick and Barbara K. Moran. New York: Basic Books, 1971.

Svartengren, T. Hilding. "The Use of Feminine Gender for Inanimate Things in American Colloquial Speech." *Moderna Sprak* 48 (1954): 261–92.

Tiedt, Iris M. "Sexism in Language: An Editor's Plague." *Elementary English* 50 (October 1973): 1073–74.

Troth, Emily. "How Can a Woman MAN the Barricades?: Or Linguistic Sexism up against the Wall." *Women: A Journal of Liberation* 2:1 (Fall, 1970): 57.

Withington, Robert. " 'Lady,' 'Woman' and 'Person.' " *American Speech* 12:2 (April 1937): 117–21.

# Part IV
# Equal Opportunity and Preferential Hiring

# Part IV
# Equal Opportunity and Preferential Hiring

## *Introduction*

We hear the phrase "equal opportunity" almost daily. Job advertisements tell us that some institutions and businesses are "equal opportunity" employers. Some schools offer women and minority groups an "equal opportunity" to advance themselves educationally or professionally. Feminists are' demanding an "equal opportunity" to succeed. Just what does this phrase mean?

As ONORA O'NEILL points out, "to complete the predicate 'equal opportunity' we need only note that all opportunities are opportunities to do or enjoy some activity or benefit." She adds that those opportunities "usually thought important for a just society are mainly educational and occupational opportunities." A woman is not asking to have the same chance as a man to grow a beard, for example, when she asks for opportunities equal to his. But she may well be asking for an equal chance to become a Ph.D., to earn $20,000 a year, or to become a lawyer. However, women may well disagree with one another as to what actually constitutes having this equal opportunity for educational or occupational attainment. One woman may think that she has an opportunity equal to a man's to obtain a particular job if they both face precisely the same criteria for hiring. But, because she has not had the same chance as the man to acquire the qualifications for the job, another woman may insist that she and the man share an equal opportunity to obtain the job only if she is given some extra consideration by the employer. In order to spell out these different notions more clearly, let us take a look at the sorts of hiring procedures defenders of the first and second types of "equal opportunity" might require in order to be satisfied that a woman has an opportunity equal to a man's to obtain a job.

Defenders of the first notion generally agree that a woman and a man have an equal opportunity to obtain a job if the hiring system they both face is a "meritocratic" one. According to a meritocratic hiring system, a person ought to be hired if and only if he or she is the best-qualified applicant. In those cases where two or more applicants are equally (and best) qualified, the choice is to be made on the basis of some fair random method (such as the toss of a "fair" coin). Justified standards for determining who is best-qualified should be used: for example, there can be no rules stipulating that women may not apply to be taxi drivers.[1]

But even if a woman and a man have equal opportunities in this first sense, the woman may still not get the job. She may not have had the same chance as the man to gain his educational background or his financial, emotional, parental, or societal support. Thus, she may have had far less of an opportunity than he to become the best-qualified candidate. Meritocratic hiring systems, in short, are quite clearly compatible with a state of affairs in which all applicants share equal opportunities in the first sense of the term, and yet in which no women and/or minority-group members actually obtain jobs. Perhaps meritocracies would not be unjust were the unequal results they produce due to the willful choice or capacities of the applicants. But, as ONORA O'NEILL puts it, "if the desires and capacities have themselves been produced or modified by earlier educational and occupational experiences, the justice of conferring success on their basis becomes questionable."

Philosophers convinced by this reasoning generally fall into one of two camps. According to the first, meritocratic systems must be reinforced by distributive educational systems if women are to enter the work force in substantial numbers at all levels. A distributive educational system is one in which all children are given the same share of support, diet, and education, much as Plato envisioned in his *Republic*. This proposal presents immediate difficulties: parents of the above-average children will complain that their children do not receive enough, and parents of the below-average children will complain that their children receive too much. Moreover, it would be extremely costly, in terms of both time and money, to institute such a system.

The second camp reasons that even if a system of distributive education were begun for the future, some system other than a meritocracy must be devised now in order to redress the disadvantages that women and/or minority-group members have had during the period in which distributive education was not available to all. Some sort of preferential treatment system is therefore usually advocated. While some in this camp argue that distributive educational systems are eventually achievable and that preferential hiring systems need only be used temporarily, others hold that distributive educational systems are unrealistic and that preferential hiring systems must permanently replace meritocracies.

We are now in a position to understand what a woman means when she asks for the second sort of "equal opportunity" in the job market. Since she has probably not had the same chance as the male applicant to obtain self-respect, encouragement, and education, she will ask for some extra consideration. Given that there was no distributive educational system in effect when she was a child, she will not be satisfied that she *really* has an equal opportunity to succeed unless preferential hiring systems are instituted.

At least two sorts of preferential hiring systems have been defended in the philosophical literature on the subject. According to the more moderate of the two positions, a woman and/or minority candidate ought to be hired only if he or she is either the best-qualified candidate for the job or if he or she is equally as qualified as the other best-qualified candidate. Judith Thomson, for example, defends this sort of preferential system by appeal to compensatory principles.[2] ROBERT K. FULLINWIDER, on the other hand, does not think that compensatory principles justify the preferential hiring of women and/or minority-group candidates over white male applicants. He admits, however, that compensatory principles may justify the preferential hiring of women and/or minority-group candidates to the detriment of some other group.

A stronger stance on preferential hiring holds that, provided that they are at least minimally qualified for the job, women and/or minority-group candidates ought to be hired even if they are not as qualified as the best-qualified non-female non-minority candidate. Thomas Nagel has suggested that this latter sort of system is not unjust because the system from which it departs (namely, meritocracy) is not just.[3] LAWRENCE CROCKER defends a system that is stronger than Thomson's yet weaker than Nagel's. He tries to show that employers are justified in hiring women and/or minority candidates who are only marginally less qualified than better qualified non-female and/or non-minority candidates.

A number of ancillary issues often accompany any discussion about the justification of preferential hiring. The two most prominent are the following:

(1) If preferential hiring is just, should a particular woman and/or minority candidate be preferentially hired because he or she is a member of a *class* that has been systematically discriminated against in the past? Or should only those women and/or minority-group members who have themselves suffered from discrimination be preferentially hired? ALAN H. GOLDMAN argues that not all women and/or minorities have suffered from discrimination, and that it is unjust to hire them preferentially on the grounds that they are members of a discriminated-against class. Judith Thomson, on the other hand, disagrees. She says,

But what of the blacks and women who haven't actually been deprived of what they have a right to, but only made to suffer the consequences of injustice to other blacks and women? *Perhaps* justice doesn't require making amends to them as well; but common decency certainly does. To fail, at the very least, to make what counts as a public apology to all, and to take positive steps to show that it is sincerely meant, is, if not injustice, then anyway a fault at least as serious as ingratitude.[4]

(This issue is also discussed by Irving Thalberg, J. L. Cowan, Michael Bayles, J. W. Nickel, Roger Shiner, and Paul Taylor, among others.)

(2) If preferential hiring is just, and if the number of jobs available is finite, from whom can jobs be justly taken in order that women and/or minorities gain them? Thomson argues that white males will (justly) go without the jobs that they might have received under meritocracies. FULLINWIDER replies that such a move would represent an injustice to white males. Vir-

ginia Held suggests the possibility of emptying all present job positions and refilling them.[5] (In the case of the university, emptying all positions, including tenured ones, and refilling them might result in the replacement of some white males with better-qualified women and/or minority-group applicants.) Marlene Fried holds that those who have discriminated in the past must be the ones to lose future benefits. She says, "in a context of hierarchical institutions where the power to make policy resides with elites, responsibility is to be located with those elites—not with everyone."[6]

M. V. B.

## NOTES

1. I have argued elsewhere that these "justified rules" should include at least the following two:
     (1) Only those properties ought to count as "qualifications" which (a) are positively causally correlated with successful job performance, and which (b) the employer has the right to count as relevant.
     (2) "Best-qualified," "less than best-qualified," and "least-qualified" ought to be determined by appeal to standardized tests.
2. Judith Thomson, "Preferential Hiring," *Philosophy and Public Affairs* 2 (Summer 1973): 364–84.
3. Thomas Nagel, "Equal Treatment and Compensatory Discrimination," *Philosophy and Public Affairs* 2 (Summer 1973): 348–63.
4. Thomson, "Preferential Hiring," pp. 381–82.
5. Virginia Held, "Reasonable Progress and Self-Respect," *Monist* 57 (January 1973): 12–27.
6. Marlene Gerber Fried, "In Defense of Preferential Hiring," *Philosophical Forum* 5 (Fall-Winter 1973–74): 318.

Onora O'Neill

# How Do We Know When Opportunities Are Equal?

I shall start my argument from the very simple observation that "equal" is an incomplete predicate. If someone asks whether $A$ and $B$ are equal we have to ask "equal in which respect?" before we can answer the question. Once we know that we are being asked whether they are equal in height or weight or wealth or health, we know which sorts of measurements and observations are relevant to answering the question. Yet when we are asked whether $A$ and $B$ are equal *in opportunity*, it is not at all obvious which measurements or observations are relevant to answering the question.

I believe that this unclarity has two separate sources. It is attributable in the first place to the fact that "equal in oppor-

Earlier versions of this paper were read during 1974 at the Conference on Method, at Tufts University and at Union College; I am grateful for comments and suggestions made on each occasion. Substantially the same paper was published in *Philosophical Forum* 5 (1975): 334–46, and reprinted in *Women and Philosophy: Toward a Theory of Liberation*, ed. Carol C. Gould and Marx W. Wartofsky (New York: Putnam's, 1976). I have discussed various conceptions of equal educational opportunity in more detail in "Equalities, Opportunities and Education," *Theory and Decision* (1976).

tunity" is still an incomplete predicate; secondly to an ambiguity in the concept of "opportunity." I shall deal with these unclarities in turn, and hope in doing so to reach some substantive as well as some analytical conclusions.

To complete the predicate "equal in opportunity" we need only note that all opportunities are opportunities to do or enjoy some activity or benefit. Schematically, any opportunity is an opportunity to do $x$—an opportunity to visit Tokyo or an opportunity to earn $20,000 or an opportunity to win a lottery. There are many sorts of opportunities whose equal distribution is not of particular concern to us. A society can choose to equalize the opportunity to live in a home fit for a hero or the opportunity to have a chicken in every pot, but the opportunities which these symbolize and which are usually thought important for a just society are mainly educational and occupational opportunities. An equal-opportunity society does not have to offer each person exactly the same work, commodities, recreation, friends and so on, but in a broad sense it is supposed to give each person an equal opportunity for educational and occupational attainment, where "attainment" is interpreted so as to cover both the learning or work and the credentials or pay that schools and jobs provide.

But when we complete the predicate "'equal in opportunity" as "equal in opportunities for educational and occupational attainment" we are little the wiser about the criteria for attributing equal opportunities for such attainment. The problem is not merely that educational and occupational attainment may be harder to measure than height and weight, wealth and health. It lies rather in a systematic ambiguity in the criteria for judging when opportunities are equal. I shall call them respectively the formal and the substantive interpretation of equal opportunity. I shall spend no time investigating the grounds for preferring either of these interpretations; my aim is to disentangle them.

## THE FORMAL INTERPRETATION OF "EQUAL IN OPPORTUNITY"

A familiar interpretation of equal opportunity sees two persons, $A$ and $B$, as having equal opportunities in some respect if neither faces a legal or quasi-legal obstacle in doing something which the other does not face. Under this formal interpretation $A$ and $B$ can have equal opportunities with respect to $x$ without being likely to enjoy $x$. Jencks and his associates start from this formal interpretation of equal opportunity; they describe it as the demand "that the rules determining who succeeds and who fails should be fair," and argue that "equal opportunity is not enough to ensure equal results."[1]

On this view, once the rules governing admissions to places of education, appointments to jobs and promotions are fair, a society is an equal-opportunity society. If no classes of persons are debarred by law or the policies of medical schools and licensing bodies from qualifying and practicing as doctors, then all persons have equal opportunities to become doctors—even though it might turn out that a derisory number of women or blacks succeed in being doctors. If women are not barred from engineering school on account of their sex, then they have equal opportunity to become engineers—and the fact that very few do so cannot be attributed to any inequality of opportunity.

This formal interpretation of equal opportunity is part and parcel of the classical liberal tradition of political thought, in that it is mainly an extension of the idea of securing the equal liberties of all persons. Just as the removal of class, income, race and sex obstacles could make all persons able to vote, hold property, serve on juries, hold office, and so on, so a removal of legal obstacles could open up places of education and employment to persons from all social groups. Where access to a place of education or a type of employment had to be restricted, selection procedures which took account not of social status, but of relevant qualifications, were devised. The career open to talents is a career entered by competitive examination.

The selection procedures devised to admit, employ and promote on "non-discriminating" criteria have generally produced results which were highly unequal in two respects. First, they have produced societies whose members were extremely unequal in educational and occupational attainment whether measured by competence, credentials, income or status. This in itself is not worrying to liberals who regard the unequal results as justifiable if everyone had an equal opportunity to succeed. After all, selection procedures are needed in the first place only in societies where certain sorts of positions are fewer than the number of people wanting them, so candidates cannot all succeed. But the second type of unequal results of the supposedly "non-discriminating" selection procedures has worried liberals of certain sorts. For these selection procedures frequently lead to disproportionate success in some social groups and correspondingly disproportionate failure in others.

If such disproportion is to be justifiable according to liberals, it must be the result only of the varying capacities and desires of those to whom the selection procedures are applied. So males might justifiably be under-represented as nurses or secretaries if they lack the appropriate desires/capacities, and for the same reasons females might justifiably be under-represented among executives and undertakers. Blacks might be under-represented among upper-income groups either unjustifiably because of the effects of legal obstacles at some earlier stage of their education and careers, or justifiably because of different desires and capacities. In the view of the classical liberal, a complete equality of opportunity will prevail when all remaining legal and quasi-legal obstacles to educational and occupational attainment have been eliminated, and when sufficient time has passed for the people who may once have been hindered by such obstacles to have died. Such an "equal-opportunity society" would, however, not be characterized by equal incomes or equal property holdings or equal standards of living or of education. Nor need it be characterized by the proportionate representation of all social groups in all lines of activity and income strata. Equal opportunity in the formal sense does not ensure equal success or equal health or equal status, but only the fair application of the rules governing the pursuit of such goods. This is the equality of opportunity of a competitive, meritocratic society, a society in which there are winners and losers, and in which winning appears often as merited by the winners and losing as deserved by the losers—for did they not all have equal opportunity to win?

While the liberals are not bothered by unequal educational and occupational attainments, many of them have been concerned that at least some of the disproportionate success and failure rates of certain social groups reflect more than capacities and desires, and they have often inferred from this that selection procedures have not yet been devised that are truly non-discriminating. Two types of response are commonly made to this problem. The narrower one is to claim that certain allegedly non-discriminating procedures are in fact culturally biased: for example, I.Q. tests discriminate against children from certain backgrounds; employment agencies treat applicants of different sexes and races differently; promotions are often made on criteria other than on-the-job performance. These problems, and they are surely still common, are exactly the ones which the formal interpretation of equal opportunity is equipped to handle. A broader response to this problem is to look at a person's educational and occupational attainments over a longer stretch of time and hence to uncover a wider range of selection procedures which may have been discriminating. For example, the disproportionately low representation of persons from poor families in college preparatory high-school programs or of women in mathematics programs may be due to their lack of opportunity at an earlier stage of life and the consequent redirection of their capacities and desires. They may have had access only to an inferior school with less financing, less varied curriculum, and so on, or they may have had their aspirations and ambitions systematically belittled and questioned. If the desires and capacities have themselves been produced or modified by earlier educational and occupational experiences, the justice of conferring success on their basis becomes questionable. Hence, in the name of redressing past discrimination a limited sort of favoritism is often advocated: colleges and professional schools may set a lower admissions hurdle for certain sorts of applicants; employers may (at least apparently) make special efforts to employ persons from groups that are underrepresented. Such moves mark a shift from a purely formal conception of equal opportunity toward a more substantive one, to which I shall now turn.

## THE SUBSTANTIVE INTERPRETATION OF "EQUAL IN OPPORTUNITY"

The one selection procedure which all agree is non-discriminating is the lottery. If each major social group had a number of tickets in a lottery proportionate to its representation in the population, then we would expect the prizes to be distributed to each major social group in the same proportion. The same proportion of women as of men, of blacks as of whites, of old as of young would win the prizes. This situation provides the paradigm of the view which I shall call the substantive or actuarial interpretation of equality of opportunity. On this view, opportunities for $A$ and $B$ with respect to $x$ are to be regarded as equal not because neither faces legal or quasi-legal obstacles which the other does not face, but because they belong to social groups whose rates of success at obtaining $x$ are equal. An equal-opportunity society on the substantive view is one in which the success rates of all major social groups are the same. On the substantive interpretation of equal opportunity, preferential and quota admissions and hirings and promotions are justifiable not because they apply standards in a non-discriminating way (they don't) but because they confer equal (or at least less unequal) rewards.

On the substantive view of equal opportunity, women have an equal opportunity to enter law school only if they are admitted in proportions appropriate to the number who apply, and their applications are not being deterred or reduced by any policy of the school so that the pool of applicants contains all women who wish to go to that law school. And on this view a company can truthfully claim to be an equal-opportunity employer only if appropriate proportions of its jobs at all levels are held by workers from various minority groups, or, where this is not the case, there is evidence of serious attempts to recruit and promote members of the under-represented groups. A strong commitment to substantive equality of opportunity demands that any under-representation of some group in some line of employment/income group/educational group be due solely to the unmanipulated choice of members of that group. Substantive equality of opportunity is not breached if Hassidic Jews are under-represented among those who have Saturday jobs; it is breached if women are under-represented among those promoted to supervisory rank. In many cases it may be harder than this to tell when choices are unmanipulated.

A society which confers substantive or actuarial equal opportunity is very different from one which aims at equal results, such as equal incomes, equal education, equal health and welfare or equal standards of living. Substantively equal opportunity is achieved when the success rates of certain major social groups—such as the two sexes, various ethnic groups and perhaps various age groups—are equalized. It is not breached when there are large differences between the most- and least-successful members of these groups, provided that there are equally large differences between the most- and least-successful members of the other major social groups. It is not true in a society which aims at substantively equal opportunities that all individuals have the same chance of any given type of success. For individuals are all members of many differently defined groups, and substantive equal opportunity seeks only to equalize their chances of success qua members of certain major social groups; it seeks to eliminate inter-group differences, but not to alter intra-group ones. If $A$ is a highly qualified woman, and $B$ a slightly retarded man, then substantively equal opportunity would give them the same chance, qua woman and qua man, of earning, say, $20,000 a year, but it would not alter the fact that $A$ has, qua highly qualified, a far greater chance of doing so. Substantively equal opportunity would yield equal results only if the groups whose success rates were to be equalized included all those groups consisting of a single person.

By and large, a move from a formal to a substantive view of equal opportunity becomes controversial only when a scarce and widely coveted educational or occupational attainment is at issue. Nobody objects if the opportunity to enter the second grade, which is almost universally available, results in a proportionate representation among all second-graders of all social groups. And nobody objects because disproportionately many steeplejacks are Mohawks, or tries to gain proportionate representation for other groups. But if a substantive interpretation of equal opportunity to enter law school would result in a proportionate representation among law students and, later, lawyers, of all social groups, then (given that not all groups have the same distribution of qualifications) there is likely to be considerable opposition to a move from a formal to a substantive interpretation of equal opportunity from members of groups which are disproportionately successful under the formal interpretation. In particular, it has been urged that preferential and quota admissions and hiring policies which fail to prefer the more qualified will lead to a less competent performance and are both unjust and inefficient.

Advocates of preferential and quota admissions and hiring policies concede that a certain price in efficiency is (reasonably) incurred in pursuit of justice, but they claim that the price will not be high (at least for many jobs) since the relevance of job qualifications to job performance is often meager, and, in any case, people grow on the job. In return, they can point to certain longer-run increases in efficiency which a break in favor of the disadvantaged might bring, for, in the long run, substantive equal opportunity maximizes the size of the pool of applicants for the position, affording the greatest choice among candidates. But they have a less ready answer on the question of justice. Some concede that an injustice is done to those better-qualified candidates who are passed over, but contend that to pass them over is the only solution to the variation in the proportion of qualified candidates which past discrimination has produced in each social group. In the long run, it is supposed, the cumulative elimination of differential rates of attainment in different social groups at successive stages in their careers may eliminate the need for compensatory educational programs and for preferential admissions, hiring and promotion. Eventually justice can be done to all groups without injustice being done to any individuals.

The substantive interpretation of equal opportunity builds on a central feature of the idea of opportunity. To have an opportunity to do $x$ is to have a chance to do $x$, and for $A$ and $B$ to have an equal opportunity to do $x$ is for them to be equally likely (qua members of certain reference classes) to do $x$. A substantively equal-opportunity society equalizes the rate of educational and occupational attainment of all major social groups. If it wants *also* to demand certain prerequisites or qualifications for certain positions, then it has to ensure that these prerequisites and qualifications are met equally frequently by members of all social groups. Only so can the demands of meritocratic admissions, hiring and promotions be combined with substantively equal opportunities. This combination of demands makes a commitment to substantive equal opportunity an embarrassing position for liberals to take.

## SUBSTANTIVELY EQUAL OPPORTUNITY AND SELECTION PROCEDURES

The work of Jencks and his associates shows very clearly how enormous the task of equalizing the distribution of qualifications and competences in all social groups would be. Schools as we know them are hardly equipped for the task. Still, schools need not remain as we know them. Could not a more radical restructuring of education achieve just what the compensatory programs had in mind: a situation where all people are prepared to grasp the opportunities available for them, and so one in which the distribution of qualifications for educational and occupational success are equalized for all groups? If this were possible, meritocratic selection procedures could be combined with substantive equality of opportunity, at least in the long run.

The evidence on such an issue is, of course, incomplete, and any conclusion must be tentative. But it seems that an effective equalization of the distribution of handicaps and advantages would have to take control of children's lives to an extent not envisaged by school systems today. Children from each major social group would have to be given a distribution of health care, diet, socialization, consideration and respect, as well as of schooling, which would ensure the same distribution of competences: for the treatment of all groups would have to provide the same distribution of intra-group differences. But such a control of children's lives would not be acceptable to classical liberals or even probably to ordinary or woolly-minded ones. Liberals of all sorts do not object to the control of children (within reason), but they are committed to respect the rights of parents and thereby to denounce attempts to remove such rights and place the control of children in the hands of government agencies. Yet short of such measures it is difficult to see how equality of opportunity can ever be more than formal and from one standpoint a sham: a pretense that certain goods are equally accessible to persons of all backgrounds when in fact they are far more easily available to persons from some groups than others. A pretense, furthermore, which unfairly shifts the burden of failure and the pride of success onto those who have in the first place been denied or granted the advantages which enable people to win in the system of selection for success.

But it is not only liberals who will find some difficulty in accepting a complete program of engineering substantive equality of opportunity by producing the same distribution of competences and incompetences in all social groups. The institutions needed to achieve these distributions end up imposing far more than substantive equality of opportunity: they demand actual equality of attainment at earlier stages of a career as the only basis for substantive equality achieved on meritocratic principles at later stages. To use meritocratic principles at later stages we would have to avoid them at earlier stages—lest any group end up disproportionately likely to succeed or fail on these selection procedures. Something, it seems, must give: if we abandon a commitment to meritocratic selection procedures within the schools, we can engineer some substantive equality of attainment which in turn can be the basis for a stage of substantive equality of opportunity. If we use meritocratic selection procedures from early on in the educational/career ladder to produce different proportions of different competences in different social groups, we will not later be able to combine substantive equality of opportunity with meritocratic selection procedures. The option which is closed is that of consistently using meritocratic selection procedures and yet expecting all social groups to develop the same distribution of competences and so to have substantively equal opportunities at later stages of their careers. This point does not depend on assuming that different social groups differ genetically and that their performance will accordingly diverge under meritocratic selection; it depends only on the assumption that different social groups differ and so will have different success rates on various selection tests, and that a succession of such tests, where success in earlier ones earns privileges in preparation for later ones, will produce quite sharply divergent success rates.

Under competitive, meritocratic selection procedures, substantive equality of opportunity is an inherently transitory phenomenon. For it presupposes a uniform distribution of competences among members of each major social group which could only have been produced by an imposed distribution of treatment—that is, by social institutions in which opportunity is no issue. But it leads to a diversity of attainment, which will be reflected in different abilities to grasp future opportunities, and so to a diminution of substantive equality of opportunity. Only a society whose various social groups have lost their diversity and consistently turn out to have the same distribution of competences could remain a substantively equal-opportunity society over a long period.

I don't believe that this means that there is no choice in these matters, but rather that there are many choices. The task is to balance liberty against both equality and efficiency, and there are many ways of doing so. If we want both liberty and short-run efficiency, then we must choose competitive selection procedures and settle for formal equal opportunity. If we want to retain liberty but are willing to sacrifice some short-run efficiency, then we can equalize the occupational attainments of different social groups to the extent we wish to by selection procedures which disregard competence to some extent and aim at proportionate representation of all major social groups. All selection procedures would require quotas to be met; success and failure would depend on social origin as well as competence; substantive equality of opportunity would be institutionalized. If we want to have short- and long-run efficiency and a considerable range of equalities, the price must be paid in liberty. We can combine meritocratic selection procedures with various sorts of equality if we choose to minimize differential rewards for different attainments. If incomes and wealth and prestige were more equal, the pain of failure and the joy of success would be lessened, and though there would (given meritocratic selection procedures) be no substantive equality of opportunity, this might be compensated for by more equal results. The lives of the successful and unsuccessful would be more similar.

Apart from these three pure policies, there is possible any number of interim or combination policies. For example, one might choose to sacrifice some efficiency or some liberty at some stages of an educational system in return for a less glaringly uneven distribution of competences. The consequence would be that a subsequent application of meritocratic selection procedures would, while still producing an inegalitarian society, produce less divergent success rates for different major social groups. Policies which tend in this direction (that is, toward substantive equal opportunity) include compensatory educational programs, the abolition of tracking and acceleration, and the extension of open admissions. Or one could choose to bypass substantive equality of opportunity in favor of some increase in equality of results with a sacrifice of liberty but not of efficiency. Policies which tend in this direction include income redistribution and ensuring more equal access to good schools, good medical care and good transport.

Affirmative-action plans are among the mildest of such compromise policies. They try to achieve somewhat greater substantive equality of opportunity without sacrificing either liberty or efficiency. Although affirmative-action plans may set target employment goals, these are not enforced,[2] provided that employers show that they have made good-faith efforts to meet them. Affirmative action in a context in which candidates from certain social groups are hardly ever successful in practice achieves no more than formal equality of opportunity, by requiring selection procedures to disregard certain traditional but irrelevant "qualifications" such as candidates' personal appearance. An employer who has filed an affirmative-action plan is committed to tip evenly balanced scales in favor of a candidate from an under-represented group. But this degree of "favoritism" does not require any sacrifice of efficiency either in the short or in the long run: no more qualified candidate was available. Nor can it be regarded as an injustice to the unsuccessful candidates, whose qualifications were not superior to those of the successful candidate. In spite of this, candidates from groups accustomed to favoritism may resent its loss.

Preferential and quota admissions, hiring and promotion are rather stronger policies aiming at greater substantive equality of opportunity at the expense of some sacrifices of liberty and efficiency. But these policies, too, hardly threaten the whole system of differential rewards and meritocratic selection procedures. Candidates from any major social group are still ranked on the basis of their qualifications, but candidates from different major social groups may not be ranked against one another. The result may be that some groups of successful candidates are on the average less qualified than others. This may involve at least short-run sacrifices of efficiency, but the impact of this sacrifice can vary greatly in its seriousness. Most jobs can be adequately filled by a great range of candidates, and the penalty for having less than the best is not great, though there are exceptions, such as neurosurgeons and pilots, whose rarity may be suggested by the frequency with which the same examples recur in discussions. Further, most qualifications are imperfect predictors of job performance; there are enormous numbers of positions for which the main qualification is to be appointed to them. Preferential and quota policies also pass over some candidates with superior qualifications. But if these qualifications are in some measure the result of earlier special treatment, rather than of intrinsic merit, then the injustice of failing to reward these candidates further is slight. It amounts only to a refusal to allow those who have won earlier races head-starts in later races.

## SUBSTANTIVELY EQUAL OPPORTUNITIES
## AND EQUAL RESULTS

An increase in substantive equality of opportunity is the avowed goal of many reforms in educational and employment practices in the United States today. I have argued that the cost of such reforms in terms of efficiency may be relatively slight, and that the injustice to those whose qualifications are passed over is not great if qualifications are capacities and desires conferred by earlier success. But the justice of substantively equal opportunities should also be looked at from the point of view of the results they produce.

In principle, substantive equality of opportunity could be produced without any overall decrease in the inequality of results. The distribution of income, wealth, education and prestige could remain as sharply pyramidal as in a society without substantively equal opportunity. The difference would be that each segment of the pyramid would contain the same proportion of persons from each major social group. Yet if there are grounds for objecting to unequal results for different groups, are there not also grounds for objecting to unequal results for different individuals? Is privilege conferred on the qualified less objectionable than privilege conferred by race, sex, or social background? This raises deeper considerations about efficiency and incentives, and about the grounds of obligation, than I intend to handle here. I shall note only that practice may go further than principle. The actuarial basis of substantively equal opportunity is neutral on the justifiability of unequal results. But a society which tries to equalize the success rates for different major social groups may set up powerful incentives for conferring more equal results on all individuals.

The educational arrangements needed to combine substantively equal opportunities with some concern for qualifications and efficiency must produce the same distribution of competences in each social group. Hence, access to certain sorts of training could not be limited to any one social group. The exclusiveness of institutions which are de facto (let alone de jure) segregated by race, ethnic background or sex would be eliminated. It does not follow that the heritability of success and failure would be eliminated; but it would at least be reduced. Social groups and families would be less able to ensure the success of their members than they would in a society in which success and failure rates differ in different groups, and this provides the successful with a powerful incentive for making even failure tolerable.

## NOTES

1. Christopher Jencks, *Inequality: A Reassessment of the Effect of Family and Schooling in America* (New York: Basic Books, 1972), pp. 3, 37.
2. See Gertrude Ezorsky, "The Fight over University Women," *New York Review of Books*, 16 May 1974, pp. 32–39.

Lawrence Crocker

# Preferential Treatment

Is it ever justified to adopt a policy favoring women or blacks (or American Indians, Chicanos, or Puerto Ricans) in employment or in admission to colleges or professional schools? In particular, ought we to follow this policy:

> (A) Award the position to any (at least minimally qualified) black or woman over any only marginally more qualified white or male competitor.[1]

I will consider possible justifications of this policy in terms of both individual compensation and group compensation. While either group or individual compensation may justify preferring blacks or women in particular cases, neither will justify our use of (A) unless, for practical reasons, no more suitable compensatory policy is possible. Having rejected compensatory arguments for (A), I will argue that a policy similar to (A) is justified in terms of its non-compensatory consequences.

## I. INDIVIDUAL COMPENSATION

We might want to give preference to an individual as a way of compensating for injustices suffered by that individual. Of special interest are injustices that affect the competitive qualifications of the individual for the position in question.[2] For exam-

---

My thanks to Jane English and to the participants of colloquia at the University of Washington and the University of North Carolina for valuable comments on earlier versions of this paper.

ple, we might favor a black applicant for college admission over a white candidate who had written a better essay, if we believe that the black would have written an essay better than the white's were it not for the black's weaker secondary education. In some such cases we believe that the black candidate is really more qualified than the white——or at least shows greater promise. This, then, is actually more an adjustment of our evidence or criteria for qualification than it is an instance of compensation.

Consider the case, however, where we believe the following of candidate $X$: (1) $X$'s achievement and skill level fall short of what they would have been, given $X$'s actual talent and effort, because of the weakness of $X$'s early training. (2) If $X$ had benefited from the same early training as the best-qualified candidate, $Y$, then $X$'s skill and achievement level, given $X$'s actual talent and effort, would be greater than those of $Y$. (3) $X$ never will quite reach $Y$'s level of skill or achievement.

In some such cases there is a fairly compelling argument for giving the position to $X$ as a form of compensation. We may also feel that $Y$ has no grounds for complaint since we are simply redressing an unfair advantage that $Y$ had over $X$, which was beyond $X$'s control and had nothing to do with $X$'s natural ability. I believe that this sort of individual compensation is sometimes justifiable, but I will not argue that here, because neither it nor any other sort of individual compensation will justify (A) or anything like (A).

Specific qualificational compensation of the sort considered above is, of course, only one sort of individual compensation. Educational opportunities and certain jobs (increasingly, all jobs) are scarce benefits. As benefits, they might possibly be used as compensation for any sort of unjust injury or disadvantage, whether related to the qualifications for the position or not. Certain other sorts of benefits may in particular cases be more appropriate compensation, but there may well be cases of unjust injuries unrelated to qualifications for which the only available or workable form of compensation is the preferential awarding of a position. (Preferential hiring of Indians in North Dakota might, for example, be both politically more feasible and more productive in terms of self-respect than would reparation payments to Indians.)

In cases where the injury to be compensated for does not affect qualifications, the better-qualified candidate has a complaint unavailable in the previous case of specifically qualificational compensation, since that candidate's being better qualified is not here the result of the other candidate's unjust disadvantages. But even if we grant that we may do the passedover candidate an injustice, that may be outweighed in a particular case by a morally more compelling need to compensate for serious past injustices that would otherwise go uncompensated.

But the proviso "in a particular case" is crucial. A policy of indvidual compensation, whether qualificational or general, must look to the particular case in a way that (A) does not. Compensation depends upon injury, not upon race or sex. We cannot compensate an uninjured party, nor ought we to compensate an individual $X$ at the expense of an individual $Y$ where $Y$ has suffered under a greater burden of injustice than has $X$. There are some blacks and women who have not suffered disadvantages of a sort affecting their qualifications for the competitive positions that they seek. Perhaps (though less likely) there are even blacks and women who have suffered no significant injustices of any sort. Certainly there are some white males who have suffered greater unjust injuries than some blacks and some women.

In short, individual compensation cannot justify (A), but only some such policy as the following:

> (B) Award the position to any (at least minimally qualified) person $X$ over any only marginally more qualified competitor $Y$ if $X$ has suffered significantly greater unjust injury than has $Y$.

## II. FROM INDIVIDUAL COMPENSATION TO GROUP PREFERENCE VIA STATISTICS

Policy (B) recommends itself as a compensatory policy as against (A) on the principle that we ought not to compensate one less unjustly injured at the expense of one more unjustly injured. There do, however, seem to be practical considerations that give rise to exceptions to this principle. Perhaps such considerations can lead to a form of individual compensatory justification for (A) after all.

Consider a system of compensation for the victims of violent crimes. Funded from general tax revenues, such systems inevitably funnel some money from the unjustly poor into the pockets of well-to-do victims of crimes. Perhaps the really poor should not pay a tax for such purposes (or any others), and perhaps the really rich should not be compensated. But even a heavily graduated version of a violent-crime compensation scheme would involve occasional transfers up the income scale. So presumably the overall-more-injured would sometimes compensate the overall-less-injured who are more injured in the particular respect of having been victims of violent crime. Since there is probably no workable crime compensation system free of this "locally unjust" consequence, and since such a crime compensation system might be conducive to justice on the whole, we should perhaps be willing to accept the local injustice.

A similar situation might arise in college admissions. Suppose that we would like to compensate for the unjust disadvantages under which some of our applicants have suffered. On a case-by-case basis, unjust disadvantages are hard to identify, document, and weigh. On the other hand, sex and race are relatively easy to identify and are known to be highly correlated with such disadvantages. Therefore, we may be confident that policy (A) would constitute desirable compensation in the majority of cases, and would work injustice in relatively few cases. So (A) would probably bring about more justice on the whole than would any feasible alternative. We might call this a "statistical compensatory justification" of (A).

Any such justification rests on the premise that under some circumstances the best we can do is to redress some injustices and not others, or even redress some injustices at the cost of creating other, lesser injustices. Suppose that I believe that all homosexuals suffer unjust disadvantages similar in importance to, if partially different in kind from, those suffered by women or blacks. I am asked to vote on whether or not to give some benefit (say, money from the general fund) to each of these groups in turn.

Believing that members of all three groups are deserving of compensation, I intend to vote "yes" in each case. However, the vote on homosexuals is taken first, and I find myself in the minority. I might now change my mind and vote against compensation for women and blacks on the basis that I believe they are no more unjustly disadvantaged than homosexuals. Would it be fair to give a benefit to women and blacks and not to homosexuals? There is a respect in which it is unfair, but surely this should not lead me to vote against compensation for women and blacks. It is normally a good thing to remedy some injustices even if one cannot remedy all of them. By voting "yes" on the remaining two motions, I vote for an increase in justice, if not for a situation of perfect justice.

Now suppose that the benefit to be awarded is of a competitive sort, as in admissions or hiring. Suppose, also, that the only workable way of compensating is to favor whole groups by giving their members extra points—points that one does not give to members of other groups. No case-by-case method will work (perhaps because those who would have to carry out a case-by-case evaluation of disadvantage cannot be trusted). I have lost the first vote as above, and know that if any of the subsequent motions wins, some members of other disadvantaged groups will be given preference over some homosexuals. Ought I to vote "yes"? I think that in most circumstances I should. It is true that the policy that will result if I am in the majority on either of the subsequent votes is likely to conflict with our principle of just compensation. It can be expected to do a direct *additional injustice* by compensating, for example, some less-injured blacks at the expense of some more-injured homosexuals. That this is likely to happen is unfortunate, but it is a price that I may be willing to pay in exchange for the (presumably more numerous) cases where blacks are given preference over uninjured competitors. (This rationale for voting "yes" on the second and third motions of course vanishes if there is reason to believe that homosexuals dominate the upper level of the candidate pool.) In voting to compensate blacks, even though I lost on the vote to compensate homosexuals, I vote for the maximum obtainable justice. In these circumstances, the homosexuals may have a prima facie right to equal consideration with other equally injured persons, but this right is outweighed by the importance of compensating the other injured individuals.

Such a "maximum obtainable justice" argument may be used to give a statistical compensatory justification for (A) under certain circumstances. But this gives (A) only a weak sort of justification. The policy is not an instance of the theoretically proper principle; it is merely the best we can do under the circumstances. Such circumstances ought to be changed, and frequently with a little effort they can be, since the problems are only those of administering more appropriate policies like (B).

## III. GROUP COMPENSATION

There is, however, another compensatory argument, one that does not rely on the practical difficulties of administering the "proper" compensatory policy (B). It will not actually justify (A), either; but it is of interest because it gives grounds for preferring a policy that calls for many instances of preferential treatment which would follow from (A) but are disallowed under (B). In particular, the new policy does not require the preferred candidate himself or herself to have been unjustly injured.

The sort of compensatory argument I have in mind is also of interest because it is a form of "group compensation" and not merely a statistical form as discussed above. Group compensation has seemed obviously wrong to many, either because groups are not moral persons or because we cannot compensate some group members by giving a benefit to other group members. "Persons are distinct." While I agree that groups are neither persons nor quasi-persons, I do believe that we can compensate members of some groups by giving a benefit to *any* member of the group—even a member who has not been unjustly injured.

Obviously, such a possibility would be absurd for many groups. Consider the group consisting of a randomly selected unjustly convicted prisoner and your favorite multimillionaire. Surely we would not compensate the convict if we gave (as we surely will) a civic award to the capitalist.

But how about more "natural" groups—racial, sexual, national, or religious? In such cases, the possibility of some form of group compensation seems at least not entirely crazy. For the sort of compensation I have in mind, however, it is neither necessary nor sufficient that the group be in any sense natural—though typically it will be. A sufficient condition is that the group be what might be called a "community of concern." If every member of the group (or at least most members) would prefer, other things being equal, that certain benefits go to any other member of the group rather than to an outsider, then we have such a community. We can compensate the unjustly disadvantaged members of the community by giving a benefit to another member of the community—even if that member has not been treated unjustly. Since each disadvantaged member wants (or wanted, or would have wanted) the non-disadvantaged member to prosper, benefiting the latter also benefits the former in that it fulfills one of his or her desires. We often compensate a person by directly benefiting those about whom that person cares. The practice of compensating estates is one example. Underlying the possibility of this sort of compensation is the fact that people do care about the welfare of other people, and the fact that this care is not always divided equally among all persons.

To cite a controversial example, this mechanism makes possible the (partial) compensation of American slaves for the injustices of slavery. We might simply give a lump-sum reparation payment to all black citizens of the United States on July 4 of a certain year. At least a significant number of slaves had a racial identification that led them (or would have led them had the question been raised) to care more about blacks than about non-blacks of subsequent generations. (And, of course, many of the persons to whom the payments would be made would be their direct descendants. Presumably many people care more about direct descendants than about non-descendants.)

Obviously this sort of compensation, when applied to past generations, raises not only theoretical problems, but also monumental practical difficulties. It would not always be easy to determine whether people long dead had, explicitly or implicitly, the appropriate sorts of desires about the future. Assessing the extent of the injury and its present monetary equivalent (or equivalent in, say, educational opportunity) would be even more difficult.

But assuming that the practical problems could be worked out, will a correct moral theory really place us under a prima facie obligation to compensate people long dead? Is such compensation really possible? Compensation requires giving someone a benefit. Do we benefit the dead by fulfilling desires that they had while alive? Does it seem right that some injuries of the distant past should be compensable and others not, just because one set of victims did, and the other did not, have desires about the future?

I doubt that a satisfactory position denying the compensability of the long-dead can be worked out without denying moral status in general to the dead. Most people believe that certain wishes of the recently deceased have moral force (at least in matters of inheritance and funeral arrangements). If we are right in thinking this, can the wishes and desires of the long-dead about the present be different except by degree? We can benefit a living person, $X$, by fulfilling $X$'s desires, even where $X$ may not know that his or her desires are being fulfilled. It seems fairly obvious that there are desires of the appropriate non-egoistic sort (for example, for the welfare of a lost friend). And there are no grounds other than those of psychological egoism to treat the fulfillment of these apparent desires differently from the fulfillment of any other desires. If all this is granted, then death appears as just one among many situations which may make $X$ unaware that his or her desire is being fulfilled.

It is likely that the long-dead had very few intense desires about the present. This might in itself be enough to justify our feeling that the moral weight of those desires is not very great. Or perhaps, independent of the strength of their desires, long-dead persons (and those to be born in the distant future) are only part, not full, members of our present moral community. (Surely our human ancestors of a million years ago have negligible moral significance today, even if they all very strongly desired, say for religious reasons, that males in all future generations should wear beards.) But, of course, to say that the moral weight of the long-dead is not very great is not to say that they have no moral weight.

That one dead person may be compensable and another not (though both were equally injured) seems to me no stranger than that some living persons are compensable and others, equally injured, are not, solely for the reason that we are in a position to benefit the former but not the latter. Dead persons who had no wishes or desires about the present have simply lost the last channel by which they could be benefited.

I realize that these few remarks fall far short of straightening out all the tantalizing problems about the compensability of the dead.[3] Fortunately, for the present purposes is is not absolutely necessary to settle them. Taking into account the interests and injuries of dead women and blacks might increase somewhat the weight of group compensation, but we do not have to look into the past at all to establish the basis for group compensation for blacks and women. Present blacks and women have been unjustly disadvantaged, and they identify sufficiently strongly with other blacks or women to meet the conditions for this sort of group compensation. The community of concern is probably not as strong among women as it is among blacks, and yet there are now a considerable number of women who have been unjustly disadvantaged and who would prefer that certain benefits, like jobs, go to women rather than to men—at least where the women are, at worst, only marginally less qualified. Note that, for the purposes of this sort of compensation, it does not matter why they prefer this, or whether they ought to.

This sort of compensation, then, is properly blind to the disadvantages suffered by the particular person to whom we propose to give preferential treatment. But it still is not properly blind to the claims of other candidates in competition for the position. It is one thing to give a position to an affluent black in competition with an affluent white; it is another to give the position to an affluent black in competition with a framed, impoverished, white ex-convict. Doubtless there are some blacks even more unjustly injured than our ex-convict, and among these, perhaps most would want the position to go to the affluent black. I cannot suggest any method for weighing the interests and injuries of these blacks against the interests and injuries of the white competitor. My intuition, however, is that the group-compensation mechanism, because of its indirectness, transmits interests and injuries with a considerable discount in their moral weight. Group compensation ought not to overwhelm the interests of the persons directly involved (in our case, the competitors for a position), leaving them as moral bystanders with regard to their own affairs.

A preferential policy combining the individual-compensation policy (B) with the considerations of this section might go as follows:

(C) (1) Award the position to any (at least minimally qualified) person $X$ over any only marginally more qualified competitor $Y$ if $X$ has suffered significantly greater unjust injury than has $Y$.

   (2) Award the position to any (at least minimally qualified) person $X$ over any only marginally more qualified competitor $Y$ even if $X$ and $Y$ do not differ significantly with respect to unjust injuries, but the people who would prefer that $X$ be awarded the position have suffered under a significantly

> greater total burden of unjust injury than
> the people who would prefer that $Y$ be
> awarded the position (where the preferen-
> tial attitudes need not refer to the candi-
> dates personally, but may involve such
> descriptions as "a black" or "a Mason").[4]

The distance this policy remains from (A) is obviously still
very great. (C-2) is like (A) in its indifference as to whether
the preferred party has himself or herself suffered unjust disadvantages; but (A) is indifferent as well to any claims by the
competitors other than those based on race or sex.

## IV. THE CHANGING OF RACIAL
## AND SEXUAL ATTITUDES

Having found no compensatory arguments that can justify (A),
or anything close to (A)—except perhaps in the face of practical difficulties that stand in the way of such properly compensatory policies as (B) or (C)—I want now to turn to a justification that focuses on non-compensatory consequences of a
preferential policy. I think that a policy in the general spirit of
(A) can probably be justified by an important social goal.

This goal is so central to the moral health of our civilization
that it might override even the injustice a preferential policy
would do to our framed ex-convict. It will certainly override
lesser injustices of the same sort. The goal is not at all new, but
it has received surprisingly little attention in the philosophical
debate about preferential treatment. The goal I have in mind is
the complete eradication of the attitude structures of racism and
sexism: hatred, prejudice, suspicion, stereotyping, and the rest.

These attitudes have to be eliminated for three reasons. First,
they breed and perpetuate injustices of a thousand different
sorts—too numerous, too pervasive, and often too subtle to
eliminate directly. Second, they are evil in themselves. Third,
they have a wide range of undesirable consequences that are
not, strictly speaking, injustices. (The racist or sexist is often a
victim of his or her own hatred and distorted perceptions. This
is not an injustice, but it is an evil.)

The occupation by blacks and women of sought-after positions of prestige and power is certainly not sufficient to eliminate racism or sexism. Perhaps it is not even necessary. But it

is a means well suited to the goal of eliminating racist and sexist attitudes. Blacks and women in positions of prestige and power undermine stereotypes. Their success encourages other blacks and women to set their sights high. Contact between the races increases, as does the level and variety of contacts between the sexes. In short, preferential treatment should encourage a homogenization of the society along the lines of the no-longer-so-popular integrationist ideal. My suspicion is that racism and sexism go so deep that they will not be eliminated short of a very thorough integration indeed (an integration which, on the racial side, would lead, through intermarriage, to the eradication of separate races). Thorough and systematic integration of blacks and women in and into all levels of society will, I think, require institutional changes going far beyond the preferential policy under consideration here. But the preferential policy is probably a good start.

Taking integration to be the proximate goal of the policy, (A) is obviously not quite appropriate. (A) would urge us to give preference to women over men for admission to nursing schools and would not distinguish between white women and black men with respect to a field where white women were unrepresented while black men constituted half the members of the field. To avoid such non-integrative consequences we need to modify (A) as follows:

> (A′)  Award the position to any (at least minimally qualified) candidate $X$ over any only marginally more qualified competitor $Y$ if $X$ is the member of racial and sexual groups that are significantly less represented in the field or position (in proportion to the general population) than are the racial and sexual groups to which $Y$ belongs.

(A′) needs to be filled in by specifying just what racial and sexual groups are relevant. But the anti-racist and anti-sexist motivation of the policy makes this easy, at least in principle. The relevant groups are those racial and sexual groups associated with significant racist and sexist attitudes. (I say "associated with" rather than "the target of" because I intend to include not only the victims of these attitudes but also the complement classes: men as well as women, non-blacks as well as blacks.) Obviously, under this formulation homosexuals ought to be counted as a sexual group. In addition, in some situations religious groups (for example in Northern Ireland) ought to be included. For simplicity, think of such groups as covered by a widened notion of "racial groups."

In cases where candidates belong to more than one such group, we can take the degree of representation of all the groups into account by assigning an under-representation index to each candidate, as follows. First, for each group to which the candidate belongs find $f$, the proportion of that group in the field or position. Then find $g$, the proportion of that group in the general population. The "degree of representation" for that group in that field or position is the ratio $f/g$. (Where $f/g < 1$, the group is under-represented; the smaller $f/g$ is, the more under-represented.) To compute the representation index, $I$, for a given candidate relative to that field or position, add these degree-of-representation ratios for each group to which the candidate belongs:

$$I = \sum_{i=1}^{n} \frac{f_i}{g_i}$$

(where $i$ enumerates the $n$ groups to which the candidate belongs. Note that $n$ will be the same for all candidates for a given position. Everyone is either male or female, black or non-black, so there are $2n$ total groups.) If $X$'s index number is significantly less than $Y$'s, then $X$ and $Y$ satisfy the antecedent of (A′).[5]

(A′) takes as relevant the proportion of a group in the general population rather than the proportion in the candidate pool for the field. HEW guidelines are keyed to proportions in the candidate pool. This is appropriate for certain considerations of justice, but when our purpose is an overall social integration it would frequently be self-defeating. The candidate pools are often far from integrated themselves.

Consider the following illustration. Who ought to be hired for a job as a secretary following policy (A′), where the candidates are a white female, a black female, and a white male, and the best of them is at most only marginally more qualified than the others? The figures used below have been made up out of thin air, solely for the purposes of illustration:

|                                      | Non-blacks | Blacks | Males | Females |
|--------------------------------------|------------|--------|-------|---------|
| Proportion among secretaries         | .9         | .1     | .03   | .97     |
| Proportion in general population     | .8         | .2     | .5    | .5      |

White female candidate $\quad I = \dfrac{.9}{.8} + \dfrac{.97}{.5} = 3.065$

Black female candidate $\quad I = \dfrac{.1}{.2} + \dfrac{.97}{.5} = 2.44$

White male candidate $\quad I = \dfrac{.9}{.8} + \dfrac{.03}{.5} = 1.185$

Here, then, we ought to hire the white male. This sort of conse-quence of (A′), in which it differs from (A), promotes the integration of the less prestigious and powerful positions which have been dominated by women and minorities. The importance of this sort of integration for anti-racist and anti-sexist purposes is less than the integration of positions of power and prestige, and yet it does break down stereotypes, increase contact, and in other ways directly and indirectly change attitudes.

## V. INCENTIVES: AN ALTERNATIVE POLICY

A preferential policy like (A′) is not, of course, the only possi-ble way to produce the desired integration. An alternative would be to offer other sorts of special incentives to members of under-represented groups. For example we might give $5,000 bonuses to blacks and women who complete B.A. degrees, and $20,000 bonuses to those who complete J.D., M.D., or Ph.D. degrees. Such bonuses might come from private charity, the general fund, or from a special tax on those who have benefited from racism and sexism in the past.[6] It is possible that such a system would encourage enough members of under-represented groups to undertake advanced training so that the fields requir-ing that training would be thoroughly integrated within a rea-sonable period of time and without any sort of preferential treatment within the competitive process itself. If such an incen-tive system were to succeed, I think that it would be preferable to anything remotely like (A) or (A′); however, (B) or (C) might still be desirable.

# VI. THE JUSTIFICATION OF PREFERENTIAL TREATMENT FOR CHANGING RACIAL AND SEXUAL ATTITUDES

There may be other methods in addition to special bonuses or preferential competitive treatment for promoting rapid and thorough integration. And there may be ways of ending racism and sexism without integration (though I doubt it). The general condition for the justification of the preferential policy (A′) is that the moral value of the decrease in racism and sexism that it produces (plus any side benefits it may have), minus its costs, leaves it morally superior to any practicable alternative policy.

Certainly, there are advantages to other policies. (C), for example, is more just than (A′). Moderate monetary bonuses as incentives have the advantage that they do not tamper with highly sensitive competitive situations as (A′) does. But monetary incentives are not politically feasible at this time. And it is possible that (C) would lead to integration at a rate enough slower than (A′) to give (A′) the overall advantage despite its rough edges with respect to justice.

There are, however, two necessary conditions which (A′) must meet if it is to be seriously considered:

(1) (A′) must be sufficient to bring about a significant increase in the rate of integration.

(2) The integration that (A′) produces, minus any backlash effect it has, must significantly decrease the level of racist or sexist attitudes.

The first condition is obvious. We cannot give an integrationist justification for a policy that fails to integrate. There are probably some competitions where (A′) won't even apply because there are *no* minimally qualified members of under-represented groups in the candidate pool. There may be other cases where there are minimally qualified under-represented candidates but, among those who would be passed over if there were no preferential policy, none is only *marginally* less qualified than the selected candidates. In such cases, we might consider a stronger version of (A′) which substitutes for "only marginally" a phrase allowing a wider range of differences in qualification. Unfortunately a version of (A′) strengthened along these lines is very likely to come into conflict with (2), and also very likely to increase certain other costs discussed below. However, there are, I think, a wide range of cases where (A'), as it stands, will promote integration. This will happen wherever there are at least a few candidates from under-represented groups who are only marginally less qualified than the candidates who would otherwise be selected.

Assuming that the first condition is met, and that integration is *usually* destructive of racist and sexist attitudes, we still need to know whether (A') as a mechanism of integration will lead to a significant net decrease in racism or sexism. In particular we have to be concerned about possible backlash effects from the use of (A'). Various sorts of compensatory policies, as well as other policies aimed at directly eliminating injustices, may be justified even if they create very great backlashes. We cannot always let justice wait on the more backward members of society. But a policy intended to eliminate racist and sexist attitudes obviously fails if it contributes more to those attitudes, directly or indirectly, than it takes from them.

It is equally obvious that there is a danger that preferential policies will encourage racist and sexist attitudes. The policies themselves make use of the very racial and sexual categories that we wish people would stop using for most purposes. Moreover, the people who administer and defend preferential policies are sometimes guilty of holding fairly serious racist or sexist attitudes. People think, and occasionally even say, of unqualified candidates, "this is the best we can expect from a woman [or black]!" Those who have lost competitions and those (probably more numerous) who mistakenly believe that they have lost competitions as the result of preferential policies are likely to harbor resentments that may grow into or feed racist or sexist attitudes. But probably the greatest backlash danger from integrating through preferential competitive treatment is that women or blacks (or other minorities) will come to be perceived as less-qualified, second-class holders of their positions of power and prestige. If it came to be believed that most women or blacks were less able students or less qualified than their white male co-workers in the professions and skilled trades, that would likely strengthen racist and sexist attitudes. Obviously, those women and blacks who would have won their positions without preference would, in some cases, be less effective counter-examples to racist and sexist beliefs than they would have been if there were no preferential policy. No matter how obviously qualified they are, some people will believe that they owe their positions to race or sex.

Increased contact between the races and sexes may itself reinforce racist and sexist attitudes if people are able to perceive that women or blacks really are less qualified than their fellow students or co-workers. Of course, even in such cases some racist or sexist attitudes, especially the most extreme, may be weakened. Even the minimally qualified black or woman surgeon or physicist undermines stereotypes. Minimal qualifications are, after all, sometimes very demanding.

On the whole, it seems to me that under a preferential policy like (A') there is danger of a backlash sufficient to overwhelm the positive consequences of integration—enough of a danger that we should insist that the position be awarded on the basis of race or sex solely where the best-qualified candidate is really only marginally better. In effect, under this policy we would treat being a member of an under-represented group as if it were a minor qualification. Ideally, it should be impossible for anyone outside the admissions or hiring committee to tell whether the candidate was the beneficiary of the preferential policy. Better still, for these purposes, would be a preferential policy that committee members apply unconsciously so that they can sincerely say that the position went to the most qualified candidate. (But of course self-deception would be undesirable for other reasons.)

If (A') succeeds in integrating, and this integration produces a significant decrease in net racism and sexism, it still must show itself superior to its competitors with respect to overall benefits and costs.

The costs of (A') can be classified according to the bearers of those costs. First, the passed-over candidate is sure to suffer under (A'). Especially weighty are any injustices that (A') does to him or her. Second, the preferred candidate may pay some cost in self-respect in knowing that his or her success was in part due to race or sex. Third, a candidate from an under-represented group who was, in fact, the best-qualified candidate may also lose self-respect if others wrongly believe that preferential treatment was involved in his or her success. And perhaps more important, the candidate himself or herself may wrongly suspect that preferential treatment was involved, and thus suffer a loss of self-esteem.

Finally, the cost to the ultimate consumers of the candidate's services has to be brought into the balance. The difference in the quality of work between one cabinetmaker and another only slightly less qualified is probably not much. It is easy to reconcile oneself to a less well-finished bookcase as part of an effective campaign against racism and sexism. But slightly less effective teachers represent a somewhat more troubling cost, and slightly less effective neurosurgeons are more troubling still. Perhaps there are some fields where we should never tolerate anyone but the best available candidate—no matter what social benefits a preferential policy would promise. Most likely are those fields where less qualification means a statistically increased risk of death or serious injury to the consumers of the service. But even in such cases the risks ought to be weighed against the benefits. Suppose that a preferential policy that would effectively eliminate racism and sexism in fifty years would, in that period, cost one hundred lives in the operating room. No other policy would eliminate racism and sexism nearly as quickly. Whether one thinks the hundred lives is a cost worth paying will depend largely on how serious one believes the evils of racism and sexism to be. My own view is that racism and sexism so thoroughly poison our society that a slight annual increase in surgical fatalities would be a small price to pay for their elimination. (How many people die in wars and riots that are in part racially motivated?)

I suppose that there may be a few people who would argue that the loss of certain sorts of achievements—symphonies, mathematical and philosophical discoveries, and the like—is a cost we should not pay for the eradication of racism and sexism. But it is quite unlikely that (A′) would lead to the loss of many really important achievements, because the potential authors of such works are unlikely to be only marginally more qualified than the least-qualified candidate from an under-represented group to win a position under (A′). Even if we did lose some achievements, however, that may be a price worth paying for a policy that eliminates racism and sexism with significantly greater speed than any other policy.

Some of the costs of (A′) may be eliminated by minor variations on the theme. We might, for example, exempt neurosurgery, or instances where the best-qualified candidate had already been the victim of extreme injustices—as in the case of the framed ex-convict. Such variants of (A′) presumably integrate nearly as quickly while eliminating special sorts of particularly high costs. (Probably, therefore, we can avoid the life-and-death calculations mentioned above.)

(A′) and its variants have some side benefits worth noting. In particular there will be a large range of cases where (A′) gives the same results as (B) or (C). This compensatory side-effect will be a plus on the side of justice. Then there are the desirable consequences of integration independent of the changes in people's attitudes.

Even with modifications, however, and bearing in mind its side benefits, it must be granted that (A′) will have serious costs. But any way of eliminating racism and sexism reasonably quickly will have serious costs. We mustn't be so intimidated by these costs that we fail to weigh them against the very high costs of racism and sexism.

In the absence of strong and feasible alternatives, I think that, even given its costs, (A′) (or minor variants thereof) should be adopted for a wide range of competitions for educational opportunities and jobs until such time as more desirable policies (like special bonuses) become feasible or integration is complete.

## NOTES

1. I intend this formulation to give preference to black women over black men and white women, and to black men and white women over white men. It does not give preference to black men over white women or vice versa.
2. See George Sher, "Justifying Reverse Discrimination in Employment," *Philosophy and Public Affairs* 4 (Winter 1975): 159–70.
3. For example, what if the dead person had contradictory desires at different times in his or her life? As is not the case with a living person, there is no *present* desire to which we might give priority. There do seem to be two reasons, however, for preferring later desires of dead persons over earlier ones.

   First, the later portions of the lives of the recently deceased are significantly closer to us than the earlier portions. The later "selves" of the recently deceased may, then, be more fully members of our moral community.

   The second consideration is more general, applying to the long-dead as well as the recently dead. Assume that the person in question's later desires or wishes were not the product of outside coercion or manipulation. To have respect for the autonomy of the individual requires us to give more weight to what $X$ became than to what $X$ grew out of or changed his or her mind about. Hence the priority of the later desires. But what are we to say if $X$ was a lifelong crusader for $Y$-ism who, on his or her deathbed, becomes converted to anti-$Y$-ism? Do $X$'s former wishes and desires—steadfast over many years—lose all their moral weight? I suspect that they do, so long as $X$ really did change his or her mind freely, competently, and completely. Wishes and desires only have moral weight as the wishes and desires of persons, and so they lose all their weight when disowned. (To believe otherwise would seem to commit one to a less than unitary metaphysics of personal identity over time.)

4. Note that this principle applies to a wider range of cases than the communities of concern. The unjustly injured individuals who want $X$ to have the job may not care at all about each other, nor need $X$ care about them. So if the slaves had been sufficiently brainwashed to prefer whites of later generations to blacks, we might compensate the slaves by giving a "reparation" payment to whites. (Presumably other considerations of justice would rule this out.)

5. This formula probably doesn't match our intuitions about the degree of representation exactly. For example, if $X$ and $Y$ belong to different entirely unrepresented groups, but $X$'s group is much larger than $Y$'s, we would like to give preference to $X$, other things being equal. The formula leaves them equal. This could be corrected by performing the calculations on the artificial assumption that each group has at least $1/100$ person in the field.

Instead of letting preference hinge on degree of representation, we could use a degree of correction: how much a given candidate's winning the position would correct under-representation. One way to do this would be to recalculate

$$\sum_{i=1}^{n} \frac{f_i}{g_i}$$

on the assumption that the given candidate did win the position. Then subtract $I$ for that candidate from this sum, giving the degree of correction for that candidate. The candidate with the larger degree of correction would be the preferred one. This procedure would give priority to smaller over larger under-represented groups, which is probably undesirable for anti-racist anti-sexist purposes.

6. If the public revenues are used for these bonuses, the scheme may have constitutional problems, since it discriminates along racial and sexual lines. Wherever the funds come from, certain safeguards will have to be built in to prevent the scheme from giving an indirect competitive advantage, rather than simply an incentive. An example of an indirect advantage would be if the bonuses

made it possible for poor members of under-represented racial and sexual groups to secure loans to finance their education—loans which poor members of over-represented groups would not be in a position to secure. If this were allowed, the incentives would lead to differential opportunity, which, I am assuming, it is the point of the incentives to avoid.

Robert K. Fullinwider

# On Preferential Hiring

## I

Is it justified, as a matter of social policy, to give general prefer
ence in employment to blacks and women? What consideration
favor such a policy? Defenders of preferential hiring of black
and women have offered a number of different grounds for it
justification. I subject the three most important justifications to
examination in this essay. I shall briefly consider the argumen
from social utility and the argument from distributive justice
and I shall take up at greater length the argument from com
pensatory justice.

Defenders of preferential hiring[1] of blacks and women ca
point to many social goals that such a policy would likely serve
It would increase the well-being of many persons, provide addi
tional role-models for young women and blacks, undermin
racial and sexual stereotypes, and make available better service
to women and blacks. These gains, of course, will be bought a
a certain cost, but perhaps it plausibly can be argued that th
long-run gains outweigh the costs.[2]

Such a defense of preferential hiring of women and black
does not fully explain, however, why preferential treatmer
should be accorded to *blacks* and *women*. It is probable that th
enumerated goals, and others, could be accomplished by a po
icy of preferring in employment some blacks, some women, an
some non-black males; and that the net gains from such a polic
would be greater than the net gains from preferring *all and on
women and blacks*. A similar problem besets a second groun

for justifying preferential hiring. The argument in this case is that distributive justice requires society to channel resources (including jobs) so as to increase the opportunities and well-being of those who "are toward the bottom of the socio-economic-political pecking order, and unlikely to rise as things are presently arranged."[3] By such means as preferential hiring policies deficiencies in opportunity can be ameliorated.[4]

A policy of preferring blacks and women would make little sense on this ground. The class of blacks and women fails by a wide margin to fit the class of persons eligible to be preferred on the distributive-justice criterion. Thus, appeal to considerations of distributive justice does not explain why a policy of preferring blacks and women is justified.[5] Since both the utilitarian argument and the distributive-justice argument seem unable to explain this, I am inclined to think that the strongest defense for preferential hiring of women and blacks lies elsewhere.

There is yet another more troubling difficulty with the two foregoing defenses of preferential hiring. The utilitarian argument requires social policy that channels resources so as to create the most social good. The distributive-justice argument requires social policy that channels resources to the bottom sector of society. What these simplified utilitarian and distributive-justice arguments fail to do is to take into account the existing rights of individuals to some or all of the resources to be channeled. These defenses of preferential hiring leave out of account the existing rights of persons—rights that may be violated by a policy of preferential hiring. How can a social policy preferring some in employment because of their race or sex be consistent with the Constitutional right to equal protection of the laws? How can we concede to all citizens the right to equal consideration or equal access to any position or job and at the same time support a policy of preferential hiring? Were it not for individuals' rights, social policy might be able more efficiently to achieve many social goals by re-allocating the various holdings and opportunities of persons; we might more efficiently realize the pattern of opportunities and advantages that pleases us most. But people's rights stand in the way of our treating social problems as if they required managerial decisions regarding efficient utilization and allocation of resources and goods. For many, at any rate, a social policy stands condemned if it is shown to violate or sacrifice persons' important rights.[6]

If preferential hiring of blacks and women is to be fully justified, it must deal with the fact of people's preexisting rights. It needs to be shown that where preferential hiring appears to conflict with some individual's rights there is a valid basis for setting aside the putative right; or that the individual actually does not have the apparent right. How can this be shown? A natural recourse lies in the appeal to compensatory justice. It is arguments from this ground that seem to promise a more adequate defense of preferential hiring of blacks and women, and it is to arguments of this kind that I now turn.

## II

I have a right (liberty or privilege)[7] not to give anyone a sum of money. That is to say, I am at liberty to do as I please in this respect, to give or not to give anyone money. But suppose, in exchange for a service, I promise another person a certain sum, $S$. Now the situation is altered; I no longer am completely at liberty to dispose of my money as I will. I have incurred an obligation to yield $S$ to the promisee, and he has a right (claim-right) to have $S$ from me. By my act of promising $S$, I have *waived* a portion of my liberty; I have given another a rightful claim to a portion of my money.

The same effect occurs when I wrongfully injure or harm someone. *By being at fault I incur an obligation* to repair the damage I have done, and to do so with my money if necessary. Whereas previous to my action I was completely at liberty to spend or not spend my money, now, by my action, I have *forfeited* a portion of my liberty. I *owe* the wronged party whatever I have that will make good the harm I caused.

It would seem that a promising defense for preferential hiring lies in seeing it as a form of reparation or compensation[8] for harms or injustices. This mode of defense would seem to promise avoidance of the two difficulties of the utilitarian and distributive-justice defenses. In the first place, we would seem to have at hand an account of individual cases of preferential treatment which showed that no one's rights were being violated, because it was evident that the relevant rights had been forfeited. And, moreover, we could apparently account for the justification for preferring blacks and women. For unlike any other major group,[9] both blacks and women have been subjected to legally enforced denial of their basic rights. Blacks were sub-

jected to legal slavery and then to legally sanctioned discrimination, the latter circumstance persisting into the middle of this
century. They have been severely deprived of opportunities for
advancement; and, though the legal apparatus of discrimination
has been dismantled, residual discrimination still persists. There
are many living blacks who have suffered from the legal or the
residual discrimination or both. Perhaps most have suffered
from the general effects of discrimination.

Women were not admitted to full legal citizenship in this
country until the early 20th century, and even thereafter they
have labored under legal restrictions that have greatly narrowed
the range of opportunities open to them. Many living women
can establish a plausible case for having suffered under arrangements and policies now recognized as unjust. A larger number
have experienced the general effects of discrimination. Of
course, not only women and blacks but other social groups have
suffered from informal social discrimination. Women and blacks,
however, having suffered under the weight of unjust state action,
would seem to have legitimate ground for advancing a claim for
state compensation; and preferential hiring might be seen as a
form of reparation or compensation warranted by this claim.

There are two problems facing this justification of preferential
hiring of blacks and women as a social policy. The first has to
do with who receives the benefits of compensation, and the
second, with who bears the costs of compensation. In discussing
a policy of preferential hiring we are not talking about individual
women or blacks bringing legal action for damages against
identifiable individuals who have deprived them of their rights,
nor are we talking about bringing such action against governmental bodies. What we are talking about is a general policy
favoring blacks and women in employment. The policy will
therefore favor individual blacks and women who have actually
suffered under legal racism and legal sexism and, in addition,
it will favor blacks and women who have not so suffered.[10]
Moreover, those who will bear the costs of this policy, primarily
young white male job seekers, are least likely to be those with
any fault or having any responsibility for the wrongs now requiring compensation.

The problem of who receives the benefits I believe to be comparatively minor; if it is the only objection to preferential hiring,
it can be overcome or tolerated. This problem with the com-
pensatory-justice defense of preferential hiring is not like the

parallel problem of the utilitarian and distributive-justice defenses. In their cases, the policy of preferential hiring grossly failed to include individuals who should have been included, given the justifications of the policy. In a policy of bestowing benefits, this is a far graver fault than the fault of not excluding some who ought to be excluded.

Much more serious is the problem of who bears the costs of compensation in preferential hiring. If those who are (involuntarily) paying the costs are not at fault for the wrongs being compensated, then we can no longer be assured that a compensatory program does not violate anyone's rights. And this was precisely the assurance that we were looking for with respect to preferential hiring. Is there a way around this difficulty?

Let us consider two job applicants, $X$, a white male, and $Y$, a black or a woman. Both $X$ and $Y$ are minimally qualified for the job. Let us further assume that $X$ and $Y$ (and all job applicants) have the basic right to equal consideration.[11] I mean by this that they have the right that the successful applicant be chosen on the basis of job-related qualifications. (In the present case, by hypothesis, neither color nor sex are job-related qualifications.) A policy of preferring blacks and women would prefer $Y$ over $X$ on account of features of $Y$ that are not job-related. How has $X$'s right not been violated?

Consider the following argument:

(1) The community owes compensation to women and blacks.

(2) In order to pay its debt, it may deny $X$ his right.

(3) Thus, assuming that the community may repay its debt by paying $Y$ (and other individual blacks and women), then the community may adopt a policy of preferential hiring.

I attribute an argument like this to Judith Thomson, whose important paper "Preferential Hiring"[12] attempts to justify such a policy by appeal to compensatory justice. The puzzle in this argument is premise (2). Why may the community deny $X$ his right? $X$ is not at fault. But Thomson declares that it is "wrongheaded" to ask whether $X$ has harmed $Y$ or any other black or woman.[13]

This is surely mistaken. Thomson asks us to consider "those debts which are incurred by one who wrongs another. It is here [she continues] that we find what seems to me the most powerful argument for the conclusion that preferential hiring . . . is not unjust."[14] This "powerful argument" relies on *those debts that are incurred by one who wrongs another.* The debt is incurred by the one who wrongs and is incurred as a consequence of his fault. How, then, can it be wrongheaded to ask about $X$'s fault? If $X$ has fault in the situation, then he has a debt to $Y$. If the community subsequently exacts an appropriate sacrifice from him to pay $Y$, $X$ has no right that is being denied or violated; the community is simply requiring $X$ to discharge *his* obligation to $Y$.

But if $X$ has no fault, then he has no debt (not directly, and not to $Y$). He has not forfeited or otherwise lost any of his rights. If the community denies $X$ his right to equal consideration, does it not violate his right? Perhaps it will be contended that the morally relevant debt in this case is the community's, so that the question of $X$'s fault need not arise. This brings us back to premise (2). Does the mere fact that the community owes something justify it in taking any action it pleases to discharge its debt? Does it justify the community in taking something from $X$? Specifically, in the present case does it justify the community in denying $X$ one of his fundamental rights, the right to equal consideration in employment? Thomson offers remarks that might be taken as defenses or explanations of (2).[15] She says that the community is justified in having preferential hiring because it is the *best* form of compensation for blacks and women. And she says that debts of compensation provide a ground for overriding rights. I look at both of these claims in turn in the following section.

### III

Thomson seems to be addressing the problem of the defensibility of premise (2) when she says:

Still, the community does impose a burden upon him [$X$, the white male applicant]: it is able to make amends for its wrongs only by taking something away from him, something which, after all, we are supposing he has a right to. And why should *he* pay the cost of the community's amends-making?
If there were some appropriate way in which the community could make amends to its blacks and women, some way which did not require depriving anyone of anything he has a right to, then that would be the best course of action to take. Or if there were anyway

some way in which the costs could be shared by everyone, and not imposed entirely on the young white male applicants, then that would be, if not the best, then anyway better than opting for a policy of preferential hiring. *But in fact the nature of the wrongs done is such as to make jobs the best and most suitable form of compensation.*[16]

The last line of this passage appears to contain the defense of the community's paying its debt in a way that deprives $X$ of his right. The "defense" rests on a confusion and will not withstand scrutiny.

Consider the following example.[17] Suppose you have stolen from me a rare ancient musket, the centerpiece of my gun collection. Before you can be made to return it, it is somehow irretrievably lost or destroyed. Suppose further that, by coincidence, there is one other such gun in existence in the world, and it is possessed by your brother. Unquestionably, from my point of view, the "best and most suitable form of compensation" I can have from you, since I cannot have my gun back, is to have a gun exactly like the one you have stolen. Neither any other kind of gun nor money can fully make up my loss. You can pay me the "best and most suitable form of compensation" by giving me your brother's gun. Are you thereby under an obligation to give me your brother's gun? Obviously not. Do you have the right to give me your brother's gun? You do not. If you take the gun and give it to me, you pay your debt to me with what is not yours to pay. You steal from your brother; and your act, though done to discharge your debt to me, is no different from your original act of stealing from me.

Alter the example in this way: imagine that the owner of the first musket is a French citizen. The musket is destroyed wrongfully by a United States customs agent. The French citizen demands compensation from the United States government. It so happens that the second musket is owned by a United States citizen. Is the United States government obligated to expropriate its citizen's musket to compensate the Frenchman, on the grounds that this constitutes the "best and most suitable" compensation? Obviously not. Does the United States government have the right to expropriate the musket? It does not.

Of the optional means of compensating me/Frenchman morally open to you/United States government, giving me/Frenchman the musket is not one of them. Its being the best form of compensation is irrelevant to its justifiability. The question of the best form of compensation becomes relevant only after we have settled the moral justifiability of exacting something from someone and settled on what the debtor has that he can pay. With reference to the community's paying $Y$ (and other blacks and women) by taking something from $X$ that $X$ has a right to, it *first* must be established that this is a morally legitimate option of the community before the "suitability" of this payment to $Y$ becomes a relevant question. By arguing that preferential hiring is the best and most suitable form of compensation to women and blacks, Thomson has not succeeded in establishing the defensibility of premise (2).

Thomson's other defense of premise (2) is more complicated. In the usual case of compensation, the person who pays the compensation has no right not to pay it. Thus, no right of that person is violated (or denied) by making him or her pay. In our present case, however, $X$'s right to not pay compensation to $Y$ has not been shown to have been forfeited or waived, and thus it still exists. The community, in establishing preferential hiring, simply *overrides* $X$'s right not to pay (that is, his right to equal consideration).[18] I have been taking such overriding as a violating of $X$'s right. But Thomson believes that sometimes a person's rights may be overridden without this being a violation. Thomson relies on the use of examples to persuade us that this is so. One example involves an eating club that gives a seating preference to one of its members over others because the club owes him a debt of gratitude. Another example is this:

suppose two candidates for a civil service job have equally good test scores, but that there is only one job available. We could decide between them by coin-tossing. But in fact we do allow for declaring for A straightway, where A is a veteran, and B is not. It may be that B is a nonveteran through no fault of his own. . . . Yet the fact is that B is not a veteran and A is. On the assumption that the veteran has served his country, the country owes him something. And it seems plain that giving him preference is a not unjust way in which part of that debt of gratitude can be paid.[19]

But, contrary to Thomson's confident claim in the last sentence, it is not plain that veterans' preference is just, although it is embodied in law. Veterans' preference can be objected to on the same grounds that preferential hiring of blacks and women can be objected to: the community acts unfairly in discharging its debt by imposing the cost not on all its members but only upon a few of its (nonculpable or nonresponsible) members.[20] It certainly is not plain that this charge of unfairness is ill-founded, if it is in fact ill-founded. It is not plain that overriding $B$'s right to equal consideration is not simply a violation of his right. Thomson's example is insufficient to show us how $X$'s right can be overridden without being violated.[21]

Thomson remarks that

> it is . . . widely believed that we may, without injustice, refuse to grant a man what he has a right to only if *either* someone else has a conflicting and more stringent right, *or* there is some very great benefit to be obtained by doing so—perhaps that a disaster of some kind is thereby averted. If so, then there is really trouble for preferential hiring.

She goes on to claim that "there are other ways in which a right may be overridden."[22] But the other ways turn out to be the way $B$'s right is denied in the veteran's case. Insofar as we have no confidence that $B$'s right is overridden without injustice in this case, we can have no confidence that $X$'s right is overridden without injustice in the case of preferring women and blacks. Thus, we have no reason to believe that preferential hiring has surmounted the major objection against it: that it violates some persons' fundamental rights.

# IV

Suppose it is argued that there is a basis for overriding $X$'s right after all, and it lies in the existence of a conflict of rights (a conflict of rights being one of the grounds listed by Thomson above). The argument might go like this: $X$ has a right to equal consideration, but $Y$ has a right to compensation. In the present case the two rights conflict—to adopt preferential hiring is to override $X$'s right, while to refuse to adopt it is to deny $Y$'s right. My argument against preferential hiring rests on the fact that such a policy overrides someone's rights; but, in fact, someone's rights will be overridden both by the adoption of a policy of preferential hiring and by the nonadoption of such a policy. So my argument fails. It rests on a covert and undefended assumption that $X$'s right is more important than $Y$'s right.

This line of reasoning is mistaken. In the first place, preferential hiring is not the only way $Y$ can be compensated. To fail to prefer $Y$ in employment is not necessarily to fail to compensate

$Y$ at all. But even if preferential hiring were the only possible mode of compensation, the situation is still not as represented by the above argument. There is no conflict of rights.

If $Y$'s having a right to compensation were his having a right from anyone to anything and everything that would make up for his loss, then perhaps there would be a conflict between $Y$'s right and $X$'s right. But $Y$'s right to compensation is not to be understood this way at all, as our gun example above should have made clear. In the first place, $Y$'s right is against a specific agent, the community. $X$ does not owe $Y$. Secondly, $Y$'s right is to whatever resources necessary for compensation that are legitimately available to the community to give him. $X$'s right to equal consideration is not among the eligible items that the community may yield to $Y$ as compensation. Whatever the scope of $Y$'s right to compensation, it does not encompass $X$'s right to equal consideration. Thus, there is no conflict of rights between $X$ and $Y$. It cannot be argued that $X$'s right to equal consideration may be justly put aside on grounds of a conflict of rights.[23]

It is worth considering here one other attempt to undercut my criticism of preferential hiring. I have conceded that the community owes $Y$ but I have claimed that $X$ does not. Yet $X$ is part of the community. If the community owes $Y$, must not $X$ owe $Y$? If so, then the major premise of my criticism collapses. However, I deny that because the community owes $Y$ it follows *from this alone* that $X$ owes $Y$.

If the community owes $Y$, then its members *collectively* owe $Y$. But the debt does not *distribute* through the members. The community is a corporate agent. If General Motors owes damages to the unlucky owner of a defective Corvair, it does not follow that a General Motors employee in Flint owes the Corvair owner anything. If the United States owes Japanese companies damages because it has imposed an illegal surcharge on imports, it does not follow that, say, Judith Thomson, a United States citizen, owes anything to any Japanese. If the community seeks through taxation to raise resources for paying $Y$ (and other blacks and women), then $X$, as a member of the community, *owes his share of taxes* to support the community's discharge of its legitimate obligation. But this is not to say that $X$ owes $Y$.

## V

A justified program to remedy past wrongs cannot itself create new wrongs. Though the wrongs done blacks and women provide a plausible ground for supporting their claims to compensation by the community, their legitimate claims seem to provide no justification for a policy of preferential hiring. Such a program will invariably violate the basic rights of some persons, primarily young white male applicants.[24] It will do so because the applicants who will be discriminated against by preferential hiring have not lost their rights due to any culpability in wrongdoing.[25] And we have found no valid basis for overriding their rights.[26] The compensation argument may justify individual cases of preferential hiring of blacks and women but not a general policy.[27] The utilitarian argument and the distributive-justice argument seem even less likely to justify a policy of preferring blacks and women in employment. Unless it is shown that valid, in-force fundamental rights of individuals may be overridden for *weaker* reasons than conflict of rights or to avoid disaster, then a policy of preferential hiring of women and blacks must be deemed unjust.

That we have failed to find in the claims to compensation a justification for preferential hiring does not mean, however, that we thus dismiss the claims to compensation themselves as illegitimate. Preferential hiring is not the only way, nor is it indisputably the best way (Judith Thomson to the contrary notwithstanding) to compensate most blacks and women for the wrongs done them, or for the effects of wrongs done their predecessors. In principle, any program that distributes its costs fairly and does not violate anyone's rights is open to consideration. Many programs for increasing representation of blacks and women in industry, business, education, and so on are thus not ruled out. Practical problems of implementation and political problems of adoption may, of course, diminish the likelihood of any particular program, or any program at all, coming into being. It may be that entrenched interests are strong enough to prevent any effective compensatory program.[28] In this unfortunate event, no general governmental program will be available, and compensatory remedies, if any, will have to come through individual actions for judicial relief.[29]

# NOTES

1. I mean by preferential hiring the deliberate preferring of blacks or women over equally or better qualified candidates. Affirmative-action programs do not entail preferential hiring, and they are not the subject of this paper.
2. For an analysis of costs and gains which comes to the opposite conclusion, see Virginia Black, "The Erosion of Legal Principles in the Creation of Legal Policies," *Ethics* 84 (January 1974).
3. Irving Thalberg, "Reverse Discrimination and the Future," *Philosophical Forum* 5 (Fall-Winter 1973–74): 300. See also Bernard Boxhill, "The Morality of Reparations," *Social Theory and Practice* 2 (1972).
4. See Marlene Fried, "In Defense of Preferential Hiring," *Philosophical Forum* 5 (Fall-Winter 1973–74): 309, 310.
5. Considering the following (extremely rough) estimates and calculations will show this. In adopting a policy of distributing resources to lower sectors, and using employment preference as a tool, let us suppose that those who are members of families making less than $5,000 a year are eligible for preference. In 1970, 45 percent of black families and 20 percent of white families were below this line. In order to simplify calculations, consider a population of 20 million blacks and 180 million whites; and assume 5 members per family, and 1.5 job-seeking members of each family. Then in 1970, 2,700,000 blacks and 10,800,000 whites would have been eligible for preference, constituting an eligibility class of 13,500,000. A policy which preferred blacks and women who were below the cutoff point would prefer 8,100,000 (assuming half the whites are women), fully 39 percent *less* than all those entitled. A policy which preferred all and only blacks and women *regardless of their income* would fall far short of preferring all those who were entitled, and would prefer fully 50 percent not entitled to preference by the distributive-justice criterion and the cutoff point. Altering the assumptions or the cutoff point will not affect the ratios involved in this analysis. Figures on family income levels are taken from *The World Almanac 1971* (New York: Newspaper Enterprise Association, 1970), p. 45.
6. Consider: ". . . there is no moral outweighing of one of our lives by others so as to lead to a greater overall *social* good. There is no justified sacrifice of some of us for others" (Robert Nozick, *Anarchy, State, and Utopia* [New York: Basic Books, 1974], p. 33). It is possession of basic rights which reflects this fact of individual worth and inviolability; and violating a person's rights to attain a worthy social goal or to benefit others (or even to

gain others *their* rights) amounts to sacrificing the person for others.

7. See Wesley N. Hohfeld, *Fundamental Legal Conceptions* (New Haven: Yale University Press, 1964), pp. 36, 38f, 42–43, 47; and Joel Feinberg, *Social Philosophy* (Englewood Cliffs, N.J.: Prentice-Hall, 1973), pp. 55–59.

8. I use "compensation" throughout synonymously with "reparation." It need not be used this way; for example, see the role it plays in Bernard Boxhill's argument in "The Morality of Reparations," op. cit.

9. American Indians excepted.

10. Certainly, some women have benefited from sexism. Consider merely the well-endowed starlet who makes $100,000 a year entirely because of her possession of attributes valued as a consequence of the special attitudes toward women and sexuality promulgated by the regnant form of sexism. It is less the case that many blacks have benefited from racism.

11. If one is not willing to grant this generally, then restrict my example to a job in the public sector. Government and public institutions are certainly required to acknowledge this right.

12. Judith Thomson, "Preferential Hiring," *Philosophy and Public Affairs* 2 (Summer 1973). I have examined this argument in detail in my "Preferential Hiring and Compensation," *Social Theory and Practice* 3 (Spring 1975). Some of what follows parallels arguments therein.

13. Thomson, pp. 380–81.

14. Ibid., p. 380.

15. Since Thomson never explicitly states premise (2), there is no explicit argument for it. However, the premise seems necessary to her position, and there are remarks throughout her paper that can be seen as relevant to the justification of (2). It is from these that I reconstruct the argument for (2). For more detail, see "Preferential Hiring and Compensation," pp. 307–10.

16. Thomson, p. 383. Emphasis added.

17. Borrowed from "Preferential Hiring and Compensation," pp. 314–15.

18. My argument in "Preferential Hiring and Compensation" is obscured by my not distinguishing between the situation where a person forfeits or loses a right (and thus it is no longer in force) and where a person still retains a right (it is still in force) but the right is simply ignored or denied (overridden). Thus, I do not give sufficient attention there to the parts of Thomson's argument that I discuss at this point.

19. Thomson, pp. 379–80.

20. Such, in fact, was the argument in the legal challenge to veterans' preference in *McNamara v. Director of Civil Service*, 330

Mass. 22, 22–26, 110 N.E. 2d 840, 842–43 (1952). See James Nickel, "Preferential Policies in Hiring and Admissions: A Jurisprudential Approach," *Columbia Law Review* 75 (April 1975): 546: "Thus, it might be argued that putting the burden of helping to compensate and meet the needs of veterans on those who are excluded from government jobs by policies which prefer veterans is an unfair way of distributing the cost of a legitimate goal. A well-qualified nonveteran who hoped to get a government job but who was denied it because of a policy which gives veterans an advantage may feel that too much of the cost of helping veterans was placed on him. This person may feel that providing benefits from taxes—where the cost can be spread among many taxpayers—is preferable as a means of helping veterans to programs which impose the burden on a few people whose opportunities are reduced by preferential policies."

21. The eating-club example is no more persuasive, and is less apt. In this example, one member of an eating club is voted, out of gratitude, preference in being seated. Thomson sees no impropriety in this and views any member who complains as insensitive (pp. 378–79). Even if we were all to agree that there is no impropriety here, this intuition is too tenuous a base upon which to rest an argument for preferential hiring. For one thing, the eating-club example lacks precisely the factors—the overriding of a basic right, and a potentially serious harm—so crucial to our appraisal of preferential hiring.

22. Thomson, p. 378.

23. Suppose that the loss of my gun (see section III above) is such that nothing except having one like it could conceivably count as compensating for my loss. Even so, I don't have a right to your brother's gun; and there is no conflict between my right to compensation and your brother's right to his gun. *A conflict of rights would exist only where your brother has a right to the gun and I have a right to it as well, and both rights cannot be honored.*

The following kind of situation may be confused with a conflict of rights: I have a right to do something (or have something), but I cannot do (have) what I have a right to do (have) so long as we honor other's rights. For example, each man has a right to marry; but suppose all the females of age marry other men, there being more males than females. Then, I cannot marry though I have a right to. This is unfortunate, but it is not the case that my right to marry has been denied me, or overridden; nor is there a conflict between my right to marry and anyone else's right.

24. Assuming, of course, that we grant that everyone has the right to equal consideration for jobs and offices.

25. Even though Thomson claims it is "wrongheaded" to ask about the fault of white male applicants, she seems to recognize the implausibility of her position when, in the end, she tries to persuade us that they are not so innocent after all: ". . . it is not entirely inappropriate that these applicants [white males] should pay the cost. No doubt few, if any, have themselves individually, done any wrongs to blacks and women. But they have profited from the wrongs the community did" (p. 383). This will not do. In order to become an "accessory" to a wrong, and thereby less than innocent, one must benefit *knowingly* and *voluntarily* from the wrong. See "Preferential Hiring and Compensation," pp. 316–18, for a more detailed discussion of this point.

26. There is no conflict of rights; there is no catastrophe to be averted; and, contrary to Thomson's claim, debts of gratitude and compensation do not standardly legitimize overriding anyone's fundamental rights.

27. Suppose $X$ *has* wronged $Y$, and in such a way as to undercut $Y$'s job opportunities. Then, if $Y$ and $X$ are again in competition for the same job it might be legitimate remedy here to prefer $Y$ for the job (even if $X$ is more qualified).

28. Or it may be that they will yield *only* to a program of preferential hiring. For one who thinks *this* justifies preferential hiring see Marlene Fried, op. cit. (above, n. 4), pp. 317–18.

29. For the limited possibilities in individual action see Boris Bittker, *The Case for Black Reparations* (New York: Random House, 1973).

Alan H. Goldman

# Limits to the
# Justification of Reverse
# Discrimination

## I

I will argue here that reverse discrimination is prima facie unjust in violating a currently accepted and fair rule for hiring; that it can nevertheless be justified as compensation for those individuals previously discriminated against; that it cannot be justified in addition as compensation for groups as a whole, when these groups are defined only by race or sex; and finally, that it is also just for socially and economically deprived groups and individuals in order to create a true equality of opportunity for generations to come.

The first question to consider is whether society has the right to enforce a rule for hiring at all, and, if so, what rule is generally fair. This preliminary matter is crucial to the present issue for two reasons. First, discrimination (and thus reverse discrimination, which attempts to correct for it) can only be defined relative to some rule of hiring held just. Since discriminatory practices in hiring consist of granting jobs to some and exclud-

Reprinted by permission from *Social Theory and Practice* 3 (Spring 1975): 289–306. My thanks to the editors of this journal for their very helpful criticisms. An earlier abridged version of this paper was read at the Eastern APA meetings, December 1974, and I profited from the discussion which followed.

ing others on morally irrelevant grounds, criteria for their occurrence presuppose knowledge of morally relevant grounds for awarding positions. Second, unless reverse discrimination violates some presently accepted rule for hiring, it will not be seriously unjust in the current social context, and there will be little of practical interest left to discuss on the issue.

The currently accepted rule, which I believe to be just, is that of hiring by competence. Although this practice has seemed to remain sacrosanct in political debates on the issue, it has been attacked from both the philosophical right and left; neither viewpoint, however, has provided alternatives that are preferable from a moral point of view.

Libertarians argue that society has no right to require conformity to any rule by private corporations with jobs to disburse.[1] They appeal both to the property rights of the corporations in their own assets (including the right to disburse them as or to whom they please) and to the right of free association of the members of these corporations. The proper reply is that while both these rights may be recognized within their proper spheres, neither must be recognized as absolute, and therefore either may be limited by a rule for hiring in the social interest. The right to property, for example, is created through social systems and can be varied according to social needs (for example, limited by taxation, eminent domain, zoning regulations, etc.); and the rule for hiring the competent can be seen as a further limitation for the purpose of substantial increases in social utility. The right of free association can be viewed as limited here by another right more fundamental: that of equality of opportunity for individuals likely, in the absence of any rule, to be summarily denied jobs. (The right of free association is limited for the same reason by open housing and desegregated school directives.) Thus, neither property nor free-association rights in relation to corporation jobs need prevent the government from protecting social interest and individual equal opportunity by regulating hiring procedures.

Egalitarians, on the other hand, argue against hiring according to competence by pointing out that the present educational and social context tends to reward native factors like intelligence, which are arbitrary from a moral point of view. The attempt is made here to separate justice from efficiency altogether, and to argue that abilities relevant to hiring from the point of view of efficiency are not relevant to the candidate deserving the job or its rewards from the point of view of justice.[2] The problem with this is that no such radical separation of justice from utility could accord with our intuitions regarding justice. Following Rescher,[3] I would argue, for example, that, despite its greater inequality, a principle that achieves a distribution of goods in units of 4, 4, 4, 3 is preferable from the point of view of justice to one that generates a distribution of 2, 2, 2, 2. Those who could have received 4 units under the first plan could claim injustice at having to settle for 2 under the second. Equality of opportunity ideally demands remedial efforts by the educational system and substantial equalization of pay scales. But even without these, if the major complaint against hiring by competence is that it rewards chance factors rather than desert, it seems better to reward those who have made efforts to attain competence (a socially useful goal) and succeeded, than to make all hiring a matter of chance (as in a job lottery). Equality of opportunity should be interpreted as an equal chance to succeed through effort, not as an equal chance at benefits through some random process of distribution. And in addition to its vast social utility, competence is one barometer of prior effort.

Thus society, it seems, does have a right in the name of welfare and equal opportunity to impose a rule for hiring, and the general rule ought to be that of hiring the most competent.[4] This means that those individuals who attain maximal competence for various positions acquire rights to those positions through their own efforts. It then becomes wrong to thwart the legitimate expectations of these people by denying them the jobs, and a case is established for compensating those individuals so denied.

## II

Since reverse discrimination violates this principle of justice implied by our moral intuitions (and since violating this principle may in any case be unjust to individuals if it is widely accepted and generally adhered to), the practice of reverse discrimination can be justified only if this evil is overridden by a greater good resulting from it—or, more precisely, if the rights of most competent individuals to jobs are overridden by other rights of other individuals to those positions. The principle that is usually appealed to as overriding is that of compensatory justice suggested above: injured parties should be compensated, and compensated in kind if possible. According to this principle, if certain persons have been discriminated against in the past in violation of the rule of hiring by competence, it would seem that awarding them jobs in the present constitutes just and fitting compensation in kind.

The recent philosophical debate on the issue thus far has centered around the question of whether it can be just to treat a characteristic such as being black or being a woman, which is irrelevant to hiring from the point of view of distributive justice, as relevant in any hiring practices. In favor of the practice of reverse discrimination it has been argued that the relevant characteristic is not being black, for example, but having been discriminated against because one is black.[5] Opponents reply that the only relevant characteristic is that of having been discriminated against (and not being black), and that therefore compensation is owed only to those discriminated against and not to the group of blacks.[6] The rejoinder is that being black is made a morally relevant basis for hiring because discrimination has in the past been a general policy throughout society.[7] The outcome of this debate is simply that a characteristic morally irrelevant from the point of view of distributive justice may be relevant from the point of view of compensation. But the central questions remain first, whether, when, and in what sense compensation can be owed to a group as a whole; second, whether blacks or women qualify as the proper *kind* of group; third, to what degree owed compensation should override the principle of distributive justice operating in the present; and finally, whether reverse discrimination can be justified on grounds other than that of compensatory justice. I will address these questions in turn in the remainder of the paper, and consider the first two in this section.

Regarding the question of whether compensation can be owed to a group as a whole rather than to specific individuals, I believe that the necessary distinctions between kinds of groups have not been drawn in the previous philosophical literature. In fact, blacks or women do not qualify as genuine groups or social organizations in the sense in which sociologists generally use these terms. A group in this latter sense is defined in terms of actual interaction among members, each of whom occupies a certain position or plays a certain role in the group reciprocal to other roles (roles being reciprocal when their performances are mutually dependent).[8] With regard to groups defined in this way, I believe that compensation for injury or damages can be owed to the group as a whole. But this is only because injury to one member affecting his duties as a member harms all members, and because many damages cannot be assigned to specific members, but only to the group as a whole. Both features result from the reciprocity of roles within such groups. If, to take a trivial example of the first feature, members of some athletic team non-accidentally break the arm of their rival team's star in the midst of a crucial game, then compensation might be owed the latter team as a whole. Here, injury to one member of the group negatively affects the performance potential of the entire group and hence harms all its members. If the team is forced to forfeit a game because of an unfair decision of the referees, we have an example of the second feature—that is, of injustice to the group which cannot be more narrowly assigned to specific members. Again, compensation is therefore owed to the group as a whole. There can also be cases of injustice to multi-group systems or organizations, such as nations, in which damages cannot be assigned to specific groups or individuals within the larger systems. If some economic alliance unjustly imposes sanctions against American exports, compensation might be owed the United States without being disbursed to particular groups or individuals. Again, however, there must be a formal organization to receive the compensation and an inability to assign more specific damages. Fairness would in every case call for assigning damages as specifically as possible and reimbursing individuals always in proportion to the actual damages suffered under the unjust policy.

The upshot of the last paragraph is that regarding groups defined only intensionally according to some shared characteristic—groups whose members have no formal interaction, and for whom injuries are assignable to specific individuals and do not necessarily affect others—compensation can be owed only to those individuals and not to the group as a whole. Even if all members of such a group have been injured, compensation is owed to them as injured individuals and not simply as members of the group. This may seem a fine point, but it becomes crucial when it is questionable whether all members have actually been unjustly treated, and when it is apparent that some have been more unjustly treated than others. To claim otherwise —to claim that compensation can be owed to such groups as a whole, given only that they be defined in terms of the characteristic that was the basis for the unjust treatment[9]—is to lead oneself into paradoxes regarding the amount of just compensation owed, to whom it is owed, and by whom it should be paid.

One possibility is to claim not only that society has a duty to compensate groups as a whole that have suffered widespread discrimination in the past, but also that particular organizations that have unjustly denied jobs to particular qualified individuals have thereby incurred debts to those individuals.[10] But this alternative would imply that these individuals are owed reimbursement twice—once from society as members of the group, and once from the particular organizations that treated them unjustly. If a fair monetary value were assigned to the compensation owed, they would be owed twice the fair amount, which is inconsistent. This may again seem like splitting hairs, in that these individuals would be satisfied if paid their due by anyone; but the further point is that, ideally, only those institutions should pay that were responsible for the discrimination. Payment by society means that specific individuals who have not caused or benefited from discrimination will be forced to pay through the general social policy of preferential treatment for groups. Just as our notions regarding collective desert or rights do not seem to apply here, as shown above, neither do our notions of collective responsibility or guilt. As in the area of collective desert, in the case of collective guilt we generally require some joint causal relation to the injustice, and this generally only occurs within groups whose members are related to each other in terms of reciprocal roles.

There are further difficulties as well with the remaining alternative, that which holds that society owes reverse discrimination to groups as a whole while denying that it is owed separately by particular organizations to particular individuals who have been unjustly treated by them.[11] This would mean that a company or organization incurs no obligation over other organizations to compensate damages when it treats individuals unjustly, as long as the practice is widespread. It also means that those individuals who have actually been treated unjustly deserve no preference over those who have never suffered discrimination, but who only happen to have the characteristic that was the basis for discrimination against others. Since blacks and women, for example, do not constitute formal groups as defined above,[12] and since compensation *must* therefore be paid only to particular individuals within those groups, this implies that individuals actually treated unjustly may have nothing coming to them at all if someone else who happens to share the group characteristic has been compensated for their damages. These unwanted implications are unimportant only if every organization has discriminated against a given group, and only if in addition every member of the group has suffered from the unjust denial of a job or of a decent education. Although discrimination against minority groups has been widespread, I do not believe that any of the present-generation groups usually singled out for reverse discrimination can support this drastic a claim.[13] And in any case, injuries have not all been of the same degree; this means, according to our principle of compensation, that individuals should be compensated differentially and in proportion to past harm. Thus it certainly seems that some group members (those who have actually suffered discrimination) are more deserving of compensation than others, which would not be the case if compensation were owed simply to the groups as a whole. In fact, given the operation of the market in selecting individuals within these groups for compensation, the policy as directed toward groups works to select just those members for compensation who have been discriminated against least (those who are presently best qualified), and forces those to pay who least share the guilt.[14]

It is sometimes argued that those individuals not actually discriminated against directly at the level of job hiring nevertheless are inevitably adversely affected through such practices directed against members of their race or sex. Proponents of this argument say that, because of discriminatory hiring, such individuals suffer loss of self-respect, ambition, confidence, etc.; and that these motivational damages destroy equality of opportunity. It is then argued that only reverse discrimination as a general social policy can restore self-esteem to the race or sex as a whole.[15] I would reply to this by arguing first that motivational problems, at least when produced by discrimination that has not resulted in general economic deprivation for members of the group, are not as fixed and intractable as this argument would have it appear. Career motivation for white males is generally at least partially a function of the dubious blessing of external social pressure, the recognized necessity of self-support. If society began to adopt the same attitude and apply the same competitive pressures to women, and this were coupled with an end to all first-level discrimination, I cannot see motivational problems lingering. Or at least where they did in individual cases, it would be less plausible to attribute them to social inequalities and injustices. (Perhaps they might be attributed rather to rational resistance to the pressures of the work ethic.) Second, if all compensation owed to individuals were paid, this would restore the balance among groups and should restore the vicarious self-esteem of other members of minority groups. Finally, a policy of attacking differences in qualifications (including motivational differences) directly, rather than ignoring them in hiring, is preferable from the point of view of justice, if justice is to be linked to efficiency in generating and distributing goods (as is argued in section I).

To sum up, one alternative holds that compensation in the form of reverse discrimination can be owed both to groups as a whole (that is, groups defined only in terms of some characteristic on the basis of which certain assignable members were discriminated against) and to actually injured members as individuals. Another view has it that compensation is owed only to the groups and not to particular members. Both alternatives generate inconsistent or counterintuitive implications. The only resolution is to deny the premise that compensation is owed to groups and admit that while particular organizations owe reparations in kind to those individuals they treated unjustly or who suffered damages from their unfair hiring practices, society owes no additional compensation to those individuals or to others who happen to share the characteristic upon which the discrimination was based. This of course does not mean that the only individuals who suffer damages are necessarily those who suffer actual discrimination, although I have argued that not all of the same sex or race necessarily suffer. A man's family, for example, may suffer additional damages if he is denied a job, and members for whom such additional damages can be shown are also owed compensation, although the latter will not be in the form of additional jobs. But I believe we must draw the line at indirect psychological pressures, which affect different individuals in different ways (including white males who succumb to opposite pressures by working at jobs they hate). And since, with regard to members of minority groups, discrimination always affects particular individuals, and payment must be made to specific individuals (there being no formal organizations to whom payment can be made), common sense and the principle of compensatory justice demand that payment be made to those individuals who actually suffer damages rather than to others.

### III

The next question that must be raised is whether reverse discrimination in the form of compensation in kind for individuals actually discriminated against in the past requires that they be awarded jobs when others are more highly qualified, or only jobs for which they are as highly qualified as any other candidates. We might argue that the answer from the principle of compensatory justice is only the latter (I did so argue in an earlier version of this paper).

Two reasons can be cited in support of this claim. First, compensation is to be reciprocal to injury (that is, it is to be compensation in kind), and the individuals in question suffered injustice only by being denied jobs for which they were as highly qualified as any other candidates. If they were not as highly qualified as those to whom the jobs were awarded, then, according to our original principle of distributive justice, no injustice was committed in the hiring practice, and so no compensation is owed. Thus it might be reasoned that they should only be awarded jobs in the present for which they are as highly qualified as others.

This argument, however, is not compelling, given the shift in time reference. It could equally be reasoned along these lines that candidates should only *not* be awarded the positions denied to them in the past if it can be proved that they would in any case have been replaced by more highly qualified persons in the interim. (In such a case they would even have monetary compensation coming to them.)

Seemingly more important here is the argument that, if past victims of discrimination are now awarded jobs for which others are more highly qualified, then those others will suffer injustice from the point of view of distributive justice, and will thus have compensation owed *them*. Michael Bayles argues[16] that these latter individuals as a group suffer no injustice because the practice is, overall, just; but, taken by itself, his argument holds no water against this claim. For one thing, it begs the question of whether the practice really is just; and for another, it ignores the fact that even overall just practices can involve injustices resulting in damages to some individuals for which compensation is then owed. Given, then, that these new damages would require compensation, new reverse discrimination would be owed the second set of persons. A progression of damages and compensations would be established until no jobs were being awarded on the basis of merit, as they all should be according to our original principle. It seems clear that this practice cannot be justified on the grounds of original and limited violation of the principle, and that compensation must therefore be in the form of jobs for which the applicants are maximally qualified.

On the other hand, the way to avoid this last argument as applied in this context is to hold that since the person discriminated against had a right to a job in the corporation in question, he or she still has a right to that same job, and so no opening exists at all in the present for which others can apply. Once individuals have justly acquired jobs, they do not lose their rights to these positions simply because others in the meantime have become somewhat more proficient. The utility that would be gained in competence would be more than offset by losses in job security if this were not admitted. Thus, once individuals have acquired rights to positions, they continue to have these rights, and this implies in the present context that individuals formerly discriminated against have rights to the first available similar positions in the corporations in question. In refusing to grant them jobs, the corporations would have to show that such positions no longer exist and cannot be reasonably created, and would then have to pay adequate monetary compensation. In regard to other individuals maximally competent for such positions in the present (assuming for the sake of argument that the positions do exist), they are being discriminated against and are owed compensation if minority-group members who were not previously unjustly denied jobs are now given these; but they are owed nothing if individuals who previously acquired rights to these positions now have those rights honored.

## IV

Our argument so far has established that compensation in the form of reverse discrimination is justified only for individuals actually discriminated against in the past. This does not take us very far in justifying the general practice of reverse discrimination. It certainly does not take us as far as most recent proponents advocate. Is there, then, any other way than to appeal to the principle of compensatory justice to justify a more widespread practice, or a practice applied to a minority group as a whole? It is sometimes suggested that the policy of reverse discrimination is necessary as a form of advertisement that discrimination with regard to certain types of jobs has ended. It is claimed that for jobs in which discrimination has long been practiced, simply ending the practice and following the principle of hiring by competence alone is not enough, for there will no longer be any qualified minority-group candidates applying. Proponents of this view argue that reverse discrimination is necessary to provide "role models" demonstrating that minority-group members can acquire and succeed at such positions. Such models are then held to be a necessary ingredient of the right to equality of opportunity. This claim is similar to the argument from motivational problems mentioned in section II, and the reply is the same. It seems to me, once again, that the additional advertisement to be gained from reverse discrimination does not justify the violation of the principle of distributive justice involved in its practice. Provided that we end all discrimination and give sufficient compensation where that is due, and provided that there are potential qualified minority-group candidates, I believe that a direct advertisement of an open policy is enough. Of course, direct advertisement can include encouragement or even recruitment of qualified minority-group applicants, which does not constitute reverse discrimination as long as the actual hiring is on the basis of competence alone.

The qualification "provided that there are potential qualified minority-group applicants" points, however, to another consideration relevant to the justification of reverse discrimination. Much discrimination, especially for the more socially prestigious positions in society, occurs not at the level of actual hiring practices, but at the level of denying equality of opportunity to acquire job competence—that is, it occurs in the educational system, especially in higher education (at least until recently). It is problems at the educational level, I believe, which will afford justification for reverse discrimination in job hiring for certain groups and certain individuals not actually discriminated against in the past. The groups and individuals for whom reverse discrimination is currently advocated and being practiced are, however, for the most part not those for whom I will suggest it may be justified.

First, it must be held (as I have already briefly argued in section II) that injustice at the level of equality of opportunity should be corrected or compensated at that level if possible. This is demanded first of all by the principle of compensation in kind, but even more importantly by the fact that compensation at that level is less likely to violate initial principles of distributive justice. This is partly because the educational system is more easily expanded than is the job market itself. Provided that the educational system can be expanded, educating or training those who have been unjustly denied the opportunity to acquire task competence is less likely to prevent that opportunity from being enjoyed in the present by some other potentially qualified individuals. Thus, compensation in the form of granting education or training to those who have been denied it may not have to constitute reverse discrimination at all at that level. This reaches its limits, however, in graduate and professional schools, where the size of a class should be limited by the potential job market for graduates. But even in that case, remedial programs can be instituted to raise the levels of competence of those previously denied educational opportunities. And if admissions to the schools themselves is still based upon relative qualifications, other candidates cannot legitimately complain. No one has a right to limited or restricted competition, and remedial programs for those previously discriminated against in education only stiffen the competition by allowing these people to compete fairly. Of course, given our prior arguments, admission to these programs must be based upon prior discrimination or disadvantage and not simply on race or sex. But keeping these criteria in mind, such programs provide the fairest and most fitting means of compensation at this level. Nor will society suffer by having persons without full qualifications filling positions of responsibility (which is the result of reverse discrimination at the level of job hiring).

Thus, these considerations of both distributive and compensatory justice demand that, if an individual is not highly qualified for a particular job because he has been denied the opportunity to acquire the qualifications, he should be afforded that opportunity now by the system or institution that denied it to him, rather than being awarded the job for which he is unqualified. Regarding other members of the group who are still at school and who have not yet been discriminated against, simply ending all discrimination at this level and providing for sufficient advertisement of that fact will in most cases ensure just treatment for them. The difficult cases in this area are those in which a person has been unjustly denied the opportunity to acquire qualifications for a particular position and is no longer able to acquire them (for example, because of age). Where such cases occur, various factors must be weighed in deciding whether simply to award the job to the person not maximally qualified. These include the responsibility involved in the job and the job's importance to society, the degree of qualification of the candidate, past damages to him, and the benefits or attractiveness of the job. In those cases in which the job carries heavy responsibility and there are others more qualified in important ways, fair monetary compensation is probably the best alternative if damages from unjust denial of equal opportunity can be shown. To take the case of a surgeon, no one would advocate awarding a position to an unqualified candidate on the grounds of discrimination in acceptance to medical schools, even if the candidate in question has clearly been discriminated against and can no longer afford to spend years studying. In the case of a desk job in a government office, on the other hand, denial of adequate training in the past may be grounds for simply awarding the position and training the person on the job in the present, if prior training is no longer feasible and there are numerous positions available. Utilitarian consideration of consequences, in other words, is all-important in these cases for deciding where justice lies.

This is not to suggest in general that questions of justice in this area reduce to questions of utility. Those concerned with political policy might consider reverse discrimination as a way to ease group pressures and create social harmony. These utilitarian benefits are themselves debatable, given backlash resentment aroused by the policy. In addition, utilitarian considerations should be distinguished from considerations regarding the rights of certain individuals to jobs according to the rule of hiring by competence, and the rights of others to compensation for prior infractions of that rule. While rights can be created or recognized in the name of various social values including welfare, they lose all meaning if they do not function to at least limit further application of utilitarian calculations. Questions of justice here are to be decided in terms of honoring rights, and not in terms of appeasing pressures or maximizing social harmony or welfare, although this is compatible with the justification of recognizing rights themselves partially in terms of utility.

## V

All along, I have been speaking of compensation to individuals actually discriminated against: I have gone no way toward other justification of reverse discrimination in hiring. This is because I argue that injustice at the level of equality of opportunity does not generally justify such a practice according to fair principles of compensation, especially if the injustice can be compensated at the prior level itself, which it most often can.

There was again an important qualification in the last argument, however, one which will open the way to that other justification of reverse discrimination for certain groups and individuals. I said there that ending discrimination at the level of education or training would ensure equality of opportunity for most, but this is not always the case. In regard especially to socially and economically depressed groups against whom there is a long history of discrimination at all levels, simply creating formal equality of means to education (and even making efforts to correct for initial inequalities within the educational system) is often not enough. Here, motivational problems resulting from deprived home environments are often obstinate and acute. It is a familiar story to those in the educational system (I speak here from the personal experience of a wife in the public school system of New York City) that children from socially deprived environments suffer problems of motivation and even aptitude and that extra effort at the level of education meets with failure more often than not. Reverse discrimination at the level of job hiring for the parents of such children, by raising the living standard in the long run, is perhaps the only way to prevent an endless progression of socially deprived generations, for whom the educational process fails even when seemingly fair. Here the practice of reverse discrimination directed toward economically deprived groups and toward individuals within those groups who are economically deprived can be justified not by any principle of compensatory justice, but as a means of creating that true equality of opportunity without which hiring by competence does not qualify as a fully valid principle of distributive justice in the first place.

This argument is easier to maintain in the context of an expanding economy. In a relatively stagnant situation, on the other hand, the problem is that giving the present poor decent jobs may lower others into that same situation. In a time of scarcity in which the number of jobs (and hence the number of unemployed) is fixed, awarding jobs to some will necessarily leave others without the means to self-support. Given losses in efficiency which generally follow from reverse discrimination in lieu of hiring by competence, not only will it then appear that nothing has been gained by this preferential policy, but there will appear to be losses, at least in welfare. Nevertheless, I maintain that there are differences between the chronic poor and socially deprived and others who may be temporarily unemployed, and I believe that these differences justify the policy even in times of scarcity. The main difference between the chronic and the newly poor relates precisely to the above-mentioned motivational problems of their children. I am not suggesting that giving parents of these children decent jobs will immediately cure the problems or alter attitudes ingrained by hundreds of years of injustice. But there seems no other first step out of an endless circle of poverty and unequal opportunity.

## VI

Thus, although the principle of compensatory justice demands that only particular individuals who have been discriminated against in the past receive reverse discrimination in the present, and although that principle to which appeal is usually made cannot justify a more widespread and extreme practice directed toward minority groups as a whole, the policy can be justified for additional individuals by appeal to the principle of equality of opportunity for the future. We might view this, too, as compensation for initially deprived environments and unequal chances, but the emphasis here is rather on the present state of current deprivation and on an attempt to break the chronic cycle for the benefit of future generations.

It must finally be noted that the practice of reverse discrimination as it is advocated and actually practiced is, for the most part (and with the exception of certain blue-collar industries like construction), unjustified, and even ironic, in relation to the above argument. For it is generally individuals who have not been discriminated against in the past, and whose children do not suffer from economically deprived environments, who are being awarded jobs in the name of the practice. Regarding women as a group, for example, I would hold that inequalities in the educational system and in hiring, as widespread as they may be, can be effectively ended. I think that reverse discrimination (on the principle that equality of opportunity must be created before job hiring by competence is fair) is not justified in the case of women as a group. It does not apply because women are not usually economically depressed so that their children suffer from poor environments. Regarding economically deprived groups, such as blacks, for whom that principle is relevant, members who are economically deprived should be given preference over those who are not when preferential policies are designed according to this second justification for the practice. That is, if we are to award jobs in order to create motivation and decent environments for the future, it is those who presently lack these benefits for whom special efforts should be made, even if these individuals deserve special treatment for no other reasons.

Social policies are in practice determined more by the articulateness and organization of the pressure groups advocating them than by rational considerations of justice. Thus, those organized enough to win special consideration are often those least deserving of it according to the above arguments. This is not to deny that discrimination has been practiced against these groups; it is only to claim that such unjust practices can often be ended directly on the level at which they occur, without further violation of fair principles of distributive justice. In all cases, it seems to me, the above arguments indicate that there are grounds for taking into account particular conditions and past histories of individuals for whom reverse discrimination is being considered—conditions beyond the fact that they are members of minority groups as these are usually defined.

## NOTES

1. See Robert Nozick, *Anarchy, State, and Utopia* (New York: Basic Books, 1974), part 2; also Judith Thomson, "Preferential Hiring," *Philosophy and Public Affairs* 2 (Summer 1973): 364–84.
2. See Thomas Nagel, "Equal Treatment and Compensatory Discrimination," *Philosophy and Public Affairs* 2 (Summer 1973): 348–63.
3. Nicholas Rescher, *Distributive Justice* (Indianapolis: Bobbs-Merrill, 1966), chaps. 1, 2, 5.
4. For a fuller discussion of this preliminary issue, see my "Justice

and Hiring by Competence," *American Philosophical Quarterly* 14 (January 1977).

5. J. W. Nickel, "Discrimination and Morally Relevant Characteristics," *Analysis* 32 (March 1972): 113–14.

6. J. L. Cowan, "Inverse Discrimination," *Analysis* 33 (October 1972): 10–12.

7. Paul Taylor, "Reverse Discrimination and Compensatory Justice," *Analysis* 33 (June 1973): 177–82.

8. See, for example, A. L. Bertrand, *Basic Sociology* (New York: Appleton-Century-Crofts, 1967), pp. 146–49; also F. L. Bates, "A Conceptual Analysis of Group Structure," *Social Forces* 36 (December 1957): 103–11.

9. This is the only restriction placed upon the definition of groups relevant to reverse discrimination in the previous literature. Thus, according to this distinction, simply the fact that a Jewish person was discriminated against does not give other Jews the right to reverse discrimination unless the person's being Jewish was the basis for the discrimination. I argue that this restriction upon the intensional definition of the group is not enough.

0. This is the position of Taylor, op. cit., p. 181.

1. This is the position of Michael Bayles, "Reparations to Wronged Groups," *Analysis* 33 (June 1973): 182–84. See also his "Compensatory Reverse Discrimination in Hiring," *Social Theory and Practice* 2 (Spring 1973): 301–12.

2. I exclude formal organizations of women or blacks, such as CORE. No one claims that compensation for discrimination is owed to such organizations, but to the broader groups they claim to represent.

3. Roger Shiner in "Individuals, Groups and Inverse Discrimination," *Analysis* 33 (June 1973): 185–87, admits that the statement "George deserves reverse discrimination because he is black" presupposes as an additional premise that all blacks have been discriminated against, but he seems to believe that the latter is true. I have claimed and will argue further that it is not true in the sense just defined, which is the only relevant sense.

4. For a fuller analysis of this point, see my "Reparations to Individuals or Groups?" *Analysis* 35 (April 1975): 168–70.

5. See Judith Thomson, op. cit., p. 381.

6. Michael Bayles, "Compensatory Reverse Discrimination in Hiring," op. cit., pp. 307–8. Bayles actually applies his argument only to the claim that the majority as a group is not wronged by reverse discrimination in favor of the minority. Since no groups of this type are wronged by any discrimination, I would agree. But Bayles does not show that reverse discrimination of the type being discussed does not involve an infinite regress of damages.

# Equal Opportunity and Preferential Hiring

# *Further References*

Starred items are those of philosophical interest.

*Aristotle. *Politics*. Book 1, chapters 1–7, 12, 13.
*Bayles, Michael. "Compensatory Reverse Discrimination in Hir ing." *Social Theory and Practice* 2:3 (Spring 1973): 301–12.
*————. "Reparations to Wronged Groups." *Analysis* 33:6 (1972) 182–84.
*Bedau, Hugo Adam. "Compensatory Justice and the Black Man festo." *Monist* 56 (1972): 20–42.
*Bhattacharya, R. D. "Because He Is a Man." *Philosophy* 49 (Jar uary 1974): 96.
Bittker, Boris I. *The Case for Black Reparations*. New York: Rar dom House, 1973.
*Black, Virginia. "The Erosion of Legal Principles in the Creatio of Legal Policies." *Ethics* 84:2 (January 1974): 93–115.
*Blackstone, William T. "Reverse Discrimination and Compensa tory Justice." *Social Theory and Practice* 3 (Spring 1975): 253 88.
*Boxhill, Bernard K. "The Morality of Reparation." In *Today Moral Problems*, edited by Richard Wasserstrom. New York Macmillan, 1975.
Brown, Barbara; Emerson, Thomas I.; Falk, Gail; and Freedmar Anne E. "The Equal Rights Amendment: A Constitutional Bas for Equal Rights for Women." *Yale Law Journal* 80 (1970–71) 871–985.
*Cowan, J. L. "Inverse Discrimination." *Analysis* 33 (1972): 10–1
Ely, John Hart. "The Constitutionality of Reverse Discrimination *University of Chicago Law Review* 41 (Summer 1974): 723–41.

*Ezorsky, Gertrude. "The Fight over University Women." *New York Review of Books*, 16 May 1974, pp. 32–39.

*———. "It's Mine." *Philosophy and Public Affairs* 3 (Spring 1974): 321–30.

Fiss, Owen M. "A Theory of Fair Employment Laws." *University of Chicago Law Review* 38 (1971): 235–314.

*Fried, Marlene. "In Defense of Preferential Hiring." *Philosophical Forum* 5:1–2 (Fall-Winter 1973–74): 289–93.

*Fullinwider, Robert. "Preferential Hiring and Compensation." *Social Theory and Practice* 3 (Spring 1975).

Ginsburg, Ruth Bader. "Equal Opportunity Free from Gender-Based Discrimination." *Key Reporter* 39:4 (Summer 1974): 2–4.

*Goldman, Alan. "Affirmative Action." To appear in a forthcoming *Philosophy and Public Affairs* reader.

*———. "Reparations to Individuals or Groups?" *Analysis* 35 (April 1975): 168–70.

*Govier, Trudy R. "Woman's Place." *Philosophy* 49 (July 1974): 303–9.

*Haack, Susan. "On the Moral Relevance of Sex." *Philosophy* 49 (January 1974): 90–95.

*Held, Virginia. "Reasonable Progress and Self-Respect." *Monist* 57:1 (January 1973): 12–27.

*Hill, Jim. "What Justice Requires: Some Comments on Professor Schoeman's Views on Compensatory Justice." *Personalist* 56:1 (Winter 1975): 96–103.

Hughes, G. "The Right to Special Treatment." In *The Rights of Americans: What They Are, What They Should Be*, edited by Norman Dorson. New York: Pantheon Books, 1971.

*Lucas, J. R. "Against Equality." In *Justice and Equality*, edited by Hugo Bedau. Englewood Cliffs, N.J.: Prentice-Hall, 1971.

*———. "Because You Are a Woman." *Philosophy* 48 (April 1973): 161–71.

*Ludwig, Jan, and Enteman, Willard. Unpublished, untitled piece on preferential hiring. Schenectady, N.Y.: Union College, Department of Philosophy, 1975.

*Martin, Michael. "Pedagogical Arguments for Preferential Hiring and Tenuring of Women Teachers in the University." *Philosophical Forum* 5:1–2 (Fall-Winter 1973–74): 297–307.

*Mill, John Stuart. *The Subjection of Women*. 1869. Reprint. Cambridge, Mass.: MIT Press, 1970.

*Nagel, Thomas. "Equal Treatment and Compensatory Discrimination." *Philosophy and Public Affairs* 2:4 (Summer 1973): 348–63.

*Newton, Lisa H. "Reverse Discrimination As Unjustified." *Ethics* 83:4 (July 1973): 308–12.

*Nickel, James W. "Classification by Race in Compensatory Programs." *Ethics* 84 (January 1974): 146–50.

*————. "Discrimination and Morally Relevant Characteristics." *Analysis* 32:4 (1972): 113–14.

O'Neill, Robert. "Preferential Admissions: Equalizing the Access of Minority Groups to Higher Education." *Yale Law Journal* 80 (1970–71): 699–767.

*Pierce, Christine. "Equality: *Republic* V." *Monist* 57:1 (1973): 1–11.

*Plato. *Republic*. Book 5.

Richards, David A. J. "Equal Opportunity and School Financing: Towards a Moral Theory of Constitutional Adjudication." *University of Chicago Law Review* 41:1 (Fall 1973): 32–71.

Rossi, Alice. "Equality between the Sexes: An Immodest Proposal." *Daedalus* 93:2 (1964): 607–52. (Bobbs-Merrill reprint S-750.)

*Shiner, Roger A. "Individuals, Groups and Inverse Discrimination." *Analysis* 33:6 (1973): 185–87.

*Shoeman, Ferdinand. "When Is It Just to Discriminate?" Paper read at American Philosophical Association, Western Division Meetings, St. Louis, April 1974.

*Silvestri, Robert. "The Justification of Inverse Discrimination." *Analysis* 34 (1973): 31.

*Simon, Robert. "Preferential Hiring." *Philosophy and Public Affairs* 3:3 (Spring 1974): 312–30.

Stegeman, Beatrice. "The Preference Problem." Unpublished. Available from 306 Dana Street, Collinsville, Ill. 62234.

*Taylor, Paul W. "Reverse Discrimination and Compensatory Justice." *Analysis* 33:6 (1973): 177–82.

*Thalberg, Irving. "Reverse Discrimination and the Future." *Philosophical Forum* 5:1–2 (Fall-Winter 1973–74): 263–81.

*Thomson, Judith. "Preferential Hiring." *Philosophy and Public Affairs* 2:4 (Summer 1973): 364–84.

*Vetterling, Mary K. "Some Common Sense Notes on Preferential Hiring." *Philosophical Forum* 5:1–2 (Fall-Winter 1973–74): 294–97.

*Wasserstrom, Richard. "Rights, Human Rights and Racial Discrimination." In *Moral Problems*, 2d ed., edited by James Rachels. New York: Harper & Row, 1975.

*Williams, Bernard A. O. "The Idea of Equality." In *Justice and Equality*, edited by Hugo Bedau. Englewood Cliffs, N.J.: Prentice-Hall, 1971.

Part V

# Marriage

# Part V

# Marriage

## Introduction

The ideology that surrounds marriage accounts for a significant portion of the thinking on sex roles and gender discussed earlier in Part II: women are expected to be homemakers and mothers; men are expected to be breadwinners and fathers. The movement toward greater sexual equality has led not only to linguistic innovations (see Part III) and to the demand for greater job opportunities (see Part IV), but also to new terms for the marriage contract. Such changes pose a complex set of interrelated conceptual and moral dilemmas. Is marriage necessarily exploitive and oppressive for women? Does it have to be heterosexual and exclusive, or are lesbian and multilateral marriages possible and desirable? What can legitimately be expected of marriage? How is it related to the family, and how could or should this relationship be changed?

LYLA H. O'DRISCOLL provides an analysis of marriage both as a legal institution in our culture and as a social institution more generally, and offers a defense of it based on friendship. Heterosexual monogamy, she points out, is the only form of marriage recognized by our laws. These require that the partners be of the opposite sex, that they be at least two and no more than two, that they not be blood relatives, that they be a minimum legal age, and that they freely consent to the marriage contract. No matter what form it takes (polyandry, polygamy, and multilateral marriages, though illegal, are still forms of marriage), marriage can be recognized across cultures by its two functions: to confer legitimacy on progeny and on sexual liaisons. Whatever its instrumental value in promoting these or other social ends, O'Driscoll argues that it can have intrinsic value as an expression of friendship. By contrast to the impersonal functional encounters that typify so much of our social life, friendship is distinguished by respect and trust, by a desire to be together and to help one another not because of self-interest but because of genuine affection. As a locus for friendship, marriage can have intrinsic value—whether it be heterosexual or homosexual, monogamous or polygamous.

O'Driscoll's reconceptionalization of the importance of marriage generates a paradox, however: friendship is essentially a personal and private relationship, yet marriage is essentially a legal and public institution. Is the legal regulation of such an intimate affair within the scope of social criticism? SARA ANN KETCHUM assesses some liberal arguments that try to justify a negative response to this question even in the face of obvious sexual inequities.

Under our present practices, marriage is not an equal-opportunity employer. The traditional division of labor within marriage typically imposes greater burdens on the wife than on the husband. This inequity is compounded by legal ones that Ketchum emphasizes: marriage fails to provide women with the protection of the law they would otherwise enjoy against physical and psychological abuse (husbands, for example, cannot be charged with raping their wives). The marriage contract itself violates three general principles regulating contracts: the religious embellishment and romantic mystification of the matrimonial service discourage people from reading the contract carefully in order that their consent be both free and informed; the roles of the contractees are not negotiable but are dictated by the biological contingencies of birth; and the allocation of duties and rights is fixed—unlike most contracts, where the terms can be altered by mutual agreement.

Can these marital injustices and anomalies be defended? Liberal theorists, who are usually harsh critics of unfair legal practices, have tended to place marriage and the family beyond the purview of political criticism by relegating them to the private sphere. Such avoidance of the issue might be dismissed as simply the male-chauvinistic bias of sexist liberal theories. Nevertheless, Ketchum gives serious consideration to three common defenses for this limitation of otherwise universal principles of justice and equality: marriage is too central to the fabric of society to alter; as a religious sacrament it falls outside the law; and as an expression of personal affection it is immune to ordinary moral principles.

She is critical of all three defenses. The first ignores research now under way and could analogously lead to the reductio ad absurdum justification of slavery. The second violates the principle of the separation of state and church by legislating simply one group's religious preference for a form of marriage. The third relies on the problematical psychological thesis that inequities promote love, and it inconsistently ignores the actual legal regulation of present marital inequities.

Our thinking about marriage is further confused by two myths that tie it to completeness and the family. JOSEPH BARNHART and MARY ANN BARNHART explode one of these— the myth that marriage is the path to fulfillment. Whereas religion had once been regarded as the way to full personhood, a secularized society came to impose this function on the institution of marriage. Individuals are treated as incomplete by themselves, in need of a unity with some other of the opposite sex, the full richness of which unity only monogamy can provide. According to the Barnharts, the ironic result of this myth is the opposite of its intent: in fact, marriage leads to a reliance on another which may frustrate human growth. Paradoxically, the exit from marriage is also seen in these terms: divorce is regarded by many as freedom from dependence on a spouse and hence a step toward complete independence. This myth about divorce likewise ignores the social context of everyday life, the matrices of interpersonal relations with varying degrees of dependence from which it is impossible to extricate oneself. A more realistic view of marriage requires that we rid ourselves of this myth of completeness through a conjugal partner, for to be human is to be incomplete.

A second myth that has confused our thinking about marriage and limited its positive value is its reputed inseparability from the family. JOSEPH MARGOLIS and CLORINDA MARGOLIS argue that the conceptual separation of these two institutions has become a practical one through advancing technology. The pill, artificial insemination by a donor, and other scientific developments have made marriages without children and families without marriages more feasible.

According to the Margolises, the social and conceptual possibilities are far-reaching. Changes in taxation laws, adoption procedures, and divorce regulations could be tried. The concepts of adultery, open marriage, trial marriage, group marriage, and homosexual marriage would need to be rethought as contractual relationships. Adultery, for example, would not necessarily be prima facie immoral, since whether or not it is a breach of promise would depend on the nature of the marriage contract.

Experiments in alternative life styles are now under way. Their value can only be assessed through the test of time—not through independent religious pronouncements that assert the divinely sanctioned inseparability of these two institutions. To recognize and dispel the myths that surround marriage is to clear the way for these experiments.

F. E.

Lyla H. O'Driscoll

# On the Nature and Value of Marriage

[Marriage] should be a school of sympathy in equality, of living together in love, without power on one side or obedience on the other.

> John Stuart Mill
> *On the Subjection of Women*

[The married woman] is locked into a relationship which is oppressive politically, exhausting physically, stereotyped emotionally and sexually, and atrophying intellectually.

> Judith Brown
> *Toward a Female Liberation Movement*

Marriage—recently condemned as psychologically destructive, as socially pointless or ineffective, as oppressive, sexist, and morally repugnant—is the focus of new and lively scholarly and popular controversy.[1] This paper is an attempt to clarify some of the issues comprehended in this debate, in particular, certain conceptual issues that seem to have been neglected or misconstrued by both advocates and critics of marriage. The marriage controversy is not merely conceptual, of course; normative issues, including the justifiability of the institution, are familiar themes in the debate. Formulation of normative issues involves

---

I would like to thank Robert Hollinger, Gerald P. O'Driscoll, Jr., Warren S. Quinn, Alyce Vrolyk, and Virginia Warren for helpful comments on earlier versions of this paper.

conceptual assumptions, however, including assumptions about the kinds of value that institutions and formal relations might have.

This paper does not directly treat the justifiability of marriage. Instead, it attempts to articulate a concept of marriage and suggests that partisans on both sides of the controversy, in conceiving of marriage as an instrument, have misjudged its value. The discussion may have some significance for the issue of justification, however: without a clearly formulated concept of marriage and of the kinds of value it might have, attempts to assess its justifiability are likely to be futile.

# I

One concept of marriage is the legal concept. Since the Anglo-American institution of heterosexual monogamy is frequently a target of criticism, it will be examined in order to ascertain some of the features of marriage as a legal institution.

According to Anglo-American custom and law, marriage is a social and legal status brought into existence by a civil contract. In the standard case, a marriage originates in a properly witnessed formal contract (distinct from any antenuptial financial contract) entered into by two persons, one male and one female; each party must be of legal age, must possess other requisites of contractual capacity, and must freely consent to the agreement.

The contract initiating a marriage differs in several ways from an ordinary business contract. Contracting a marriage requires the performance of special formalities; the contract cannot be terminated or rendered void except by action of a competent official. Business contractors have considerable leeway in formulating the terms of their agreement; those who contract a marriage are limited to the terms uniformly specified by law. The requirements of contractual capacity are especially stringent for marriage contracts. Marriage contractors are prohibited from having certain degrees of blood kinship and may be required to submit to a physician's examination. Furthermore, marriage contractors may have no prior marital relationships (unless legally dissolved), no concurrent marriages, and must enter the contractual relationship in pairs consisting of one male and one female.[2]

Each party to the marriage contract obtains certain rights and

duties, including rights regarding support, fidelity, companionship, sexual congress, inheritance, confidentiality, and protection from interference by third parties.[3] In some cases, spouses
choose not to seek enforcement of these rights; persons may
even enter the legal relation intending not to seek enforcement
—as in the case of a marriage of convenience or marriage to
prevent the deportation of one contractor.

In jurisdictions recognizing common-law marriage, mutual
rights to support, companionship, sexual congress, inheritance,
etc. arise from an overt agreement to become spouses, cohabitation over a legally specified period of time, and public presentation and reputation as spouses.[4]

A leading English case characterizes marriage as "the voluntary union for life of one man and one woman, to the exclusion
of all others."[5] The accuracy of the restriction, "for life," is
dubious, for even at the time of the decision (1866), divorce
was legal in England.[6]

English and American jurists disagree about whether procreation is a principal end of marriage. The leading English case is
a 1948 ruling that one spouse's insistence on the use of contraceptives did not constitute willful refusal to consummate the
marriage. The judge pointed out that

the institution of marriage generally is not necessary for the procreation of children; nor does it appear to be a principal end of marriage
as understood in Christendom. . . . In any view of Christian marriage, the essence of the matter, as it seems to me, is that the children, *if there be any*, should be born into a family, as that word is
understood in Christendom generally, and in the case of a marriage
between spouses of a particular faith that they should be brought up
and nurtured in that faith. But this is not the same thing as saying
that a marriage is not consummated or that procreation is the principal end of marriage.[7]

The judge also noted that it was not alleged in the suit that the
sterility of a husband or the barrenness of a wife had some
bearing on the question whether a marriage had been consummated.[8]

In the past, American jurists have regarded procreation as
"the controlling purpose" of marriage, ruling that a wife's refusal to engage in uncontracepted intercourse constituted deser-
tion of her husband or cruelty to him. In another case, the
wife's refusal was adjudged a breach of her marital obligations
and resulted in dismissal of her suit for separation and sup-

port.[9] Although a few jurisdictions have even ruled that a spouse's premarital sterility renders a marriage void, most have concurred with recent decisions more carefully distinguishing canon law from civil law and rejecting the claim that in civil law procreation is the chief end of marriage.[10]

A recent decision in a suit requesting legal recognition of homosexual alliances was rejected on the grounds that the common usage of the term "marriage" restricted its application to unions of persons of opposite sexes and that marriage is a union "uniquely involving procreation."[11]

The advocacy and existence of deliberately child-free marriages controverts the traditional assumption that the "unique involvement" of procreation in marriage is that it is the *purpose* of marriage. It also controverts the assumption that there is a necessary connection between the intention to become spouses and the intention to become parents. Once those assumptions are discarded, one rationale for nonrecognition of homosexual alliances is weakened.

The characterization of marriage as a legal institution is one concept of marriage; or, to be more precise, it is a concept of a form of marriage. Nonterminable, monogamous heterosexual marriage is one form of marriage. The qualifications can be variously altered to specify other logically possible forms of marriage. Legal recognition of polyandry, for example, could be accomplished by altering the rules of contractual capacity so that a female could maintain prior or concurrent marital relationships. Legal recognition of homosexual monogamy could be accomplished by abolition of the requirement that persons enter the relationship in pairs consisting of one male and one female.

A multilateral marriage, which consists of three or more partners, "each of whom considers himself/herself to be married (or committed in a functionally analogous way) to more than one of the other partners,"[12] could be legally recognized if the requirement of pairing were deleted and the requirement that spouses have no previous or concurrent marriages were deleted. (Multilateral marriage is distinct from polygyny, the marriage of one male to more than one female, and from polyandry. In polygyny, the females are not married to more than one person. It is characteristic of multilateral marriage that each spouse has more than one spouse.)

Successful criticisms of heterosexual monogamy do not suffice to demonstrate the unacceptability of the institution of marriage any more than successful criticisms of absolute monarchy demonstrate the unacceptability of the institution of government. The concept of marriage is more abstract and general than the concept of heterosexual monogamy. Thus, for example, John McMurtry's critique of heterosexual monogamy, if well taken, demonstrates at most the unacceptability of that form of marriage (and then only when it has the consequences he attributes to it.)[13]

Some constituents of the legal characterization of the institution, including the restriction of entry to male-female pairs, are not part of the concept of marriage. Other features characterize marriage as a legal institution, regardless of form: in law, marriage is a formalized relationship between legal adults, initiated by a more or less explicit agreement, and defined by legally specified rights and duties.

## II

Although they are important, the legal aspects of marriage do not exhaust the concept of marriage. A broader conceptual problem remains, and it is one that cannot be resolved by a descriptive study of marriage in various cultures, a study in which common features, if any, are noted and combined as the essence of marriage.

Indeed, resolution of the broader conceptual problem is logically prior to empirical or descriptive study of the institution. The conceptual problem here is one of discerning the characteristics that distinguish a society having an institution of marriage from one lacking it. It is also a problem of determining what features of human association would have to be examined in order to resolve the question whether the institution of marriage exists.

Part of the solution to the broader conceptual problem is evident enough: whatever else it is, marriage is a social institution. The marital relation is not captured in a catalogue of changes in the spatial and temporal locations of human bodies; still less is it comprehended in a list of pieces of behavior. Marriage is a social institution that typically regulates (some) sexual activities and (in some way) the production of offspring. Marriage is of course not the only social institution that serves these functions. In order to determine whether the institution of marriage exists in a society, however, one would examine the social institutions that regulate sexual conduct and procreation.

The difference between a society with marriage and one without it is that in the former the rules constituting an existing social institution distinguish between illegitimate and legitimate progeny and characterize actual or possible instances of sexual congress as conjugal relations. The institution of marriage is partly constituted by rules that structure certain activities and define certain roles. Two-party heterosexual copulation, for example, cannot be adultery unless one of the participants is the spouse of a nonparticipant; it cannot be an instance of conjugal relations unless the participants are married to one another. Other activities structured by the rules constituting marriage include courtship, engagement, payment of dowry, divorce, and bigamy. By reference to the rules defining marriage, the bachelor can be distinguished from the husband, the spinster from the wife, the fiancée from the divorcée, the in-law from the parent, the bastard from the legitimate offspring.

Whatever its form, marriage is a social institution in which sexual intercourse is socially and legally legitimate and in which the production of socially and legally legitimate offspring is possible. Until effective contraception was generally available, it was tempting, in view of the connection between marriage and the production of *legitimate* offspring, to regard procreation as the purpose of marriage. It is important, however, to distinguish the device used to identify an institution as marriage from a specification of the purpose of the institution. The logical connection between marriage and procreation is not that procreation is the purpose of marriage but that it is in marriage that legitimate offspring can be produced.

Social and legal legitimacy are not always all-or-nothing matters. Some societies have not only marriages that confer full legitimacy on sexual intercourse and offspring but also legally recognized systems of concubinage. The legitimacy of sexual congress with a concubine and of the offspring of such a union may be more social than legal, but the relationship is nevertheless distinguished from, and more legitimate than, casual, fleeting sexual encounters or incestuous relationships.[14]

This concept of marriage, an explication by reference to the social functions of the institution, provides a general characterization compatible with the logical possibility of various forms of marriage and usable in deciding whether the institution exists in a particular society. A society lacks the institution if there is no social institution by reference to which one can distinguish conjugal and nonconjugal relations, legitimate offspring and bastards. (Such a society can nevertheless have rules to distinguish rape from consensual intercourse.)

Articulation of this concept of marriage will not end the marriage controversy, but it does indicate that the disputants may share some common ground. Critics of marriage have not generally advocated a society in which marriage does not exist, although some have ventured in the direction of such a proposal.[15] Individuals on both sides of the marriage controversy largely agree that a society will (and perhaps even should) have an institution or institutions to perform these functions.

Part of the marriage controversy is a dispute about whether the institution or institutions performing these functions should be legally defined and should be limited by law to a single form. Another aspect of the dispute focuses on the fact that if spouses become parents, they customarily take on the task of rearing the young. Some, who claim that the additional burden of childrearing inflicts excessive strain on marriages, suggest that this function can and should be separated from the legitimating function of marriage.

The purpose of this paper is not to resolve these disputes, but to formulate the issues more clearly and precisely so that others may approach them with a greater awareness of what is at stake.

## III

Participants in the marriage controversy frequently assimilate the question of the justifiability of the institution with the question of the aptness of the institution as a means to the achievement of certain good ends such as human happiness. The issue is then treated as a problem of assessing the costs and benefits of particular arrangements, a problem whose resolution depends essentially on empirical evidence regarding the effects of the arrangements on the psychological, pecuniary, legal, and social well-being of spouses and offspring, and evidence regarding social advantages and disadvantages. Much of the feminist critique of heterosexual monogamy originates in such considerations.

But the issue of the justifiability of the institution is not as simple as this assimilation suggests. Among the complexities is the possibility that a marriage can be good even if its goodness does not lie solely in its aptness as a means of advancing good ends. Not all value is instrumental; the value of marriage, for the spouses, may lie not merely in what it *does* or can do (i.e., the effects it has) but in what it *is* or can be.

I would like to suggest that as an expression of friendship, marriage can have intrinsic value. I do not wish to deny, of course, that marriage can have instrumental value; the suggestion, rather, is that its instrumental value is not its only possible value.[16]

The thesis that marriage can have noninstrumental value for spouses is distinct from the claim that marriage is morally valuable. Something intrinsically valuable is valuable in itself, valuable because of its intrinsic properties, not because of its effects; something morally valuable is good on moral grounds, for example, its aptness as a means to morally praiseworthy ends. Something can be intrinsically good without being morally good; in the view of the hedonistic utilitarian, for example, pleasure is intrinsically and nonmorally good.[17]

It is evident that expressions of friendship can have noninstrumental value. A service performed as a gesture of friendship, for example, can be instrumentally useful, and can also be valuable because it is done by a certain person out of certain motives. In such gestures, friendship can be expressed for its own sake and not for the sake of some external objective. The pledge of marriage can be a gesture of friendship; it creates a public and relatively permanent arrangement that symbolizes the dispositions and attitudes constitutive of friendship.

It might be thought that to characterize the marriage pledge and status as expressions of friendship trivializes the relationship between spouses, reducing it to "mere friendship." To suppose this is to confuse merely being friendly and being friends. Although friendships vary in the degree of affection, intimacy, sharing, and trust involved, these attitudes and behavior are essential to friendship; in the paradigm case—close (but not the closest possible) friendship—the depth of affection amounts to love.

## IV

The difference between friendship and ordinary social associations, as described by Kant, is that in ordinary social associations

we do not enter completely into the social relation. The greater part of our disposition is withheld; there is no immediate outpouring of our feelings, dispositions and judgments. We voice only the judgments that seem advisable in the circumstances. A constraint, a mistrust of others, rests upon all of us, so that we withhold something, concealing our weaknesses to escape contempt, or even withholding our opinions.[18]

If marriage is to express friendship, friendship must exist; if there is to be friendship, certain attitudes must exist and certain kinds of shared activities must occur.[19] Two persons are friends if and only if, first, they regard one another as worthy of respect and trust; second, they are disposed to seek one another's company (for the sake of *that person's* company, not merely for the sake of company); third, they are disposed to seek one another's well-being; and fourth, they have these dispositions because they are fond of one another.

A marriage that expresses friendship reveals and symbolizes attitudes such as affection for and commitment to a particular person. Such a relation is necessarily personal. Affection *for a person* is distinct from regard for someone's virtues and admiration for someone's characteristics, although it may be causally connected with these virtues and characteristics. Admiration and approval of a person's characteristics diminish if the characteristics dwindle; admiration of an artist's ability declines with the artist's declining skill. Affection for a person, on the other hand, does not diminish in the face of diminution of admired and approved qualities in the person. Love of a person, as Shakespeare points out, does not alter when it alteration finds. Affection for a person applies to a particular being; it cannot be automatically transferred to another instantiation of similar characteristics.[20]

Mutual trust and respect underlie the sharing of confidences that is typical of friends. Friendship between two persons entails the existence of durable tendencies; the affection of friends is not transitory fondness or attraction, nor is it unrequited.

Friends do not value one another primarily or merely as means; someone who values another primarily or merely because he has certain instrumentally useful traits values him as an instrument. If customer Jones's association with grocer Smith is primarily or solely instrumentally valuable to both parties, each individual, as far as the other is concerned, is a replaceable component in the arrangement. It is a matter of indifference to Smith whether Jones or some other equally good instrument occupies the role of customer; Jones is indifferent to the particular person occupying the grocer's role, as long as the services are efficiently provided.

In short, if people value one another's characteristics as instruments, their relation is essentially impersonal, not a valuing of a particular person, but an appreciation of the usefulness of certain traits that happen to be embodied in one person but would be equally valuable if found in another. Smith values Jones's patronage, the business he brings to the store; Smith would value equally any other instantiation of the properties that make Jones a good customer. Likewise, Jones values the performance of certain services, and would value equally another instantiation of the characteristics that make Smith a good grocer.

The importance of affection in marriage is often confined to or confused with the importance of erotic love. Although erotic love is one facet of marital affection, others include the tendency to find companionship in one's spouse's company (*philia*) and the tendency to give oneself nonsexually and unselfishly—to invest oneself in the relationship.

Activities, including sexual activities, are enhanced in value by being shared with, or done for, the sake of someone of whom the agent is fond. Sexual desire can of course be satisfied in casual encounters. But the mutual respect, trust, and affection that subsist between friends can render sexual activity intrinsically as well as instrumentally valuable—valued because it is shared with a valued individual.[21]

Friends are not necessarily of the same sex; nor are friends necessarily of opposite sexes.

Friendship is neither exclusive nor necessarily transitive. Someone may have several friends, including people who are not mutual friends. It is unlikely, however, that anyone could maintain a large number of close friendships. The problem is not conceptual but empirical: intimacy and intense affection are psychologically demanding and can probably subsist only in small groups.

Not all affectionate relationships are friendships. A parent may be fond of a newborn child. Since the affection is not reciprocated and since mutual trust and respect are not possible, the relationship is not friendship.

Friends need not have made a formal or explicit pledge of friendship. In some cases, one's commitment to a friend is simply a tendency to seek his well-being for his sake. This tendency may exist without having been deliberately cultivated; the principle of action may be unformulated, and the agent may even be unable to formulate it. If the agent's behavior, attitudes, and beliefs are generally consistent with his regarding the other's well-being as a good, and if the agent is disposed to alter his behavior, attitudes, and beliefs to conform to the belief that the other person's well-being is a good, then the person may be characterized as having an inchoate principle of action committing him to seek the other person's good for that person's sake.

Implicit commitment to a friend may consist of a tendency, should the occasion arise, upon reflection to admit the existence of activities, attitudes, and dispositions essential to friendship and to identify the other as a friend.[22] There is a sense, therefore, in which friendship can be initiated and terminated voluntarily. Upon becoming aware of the existence of the relevant attitudes, dispositions, and activities, one can choose to discontinue the activities and seek to eradicate or modify the attitudes and dispositions. Such a choice amounts to refusing to make an explicit commitment to the person, a refusal to affirm the dispositions, attitudes, and activities of friendship, and a refusal to sustain a friendship.

On the other hand, people might choose to affirm the relationship, and furthermore to formalize it in a ceremony such as the ritual of blood brotherhood. Such a public declaration is a fully explicit statement of a willingness to pursue mutual well-being; it is a joint pledge of continuing association, loyalty, and fidelity. A public declaration is not necessary in order to make such a commitment explicit, but it can serve to distinguish an especially serious and significant friendship from other associations.

At any of these levels of explicitness, the commitment of friendship need not be a commitment to the exclusivity of the friendship: even when one has publicly declared the great significance of a particular friendship, it is logically possible to ascribe (and to declare publicly) the equal significance of another friendship.

## V

Marriage can single out an especially significant friendship (if monogamous) or especially significant friendships (if multilateral, polygamous, or polyandrous); it can distinguish such relationships from less profound, serious, and durable affections and commitments.

As has been pointed out, friends are disposed to seek one another's company and well-being, and they have these tendencies because they are fond of one another. Between (or among) friends, these dispositions may be manifested in the desire to share domicile and in the desire of each to participate fully in the achievement of the other's aspirations and the execution of the other's plans—the desire to share in the other's life and (good or ill) fortune. Individuals having these desires might reasonably choose a formal declaration to express, affirm, and cement their intentions, and their commitment to, and affection for, one another. They regard their relationship, and its formal expression, as having intrinsic value.

Their willingness to declare their intention to pursue joint well-being openly and in a way that creates legal and moral obligations signifies their confidence in the durability and importance of the relationship. Their willingness to make such a declaration also signifies their willingness to risk censure, from their spouses or from others, should they fail to fulfill their obligations; and it also signifies their willingness to have these obligations enforced. The willingness of friends to make such a declaration and to undertake such obligations signifies their willingness to share in one another's good (or ill) fortune, and to incur the risks inherent in an enduring and legally recognized relationship, including the risk that pursuit of mutual well-being will necessitate some compromise and sacrifice of individual well-being.[23]

No one marries all his friends, not even all his especially significant friends. But considerations of the intrinsic value of the relationship might, in some (rare) cases, account for the decision to marry. Such considerations could provide a satisfactory reason for initiating or continuing a marriage if they were (as they usually are) conjoined with judgments about the instrumental value of a legally recognized bond (for example, the supposition that the special legal and social status accorded to spouses fosters a stable, profound, and enduring affection and enhances the attitudes and commitments of friendship).

Marriage expressive of friendship can be heterosexual, homosexual, multilateral, polygynous, or polyandrous. Thus, this account of the nature and possible value of marriage for spouses is compatible with the conceivability of a variety of forms of marriage.

This discussion is not intended as proof of the justifiability of the institution of marriage. I have considered its possible value for spouses. It may be that the intrinsic value of the relationship for spouses is insufficient to show the institution acceptable from a moral point of view; there may be overriding objections based on other considerations. I have attempted only to outline a different perspective for the assessment of marriage, to suggest that the value of marriage, for spouses, may be intrinsic as well as instrumental.

## NOTES

1. Instances of such criticisms can be found in the following: Robin Morgan, ed., *Sisterhood Is Powerful* (New York: Random House, Vintage Books, 1970), pp. 438–54, 514–48; Vivian Gornick and Barbara K. Moran, eds., *Woman in Sexist Society* (New York: New American Library, Mentor Books, 1971), pp. xxvi, 145–86. On the legal effects of marriage on women, see Leo Kanowitz, *Women and the Law* (Albuquerque: University of New Mexico Press, 1969), chap. 3.
2. P. M. Bromley, *Family Law* (London: Butterworth, 1971), pp. 11–12.
3. Morris Ploscowe, Henry H. Foster, Jr., and Doris Jonas Fried, *Family Law* (Boston: Little, Brown, 1972), p. 43.
4. Ibid., pp. 79–81. See also Stuart J. Stein, "Common Law Marriage," *Journal of Family Law* 9 (1970): 271–99.
5. Ploscowe, Foster, and Fried, pp. 16–17. The case is *Hyde* v. *Hyde*.
6. Bromley, p. 12.
7. J. C. Hall, *Sources of Family Law* (Cambridge: Cambridge University Press, 1966), p. 2. The case is *Baxter* v. *Baxter*. Emphasis added.
8. Hall, p. 2.

9. Joseph Goldstein and Jay Katz, *The Family and the Law* (New York: Free Press, 1965), pp. 823–28. The cases are *Raymond* v. *Raymond*, *Forbes* v. *Forbes*, and *Baretta* v. *Baretta*.

10. Goldstein and Katz, p. 816; Monrad G. Paulsen, Walter Walington, and Julius Goebel, Jr., *Domestic Relations*, 2d ed. (Mineola, N.Y.: Foundation Press, 1974), p. 155. The cases are *Van Nierke* v. *Van Nierke* and *T*. v. *M*.

11. Paulsen, Walington, and Goebel, pp. 35–36. The cast is *Baker* v. *Nelson*.

12. Larry Constantine and Joan Constantine, *Group Marriage* (New York: Macmillan, 1973), p. 28.

13. John McMurtry, "Monogamy: A Critique," *Monist* 56 (1972): 587–99; reprinted in *Philosophy and Sex*, ed. Robert Baker and Frederick Elliston (Buffalo, N.Y.: Prometheus Books, 1975). Other relevant essays in the same anthology are David Palmer, "The Consolation of the Wedded," and Michael D. Bayles, "Marriage, Love, and Procreation."

14. See William J. Goode, *World Revolution and Family Patterns* (New York: Free Press, 1963), pp. 282–85, on concubinage in China; and idem. *The Family* (Englewood Cliffs, N.J.: Prentice-Hall, 1964), chap. 3.

15. David E. Engdahl, "Medieval Metaphysics and English Marriage Laws," *Journal of Family Law* 8 (1969): 381–97.

16. The thesis that formalized relationships can be intrinsically valuable is defended in John Rawls, *A Theory of Justice* (Cambridge: Harvard University Press, 1971), pp. 520–29. In *An Anatomy of Values* (Cambridge: Harvard University Press, 1971), pp. 117–21, Charles Fried also defends this claim and applies it to legal institutions in general and to marriage in particular. Fried defines an *expressive* relation as one that has intrinsic value (p. 118n). In this discussion, however, "express" is used in the sense of "serving to manifest, reveal, or symbolize."

17. On the notion of intrinsic value, see William Frankena, *Ethics*, 2d ed. (Englewood Cliffs, N.J.: Prentice-Hall, 1973), p. 82.

18. Immanuel Kant, *Lectures on Ethics* (New York: Harper & Row, Harper Torchbooks, 1963), p. 205.

19. This account of friendship substantially follows Elizabeth Telfer, "Friendship," *Proceedings of the Aristotelian Society* 71 (1970–71): 222–41. The view is rooted in the doctrines of Kant and Aristotle. See especially Immanuel Kant, *The Metaphysical Principles of Virtue* (Indianapolis: Bobbs-Merrill, 1964), and Aristotle, *Nichomachean Ethics* (Indianapolis: Bobbs-Merrill, 1962), book 8.

20. Cf. Gregory Vlastos, "Justice and Equality," in *Social Justice*, ed. Richard B. Brandt (Englewood Cliffs, N.J.: Prentice-Hall,

Spectrum Books, 1962), pp. 43–44, and idem, "The Individual As an Object of Love in Plato," in *Platonic Studies* (Princeton: Princeton University Press, 1973), pp. 3–34.

21. Cf. Carl Cohen, "Sex, Birth Control and Human Life," *Ethics* 79 (1969): 257. Cohen argues for the intrinsic worth of sexual passion. In "Marriage, Love, and Procreation" (above, n. 13), pp. 197–98, Michael Bayles argues for the intrinsic value of relationships intentionally of indefinite duration, claiming that they are superior to relationships of intentionally limited duration.

22. See Fried (above, n. 16), pp. 23–24, for a formulation of the distinction between inchoate and implicit principles.

23. Bayles (above, n. 13), p. 198, adduces similar considerations in discussing the value of relationships that are intentionally of indefinite duration.

Sara Ann Ketchum

# Liberalism and Marriage Law

Liberals have traditionally excluded the institution of marriage from political criticism, partly on the grounds that the public/private split relegates marriage to the realm of the private and, hence, the apolitical and uncriticizable. In doing so, liberals have left uncriticized laws that enforce with respect to gender the institutionalization of the notion of a natural place assigned by birth which, when applied to class, was the original target of liberal theory. I will deal here with the tradition of granting to marriage law immunity from principles of equality and freedom. I will do this by indicating prima facie violations of basic liberal principles,[1] and then considering some of the arguments for making an exception to these principles in the case of laws regulating marriage.

Historically, standard liberal theories (and, in particular, social-contract theory) tend to leave marriage[2] out of both descriptions and principles which are nonetheless presented as universal in scope. The major starting point of 17th- and 18th-century social-contract theory is the principle (and/or descrip-

Earlier versions of this paper were read at the Oswego Women's Center, Oswego, New York, in March 1975, and at Alive and Kicking: Women's Studies at SUNY, held on the campus of the State University of New York at Albany in June 1976.

I would like to thank Christine Pierce for helpful discussion and comments on this paper.

tion) that in the state of nature everyone is equal;[3] that there is no natural authority, and there are no natural social bonds. However, many of these philosophers assume that husband and wife form a natural society and that the authority of husbands over wives is a natural authority.[4]

It is still taken by most liberal theory to be inappropriate to apply to marriage those principles of equality and liberty that are presented as universal and hence applied to all political and legal institutions. While classical liberal theory attacked the assumption that the natural authority of lords over serfs and of kings over subjects should be respected because it was natural and not to be interfered with,[5] they left the ideology of marriage more or less intact in that respect.

According to feudal thinking, who rules over whom is given by God and/or nature; authority is assigned by the natural place of classes of people rather than by individual inclination or merit. For this reason, political structures and the organization of society are not legitimately within the realm of human decision. The assumption that males, as such, rather than particular people, are naturally and ought to be the breadwinners and decision-makers within the family is theoretically parallel to the assumption that lords, regardless of their ability, ought to manage estates and rule over peasants.

## I. THE INCONSISTENCIES

If we treat these liberal assumptions as truly universal and apply them to marriage as a political institution, it would appear that the institution would violate, at least prima facie, some very basic liberal principles.

According to one standard form of liberal theory, there are some basic general rights that everyone has, simply in virtue of being human or in virtue of having some specific characteristic such as rationality or the capacity to make choices. One can give up a basic right or acquire new obligations and rights through a voluntary alienation of that right. The rights and duties of the marriage relationship are special, rather than general rights. That is, they apply to individuals in virtue of a special relationship, rather than to everyone as human beings or citizens. Thus, these obligations and rights arise out of the marriage contract or marriage vows. There are two sets of problems that emerge when we apply this liberal theory of contracts to the legal treatment of marriage: formal problems having to do with the conditions of entering the contract, and problems arising out of the substance or particular provisions of the contract.

### Formal Problems

(1) The special rights and obligations of marriage are defined by the laws regarding married persons of the state in which the married couple are living. A man and a woman place themselves under these laws by undergoing a marriage ceremony rather than by signing a contract that specifies these rights and duties in writing. Hence, the contract that would represent the legal relationship into which a couple enters upon getting married is one that is not easily available for perusal before signing. Certainly no one is required to read it or even encouraged to read it before entering into the contract;[6] nor are couples about to be married urged to consult a lawyer as are people about to make a will. The ceremony that commits them to the contractual relationship does not specify the legal duties of marriage. In many cases, the ceremony is identical with the ceremony connected to the religious sacrament of marriage, and, at best, describes the duties of marriage as a sacrament in that particular religion. Special effort may even be taken to obscure the fact that the marriage ceremony legally commits the couple to a contractual relationship; the reason offered may be that such a realization would dampen the religious or romantic fervor of the occasion. This practice is in conflict with the standard liberal and legal principle that a contract may be void if the contractees do not have the opportunity to read it or have it read to them before signing, since the validity of contracts depends on the free, informed consent of the contracting parties.

(2) One of the major aspects of marriage law that makes it feudal rather than liberal in nature is that the roles in the contract are set by birth.[7] It is not the case that, given the two terms of the contract, I could choose to contract to fulfill either the function of husband or that of wife, and the other contractee could also choose. Nor could I choose to enter into this contract with any consenting adult who is not prohibited by other contracts from entering such a contract; women are legally unable to enter into such a contract with other women and men with other men. With respect to a real-estate or employment contract, there is nothing about my birth that would make me

legally capable only of being the buyer or employee, or only of being the seller or employer. Similarly, there is no restriction that women can only sell to men, or blacks can only sell to whites. Such restrictions would, in these cases, be seen as clear violations of liberty and equality. However, in marriage law and in marriage contracts the roles are determined by birth because they are defined by sex, rather than by the function that people choose to, or are able to, fulfill. Legally, a wife is female, and no amount of housework and child care will make a man legally capable of falling under the provisions for wives; the husband's housework is legally a gift, while a wife who performs the same work is fulfilling her legal obligations.

(3) Not only is there no choice of roles within the contract, but there is also no choice of contracts.[8] One does not have a choice between *this* contract with unequal apportionment of duties and an alternative contract that spells out an equal division of rights and duties. Presumably, one reason for having a uniform contract is that it is feared that the results of freedom of choice would be chaos. However, the law currently allows for individualized wills and individualized business contracts without undue stress. For those couples who do not devise their own contract, the law could provide a standard contract that would be analogous to laws covering intestacy. There could also be restrictions on the contract similar to laws requiring that a will make adequate provision for surviving spouses and dependent children. In the case of the marriage contract, this might include provision for care and support of children if there are any, guidelines for division of property and child custody in the event of a divorce, etc. One advantage of having such contracts, rather than the usually vaguer legal assumptions that husbands are heads of households and that wives have primary responsibility for housekeeping and child-rearing, would be that it would reduce the problems produced by leaving the details of divorce settlements up to the discretion of the courts. Such a contract might be a better guide to a divorce settlement than the judge's sometimes arbitrary or biased judgement, and would reduce the probability that property settlements and child-custody cases be turned into arenas for character assassination and playing to the prejudices of the court.

All of these aspects of marriage laws constitute prima facie violations of the liberal principle of freedom of choice. The first violates the principle that contracts are only binding if the people who enter into them do so with informed, uncoerced consent. The second violates the principle of equality of opportunity and equal treatment under the law, since it sets the terms of the contract by birth rather than by choice or ability. Such a condition is formally like a law that states that only whites can be bank presidents and only blacks can be ditch-diggers, or that certain political duties and rights apply only to descendants of peasants or only to descendants of aristocrats.

## Problems of Content

According to traditional natural-rights theory, there are some contracts that governments ought not to enforce. There are rights that cannot be alienated and, hence, some contracts that are void because of their substance. Two standard cases of such contracts are a contract to give or sell oneself into slavery and a contract under which one gives up one's civil right to protection by the law against violence and injury.

At the time of the early cooperation between the abolitionist and woman suffrage movements, the legal status of a wife was almost identical with that of a slave, and some of that similarity remains.[9] The following is a description of two legal clauses applying to slaves:

The first clause confirmed his status as property—the right of the owner to his "time, labor and services" and to his obedient compliance with all lawful commands. . . .
   The second clause acknowledged the slave's status as a person. The law required that masters be humane to their slaves, furnish them adequate food and clothing and provide care for them during sickness and old age.[10]

Compare that to the following recent description of the rights and duties of wives:

The legal responsibilities of a wife are to live in the home established by her husband; to perform the domestic chores . . . necessary to help maintain that home; to care for her husband and children.
   The legal responsibilities of a husband are to provide a home for his wife and children; to support, protect and maintain his wife and children.[11]

Even though the time separating these two legal statements is more than a hundred years, they seem remarkably similar. The legal duties of a wife entail that she has an obligation to work without pay, as does a slave; so a contract between husband and wife which stipulates that the husband will pay the wife for her labor is not legally binding: the courts will not honor a contract to pay someone to do something that she is legally required to do without pay.[12]

If it is morally illegitimate to sell oneself into slavery, and if governments ought not to honor such contracts, then such a contract ought not to be legally enforceable, let alone legally required of married couples. Liberal arguments for the position that voluntarily entered slavery contracts are such that they ought not to be honored by law vary, and some of them may not apply very clearly to this case. Arguments that base the illegitimacy of slavery contracts on the grounds that the renunciation of freedom is permanent would seem to apply only to the extent to which divorce is unavailable. However, John Stuart Mill, who uses a similar argument against voluntary slavery contracts,[13] claims that the lack of divorce only completes the analogy between slavery and marriage.[14] Arguments that base the illegitimacy of the enforcement of voluntary slavery contracts on the moral objectionability of exploitation or of ownership of people[15] might be more applicable. However, the extension of such arguments to the marriage contract would depend on whether or not such a contract would be exploitation or alienation of one's rights in important ways that go beyond legitimate limits of individual freedom.

The marriage laws also tend to exclude spouses from legal protection against violence or violation of rights by the other spouse. The most obvious and best-known example of this practice is that a wife has no legal protection against rape by her husband, since rape laws explicitly exclude such acts, no matter how forcible and violent, from criminal statutes. There is also a general legal principle of non-interference in marriage, which involves a refusal on the part of the courts to adjudicate many criminal cases and civil suits for injury between spouses.[16] Thus, to borrow the terminology of social-contract theory, spouses are, to some extent, in a state of nature with respect to each other, with no common judge between them unless they choose to file for divorce. The person who is better off in a state of nature is likely to be the one who is stronger. If there is a fight between a two-hundred-pound trained fighter and an untrained ninety-eight-pound weakling, it is fairly clear which one would benefit from outside parties refraining from interference.

Since men tend to marry women who are physically weaker than they are, and since men are culturally better trained for violence than women are and usually have greater political and economic power, the principle of non-interference in disputes between spouses will be likely to produce, in effect, a grant of unchecked power to the husband.[17]

Again, it would seem to be consistent with liberal principles as applied elsewhere to argue that no contract should be interpreted as alienating one's right to legal protection against violence and one's right to legal redress of grievance, and to argue further that such a legal principle denies spouses equal protection under the law.

## II. ARGUMENTS FOR IMMUNITY

There are three major arguments for excluding marriage law from political criticisms that are otherwise deemed universal: (1) marriage is too important to be meddled with by law; (2) marriage is a religious sacrament and thus does not fall within the realm of political decision; and (3) marriage law is a special case, because marriage is appropriately a relationship of love and mutual trust.

### *The Importance of Marriage*

The first argument is that we ought not to interfere with marriage because marriage is too important:

Our whole society is based on the absolutely fundamental proposition that: "Marriage, as creating the most important relation in life," has "more to do with the morals and civilization of a people than any other institution" (*Maynard* v. *Hill*, 125 U.S. 190, 205).[18]

However, a policy allowing people to choose their own contracts would interfere less in the marriage relationship than the laws we already have. Therefore, unless there is something more to the argument, the point that marriage is too important to interfere with would seem to be most appropriate to an argument calling for careful scrutiny and criticism of present marriage law.

The argument might be filled out as follows: It is generally more dangerous to try out new political and social forms than to stick to the ones we have already tried. Marriage, in the form we now have institutionalized in the law, is a time-honored and well-tested institution. Any attempt to make the marriage laws egalitarian would constitute a major change in the institution since it would eliminate the special duties and rights of spouses and the corresponding division of labor which have worked so well in the past. Thus, changing the laws would be choosing a risky venture over a well-tested institution. And, since marriage is such an important institution, the risk entails that, if the experiment fails, it will damage not only many individuals, but the very fabric of the society.

This is a fairly standard Burkean conservative argument,[19] and there are two lines of response to it: (1) a standard liberal response to this kind of argument in general, and (2) a criticism of this specific argument about marriage that does not dispute the general conservative thesis.

The liberal response might be as follows: Slavery was a time-hallowed institution, but that does not make it a just institution. The fact that there is uncertainty about the results of just treatment is at the least not a conclusive argument for failing to attempt to make the laws more just.

However, we could also criticize this argument on the grounds that, whether or not the basic conservative theory is correct, it does not apply in this case. This is not a case of a vast political experiment or of trying to change social institutions through government action, but rather an attempt to bring the laws into line with a social institution that has already changed, at least in some segments of the population. Many couples now share responsibilities, and among those who still follow the prescribed pattern to some extent—such that the woman does the housework and the man earns the money— many regard this arrangement as one they have chosen rather than as a necessity that ought to be enforced by law. The experiments have been performed in advance, and there have been a sufficient number of successful ones to make the fears of disaster less plausible. It might also be argued that marriage as we now know it—the patriarchal nuclear family—is a relatively recent historical phenomenon and is an experiment that has not succeeded so very spectacularly.[20] So, there is not much reason to believe that making the marriage contract less unequal is either particularly experimental or entails more risk than allowing the laws we now have to continue.

## The Religious Argument

The second argument, the one from religion, is roughly as follows: marriage is a religious sacrament, the form of which is ordained by particular religions or by God. Therefore, marriage law, which now conforms, more or less, to the religious sacrament, ought not to be changed from that form. However, if we assume that freedom of religion and separation of church and state are good things, then this would more reasonably back up the position that the state ought not to keep this legal institution. If marriage is a religious sacrament, then freedom to choose between marriage contracts would be an element of religious freedom. The exclusive enforcement of a contract that conforms to the religious sacrament of the majority religion would violate the principle of separation of church and state, since it ties the legal institution, which should be open to people of any religion or of no religion at all, to the religious sacrament of a particular religion.

## Domestic Harmony

The third argument is based on the claim that marriage laws are a special case, since marriage is appropriately a relationship of love and affection. Thus, we should not apply the same principles to such laws as we would, for example, to a purely economic relationship. This would seem to be a reasonable argument against, for example, an attempt to apply anti-discrimination laws to the choice of marriage partners in the same way that they are applied to the choice of tenants. However, it seems less relevant to an argument for the position that the roles within a marriage ought to be set by law regardless of the choices of the people who have made the contract.

This argument is most often used (1) against allowing contractual relationships other than the existing one between marriage partners, and (2) against court "interference" in the marriage relationship. That is, it is used in defense of the refusal of the courts to enforce civil and, in some cases, criminal laws when the disputants are married to each other.

Lon L. Fuller, an authority on contract law, summarizes the arguments for refusing to grant legal status to contracts that regulate the internal affairs of a marriage:

The first of these is that the success of a marriage depends on a shared sense of trust and mutual respect that would be destroyed by any attempt to spell out its implications in numbered paragraphs; unmeasured love and contractually imposed boundary markers hardly go together. A second consideration is that the management of the household is vulnerable to so many shifting contingencies that any attempt to subject it to a regime of rules would inevitably fail.[21]

But if marriages would be destroyed by any legal attempt to spell out marital duties, Fuller does not offer any explanation of how it has survived such specification by past and current common-law regulations of marriage duties. Perhaps it is only when the contract is voluntarily chosen and knowingly entered into that it has such consequences.

Fuller does not seem to notice that his criticism of inter-spousal contracts on the grounds that marriage duties should not be specified at all is inconsistent with an objection to such contracts on the grounds that they conflict with common-law specification of marriage duties. Thus, the argument he gives is in conflict with the argument used by the court in *Miller* v. *Miller*, the case he cites to support his claim.

In *Miller* v. *Miller*, Mrs. Miller had agreed to stay with her husband, despite serious misconduct on his part, on the basis of a written agreement. This contract specified, among other things, that the wife would care for their children and keep the home in good order, and that the husband would pay the household expenses and, in addition, pay her sixteen and two-thirds dollars a month. He defaulted on the payments and his wife brought suit. The objection made by the court to enforcing the contract entered into by Mr. and Mrs. Miller was that it required him to pay her for the performance of duties which, as his wife, she was already legally required to perform.[22] Fuller seems to see no inconsistency between the bond of love and the legal specification of the duty of a wife to perform housework without pay.

Nor does Fuller see such a legal specification of duties as one that would run into problems with "shifting contingencies." Surely, a marriage in which the husband loses his outside job and the wife has to work outside the home to support the family would be a shift in the situation which would make that provision of the marriage law inappropriate. As long as the courts decline to honor contracts chosen by a husband and wife, a couple will lack not only the legal option of alternative contracts designed to meet shifting contingencies but, in many cases, will not have the option of choosing a contract that fits their present situation.

The argument of dangers to "domestic harmony" is also used by the courts in refusing to adjudicate civil, and in some cases criminal, cases between spouses. "The flames which litigation would kindle on the domestic hearth would consume in an instant the conjugal bond."[23] Hence, there is a general judicial assumption that the availability of legal redress for personal injury would endanger the stability of marriages. This seems to be an empirical assumption for which no evidence is offered. One might more reasonably assume that fear of unprotected violence would damage the mutual love and trust that the courts hold to be so necessary to the stability of a marriage. The availability of legal redress might serve as a deterrent (at least to cases of intentional injury and refusal to honor either contracts or common-law marriage duties), whereas the refusal of courts to judge disputes between spouses who are living together leaves divorce and separation as the *only* legal recourse.[24] Requiring spouses to separate in order to be eligible for legal protection would appear likely to encourage the dissolution rather than the stability of marriage.

I have argued that the reasons typically advanced for granting to marriage immunity from basic principles of justice are untenable. As sufficient grounds for denying such basic rights as access to legal redress of civil and criminal grievances, religious and contractual freedom, and equality under the law, they are flimsy indeed.

## NOTES

1. In particular, I will deal with general principles of equality and justice and with natural-rights liberalism, rather than with utilitarian arguments. For a criticism of the institution of marriage on the grounds of its consequences (particularly for women) see Jessie Bernard, *The Future of Marriage* (New York: Bantam, 1973).

2. Most of what I will have to say about liberal treatment of marriage is also true of the treatment of other family relationships and of the family itself.

3. See, for example, Thomas Hobbes, *Leviathan*, pt. 1, chap. 13; John Locke, *The Second Treatise of Government*, chap. 2; Jean-Jacques Rousseau, *The Social Contract*, chap. 4.

4. See, e.g., Rousseau, bk. 1, chap. 2: "The oldest of all societies and the only natural one, is that of the family." Locke claims that marriage is a contractual relationship (and, thus, not a natural society), but that "the rule . . . naturally falls to the man's share" (chap. 7, par. 82). Also, in at least one place (chap. 5, "Of Property") Locke treats the family, including the wife, as an individual, and that individual is clearly the husband-father (who is the one who gains an individual right to the property which has been created by the whole family—that is, assuming that his wife and children are not simply sitting back amusing themselves).

5. Hobbes, pt. 1, chap. 14; Locke, chaps. 1, 2; Rousseau, bk. 1, chaps. 4, 5.

6. "Although every girl . . . is trained in the School for Wives, such training is no indication that she knows the legal implications of marriage. Before one can get a driver's license one must score 90 percent of the Rules of the Road. To get a marriage license, one must have a blood test and pay a couple of dollars." Karen de Crow, *Sexist Justice* (New York: Random House, 1975), p. 177.

7. John Stuart Mill, whose rigorous application of liberal principles to marriage stands as a notable exception in the history of liberals' treatment of the family, makes his one major slip on this issue. In *The Subjection of Women* ([1869]; reprinted in *Essays in Sex Equality*, ed. Alice Rossi [Chicago: University of Chicago Press, 1970]), he criticizes the claim that men ought to have legal authority over their wives (pp. 168–69). But, in direct conflict with arguments he advances elsewhere, he assumes that the jobs of housework and child-care are appropriately sex-linked: "when a woman marries, it may in general be understood that she makes choice of the management of the household, and the bringing up of a family, as the first call upon her exertions" (p. 179). Housework and child-rearing are, in his words, "the one vocation in which there is nobody to compete with them" (i.e., women) (p. 183).

8. The National Organization for Women is proposing legislation to validate marriage contracts other than the present unwritten one. *Do It NOW*, vol. 9, no. 3 (1976), p. 14.

9. Sheila Cronin, "Marriage," in *Radical Feminism*, ed. Anne Koedt, Ellen Levine, and Anita Rapone (New York: Quadrangle Books, 1973), pp. 215–17.

10. Kenneth M. Stampp, *The Peculiar Institution* (New York: Vintage Books, 1956), p. 192. Quoted in Cronin.

11. Richard T. Gallen, *Wives' Legal Rights* (New York: Dell, 1967), pp. 4–5. Quoted in Cronin.

12. Cronin, pp. 216–17; *Miller* v. *Miller*, excerpted in Lon L. Fuller and Melvin Aaron Eisenberg, *Basic Contract Law*, 3d ed., American Casebook Series (St. Paul: West Publishing Co., 1972), pp. 105–7.

13. John Stuart Mill, *On Liberty* (1859; New York: Bobbs-Merrill, 1956), p. 125.

14. *Subjection of Women*, (above, n. 7) p. 161.

15. Joel Feinberg, "Legal Paternalism," *Canadian Journal of Philosophy* 1 (1971): 118.

16. Notes: "Litigation between Husband and Wife," *Harvard Law Review* 79 (1966): 1650–65.

17. For reviews of research on the distribution of power within a marriage, see Bernard (above, n. 1), pp. 6–7, 9–15; and Dair L. Gillespie, "Who Has the Power? The Marital Struggle," in *Women: A Feminist Perspective*, ed. Jo Freeman (Palo Alto: Calif.: Mayfield, 1975), pp. 64–87.

18. *Bunim* v. *Bunim*, 298 N.Y. 391 (1949). Quoted in de Crow (above, n. 6), p. 198.

19. For a defense of the general principles on which this argument is based, see Michael Oakeshot, *Rationalism in Politics* (London: Methuen, 1967).

20. See, e.g., Bernard (above, n. 1).

21. Lon L. Fuller, "The Justification of Legal Decisions," *Archives for Philosophy of Law and Social Philosophy* (Weisbaden, Germany: Franz Steiner Verlag, 1971), no. 7; 82.

22. Fuller and Eisenberg (above, n. 12), p. 106.

23. *Ritter* v. *Ritter*, 31 Pa. 396, 398 (1858).

24. de Crow (above, n. 6), pp. 184–87.

Joseph E. Barnhart
Mary Ann Barnhart

# The Myth of the Complete Person

## STATEMENT OF THE ISSUE

The increase of desired expectations does not in itself bring an increase in freedom. Indeed, unfreedom and relative deprivation may be experienced when the individual's desired expectations fail to be actualized while the intensity of these expectations continues. In this article we contend that the unrealistic hope of becoming a complete and whole person through either marriage or divorce may easily become a source of unfreedom or suffering. It may even lead to what Nietzsche and Max Scheler refer to as *ressentiment*,[1] a kind of rancor and repressed envy that grows out of powerlessness and helplessness in failing to gain what one thinks one has a right to enjoy. Our underlying assumption is twofold: first, that the myth of personal wholeness drains away energy that is needed for the pursuit of more realistic expectations and freedom; and second, that the myth of completeness is a remythologized dogma having disguised religious roots and overtones.

## WHOLENESS THROUGH MARRIAGE

According to Plato's Aristophanes, "human nature was originally one and we were whole, and the desire and pursuit of the whole is called love." Aristophanes promises that if we are pious we will be restored to our "primeval nature," "our own nature," and "original true love." Love, he says, "will restore us to our original state, and heal us and make us happy and blessed."[2] If the true state of human being is seen as unity, separation is compared to a wound in need of healing.

According to one of the Biblical accounts of creation, after creating a single male (*Ish*), God discovered that the male was in himself incomplete. So he created various animals, but they proved less than satisfactory. Finally, out of the side of *Ish* God formed *Ishah*, a female; and that is why the two should pair off together to "become one flesh."[3]

In many religions, the word "salvation" means "wholeness." The English word "hale" is rooted in the Old English *hol*, from which is obtained the word "whole." It is related to "heal" (to make whole or sound).[4] In the twentieth century, love, with marriage as love's crowning exemplification, has come to be accepted by many as something of a religious ultimate and mystical union. For all practical purposes, marriage is the supreme sacrament in the minds of many people, even for some who profess to be atheists. According to the most well-known American preacher, Billy Graham, "Society did not make the first marriage; it was founded by God." For Christians, Dr. Graham sets forth the vision of "complete fulfillment in marriage."[5] This notion of perfect wholeness through marriage is foreshadowed in the New Testament Epistle to the Ephesians, which finds in the husband-wife union the human analogy of the mystical union of Christ and his Church.[6]

Numerous musicals, sermons, "coping" books, and marriage manuals have given forth the distinct message that until a person is married or at least romantically involved he or she is somehow not a complete person, whereas someone who is so involved stands a good chance of becoming a "whole person." Movies play violins in the background whenever there is serious talk of marriage or falling in love—as if the violins function as a kind of "invitation hymn" reinforcing an impending profound conversion in the lives of the candidates. In *The Music Man*, " 'Til There Was You" is a song of conversion. The female says that she had never really noticed the birds flying and singing " 'til there was you." In fact, nature itself took on for her a new form when she fell in love with the music man. This song may be fruitfully compared to the statements of two American evangelists—Jonathan Edwards and Dwight L. Moody—regarding their religious conversion. Very explicitly, they tell how facets of nature itself looked different to them after their conversion.[7] There is another romantic popular song in which the woman proclaims that for her "nothing is the same" since "he touched me." It takes no great leap of imagination to recall stories of the transforming touch of Jesus and other religious figures. One woman desired only to "touch the hem of his garment."

We are not denying the fact of conversion—whether through the idiom of religious experience or through that of romantic passion—but rather are challenging the very notion of a complete person, whether it is promised through religion, romantic involvement, or through marriage.

The ideal of a reasonably happy marriage for some couples is consequently in danger of being overshadowed by the myth of completeness in marriage. There is evidence to suggest that this myth might itself be a major factor leading not only to unpromising and unrealistic marriages to start with, but also to a number of divorces.[8] If disagreements and conflict of interests are regarded as somehow abnormal or unreal ingredients of the human marriage relationship, then the option of communicating plans of compromise on these conflicts may be lost or considerably reduced.

There is another argument against the myth of completeness through marriage: this myth is propaganda which unfairly pulls some people into marriage, or at least pulls them in too early. Hence, in opposing the myth, friends and relatives may help young adults to accept living without expecting to be whole or complete. In short, by eliminating this expectation, we may as a consequence eliminate the "vacuum" or emptiness that is supposed to come to those who choose a life style outside marriage. Paul C. Glick, demographer of the U.S. Census Bureau, suggests that just as "many of the women who delayed having other children reached the point where they liked it better without them than they had thought they would," so a postponement in marriage may lead women (and men) to enjoy singleness more than they had thought they would.[9] Indeed, at least one study indicates that single women are much happier and more satisfied than women who are married and in the process of raising children.[10] The contemporary single man, however, seems not to enjoy his singleness as much as single females do.[11]

The social pressure to become married was probably strongest in this country during the 1950s and 1960s. Current figures document a slowing down of marriage and a speeding up of divorce.[12] It may just be that the recent trend toward "living together" (rather than being legally married) is, despite the condemnation of the elders, a very conservative move on the part of a generation that not only has experienced divorce from the children's side, but has perhaps come to question the myth of completeness through marriage. In many ways, marriage is still a radical act, and becoming a parent is even more radical and more of a commitment—one that is extremely difficult to get out of.

Marriage may not be on the wane. Morton Hunt has probably oversimplified and overstated his case when he views divorce as simply a healthy mutation within monogamous marriage.[13] Nevertheless he is doubtless correct in seeing marriage as the major life style for most American adults in the coming decades. However, in order for marriage to retain a broad appeal, it has already had to undergo significant structural changes and revisions, and it is likely to undergo still more. Divorce may in many cases be seen as a painful adjustment within the commitment to marriage, for four out of every five who divorce eventually remarry.[14] It is possible that extramarital relations of either a sexual or nonsexual nature will become another mutation within marriage, although unless certain careful guidelines are worked out and publicly legitimated by influential and significant Americans as a viable option for some married couples, the extramarital mutation could, like most biological mutations, become lethal to the individual (which in this case would be the individual marriage).[15]

Two simple points should be made about recent attempts by some students of animal and primate behavior who contend that matrimony and parenthood are "natural" phenomena. First, it is quite difficult to say what is natural for all human beings, for the very word itself seems to be meaningful only in a relative context. Both marriage and parenthood are complex phenomena, and it is not at all clear what exactly the "it's natural" argument is saying. The second point may be expressed in the form of a question: Are those who emphasize the "marriage is natural" argument prepared to turn *every* so-called natural practice or act into a social ideal? If not, then what "extra-natural" qualifications are to be recognized?

## COMPLETENESS THROUGH DIVORCE

Some people regard divorce as a means whereby an individual can become a complete or whole person. If the marriage relationship has been one of *dependence*, then the divorce is regarded as necessary in order for the individual to become independent and thus a complete person. Here, paradoxically, completeness and wholeness are seen not in terms of the union of love, of two becoming one, but in terms of *separation and divorce.*

Whereas marriage, pregnancy, or parenthood was previously defined as the royal road to completeness as a person, now divorce is so defined. Grand promises are made on behalf of divorce in the way that they were made on behalf of falling in love and marrying. There are numerous "love songs" telling of how life takes on "meaning" when a person falls in love, or loses its meaning when the couple in love "break up." But in the Christmas season of 1974 we received from one of our friends the following note regarding a divorce:

Finally got the divorce last week. I've had a full year of that trauma. But I feel at long last I have something to live for! Hope to see you someday.

Love from _____

Disenchantment with one thing may lead to enchantment with another. Disillusionment with one life style may open the door to a new illusion, more tantalizing than the first. If people can suffer illusions about the state of matrimony, they may also suffer illusions about what divorce can offer them. Indeed, some people seem to repeat the cycle of illusion-disillusion-illusion regarding marriage and divorce. Most divorced people end up getting married again, usually not to the same person but sometimes to people very much like their former spouses. The fact that four out of five divorced persons do eventually marry again suggests that a great number find divorce to be less than a desirable state. Doubtless this is true to a considerable degree because a complex of social and economic stimuli and reinforcers punish the divorced. The attempts to change the long-legitimated practices have met with some measure of success in the past decade. For example, a growing number of the divorced are elected to important local and regional offices in an increasing number of religious denominations, including Southern Baptists. Roman Catholic practice, however, is still restricted by official pronouncements on divorce. Divorced women in particular seem to perceive themselves as very unhappy and as living an unsatisfied life so long as they remain divorced. Before any woman romanticizes divorce, she would do well to realize that divorce hits women harder than men. "Most of them have to work (71 percent) and care for their children (84 percent), without moral, economic, or psychological support from a husband or partner."[16] Furthermore, given the social structures of Western life, divorced women find it more difficult than men to get dates.[17] Usually they lack funds for someone to do household chores, which means that divorced women, after they come home from work, still have more work to do.

This is not to suggest that a particular marriage is better than a divorce. Rather it is just a way of saying that divorce, like any other life style, has its chores, limitations, and frustrations. Idealized promises about marriage, parenthood, and divorce are all alike in one respect—they tend to blind the individual to the need to prepare himself or herself for the responsibilities implicit in the newly acquired life style. In his book on divorce and readjustment, Willard Waller focuses on some of the central problems that the divorced in particular must face. First, one's love life must be reorganized. This in itself may create concerns not only of social facilitation but also of how one sees oneself as a sexually active or inactive person who is unmarried. Second, there is the question of pride and self-respect, especially if the divorce is looked upon in terms of failure. Third, the network of habits, rituals, and division of labor that in marriage provided at least a sense of familiarity is lost in the separation and divorce. What remains is often a kind of psychosocial vacuum that cannot be filled all at once. Fourth, the question of old personal relationships has to be dealt with. Some of the divorced simply move away or, less drastically, drop old friendships and in some cases lose contact with important in-laws.[18]

One of the sad notes of divorce is the reduction in standard of living that often comes when the marriage is dissolved. Also, the legal complications can be emotionally devastating, especially when children, property, and money have to be redistributed. Willard Waller was right when he classified *divorce as one of the serious crises of life* and compared it with death and birth. Just as one ought not to enter lightly into marriage or parenthood, so one would do well to count the cost before launching a divorce.

Why has divorce sometimes been glamorized as the highway to wholeness and completeness as a person? One answer is that such propaganda is an overreaction to those who, by placing a terrible social stigma on the divorced, have portrayed them as something of a social infection. The noted evangelist Billy Graham expressed the feelings of many who consider divorce as a stigma when he once said with sarcasm, "There was a time when a divorced man would have had no chance in American politics, but with our shifting ideals of today, whether or not a person is divorced seems to make little difference."[19] There is little doubt that the evangelist was longing for the day when no divorced person could be elected to public office. But to counter such a harsh attitude, others need not react in excess by idolizing divorce or even recommending it except as an option that may or may not be an improvement over one's present marriage. In any case, like marriage and parenthood, divorce is hardly a step into Paradise.

Sociologist Jessie Bernard notes, "In the 1950s women had been convinced that not to get married was indeed a fate worse than death, for without marriage, one could not be *completely fulfilled*."[20] We would add that neither in divorce does one become "completely fulfilled."

## INTEGRATING ONE'S ACTIVITIES AND INTERESTS

It is systematically misleading to tell a person that unless she does $X$ or is involved in $X$, she cannot be truly fulfilled as a person. The misleading assumption is that either (1) there is an undisputed and universal state of being to be designated as "truly fulfilled" or (2) such a state has been universally or authoritatively defined. We can say with authority that water will boil at a particular temperature at a specified elevation, but we cannot formulate a general law or even a consensus generalization that informs us when any and every person is "truly fulfilled." Not without falling into contradiction can we state what would be "true fulfillment" or "completeness of being" for even a projected Ideal Person. (The word "perfection" when applied even to the life of deity turns out to contain a bewildering thicket of conflicting emphases and cross-purposes.)[21]

To be sure, in various cultures and subcultures a variety of behaviors and experiences have been stipulated as "truly fulfilling" (or some similar phrase). But our argument in this article is that many of these stipulations eventually come into deep and profound conflict with one another. And, to the degree that it develops any depth and scope in content, any worked-out compromise becomes a new definition of expectations having rough edges and internal contradictions.

We may admit that there seems to be a general, although vague, consensus that the truly fulfilled person is one who *enjoys his activities* and is probably contributing somewhat to the *enjoyment of others*. In the empirical world, however, social realities such as marriages and divorces hit often on hard times and prove to be less than enjoyable; indeed, they sometimes bring frustration, meaninglessness, and disillusionment. Failure to admit the *finitude*—that is, the contextual and contingent nature—of all human expectations and their fulfillment adds to this disillusionment.

The integration of expectations and fulfillments is never fully completed, for either new and disturbing expectations emerge, or the supply of certain fulfillments becomes decreased or even cut off entirely. Nevertheless, many people have been able to attain an appreciable degree of integration of their expectations and fulfillments (which is sometimes called *self*-integration); and this integration, so long as it is maintained, is itself a kind of added expectation that is fulfilled somewhat.

## THE QUESTION OF DEPENDENCE AND INDEPENDENCE

The noted nineteenth-century theologian Schleiermacher defined religion as the "feeling of absolute dependency." Some traditions have perverted this to mean that while males are indeed absolutely dependent on God, females are absolutely dependent on either their fathers or their husbands. In their article "Women in the Afterlife: The Islamic View As Seen from Qur'an and Tradition" Jane I. Smith and Yvonne Y. Haddad make the following revealing comments:

If we put these several [Muslim] traditions together, we can construct the following kind of scheme which may, in fact, not be too far from the cultural attitudes of Muslims of the early centuries about the relationship of women to men. The two worst sins of Islam are *shirk* (association of anything with God) and *kufr* (ingratitude or rejection of God's signs). What these traditions seem to be saying is that the two worst things man can do in relation to God are precisely those things which, if done by woman in relation to man, earn her damnation. Specifically, this means the *shirk* of giving herself to more than one man (or not safeguarding her honor), and the *kufr* of being ungrateful for the charity and beneficence of her husband. We reach the somewhat unnerving conclusion that in these traditions there may be a real sense in which woman's sins are to man as man's sins are to God. One's confidence that this is too extreme an interpretation is not bolstered by such a *hadith* as that which cites the Prophet as saying that it is not possible for one person to worship another—but if it were, he would order a woman to worship her husband![22]

Smith and Haddad point out that there are "contemporary attempts to assure the equality of all Muslims regardless of sex" and that these attempts reflect the basic attitude of the Qur'an itself. Nevertheless, the accompanying traditions have often portrayed women as far from equals to males and "have been enormously influential in moulding the opinions and understandings of many centuries of Muslims." Indeed, "the fact that women have been seen and dealt with by the imagination of man has resulted in everything from the fanciful flights in descriptions of the *hur* to the threat of perdition for recalcitrant wives."[23]

Divorce is often said to be a means whereby a dependent individual is enabled to become his or her own independent self. But this is not necessarily the case, even in a relative sense. Just as one cannot walk out of one spatial area without walking into another, so one cannot break off old dependent relationships without taking on new or different ones. Independence is always relative—independence *of* this or that, but never independence simply. Divorce may release a person from a destructive dependence relationship, but it cannot guarantee that constructive dependence relationships will follow. What it can guarantee is that the divorced individual's life will invariably become dependent on certain stimulus and reinforcement patterns that were not in play so long as the marriage was in effect. Dependence relationships are unavoidable and are often desirable. For any human being, to be is to be related to something that is not oneself. While it is a fallacy to confuse dependence with identity —that is, to think that one is identical with what one depends upon—nevertheless there is no distinct individual identity without dependence. More precisely, the nature and quality of one's independence or uniqueness is shaped by *what* one is dependent on and the *way* one is dependent on it. A woman who chooses to think with an independent mind—without her husband's mediating her conclusions for her—will, in order to develop and maintain this independence of mind, necessarily become dependent on information, on proper logical form, and on other dimensions of her environment that make for rational thinking and discourse. Inasmuch as her husband is not the fount of knowledge, she must learn to depend on more fundamental sources of knowledge and information. She may become independent of her husband's opinions by ignoring him, but she cannot become an independent *thinker* without developing the appropriate dependency relationships that make for rationality. And, of course, the same holds true for the husband in his attempt to be an independent thinker.

The question is not whether one is to be a dependent being in the world, but rather whether one's dependent relationships are to be creative rather than destructive. George Eliot states in one of her novels that when the author of Proverbs compared a "contentious woman to a continual dripping on a very rainy day," he did not have in mind "a fury with long nails, acrid and selfish," but "a good creature, who had no joy but the happiness of the loved ones whom she contributed to make uncomfortable, . . . spending nothing on herself."[24] A dependence relationship that treats one human being as if he or she were *the* source of the joy of another is very likely to generate resentment in at least one member of the relationship. In some cases the finite mortal who is made *the* source of sustenance and guidance of another is worshiped and idolized as if the mortal were a god or goddess. (The language of worshiping and idolizing still pervades popular "love" songs. Paradoxically, in these songs the "idols" are sometimes described as possessions. Speaking of "his woman," Elvis Presley sings, "There goes my only possession; there goes my everything.")[25]

## THE MISTAKE OF ABSOLUTIZING
## RELATIVE EXPECTATIONS

It is risky indeed to try to define for others what will make their lives meaningful in their own eyes. For some, divorce opens the possibility for new and meaningful interests, activities, and relationships. For others, marriage is "the answer." Our point, however, has been that "the answer" in people's lives depends upon the problem and how it is perceived and taken by them. Furthermore, we have contended that the unrealistic expectation of completeness or wholeness as a person quite often serves to divert attention and energy from the practical tasks of better learning to enjoy the process of living. This is not to play down the important and crucial role of expectations and standards in one's life. On the contrary, some expectations and standards, while admittedly high, deserve the individual's greatest efforts and reinforcements. The quest for "completeness of being" or "wholeness," however, often serves to increase the gap of relative deprivation and to turn realistic hope into cynicism whenever the unrealistic expectation of completeness has brought about the reaction of disillusionment.

Many people seem to become involved in guilt behavior upon realizing that their vision of completeness will never be achieved by them. They regard themselves as failures in life. This vision should be demystified and replaced by more realistic dreams. Also, dreams which are risky should be seen as just that, so that in placing one's bets one will not be led to think that one is betting on a sure thing.

In his theory of induction, the philosopher of science Karl Popper shows that while we cannot be certain of avoiding disaster if we pursue what seem to be reasonable courses of action, we can be more sure that we will meet failure if we guide our lives by expectations (for example, promises, visions, conjectures, or convictions) that have already been falsified or exposed as deeply self-contradictory.[26] Like the idea of perfection, the idea of completeness has always a relative and contextual meaning. But when it becomes emotively absolutized and is taken seriously, it often becomes a source of guilt and disillusionment.

The eighteenth-century philosopher David Hume argued that there are no *necessary* connections between the phenomena of the empirical world. It has taken almost two centuries for at least Western society to begin to appreciate the radical impact of Hume's argument. Many people are beginning to see that what traditionally have been connected—marriage and procreation—are not necessarily connected. What is now needed is a more empirical inquiry into the consequences of various kinds of associations and relationships. To say that empirical phenomena are not necessarily connected is not to say that just any combination will be followed or accompanied by just any random consequence. The contextualism and relativism that we have espoused might more accurately be characterized as "empirical relatedness" in contrast to both necessary connection and pure chance-relatedness.[27]

# NOTES

1. See Max Scheler, *Ressentiment*, trans. W. H. Holdheim (New York: Schocken Books, 1972). For a profound study of "relative deprivation" see Robert K. Merton, "Social Structure and Anomie," in *Social Theory and Social Structure*, rev. ed. (Glencoe, Ill.: Free Press, 1957), pp. 132, 155–56, 464f.; see also Samuel Stouffer, et al. in *The American Soldier*, 2 vols. (Princeton: Princeton University Press, 1949), 1:125, 173.
2. Plato, *Symposium*, 192–93. B. Jowett trans.
3. See "Hale" and "Heal" in *Oxford English Dictionary*.
4. See Genesis 2:18–24.
5. *The Quotable Billy Graham*, ed. Cort R. Flint and the staff of *Quote* (Anderson, S.C.: Drake House, 1966), p. 129. For arguments that Mr. Graham represents "the mood of Middle America," see Lowell D. Streiker and Gerald S. Strober, *Religion and the New Majority: Billy Graham, Middle America, and the Politics of the 1970s* (New York: Association Press, 1972). For some critical comments on Graham's view of women, see J. E. Barnhart, *The Billy Graham Religion* (Philadelphia: Pilgrim Press, 1972), pp. 77–80.
6. See Ephesians 5:23–33. There is considerable debate as to who the author of this epistle really is. The Apostle Paul in I Corinthians 7 seems to have a less glorified view of marriage, so that he cannot be regarded as holding marriage to be either a necessary or a sufficient condition (or state) of completeness and wholeness.
7. See James W. Jones, "Reflections on the Problem of Religious Experience," *Journal of the American Academy of Religion*

11 (December 1972): 445. Jones quotes from Edwards' *Personal Narrative*. See also A. P. Fitt, *Moody Still Lives* (Chicago: Moody Press, 1936), p. 20. On the tendency to regard the extramarital relationship as a religious conversion, see Morton Hunt, *The Affair* (New York: World Publishing Co., 1969), pp. 117, 188–89, 202–3.

8. See Marion L. Schulman, "Idealization in Engaged Couples," *Journal of Marriage and the Family* 36 (February 1974): 139–46.

9. Paul C. Glick, "A Demographer Looks at American Families," *Journal of Marriage and the Family* 37 (1975), 16f.

10. See Angus Campbell, "The American Way of Mating: Marriage Si, Children Only Maybe," *Psychology Today*, May 1975, pp. 38f.

11. Ibid., p. 38.

12. See Glick (above, n. 9), p. 16.

13. Morton Hunt, "The Future of Marriage," *Playboy*, August 1971, p. 168.

14. See "Marriage, Divorce, and Remarriage by Year of Birth: June 1971," *Current Population Reports*, series P-20, no. 239 (Washington, D.C.: U.S. Government Printing Office, 1972); and Glick (above, n. 9), p. 24.

15. See Gerhard Neubeck, ed., *Extramarital Relations* (Englewood Cliffs, N.J.: Prentice-Hall, 1969); Ronald Mazur, *The New Intimacy: Open-Ended Marriage and Alternative Lifestyles* (Boston: Beacon Press, 1973).

16. Campbell, (above, n. 6), p. 43.

17. Ibid.

18. See Willard Waller, *The Old Love and the New: Divorce and Readjustment* (New York: Horace Liveright, 1930), pp. 3–14; Mel Krantzler, *Creative Divorce: A New Opportunity for Personal Growth* (New York: M. Evans, 1973), pp. 51–70, 130–32.

19. *Quotable Billy Graham* (above, n. 5), p. 62.

20. Jessie Bernard, *The Future of Marriage* (New York: Bantam Books, 1973), p. 244. Italics added.

21. See J. E. Barnhart, *Religion and the Challenge of Philosophy* (Totowa, N.J.: Littlefield, Adams, 1975), pp. 120–24.

22. *Journal of the American Academy of Religion* 43 (March 1975): 44.

23. Ibid., p. 50. The term *hur* refers to celestial women who serve in a geisha-like capacity to Muslim men in the afterlife.

24. *Adam Bede* in *The Writings of George Eliot*, 3:57–58.

25. In his book *Fatherhood: A Sociological Perspective* (New York: Random House, 1968), Leonard Benson speaks of a socially inculcated sex-role distinction. The female mode of behavior is said to be "expressive," which "is characterized by a basic pre-

disposition toward pleasing others." The male mode of behavior is said to be "instrumental," which "evokes a disciplined pursuit of goals transcending the immediate situation and encourages resistance to any emotional involvement as an end in itself" (p. 21). Benson does not hold that this distinction is biologically conditioned but rather that it is socially reinforced as "a double sex standard." Doubtless the distinction today is much too neat to fit empirical realities, but it does reflect some of the male and female "images" that have been popularized in a number of movies, churches, and elsewhere. Much has been made of the so-called lack of creativity on the part of women (see ibid., p. 23), but what needs to be pointed out is the persistent failure of male-dominated institutions and organizations to *recognize and reward* female creativity. Mary Ann Evans felt that she had to assume the name "George Eliot" in order to increase the probability of her being accepted as a creative writer. In *The Mirages of Marriage* (New York: W.W. Norton, 1968) W. J. Lederer and Don Jackson list eleven influential false assumptions about the differences between males and females (pp. 60–61).

26. See Karl Popper, *Objective Knowledge: An Evolutionary Approach* (New York: Oxford University Press, 1972), chap. 1.

27. For an excellent study of how social identities, relationships, and patterns become taken for granted as "given" realities, see Peter Berger and Thomas Luckmann, *The Social Construction of Reality: A Treatise on the Sociology of Knowledge* (Garden City, N.Y.: Doubleday, Anchor Books, 1967).

Joseph Margolis
Clorinda Margolis

# The Separation of Marriage and Family

The family and the institution of marriage are obviously so central to the history of every society that it is hopeless to suppose that one could specify, quite objectively, the proper form of either or both. Proposals can be no more than reasonable adjustments of existing practices; that is, debate tends to be dialectical, focused on those possibilities of change that actual arrangements, which are themselves no more than the latest phase of accumulating changes, may support. Furthermore, marriage and the family are the natural magnets for every important quarrel about societal arrangements—property and inheritance, personal relations, the care and education of the young, the initiation and monitoring of sex, the limits of personal freedom, the authority of the state and church, the distribution of public status. At one extreme, it is claimed that marriage is a sacrament or has a fixed and ordained function.[1] At the other, only the historical contingencies are noted by which the nuclear family and its norms are seen to be the gradual result of a certain narrowing and a certain alteration of family relations since at least the Middle Ages.[2]

The peculiarity of marriage is the intensity with which its norms are disputed, at the same time that its functional possibilities remain quite unclear. It appears simultaneously to be a purely personal relationship, a sacrament or at least a serious institution guarded by moral or religious authorities, and a mere legal contract. It is in fact easy to see how marriage may be viewed exclusively along any one of these dimensions.

An interesting experiment suggests itself. Why not consider the separation of the interests of marriage and the family within the developing forms of contemporary Western life? One might almost say that this would not even be an experiment, since it would perhaps be no more than an elaboration of an actual tendency. For example, today's ease of divorce and insistence on the privacy of sexual and other personal relationships tend, in the context of the nuclear family, to drive the interests of marriage and family apart. Marriage increasingly tends to focus on the satisfaction of certain private interests, while family tends to focus on at least some public concerns regarding the well-being of dependents, the control of property, and the like. Why not, therefore, consider what would be involved in construing marriage as essentially concerned with such private interests, and families as essentially concerned with such public interests?

This need not be taken as an attack on existing institutions. It would merely offer us a picture of certain rational options available to those who are already drifting in the direction of separating the two institutions. For instance, there is evidence of an increasing interest on the part of unmarried women to have and raise children. Wherever an older viable practice exists in which the interests of the family and the married couple converge harmoniously, there may be no need to explore the prospects for radically transforming our understanding of the marriage relationship. But—in a society committed to tolerating plural conceptions of marriage, defending sexual and personal privacy as a matter of personal liberty, liberalizing on both legal and informal grounds the acceptability of separation and divorce, and acknowledging the legitimacy of the view that the personal compatibility of mates is the primary or even exclusive justificatory basis for marriage—there is bound to be a realistic need to consider even radical possibilities.

No doubt Medieval marriage involved the institution of a personal relationship, but there is little reason to think that it was ever construed romantically (certainly not in the technical sense); in fact, it was effectively incompatible with romantic love.[3] It surely never set a premium on a sustained and exclu-

ive personal and distinctly sexualized love. The development of
hat conception resulted somehow from the gradual seculariza-
ion, then sexualization, of romance and its identification with
he utterly different notion of the functional harmony and
mutual respect of marriage mates. The Vatican Council's pronouncement, reported in Pope Paul's *Humanae Vitae*, that
'Marriage and conjugal love are by their nature ordained toward the begetting and educating of children" holds so closely
o the earlier conception of marriage that it must seem to orthodox Roman Catholics like a contradiction in terms to hear that
Dutch priests have actually attempted to extend and to defend
offering the marriage sacrament to homosexual couples. (The
ame issue of course appears outside Roman Catholic circles.)
And yet, in our own day, the matter is blandly regarded by
many as debatable, even within the Catholic tradition.

Again, *Humanae Vitae* declares explicitly that "directly
villed and procured abortions, even if for therapeutic reasons,
are to be absolutely excluded as licit means of regulating births";
also, that "direct sterilization, whether perpetual or temporary,
whether of the man or of the woman" is to be outlawed. Obviously this doctrine is rejected by many of the Christian faith,
disputed even among Catholics, and notably inoperative in
Western civil law. What is important about the pronouncement,
however, quite apart from its substance, is that it presupposes a
normative conceptual unity linking the function of individual
persons, the function of the marriage relationship, and the func-
ion of the family initiated by marriage. To concede that such a
unity may not obtain is, in our own time, hardly subversive: it is
he standard claim of a very large number of persons and is as
much institutionalized as the doctrine of *Humanae Vitae* itself.
Furthermore, even where such a unity is admitted, as in other
parts of the Christian community, the conception of the func-
ions involved differs drastically from the view advanced by the
Pope—so drastically, for instance, that divorce, abortion, steri-
ization, the legitimacy of homosexual marriage, contraception,
and the like are either flatly regarded as legitimate or, at the
very least, debatable.

Consider, then, the extreme possibility. *If* marriage were a
purely personal matter, the effective union of two (or even
several) persons (of either sex), the permanence of the rela-
ionship would depend entirely on the feelings and volitions of
he parties affected. On that assumption, there would be abso-

294 **FEMINISM AND PHILOSOPHY**

lutely no point in linking property rights, inheritance, social position, the "begetting and educating of children," and even the monitoring of sex or obligations of child support or the support of spouses, with the institution of marriage.

Two types of marriage would fit this extreme condition. First of all, there could be an *informal* marriage, a personal agreement to cohabit, not legally binding but socially (possibly even religiously or sacramentally) recognized. Second, there could be a *term* marriage, a legal agreement to cohabit for a certain period; this would be for purposes of a private nature, and renewable by mutual consent.

Here, what strikes one at once is that, however reasonable it may be to protect the legal rights of children or other wards, legal constraints on marriage (that is, constraints not arising from the initiative of contracting parties) have very little to do with the kind of personal affection, cooperation, or sexual interest that presumably would sustain either the informal or the (probably short-term) contractual marriage. In fact, families themselves might well be formed in quite different ways from those acknowledged at present. There is of course every evidence that so-called primitive societies draw rather sharp distinctions between the rights of families and the rights of marriage mates.[4] In our own society, it is quite conceivable that agreements could obtain in which, though a party of either sex be a donor toward the begetting of children, families would be legally recognized in which children begotten or adopted and only one parent (not necessarily the natural parent and not necessarily a parent made single by divorce or death) form the functioning family. The concept of a family is quite different from the concept of a marriage; even the so-called nuclear family is by no means the limiting form of viable families. Hence the legal considerations involved in protecting a family—for instance, limitations on the use of property in the interests of family or family members—may be sharply distinguished from the personal or contingent legal considerations involved in a marriage.

In this sense, a *family* is a social unit of *legal parents* and *offspring* or *wards*, whether natural or adopted; and a *marriage* is a social unit of *adults* or competent parties agreeing informally or by contract to cohabit according to whatever arrangements of personal privacy they may agree to. It may be argued that the younger natural offspring of elderly parents may be-

come the legal parents of their own natural parents (or, adop-
tively, of other wards of any age); and in general, the legal
protection and control of families and their members will be
seen to be a logically distinct matter from that of imposing legal
constraints upon marriage.

One obvious place where the confusion of marriage and family interests has regularly obtained is where the income-tax laws
apply. If, for example, persons not legally married were permitted to file joint income-tax returns, or if the tax did not favor
those legally married over those not married, there would be no
gratuitous disadvantage to those who choose to live together in
an informal marriage or who, though contractually married,
intend to have no children. It is reasonably clear that the motivation for favoring married couples over the unmarried has to
do with an anticipated link with the raising of families. But if
the management of property and the assignment of children and
wards were linked solely to families and not to marriages, there
would be no need to consider marriage in the distribution of
taxes. And the widespread use of contraception and sterilization
suggests that the linkage of marriage and family is becoming
increasingly irregular. Even now, the assignment of children to
parents must sometimes be determined where no actual marriage obtains; in particular, the very concept of illegitimacy
depends on conflating the interests of marriage and family.
Were there legal specifications for the individuation of families
—*specifications that did not depend on (or solely on) consent*
—the category of illegitimacy could be quite simply eliminated.
Obviously, the welfare laws of the United States, which bind
unwed fathers to support their natural offspring, already are
committed to the principle; nevertheless, the social and legal
stigma of illegitimacy remains. Again, if the tax advantages of a
given family were independently defensible, they could be sustained without any reference to marriage at all.

Clearly, the distinction between marriage and family requires
a third form of contract, yielding what might be called a *contractual family* (*not* a marriage). Thus, several parties might
voluntarily contract to form a family, which they might do in
either of two ways. First, whether they are married or not, they
could beget children, which they would legally signify they intend to take responsibility for as wards. Alternatively, they
could adopt children—again, whether they are married or not.
Conditions of eligibility may very reasonably be imposed, since

the public community has an understandable interest in the care of children and wards and the control and management of property. Marriage as such, however, would not be a relevant consideration, since *its* function, *ex hypothesi*, is a matter exclusively of private concern. But the character and responsibility of individuals who happen to be or not to be married would quite fairly be considered relevant. The members of a family sharing responsibility on some admissible basis need not cohabit as a marriage unit; clearly, therefore, their legal responsibilities would be unaffected by the transience and the vagaries of the marriage relationship itself. It is even conceivable that, in the absence of a family contract or where such a contract is disallowed, children begotten by a given couple, whether married or not, would be assigned involuntarily to some legally recognized family; also, contractually initiated families might well have jurisdiction only in specified contexts. Again, a family might conceivably be contractually initiated by one party of either sex, where another might serve merely as a natural donor (as is very nearly already the case in the practice of artificial insemination, where the donor need be neither a member of the resulting family nor a party to any marriage); and of course the contracting parent(s)—one, two (of either sex), or more—may merely adopt children or wards, without entering into a marriage at all. The separation of marriage and family, therefore, suggests the viability both of homosexual marriages and of families composed of parents of one sex, as well as marriages and families composed of more than two adults or two parents.

These variations suggest the relative inflexibility of our current marriage customs. In fact, the history of family organization shows that the human race has always experimented boldly and with a great deal of variety in distinguishing marriage and family structures. In primitive matrilineal societies, for instance, it is quite characteristic that the care and responsibility for children and the inheritance of property is sharply distinguished from the limited interests of those recognized as mated. Even in the most conservative setting of American life, the admission of day-care centers, boarding schools, the public educational system, compulsory health standards, the rights of children, and the like argue that the effective jurisdiction of the nuclear family is largely a myth. And in other societies—for instance, those with a strong communal if not collective organization—the authority of parents is bound to be severely circumscribed by the prerogatives of the community itself. But why this should affect the purely private relations between or among parties to a marriage is not in the least clear—unless, that is, the very notion of private relations (part of the heritage of the liberal tradition of personal rights and liberties) is itself rejected. So it is entirely fair to say that the concepts of the informal and term marriage are intelligible only within the conceptual tradition of personal liberties. In that sense, of course, they represent a partisan proposal. (Doubtless, however, analogues of these alternatives could be formulated for non-Western traditions.)

Marriages, then, need not entail families, and families need not entail marriages. Since birth control is legally permitted both in and out of marriage, it cannot consistently be maintained that marriages must be legally controlled in order to further the biological objective of the reproduction of the race. In any event, the enormous increase in the population of the world in our own century has made the restriction of births biologically more important than their encouragement. Also, artificial insemination would be a more reliable means of ensuring the birth rate (if that were actually our prime concern); and marriage interests, on the evidence, might even interfere to some extent with the biological issue. Furthermore, since the legal protection of personal privacy is one of the strongest themes of the liberal tradition, it must appear increasingly arbitrary to interfere with the discreet expression of sexual preferences on the part of consenting adults or otherwise competent parties. Hence, if the legal control of property were generally distinguished from matters affecting marriage, and if the property rights of families and members of families and the rights of children (for example, regarding constraints on child abuse) and wards were legally specified, there would seem to be no reason at all why either informal or term marriages tailored to the idiosyncratic interests of participating parties should not be tolerated within the existing legal system.

The radical implications are obvious. For instance, there would no longer be a basis for the legal status of adultery, except perhaps contingently as grounds for the breach of a *particular* contract. Adultery would be irrelevant to a marriage by informal consent, might well be precluded or ignored by some term contracts, and would in any case never as such provide grounds for a criminal action or for a civil action involving the custody of children or wards or the acquisition of property.[5] So-called "open marriages" would not be a contradiction in terms; and of course homosexual and group marriages would no longer be anomalous. Considerations of child support, child custody, alimony, and the like would be radically altered, since they would not rest, wherever still relevant, exclusively on grounds of family responsibility. The result would be to disentangle the resolution of questions of divorce, property settlement, custody of children, and so forth from just those complications that result from confusing family with marriage considerations. Conditions of divorce, for instance, might well be specified in a term contract or be legally construed as a matter of formal notice of some appropriate sort, without involving the law in any questions of intent, personal cruelty, or the like that might legitimately fall within the boundaries of personal privacy. Legal divorce proceedings, including settlement, therefore, could be entirely obviated. Neither children nor property would ever, logically or legally, involve the marriage relationship as such. The implied economies are actually startling—particularly for such a small conceptual adjustment (one that in any case is already to some extent upon us).

Accordingly, the personal and moral or religious dimensions of marriage would be affected also. For one thing, in spite of *Humanae Vitae*, there is no consensus about the natural function of marriage or the family; it is not even clear that it makes sense to speak of the natural function of such a complex pair of institutions.[6] Appeal to "the objective moral order established by God," however convincing to the faithful, is already implicitly more than questioned by a great many people.[7] Still, there is no reason to think that those who participate (or would participate) in marriage (even informal and term marriage) are (or would be) disinclined to sanctify or dignify that relationship. The "natural" function that interested parties tend to prefer is, clearly, harmonious cohabitation for whatever private purposes they may voluntarily subscribe to. In what conceivable sense, given the history of the institution to our own day, could this be said to be an illegitimate function? But if that function be conceded, it would be palpably unreasonable to disallow divorce, separation, and annulment. In fact, in the liberal tradition, it is thought to be an improper use of the law to enforce directly, merely as such, any given moral or religious practice.[8] On the other hand, the noticeable fragility of the marriage relationship—a fragility which, after all, is not the result of the innovations we are considering, but rather of the rigidity, confusion, inflexibility, and insensitivity of existing customs to historical change itself—requires, if marriage is to survive at all, a liberalized sense of the dignity or sanctity of that relationship.

One may therefore view divorce and separation less as a sign of the failure of marriage or a sign of a threat to the life of the institution, than as a natural adjunct of the relationship. *If* marriage were viewed as a wholly personal and private relationship, there would be no plausible basis for denying that short-term contracts, termination or non-renewal of a contract, and divorce or separation for cause would be legitimate sources of either relief against dissatisfaction or of continuing liberty following satisfaction within the contractual terms specified. It should be possible to liberalize the conditions of marriage so that those who wished to participate could experiment with whatever private arrangements they could jointly support in terms of personal taste and of whatever traditions of dignity and sanctity they could subscribe to. In this way, divorce, separation, and annulment would come to be construed as the appropriate forms of terminating, in a rational manner, an entirely private relationship. It could do this without affecting in the least the entirely distinct structure of whatever families the participating parties belong to and without implying anything at all of a pejorative nature about the marriage dissolved or terminated. What this means is that marriage cannot, on the hypothesis given, fail to become a relatively transient institution, at least for many. It would be a source of continuing personal freedom and renewal for competent parties, weaving in and out of contact with more permanent and more fundamental family relations.[9]

The issue is not whether it is realistic to invent new forms of marriage along the lines suggested or even to separate the concepts of marriage and family in the precise way indicated; it is rather to recognize that the impermanence, dissatisfaction, and collision of values that characterize so much of contemporary marriage are effectively yielding such a separation. As things stand, however, neither institution is protected from the dislocations due to the other, and there is no provision for the rational resolution of problems affecting either institution. For example, there is good reason to think that the incidence of juvenile delinquency and juvenile crime is in large measure due to the inertia, incompetence, and inefficiency of isolated nuclear families regarding the rearing and control of their members. The transience of marriage obviously contributes to the instability of nuclear families. But it is the nuclear family that is utterly inadequate to come to grips with the broader problems of any community. This inadequacy is both masked and confirmed against change by our insistence on subordinating the existence of families to the condition of marriage. *If* marriages are as unstable as they appear to be and *if* families are as important as they are thought to be to the stable life of a community (for instance, to the effectiveness of its moral values, and to the rational management of its resources), then it must be entirely irrational to conflate the two institutions or, worse, to make the institution of the family wholly or largely dependent on that of the more transient marriage.

There may well be, therefore, an actual need to experiment with separating the institutions in a more formal way—not just to speculate about the implications of such a change.

## NOTES

1. See, for instance, Pope Paul VI, *Humanae Vitae* (1964), reprinted in *Philosophy and Sex*, ed. Robert Baker and Frederick Elliston (Buffalo, N.Y.: Prometheus Books, 1975), pp. 131–49.
2. See, for instance, "The Family, Prison of Love" (conversation between Philippe Ariès and Jacques Mousseau), *Psychology Today*, September 1975, pp. 52–58.
3. See Denis de Rougemont, *Love in the Western World*, trans. Montgomery Belgion (New York: Pantheon, 1956).
4. See Edward Westermarck, *History of Human Marriage*, 3 vols. (New York: Macmillan, 1921); Bernard I. Murstein, *Love, Sex, and Marriage* (New York: Springer, 1974); Friedrich Engels, *The Origin of the Family, Private Property and the State*, rev. ed., trans. Alec West (New York: International Publishers, 1942, 1970); Bronislaw Malinowski, *The Family among the Australian Aborigines* (New York: Schocken, 1963).
5. See Richard Wasserstrom, "Is Adultery Immoral?," in Baker and Elliston (above, n. 1), pp. 207–21.
6. See Joseph Margolis, *Negativities: The Limits of Life* (Columbus: Charles E. Merrill, 1975).
7. *Humanae Vitae*.
8. See Ronald Dworkin, "Lord Devlin and the Enforcement of Morals," *Yale Law Journal* 75 (1965–66), reprinted in *Morality and the Law*, ed. Richard Wasserstrom (Belmont, Calif.: Wadsworth, 1971); but also Joseph Margolis (above, n. 6), chap. 5.

9. It is interesting to note that a recent development in family ther-
apy stresses "retribalization," which conceivably would permit
(though it does not specify) a distinction between family and
marriage. In Ross V. Speck and Carolyn L. Attneave, *Family
Networks* (New York: Pantheon, 1973), a "social network"
("tribe") is said to include "the nuclear family and all of the kin
of every member. But it also includes the friends, neighbors, work
associates, and significant helpers from churches, schools, social
agencies, and institutions who are willing and able to take the risk
of involvement" (p. xxii). Regarding the "retribalization goal," it
is the social network itself that "becomes the unit of treatment or
intervention" (p. 6). The movement, influenced by R. D. Laing,
appears to make no mention of divorce, separation, even marriage. Yet it centers on the "nuclear family," which of course at
once neglects the alternative possibilities of marriage and is too
restrictive, in spite of its apparent inventiveness, regarding the
possibilities of family organization.

# Marriage

# *Further References*

Starred items are those of philosophical interest.

Anthony, Susan B. "Marriage Has Ever Been a One-Sided Affair." In *Voices from Women's Liberation*, edited by Leslie B. Tanner. New York: New American Library, Signet, 1971.

*Aquinas, Thomas. *On the Truth of the Catholic Faith*. Translated by Vernon J. Bourke. Garden City, N.Y.: Doubleday, 1956. Book 3, parts 1 and 2.

*Archbishop of Canterbury (Fisher). *The Church and Marriage*. London: Church Information Board, 1954.

*Ardley, Gavin. "The Meaning of Plato's Marital Communism." *Philosophical Studies* (Ireland) 18 (1969): 36–47.

*Astell, Mary. *Reflections on Marriage*. London, 1706.

Baber, Ray E. *Marriage and the Family*. New York: McGraw-Hill, 1953.

Bach, George R., and Wyden, Peter. *The Intimate Enemy*. New York: Morrow, 1968.

*Barnhart, Joseph E., and Barnhart, Mary Ann. "Marital Faithfulness and Unfaithfulness." *Journal of Social Philosophy* 4 (1973): 10–15.

Bartell, G. D. *Group Sex*. New York: Peter H. Wyden, 1971.

Basset, William. *The Bond of Marriage*. Notre Dame, Ind.: University of Notre Dame Press, 1968.

*Bayles, Michael. "Marriage, Love and Procreation." In *Philosophy and Sex*, edited by Robert Baker and Frederick Elliston. Buffalo, N.Y.: Prometheus Books, 1975.

*Beauvoir, Simone de. *The Second Sex*. Translated by H. M. Parshley. New York: Knopf, 1953. Pages 400–55.

Becker, Howard, and Hill, Reuben, eds. *Family, Marriage, and Parenthood*. Boston: D.C. Heath, 1955.

Bell, Robert R. *Marriage and Family Interaction*. Homewood, Ill.: Dorsey Press, 1971.

————. *Premarital Sex in a Changing Society*. Englewood Cliffs, N.J.: Prentice-Hall, 1966.

————, ed. *Studies in Marriage and the Family*. New York: Thomas Y. Crowell, 1973.

Bernard, Jessie. *The Future of Marriage*. New York: Bantam Books, 1974.

————. *Remarriage*. New York: Dryden, 1956.

*Bertocci, Peter Anthony. *The Human Venture in Sex, Love and Marriage*. New York: Association Press, 1949.

Blood, Robert O. *Marriage*. New York: Free Press, 1969.

Briffault, Robert, and Malinowski, Bronislaw. *Marriage: Past and Present*. Boston: Porter Edward Sargent, 1956.

Brown, Judith. "Toward a Female Liberation Movement." In *Voices from Women's Liberation*, edited by Leslie B. Tanner. New York: New American Library, 1971.

Burgess, Ernest W., and Cottrell, Leonard S. *Predicting Success or Failure in Marriage*. New York: Prentice-Hall, 1939.

Burgess, Ernest W., and Locke, Harvey J. *The Family*. New York: American Book Co., 1953.

Burgess, Ernest W., and Wallin, Paul. *Engagement and Marriage*. Philadelphia: Lippincott, 1953.

Carter, Hugh, and Glick, Paul C. *Marriage and Divorce: A Social and Economic Study*. Cambridge: Harvard University Press, 1970.

Casler, Lawrence. "Permissive Matrimony: Proposals for the Future." *Humanist* 34:2 (March-April 1974): 4–9.

Chesser, Eustace. *Unmarried Love*. New York: David McKay, 1965.

Christensen, Harold T., ed. *Handbook of Marriage and the Family*. Chicago: Rand McNally, 1964.

*Cohen, Carl. "Sex, Birth Control, and Human Life." *Ethics* 79 (1969): 251–62.

Conley, John A., and Huffman, Warren J. *Readings in Marriage, Sex Education, Human Sexuality*. Champaign, Ill.: Stipes Publishing Co., 1972.

Cox, Frank D. *Youth, Marriage and the Seductive Society*. Dubuque, Iowa: William C. Brown Co., 1968.

Cronan, Sheila. "Marriage." In *Radical Feminism*, edited by Anne Koedt, Ellen Levine, and Anita Rapone. New York: Quadrangle Books, 1973.

Cuber, John F., and Harroff, Peggy B. *Sex and the Significant Americans*. Baltimore: Penguin Books, 1968.

Delora, Joann S., and Delora, Jack R., eds. *Intimate Life Styles*. Pacific Palisades, Calif.: Goodyear, 1972.

*Dewar, Lindsay. *Marriage without Morals: A Reply to Mr. Bertrand Russell*. London: Society for Promoting Christian Knowledge, 1931.

Ditzion, Sidney. *Marriage, Morals and Sex in America: A History of Ideas*. New York: Bookman Associates, 1953.

Duberman, Lucile. *Marriage and Its Alternatives*. New York: Praeger, 1974.

Ellis, Havelock. *The History of Marriage*. Vol. 7 in *Studies in the Psychology of Sex*. Philadelphia: F. A. Davis, 1928.

*Elliston, Frederick. "In Defense of Promiscuity." In *Philosophy and Sex*, edited by Robert Baker and Frederick Elliston. Buffalo: Prometheus Books, 1975.

*Engels, Friedrich. *The Origin of the Family, Private Property, and the State*. 1884. Reprint. New York: International Publishers, 1942.

Fishbein, Morris, and Kennedy, Ruby Jo R., eds. *Modern Marriage and Family Living*. New York: Oxford University Press, 1957.

*Friedan, Betty. *The Feminine Mystique*. New York: W.W. Norton, 1963.

Fullerton, Gail Putney. *Survival in Marriage*. New York: Holt, Rinehart & Winston, 1972.

Gillespie, D. "Who Has the Power? The Marital Struggle." *Journal of Marriage and the Family* 33 (1971): 445–58.

Glazer-Malbin, Nona, and Waehrer, Helen Youngelson, eds. *Woman in a Man-Made World*. Chicago: Rand McNally, 1972. Pages 164–207.

Goldman, E. "Marriage and Love." 1917. Reprinted in *The American Sisterhood*, edited by W. Martin. New York: Harper & Row, 1972.

Goode, William. *After Divorce*. Glencoe, Ill.: Free Press, 1956.

Gornick, Vivian, and Morgan, Barbara K., eds. *Woman in Sexist Society: Studies in Power and Powerlessness*. New York: Basic Books, 1971. Pages 35–203.

Gough, K. "The Origin of the Family." *Journal of Marriage and the Family* 33 (1971): 760–70.

Greer, Germaine. "The Middle-Class Myth of Love and Marriage." In *The Female Eunuch*. London: Paladin, 1970. Pages 198–218.

Gross, Leonard, ed. *Sexual Issues in Marriage*. New York: Spectrum Publications, 1975.

Hamilton, G. V. *A Research in Marriage*. New York: A. & C. Boni, 1929.

Hadden, Jeffrey K., and Borgatta, Marie L., eds. *Marriage and the Family*. Itasca, Ill.: F.E. Peacock Publishers, 1969.

Hart, Harold H. *Marriage: For and Against*. New York: Hart Publishing Co., 1972.

*Held, Virginia. "Marx, Sex and the Transformation of Society." *Philosophical Forum* 5 (1973–74): 168–84.

*Horney, Karen. *Feminine Psychology*. New York: W.W. Norton, 1967. Pages 84–98, 119–32.

*Hume, David. "Of Polygamy and Divorces." In *Essays Moral, Political and Literary*, vol. 2, edited by T. H. Green and T. H. Grose. London: Longmans, Green, 1875.

Hunt, Morton. *The Affair: A Portrait of Extra-Marital Love in Contemporary America*. Cleveland: World Publishing Co., 1969.

———. *The World of the Formerly Married*. New York: McGraw-Hill, 1966.

Janeway, Elizabeth. *Man's World, Woman's Place*. New York: William Morrow, 1971.

Jones, Beverly. "The Dynamics of Marriage and Motherhood." In *Sisterhood Is Powerful*, edited by Robin Morgan. New York: Random House, 1970.

*Kierkegaard, Sören. "The Aesthetic Validity of Marriage." In *Either/Or*, vol. 2, translated by W. Lowrie. Garden City, N.Y.: Doubleday, Anchor Books, 1959.

Kirkendall, Lester A. *Premarital Intercourse and Interpersonal Relationships*. New York: Julian Press, 1961.

Komarovsky, Mirra. *Blue-Collar Marriage*. New York: Random House, Vintage Books, 1970.

Leo, Evelyn. "Dependency in Marriage: Oppression in Middle-Class Marriage." In *Voices from Women's Liberation*, edited by Leslie B. Tanner. New York: New American Library, Signet, 1971.

Leslie, Gerald R., and Leslie, Elizabeth McLaughlin. *Marriage in a Changing World*. New York: John Wiley & Sons, 1977.

*Lindsey, B. B., and Evans, W. *The Companionate Marriage*. 1927. Reprint. New York: Arno Press, 1972.

McLennan, John. *Primitive Marriage*. Edinburgh: Adam & Charles Black, 1865.

*McMurtry, John. "Monogamy:A Critique." *Monist* 56 (1972): 587–99.

Masters, William H., and Johnson, Virginia E. *The Pleasure Bond*. Boston: Little, Brown, 1974.

*Mill, John Stuart, and Taylor, Harriet. "Early Essays on Marriage and Divorce." In *Essays on Sex Equality*, edited by Alice S. Rossi. Chicago: University of Chicago Press, 1970.

Mitchell, Juliet. *Woman's Estate*. New York: Random House, 1971. Chapter 8.

Mudd, Emily, et al. *Marriage Counseling: A Casebook*. New York: Association Press, 1958.

Müller-Lyer, F. C. *The Evolution of Modern Marriage*. 1913. Reprint. London: Allen & Unwin, 1930.

Murstein, Bernard I. *Love, Sex and Marriage*. New York: Springer, 1974.

Neubeck, Gerhard, ed. *Extramarital Relations*. Englewood Cliffs, N.J.: Prentice-Hall, 1970.

Nimkoff, Meyer F. *Marriage and the Family*. Boston: Houghton Mifflin, 1947.

Novak, Michael, ed. *The Experience of Marriage*. New York: Macmillan, 1964.

O'Neill, Nena, and O'Neill, George. *Open Marriage*. New York: M. Evans & Co., 1972.

————. *Shifting Gears*. New York: Avon, 1974.

Otto, Herbert A., ed. *The Family in Search of a Future*. New York: Appleton-Century-Crofts, 1970.

*Palmer, David. "The Consolation of the Wedded." In *Philosophy and Sex*, edited by Robert Baker and Frederick Elliston. Buffalo, N.Y.: Prometheus Books, 1975.

Pineo, P. "Disenchantment in the Later Years of Marriage." In *Middle Age and Aging*, edited by B. Neugarten. Chicago: University of Chicago Press, 1968.

*Plato. *The Republic*. Translated by G. M. A. Grube. New York: Hackett Publishing Co., 1974. Book 5.

Pomeroy, Hiram S. *The Ethics of Marriage*. New York: Funk & Wagnalls, 1888.

*Pope Paul VI. *Humanae Vitae*. Washington, D.C.: N.C.W.C., 1968.

*Pope Pius XI. "Casti Connubii." *Catholic Mind* 29 (22 January 1931): 21–64.

Pospishil, V. J. *Divorce and Remarriage*. New York: Herder & Herder, 1967.

Post, Louis F. *Ethical Principles of Marriage and Divorce*. Chicago: Public Publishing Co., 1906.

Reiss, Ira L. *The Social Context of Premarital Sexual Permissiveness*. New York: Holt, Rinehart & Winston, 1967.

Rodman, Hyman, ed. *Marriage, Family and Society*. New York: Random House, 1965.

Rogers, Carl R. *Becoming Partners: Marriage and Its Alternatives*. New York: Delacorte Press, 1972.

Roy, Rustum, and Roy, Della. "Is Monogamy Outdated?" *Humanist* 30:2 (March/April 1970): 19–26.

*Royal Commission on Marriage and Divorce*. Report. Cond. 9678. London: H.M.S.O., 1956.

*Russell, Bertrand. *Marriage and Morals*. New York: Liveright 1928.

*————. "Marriage and the Population Question." *International Journal of Ethics* 26 (1916): 443–61.

\*————. "My Own View of Marriage." *The Outlook* 48 (7 March 1928): 376–77.

\*————. "Ostrich Code of Marriage." *Forum* 80 (1928): 7–10.

Safilios-Rothschild, Constantina, ed. *Toward a Sociology of Women.* Lexington, Mass.: Xerox College Publishing, 1972.

Seigle, Bernard. *Marriage Today.* New York: Alba House, 1973.

Smith, James R., and Smith, Lynn G. *Beyond Monogamy.* Baltimore: Johns Hopkins University Press, 1974.

Stopes, Marie. *Married Love.* London: A. C. Fifield, 1918.

Sussman, Marvin B., ed. *Sourcebook in Marriage and the Family.* Boston: Houghton Mifflin, 1968.

Terman, Lewis M., et al. *Psychological Factors in Marital Happiness.* New York: McGraw-Hill, 1938.

Theodore, Athena. *The Professional Woman.* Cambridge, Mass.: Schenkman Publishing Co., 1971.

Van de Velde, Theodoor. *Ideal Marriage: Its Physiology and Technique.* New York: Covici Friede, 1930.

Vincent, Clark. *Unmarried Mothers.* Glencoe, Ill.: Free Press, 1961.

\*Wasserstrom, Richard. "Is Adultery Immoral?" In *Philosophy and Sex,* edited by Robert Baker and Frederick Elliston. Buffalo, N.Y.: Prometheus Books, 1975.

\*Wayne, T. G. *Morals and Marriage: The Catholic Background to Sex.* New York: Longmans, 1936.

Werth, Alvin, and Mihanovich, Clement S. *Papal Pronouncements on Marriage and the Family.* Milwaukee: Bruce Publishing Co., 1955.

Westermarck, Edward. *The History of Human Marriage.* 1889. Reprint. New York: Allerton Book Co., 1922.

White, Douglas. *Modern Light on Sex and Marriage.* London: Skeffington, 1932.

Whitehurst, Robert N. "Sex: In and Out of Marriage." *Humanist* 30:1 (Jan./Feb. 1970): 27–28.

Wilson, Thomas J. B., with Meyers, Everett. *Wife-Swapping: A Complete Eight-Year Survey of Morals in North America.* New York: Counterpoint Inc., 1965.

Winch, Robert F. *Mate Selection.* New York: Harper, 1958.

————. *The Modern Family.* New York: Henry Holt, 1952.

# Part VI
# Rape

# Part VI

# Rape

## Introduction

Feminists have recently seized on rape as a paradigmatic and dramatic symbol of the plight of women within our culture. SUSAN GRIFFIN associates a host of evils with this all-American crime. Rape is an act of coercion that forces women to do something harmful to them against their will. For women, the threat of rape curtails liberties that men freely enjoy. Rape's frequent occurrence but less frequent successful prosecution is symptomatic of women's social position as second-class citizens. The lies with which rape is disguised only perpetuate the injustice: rapists are thought to be insane, sexually repressed, and atypical males; rape is regarded as a natural sex outlet for men who cannot contain themselves; all women are believed secretly to yearn to be ravished by violent and passionate men. The ideology of patriarchy, which places social power exclusively in the hands of men (who are supposed to be strong, aggressive, domineering, and forceful), reinforces the distortion of the actual relation between the sexes and subverts the movement toward a more equitable ideal.

Is there any inner logic to this catalogue of evils associated with rape? MARILYN FRYE and CAROLYN M. SHAFER offer a moral diagnosis of rape and a social explanation for its causes. Rape is wrong because it is disrepectful: the rapist intrudes into another person's domain in a harmful way without her consent. As a type of assault, its special wrongness consists partly in the degree of intrusion: the man penetrates not the privacy of a woman's home or bedroom, but of her body. If the body is the creative center of a person's domain, then rape is a violation of personhood, the ultimate act of disrespect which denies women their equality as bearers of the same moral and legal rights men enjoy.

The myths that surround rape serve to protect and perpetuate it as a mechanism for social control: the threat of rape keeps women in their places as members of the second—that is, the subordinate—sex. Women collude in these deceptions because a realistic perception of their secondary social status would deny them the self-image necessary to function in everyday life—indeed, to survive.

PAMELA FOA argues against this diagnosis that rape is wrong as a species of assault that denies women their ontological equality. Rape of an animal, child, or mentally retarded adult lacking this equality is still morally outrageous. And the violent physical attacks of a Jack the Ripper are at least as harmful and disrespectful as rape, yet his victims would not suffer the same moral degradation.

Consequently, Foa argues that the special wrongness of rape is to be traced to our sexual code. According to our Victorian heritage, intercourse between a man and a woman is supposed to be accompanied by love and affection. Sex with strangers, or other men for whom a woman has no such feelings, violates this moral tie between intercourse and intimacy, degrading the woman as a survivor of this social transgression.

According to Foa, the solution to the problem of rape requires a reconceptualization of sex. At present, boys are taught to be sexually aggressive; girls are taught to be tolerant and passive. Foa argues alternatively for sex based on friendship and the recognition of the legitimacy of erotic pleasure. To make friends of our lovers is to expand the field of meaningful social encounters through sexual intimacy. Rape would cease to be a defilement of its victim on this new paradigm because sex had been cleansed of its dirty connotations.

SUSAN RAE PETERSON argues that rape is immoral not primarily because it violates the principle of treating women as persons, or because of the nature of our sexual morality generally, but because it forcibly restricts the bodily movements of women. She interprets rape not as an isolated series of random events but as a coercive social practice embedded in a patriarchal set of roles and rules governing the lives of both sexes. According to Peterson, the legal inequities that protect husbands from the charge of "raping" their wives, the sympathy of jurists toward rapists that makes conviction difficult, and the unusual burden of proof placed on its victims to establish their innocence all demonstrate the secondary legal and social status of women. Appeals to the "undue risks" women take in visiting bars or other public places, as well as the pervasive myth that all women secretly long to be ravished, render rape prima facie justified sexual assault and make it a type of curfew imposed by men to limit female mobility. Peterson emphasizes the aggressiveness of rape over its sexual character. She does this to counter the popular belief that its victims are seductive females inviting trouble, rather than mothers and infants esconced in the privacy of their homes. Such sex without the woman's consent may be far more normal than current mythology is willing to concede—as the erotic appeal of violence and the permissibility of male aggression (sexual or otherwise) strongly hints.

Is rape simply a seduction gone astray? The line between persuasion and coercion is so thin that the difference between reluctant compliance and final refusal is difficult to anticipate. But the male's dilemma does not obliterate this difference on which rape depends.

Peterson argues that rape is a "sex-differentiated risk": whatever dangers afflict people, rape is an additional form of sexual assault that only women undergo. And the cautious behavior of most women on dark, isolated streets is evidence for this covert threat, whether it is consciously acknowledged or not. This threat arises from the failure of the state to guarantee a basic political right: the freedom of bodily movement. And this failure betrays the state's underlying character as a male protection agency. What is wrong with rape is that it is really not wrong at all.

The immorality of rape calls into question fundamental assumptions about our sex lives. What are the sexual paradigms within our culture today, and what should they be? Once we abandon the view of sex for procreation, as many members of society (including an increasing number of Roman Catholics) have done, then we can easily relapse into a vulgar hedonism whereby sex is exclusively for pleasure. But this paradigm leads to De Sade's paradox: from his hedonistic, libertine perspective, no form of sexual activity is wrong and none should be proscribed; inasmuch as the protests of women frustrate the maximization of physical gratification, their resistance rather than rape itself is the real evil. Few if any are willing to accept his conclusion—and certainly not Frye, Shafer, Foa or Peterson. Their appeals to respect for persons, to sex based on friendship, and to the freedom of physical movement offer three ways to refute the perverse logic that underlies De Sade's paradox. They thereby raise some fundamental questions about the differences between men and women, the purpose and justification of marriage, the moral and legal rights of women, and many other issues with which this collection has been concerned.

F. E.

Susan Griffin

# Rape: The All-American Crime

## I

I have never been free of the fear of rape. From a very early age I, like most women, have thought of rape as part of my natural environment—something to be feared and prayed against like fire or lightning. I never asked why men raped; I simply thought it one of the many mysteries of human nature.

I was, however, curious enough about the violent side of humanity to read every crime magazine I was able to ferret away from my grandfather. Each issue featured at least one "sex crime," with pictures of a victim, usually in a pearl neck- lace, and of the ditch or the orchard where her body was found. I was never certain why the victims were always women, nor what the motives of the murder were, but I did guess that the world was not a safe place for women. I observed that my grandmother was meticulous about locks, and quick to draw the shades before anyone removed so much as a shoe. I sensed that danger lurked outside.

At the age of eight, my suspicions were confirmed. My grand- mother took me to the back of the house where the men wouldn't hear, and told me that strange men wanted to do harm

This article first appeared in *Ramparts*, September 1971, pp. 26–35, and is reprinted by permission of Susan T. Griffin, copyright holder.

to little girls. I learned not to walk on dark streets, not to talk to strangers, or get into strange cars, to lock doors, and to be modest. She never explained why a man would want to harm a little girl, and I never asked.

If I thought for a while that my grandmother's fears were imaginary, the illusion was brief. That year, on the way home from school, a schoolmate a few years older than I tried to rape me. Later, in an obscure aisle of the local library (while I was reading *Freddy the Pig*) I turned to discover a man exposing himself. Then, the friendly man around the corner was arrested for child molesting.

My initiation to sexuality was typical. Every woman has similar stories to tell—the first man who attacked her may have been a neighbor, a family friend, an uncle, her doctor, or perhaps her own father. And women who grow up in New York City always have tales about the subway.

But though rape and the fear of rape are a daily part of every woman's consciousness, the subject is so rarely discussed by that unofficial staff of male intellectuals (who write the books which study seemingly every other form of male activity) that one begins to suspect a conspiracy of silence. And indeed, the obscurity of rape in print exists in marked contrast to the frequency of rape in reality, for *forcible rape is the most frequently committed violent crime in America today*. The Federal Bureau of Investigation classes three crimes as violent: murder, aggravated assault and forcible rape. In 1968, 31,060 rapes were *reported*. According to the FBI and independent criminologists, however, to approach accuracy this figure must be multiplied by at least a factor of ten to compensate for the fact that most rapes are not reported; when these compensatory mathematics are used, there are more rapes committed than aggravated assaults and homicides.

When I asked Berkeley, California's, Police Inspector in charge of rape investigation if he knew why men rape women, he replied that he had not spoken with "these people and delved into what really makes them tick, because that really isn't my job. . . ." However, when I asked him how a woman might prevent being raped, he was not so reticent, "I wouldn't advise any female to go walking around alone at night . . . and she should lock her car at all times." The Inspector illustrated his warning with a grisly story about a man who lay in wait for women in the back seats of their cars, while they were shopping in a local supermarket. This man eventually murdered one of his rape victims. "Always lock your car," the Inspector repeated, and then added, without a hint of irony, "Of course, you don't have to be paranoid about this type of thing."

The inspector wondered why I wanted to write about rape. Like most men he did not understand the urgency of the topic, for, after all, men are not raped. But like most women I had spent considerable time speculating on the true nature of the rapist. When I was very young, my image of the "sexual offender" was a nightmarish amalgamation of the bogey man and Captain Hook: he wore a black cape, and he cackled. As I matured, so did my image of the rapist. Born into the psychoanalytic age, I tried to "understand" the rapist. Rape, I came to believe, was only one of many unfortunate evils produced by sexual repression. Reasoning by tautology, I concluded that any man who would rape a woman must be out of his mind.

Yet, though the theory that rapists are insane is a popular one, this belief has no basis in fact. According to Professor Menachem Amir's study of 646 rape cases in Philadelphia, *Patterns in Forcible Rape*, men who rape are not abnormal. Amir writes, "Studies indicate that sex offenders do not constitute a unique or psychopathological type; nor are they as a group invariably more disturbed than the control groups to which they are compared." Alan Taylor, a parole officer who has worked with rapists in the prison facilities at San Luis Obispo, California, stated the question in plainer language, "Those men were the most normal men there. They had a lot of hang-ups, but they were the same hang-ups as men walking out on the street."

Another canon in the apologetics of rape is that, if it were not for learned social controls, all men would rape. Rape is held to be natural behavior, and not to rape must be learned. But in truth rape is not universal to the human species. Moreover, studies of rape in our culture reveal that, far from being impulsive behavior, most rape is planned. Professor Amir's study reveals that in cases of group rape (the "gangbang" of masculine slang) 90 percent of the rapes were planned; in pair rapes, 83 percent of the rapes were planned; and in single rapes, 58 percent were planned. These figures should significantly discredit the image of the rapist as a man who is suddenly overcome by sexual needs society does not allow him to fulfill.

Far from the social control of rape being learned, comparisons with other cultures lead one to suspect that, in our society, it is rape itself that is learned. (The fact that rape is against the law should not be considered proof that rape is not in fact encouraged as part of our culture.)

This culture's concept of rape as an illegal, but still understandable, form of behavior is not a universal one. In her study *Sex and Temperament*, Margaret Mead describes a society that does not share our views. The Arapesh do not ". . . have any conception of the male nature that might make rape understandable to them." Indeed, our interpretation of rape is a product of our conception of the nature of male sexuality. A common retort to the question, why don't women rape men, is the myth that men have greater sexual needs, that their sexuality is more urgent than women's. And it is the nature of human beings to want to live up to what is expected of them.

And this same culture which expects aggression from the male expects passivity from the female. Conveniently, the companion myth about the nature of female sexuality is that all women secretly want to be raped. Lurking beneath her modest female exterior is a subconscious desire to be ravished. The following description of a stag movie, written by Brenda Starr in Los Angeles' underground paper, *Everywoman*, typifies this male fantasy. The movie "showed a woman in her underclothes reading on her bed. She is interrupted by a rapist with a knife. He immediately wins her over with his charm and they get busy sucking and fucking." An advertisement in the *Berkeley Barb* reads, "Now as all women know from their daydreams, rape has a lot of advantages. Best of all it's so simple. No preparation necessary, no planning ahead of time, no wondering if you should or shouldn't; just whang! bang!" Thanks to Masters and Johnson even the scientific canon recognizes that for the female, "whang! bang!" can scarcely be described as pleasurable.

Still, the male psyche persists in believing that, protestations and struggles to the contrary, deep inside her mysterious feminine soul, the female victim has wished for her own fate. A young woman who was raped by the husband of a friend said that days after the incident the man returned to her home, pounded on the door and screamed to her, "Jane, Jane. You loved it. You know you loved it."

The theory that women like being raped extends itself by deduction into the proposition that most or much of rape is provoked by the victim. But this, too, is only myth. Though provocation, considered a mitigating factor in a court of law, may consist of only "a gesture," according to the Federal Commission on Crimes of Violence, only 4 percent of reported rapes involved any precipitative behavior by the woman.

The notion that rape is enjoyed by the victim is also convenient for the man who, though he would not commit forcible rape, enjoys the idea of its existence, as if rape confirms that enormous sexual potency which he secretly knows to be his own. It is for the pleasure of the armchair rapist that detailed accounts of violent rapes exist in the media. Indeed, many men appear to take sexual pleasure from nearly all forms of violence. Whatever the motivation, male sexuality and violence in our culture seem to be inseparable. James Bond alternately whips out his revolver and his cock, and though there is no known connection between the skills of gun-fighting and love-making, pacifism seems suspiciously effeminate.

In a recent fictional treatment of the Manson case, Frank Conroy writes of his vicarious titillation when describing the murders to his wife:

> "Every single person there was killed." She didn't move.
> "It sounds like there was torture," I said. As the words left my mouth I knew there was no need to say them to frighten her into believing that she needed me for protection.

The pleasure he feels as his wife's protector is inextricably mixed with pleasure in the violence itself. Conroy writes, "I was excited by the killings, as one is excited by catastrophe on a grand scale, as one is alert to pre-echoes of unknown changes, hints of unrevealed secrets, rumblings of chaos. . . ."

The attraction of the male in our culture to violence and death is a tradition Manson and his admirers are carrying on with tireless avidity (even presuming Manson's innocence, he dreams of the purification of fire and destruction). It was Malraux in his *Anti-Memoirs* who said that, for the male, facing death was *the* illuminating experience analogous to childbirth for the female. Certainly our culture does glorify war and shroud the agonies of the gun-fighter in veils of mystery.

And in the spectrum of male behavior, rape, the perfect combination of sex and violence, is the penultimate act. Erotic pleasure cannot be separated from culture, and in our culture male eroticism is wedded to power. Not only should a man be taller and stronger than a female in the perfect love-match, but he must also demonstrate his superior strength in gestures of dominance which are perceived as amorous. Though the law attempts to make a clear division between rape and sexual intercourse, in fact the courts find it difficult to distinguish between a case where the decision to copulate was mutual and one where a man forced himself upon his partner.

The scenario is even further complicated by the expectation that, not only does a woman mean "yes" when she says "no," but that a really decent woman ought to begin by saying "no," and then be led down the primrose path to acquiescence. Ovid, the author of Western Civilization's most celebrated sex manual, makes this expectation perfectly clear: ". . . and when I beg you to say 'yes,' say 'no.' Then let me lie outside your bolted door. . . . So Love grows strong. . . ."

That the basic elements of rape are involved in all heterosexual relationships may explain why men often identify with the offender in this crime. But to regard the rapist as the victim, a man driven by his inherent sexual needs to take what will not be given him, reveals a basic ignorance of sexual politics. For in our culture heterosexual love finds an erotic expression through male dominance and female submission. A man who derives pleasure from raping a woman clearly must enjoy force and dominance as much or more than the simple pleasures of the flesh. Coitus cannot be experienced in isolation. The weather, the state of the nation, the level of sugar in the blood—all will affect a man's ability to achieve orgasm. If a man can achieve sexual pleasure after terrorizing and humiliating the object of his passion, and in fact while inflicting pain upon her, one must assume he derives pleasure directly from terrorizing, humiliating, and harming a woman. According to Amir's study of forcible rape, on a statistical average the man who has been convicted of rape was found to have a normal sexual personality, tending to be different from the normal, well-adjusted male only in having a greater tendency to express violence and rage.

And if the professional rapist is to be separated from the average dominant heterosexual, it may be mainly a quantitative difference. For the existence of rape as an index to masculinity is not entirely metaphorical. Though this measure of masculinity seems to be more publicly exhibited among "bad boys" or aging bikers who practice sexual initiation through group rape, in fact, "good boys" engage in the same rites to prove their manhood. In Stockton, a small town in California which epitomizes silent-majority America, a bachelor party was given last summer for a young man about to be married. A woman was hired to dance "topless" for the amusement of the guests. At the high point of the evening the bridegroom-to-be dragged the woman into a bedroom. No move was made by any of his companions to stop what was clearly going to be an attempted rape. Far from it. As the woman described, "I tried to keep him away—told him of my Herpes Genitalis, et cetera, but he couldn't face the guys if he didn't screw me." After the bridegroom had finished raping the woman and returned with her to the party, far from chastising him, his friends heckled the woman and covered her with wine.

It was fortunate for the dancer that the bridegroom's friends did not follow him into the bedroom for, though one might suppose that in group rape, since the victim is outnumbered, less force would be inflicted on her, in fact, Amir's studies indicate, "the most excessive degrees of violence occurred in group rape." Far from discouraging violence, the presence of other men may in fact encourage sadism, and even cause the behavior. In an unpublished study of group rape by Gilbert Geis and Duncan Chappell, the authors refer to a study by W. H. Blanchard which relates, "The leader of the male group . . . apparently precipitated and maintained the activity, despite misgivings, because of a need to fulfill the role that the other two men had assigned to him. 'I was scared when it began to happen,' he says. 'I wanted to leave but I didn't want to say it to the other guys—you know—that I was scared.' "

Thus it becomes clear that not only does our culture teach men the rudiments of rape, but society, or more specifically other men, encourage the practice of it.

## II

Every man I meet wants to protect me. Can't figure out what from.

—Mae West

If a male society rewards aggressive, domineering sexual behavior, it contains within itself a sexual schizophrenia. For the masculine man is also expected to prove his mettle as a protector of women. To the naive eye, this dichotomy implies that men fall into one of two categories: those who rape and those who protect. In fact, life does not prove so simple. In a study euphemistically entitled "Sex Aggression by College Men," it was discovered that men who believe in a double standard of morality for men and women, who in fact believe most fervently in the ultimate value of virginity, are more liable to commit "this aggressive variety of sexual exploitation."

(At this point in our narrative it should come as no surprise that Sir Thomas Malory, famous for that classic tale of chivalry, *Le Morte d'Arthur*, was himself arrested and found guilty of repeated incidents of rape.)

In the system of chivalry, men protect women against men. This is not unlike the protection relationship which the Mafia established with small businesses in the early part of this century. Indeed, chivalry is an age-old protection racket which depends for its existence on rape.

According to the male mythology which defines and perpetuates rape, it is an animal instinct inherent in the male. The story goes that sometime in our pre-historical past, the male, more hirsute and burly than today's counterparts, roamed about an uncivilized landscape until he found a desirable female. (Oddly enough, this female is *not* pictured as more muscular than the modern woman.) Her mate does not bother with courtship. He simply grabs her by the hair and drags her to the closest cave. Presumably, one of the major advantages of modern civilization for the female has been the civilizing of the male. We call it chivalry.

But women do not get chivalry for free. According to the logic of sexual politics, we, too, have to civilize our behavior. (Enter chastity. Enter virginity. Enter monogamy.) For the female, civilized behavior means chastity before marriage and faithfulness within it. Chivalrous behavior in the male is supposed to protect that chastity from involuntary defilement. The fly in the ointment of this otherwise peaceful system is the fallen woman. She does not behave. And therefore she does not deserve protection. Or, to use another argument, a major tenet of the same value system: what has once been defiled cannot again be violated. One begins to suspect that it is the behavior of the fallen woman, and not that of the male, that civilization aims to control.

The assumption that a woman who does not respect the double standard deserves whatever she gets (or at the very least "asks for it") operates in the courts today. While in some states a man's previous rape convictions are not considered admissible evidence, the sexual reputation of the rape victim is considered a crucial element of the facts upon which the court must decide innocence or guilt.

The court's respect for the double standard manifested itself particularly clearly in the case of *The People* v. *Jerry Plotkin*. Mr. Plotkin, a 36-year-old jeweler, was tried for rape in the spring of 1971 in a San Francisco Superior Court. According to the woman who brought the charges, Plotkin, along with three other men, forced her at gunpoint to enter a car one night in October, 1970. She was taken to Mr. Plotkin's fashionable apartment, where he and the three other men first raped her and then, in the delicate language of the *San Francisco Chronicle*, "subjected her to perverted sex acts." She was, she said, set free in the morning with the warning that she would be killed if she spoke to anyone about the event. She did report the incident to the police, who then searched Plotkin's apartment and discovered a long list of names of women. Her name was on the list and had been crossed out.

In addition to the woman's account of her abduction and rape, the prosecution submitted four of Plotkin's address books containing the names of hundreds of women. Plotkin claimed he did not know all of the women, since some of the names had been given to him by friends and he had not yet called on them. Several women, however, did testify in court that Plotkin had, to cite the *Chronicle*, "lured them up to his apartment under one pretext or another, and forced his sexual attentions on them."

Plotkin's defense rested on two premises. First, through his own testimony Plotkin established a reputation for himself as a sexual libertine who frequently picked up girls in bars and took them to his house where sexual relations often took place. He was the Playboy. He claimed that the accusation of rape, therefore, was false—this incident had simply been one of many casual sexual relationships, the victim one of many playmates. The second premise of the defense was that his accuser was also a sexual libertine. However, the picture created of the young woman (fully thirteen years younger than Plotkin) was not akin to the light-hearted, gay-bachelor image projected by the defendant. On the contrary, the day after the defense cross-examined the woman, the *Chronicle* printed a story headlined, "Grueling Day For Rape Case Victim." (A leaflet passed out by women in front of the courtroom was more succinct: "rape was committed by four men in a private apartment in October; on Thursday, it was done by a judge and a lawyer in a public courtroom.")

Through skillful questioning fraught with innuendo, Plotkin's defense attorney James Martin MacInnis portrayed the young woman as a licentious opportunist and unfit mother. MacInnis began by asking the young woman (then employed as a secretary) whether or not it was true that she was "familiar with liquor" and had worked as a "cocktail waitress." The young woman replied (the *Chronicle* wrote "admitted") that she had worked once or twice as a cocktail waitress. The attorney then asked if she had worked as a secretary in the financial district but had "left that employment after it was discovered that you had sexual intercourse on a couch in the office." The woman replied, "That is a lie. I left because I didn't like working in a one-girl office. It was too lonely." Then the defense asked if, while working as an attendant at a health club, "you were accused of having a sexual affair with a man?" Again the woman denied the story, "I was never accused of that."

Plotkin's attorney then sought to establish that his client's accuser was living with a married man. She responded that the man was separated from his wife. Finally he told the court that she had "spent the night" with another man who lived in the same building.

At this point in the testimony the woman asked Plotkin's defense attorney, "Am I on trial? . . . It is embarrassing and personal to admit these things to all these people. . . . I did not commit a crime. I am a human being." The lawyer, true to the chivalry of his class, apologized and immediately resumed questioning her, turning his attention to her children. (She is divorced, and the children at the time of the trial were in a foster home.) "Isn't it true that your two children have a sex game in which one gets on top of another and they—" "That is a lie!" the young woman interrupted him. She ended her testimony by explaining "They are wonderful children. They are not perverted."

The jury, divided in favor of acquittal ten to two, asked the court stenographer to read the woman's testimony back to them. After this reading, the Superior Court acquitted the defendant of both the charges of rape and kidnaping.

According to the double standard, a woman who has had sexual intercourse out of wedlock cannot be raped. Rape is not only a crime of aggression against the body; it is a transgression against chastity as defined by men. When a woman is forced into a sexual relationship, she has, according to the male ethos, been violated. But she is also defiled if she does not behave according to the double standard, by maintaining her chastity, or confining her sexual activities to a monogamous relationship.

One should not assume, however, that a woman can avoid the possibility of rape simply by behaving. Though myth would have it that mainly "bad girls" are raped, this theory has no basis in fact. Available statistics would lead one to believe that a safer course is promiscuity. In a study of rape done in the District of Columbia, it was found that 82 percent of the rape victims had a "good reputation." Even the Police Inspector's advice to stay off the streets is rather useless, for almost half of reported rapes occur in the home of the victim and are committed by a man she has never before seen. Like indiscriminate terrorism, rape can happen to any woman, and few women are ever without this knowledge.

But the courts and the police, both dominated by white males, continue to suspect the rape victim, *sui generis*, of provoking or asking for her own assault. According to Amir's study, the police tend to believe that a woman without a good reputation cannot be raped. The rape victim is usually submitted to countless questions about her own sexual mores and behavior by the police investigator. This preoccupation is partially justified by the legal requirements for prosecution in a rape case. The rape victim must have been penetrated, and she must have made it clear to her assailant that she did not want penetration (unless of course she is unconscious). A refusal to accompany a man to some isolated place to allow him to touch her does not in the eyes of the court, constitute rape. She must have said, "no" at the crucial genital moment. And the rape victim, to qualify as such, must also have put up a physical struggle—unless she can prove that to do so would have been to endanger her life.

But the zealous interest the police frequently exhibit in the physical details of a rape case is only partially explained by the requirements of the court. A woman who was raped in Berkeley was asked to tell the story of her rape four different times "right out in the street," while her assailant was escaping. She was then required to submit to a pelvic examination to prove that penetration had taken place. Later, she was taken to the police station where she was asked the same questions again: "Were you forced?" "Did he penetrate?" "Are you sure your life was in danger and you had no other choice?" This woman had been pulled off the street by a man who held a ten-inch knife at her throat and forcibly raped her. She was raped at midnight and was not able to return to her home until five in the morning. Police contacted her twice again in the next week, once by telephoning at two in the morning and once at four in the morning. In her words, "The rape was probably the least traumatic incident of the whole evening. If I'm ever raped again, . . . I wouldn't report it to the police because of all the degradation. . . ."

If white women are subjected to unnecessary and often hostile questioning after having been raped, third-world women are often not believed at all. According to the white male ethos (which is not only sexist but racist), third-world women are defined from birth as "impure." Thus the white male is provided with a pool of women who are fair game for sexual imperialism. Third-world women frequently do not report rape and for good reason. When blues singer Billie Holliday was ten years old, she was taken off to a local house by a neighbor and raped. Her mother brought the police to rescue her, and she was taken to the local police station crying and bleeding:

When we got there, instead of treating me and Mom like somebody who called the cops for help, they treated me like I'd killed somebody. . . . I guess they had me figured for having enticed this old goat into the whorehouse. . . . All I know for sure is they threw me into a cell . . . a fat white matron . . . saw I was still bleeding, she felt sorry for me and gave me a couple glasses of milk. But nobody else did anything for me except give me filthy looks and snicker to themselves.

After a couple of days in a cell they dragged me into a court. Mr. Dick got sentenced to five years. They sentenced me to a Catholic institution.

Clearly the white man's chivalry is aimed only to protect the chastity of "his" women.

As a final irony, that same system of sexual values from which chivalry is derived has also provided womankind with an unwritten code of behavior, called femininity, which makes a feminine woman the perfect victim of sexual aggression. If being chaste does not ward off the possibility of assault, being feminine certainly increases the chances that it will succeed. To be submissive is to defer to masculine strength; is to lack muscular development or any interest in defending oneself; is to let doors be opened, to have one's arm held when crossing the street. To be feminine is to wear shoes which make it difficult to run; skirts which inhibit one's stride; underclothes which inhibit the circulation. Is it not an intriguing observation that those very clothes which are thought to be flattering to the female and attractive to the male are those which make it impossible for a woman to defend herself against aggression?

Each girl as she grows into womanhood is taught fear. Fear is the form in which the female internalizes both chivalry and the double standard. Since, biologically speaking, women in fact have the same if not greater potential for sexual expression as do men, the woman who is taught that she must behave differently from a man must also learn to distrust her own carnality. She must deny her own feelings and learn not to act from them. She fears herself. This is the essence of passivity, and of course, a woman's passivity is not simply sexual but functions to cripple her from self-expression in every area of her life.

Passivity itself prevents a woman from ever considering her own potential for self-defense and forces her to look to men for protection. The woman is taught fear, but this time fear of the other; and yet her only relief from this fear is to seek out the other. Moreover, the passive woman is taught to regard herself as impotent, unable to act, unable even to perceive, in no way self-sufficient, and, finally, as the object and not the subject of human behavior. It is in this sense that a woman is deprived of the status of a human being. She is not free to be.

## III

Since Ibsen's Nora slammed the door on her patriarchical husband, woman's attempt to be free has been more or less fashionable. In this 19th-century portrait of a woman leaving her marriage, Nora tells her husband, "Our home has been nothing but a playroom. I have been your doll-wife just as at home I was papa's doll-child." And, at least on the stage, "The Doll's House" crumbled, leaving audiences with hope for the fate of the modern woman. And today, as in the past, womankind has not lacked examples of liberated women to emulate: Emma Goldman, Greta Garbo, and Isadora Duncan all denounced marriage and the double standard, and believed their right to freedom included sexual independence; but still their example has not affected the lives of millions of women who continue to marry, divorce, and remarry, living out their lives dependent on the status and economic power of men. Patriarchy still holds the average woman prisoner not because she lacks the courage of an Isadora Duncan, but because the material conditions of her life prevent her from being anything but an object.

In the *Elementary Structures of Kinship*, Claude Levi-Strauss gives to marriage this universal description: "It is always a system of exchange that we find at the origin of the rules of marriage." In this system of exchange, a woman is the "most precious possession." Levi-Strauss continues that the custom of including women as booty in the marketplace is still so general that "a whole volume would not be sufficient to enumerate instances of it." Levi-Strauss makes it clear that he does not exclude Western Civilization from his definition of "universal" and cites examples from modern wedding ceremonies. (The marriage ceremony is still one in which the husband and wife become one, and "that one is the husband.")

The legal proscription against rape reflects this possessory view of women. An article in the 1952–53 *Yale Law Journal* describes the legal rationale behind laws against rape: "In our society sexual taboos, often enacted into law, buttress a system of monogamy based upon the law of 'free bargaining' of the potential spouses. Within this process the woman's power to withhold or grant sexual access is an important bargaining weapon." Presumably then, laws against rape are intended to protect the right of a woman, not for physical self-determination, but for physical "bargaining." The article goes on to explain explicitly why the preservation of the bodies of women is important to men:

> The consent standard in our society does more than protect a significant item of social currency for women; it fosters, and is in turn bolstered by, a masculine pride in the exclusive possession of a sexual object. The consent of a woman to sexual intercourse awards the man a privilege of bodily access, a personal "prize" whose value is enhanced by sole ownership. An additional reason for the man's condemnation of rape may be found in the threat to his status from a decrease in the "value" of his sexual possession which would result from forcible violation.

The passage concludes by making clear whose interest the law is designed to protect: "The man responds to this undercut-

ting of his status as *possessor* of the girl with hostility toward
the rapist; no other restitution device is available. The law of
rape provides an orderly outlet for his vengeance." Presumably
the female victim in any case will have been sufficiently socialized so as not to consciously feel any strong need for vengeance.
If she does feel this need, society does not speak to it.

The laws against rape exist to protect rights of the male as
possessor of the female body, and not the right of the female
over her own body. Even without this enlightening passage from
the *Yale Law Review*, the laws themselves are clear: In no state
can a man be accused of raping his wife. How can any man
steal what already belongs to him? It is in the sense of rape as
theft of another man's property that Kate Millett writes, "Traditionally rape has been viewed as an offense one male commits
against another—a matter of abusing his woman." In raping
another man's woman, a man may aggrandize his own manhood
and concurrently reduce that of another man. Thus a man's
honor is not subject directly to rape, but only indirectly, through
"his" woman.

If the basic social unit is the family, in which the woman is a
possession of her husband, the superstructure of society is a
male hierarchy, in which men dominate other men (or patriarchal families dominate other patriarchal families). And it is no
small irony that, while the very social fabric of our male-dominated culture denies women equal access to political, economic
and legal power, the literature, myth, and humor of our culture
depict women not only as the power behind the throne, but as
the real source of the oppression of men. The religious version
of this fairy tale blames Eve for both carnality and eating of the
tree of knowledge, at the same time making her gullible to the
obvious devices of a serpent. Adam, of course, is merely the
trusting victim of love. Certainly this is a biased story. But no
more biased than the one television audiences receive today
from the latest slick comedians. Through media which are
owned by men and censored by a State dominated by men, all
the evils of this social system which make a man's life unpleasant are blamed upon "the wife." The theory is: were it not
for the female who waits and plots to "trap" the male into
marriage, modern man would be able to achieve Olympian
freedom. She is made the scapegoat for a system which is in fact
run by men.

Nowhere is this more clear than in the white racist use of the concept of white womanhood. The white male's open rape of black women, coupled with his overweening concern for the chastity and protection of his wife and daughters, represents an extreme of sexist and racist hypocrisy. While on the one hand she was held up as the standard for purity and virtue, on the other the Southern white woman was never asked if she wanted to be on a pedestal, and in fact any deviation from the male-defined standards for white womanhood was treated severely. (It is a powerful commentary on American racism that the historical role of blacks as slaves, and thus possessions without power, has robbed black women of legal and economic protection through marriage. Thus black women in Southern society and in the ghettos of the North have long been easy game for white rapists.) The fear that black men would rape white women was, and is, classic paranoia. To quote from Ann Breen's unpublished study of racism and sexism in the South, "The New South: White Man's Country": "Frederick Douglass legitimately points out that, had the black man wished to rape white women, he had ample opportunity to do so during the Civil War when white women, the wives, sisters, daughters and mothers of the rebels, were left in the care of blacks. Yet not a single act of rape was committed during this time. The Ku Klux Klan, who tarred and feathered black men and lynched them in honor of the purity of white womanhood, also applied tar and feathers to a Southern white woman accused of bigamy, which leads one to suspect that Southern white men were not so much outraged at the violation of the woman as a person, in the few instances where rape was actually committed by black men, but at the violation of his property rights." In the situation where a black man was found to be having sexual relations with a white woman, the white woman could exercise skin privilege, and claim that she had been raped, in which case the black man was lynched. But if she did not claim rape, she herself was subject to lynching.

In constructing the myth of white womanhood so as to justify the lynching and oppression of black men and women, the white male has created a convenient symbol of his own power which has resulted in black hostility toward the white "bitch," accompanied by an unreasonable fear on the part of many white women of the black rapist. Moreover, it is not surprising that after being told for two centuries that he wants to rape white women, occasionally a black man does actually commit that act. But it is crucial to note that the frequency of this practice is outrageously exaggerated in the white mythos. Ninety percent of reported rape is intra- not inter-racial.

In *Soul on Ice*, Eldridge Cleaver has described the mixing of a rage against white power with the internalized sexism of a black man raping a white woman: "Somehow I arrived at the conclusion that, as a matter of principle, it was of paramount importance for me to have an antagonistic, ruthless attitude toward white women. . . . Rape was an insurrectionary act. It delighted me that I was defying and trampling upon the white man's law, upon his system of values and that I was defiling his women—and this point, I believe, was the most satisfying to me because I was very resentful over the historical fact of how the white man has used the black woman." Thus a black man uses white women to take out his rage against white men. But in fact, whenever a rape of a white woman by a black man does take place, it is again the white man who benefits. First, the act itself terrorizes the white woman and makes her more dependent on the white male for protection. Then, if the woman prosecutes her attacker, the white man is afforded legal opportunity to exercise overt racism. Of course, the knowledge of the rape helps to perpetuate two myths which are beneficial to white male rule—the bestiality of the black man and the desirability of white women. Finally, the white man surely benefits because he himself is not the object of attack—he has been allowed to stay in power.

Indeed, the existence of rape in any form is beneficial to the ruling class of white males. For rape is a kind of terrorism which severely limits the freedom of women and makes women dependent on men. Moreover, in the act of rape, the rage that one man may harbor toward another higher in the male hierarchy can be deflected toward a female scapegoat. For every man, there is always someone lower on the social scale on whom he can take out his aggressions. And that is any woman alive.

This oppressive attitude toward women finds its institutionalization in the traditional family. For it is assumed that a man "wears the pants" in his family—he exercises the option of rule whenever he so chooses. Not that he makes all the decisions—clearly women make most of the important day-to-day decisions in a family. But when a conflict of interest arises, it is the man's interest which will prevail. His word, in itself, is more powerful.

He lords it over his wife in the same way his boss lords it over him, so that the very process of exercising his power becomes as important an act as obtaining whatever it is his power can get for him. This notion of power is the key to the male ego in this culture, for the two acceptable measures of masculinity are a man's power over women and his power over other men. A man may boast to his friends that "I have twenty men working for me." It is also aggrandizement of his ego if he has the financial power to clothe his wife in furs and jewels. And, if a man lacks the wherewithal to acquire such power, he can always express his rage through equally masculine activities—rape and theft. Since male society defines the female as a possession, it is not surprising that the felony most often committed together with rape is theft. As the following classic tale of rape points out, the elements of theft, violence, and forced sexual relations merge into an indistinguishable whole.

The woman who told this story was acquainted with the man who tried to rape her. When the man learned that she was going to be staying alone for the weekend, he began early in the day a polite campaign to get her to go out with him. When she continued to refuse his request, his chivalrous mask dropped away:

"I had locked all the doors because I was afraid, and I don't know how he got in; it was probably through the screen door. When I woke up, he was shaking my leg. His eyes were red, and I knew he had been drinking or smoking. I thought I would try to talk my way out of it. He started by saying that he wanted to sleep with me, and then he got angrier and angrier, until he started to say, 'I want pussy,' 'I want pussy.' Then, I got scared and tried to push him away. That's when he started to force himself on me. It was awful. It was the most humiliating, terrible feeling. He was forcing my legs apart and ripping my clothes off. And it was painful. I did fight him—he was slightly drunk and I was able to keep him away. I had taken judo a few years back, but I was afraid to throw a chop for fear that he'd kill me. I could see he was getting more and more violent. I was thinking wildly of some way to get out of this alive, and then I said to him, 'Do you want money. I'll give you money.' We had money but I was also thinking that if I got to the back room I could telephone the police—as if the police would have even helped. It was a stupid thing to think of because obviously he would follow me. And he did. When he saw me pick up the phone, he tried to tie the cord around my neck. I screamed at

him that I did have the money in another room, that I was going
to call the police because I was scared, but that I would never
tell anybody what happened. It would be an absolute secret. He
said, okay, and I went to get the money. But when he got it, all
of a sudden he got this crazy look in his eye and he said to me,
'Now I'm going to kill you.' Then I started saying my prayers. I
knew there was nothing I could do. He started to hit me—I still
wasn't sure if he wanted to rape me at this point—or just to kill
me. He was hurting me, but hadn't yet gotten me into a strangle-
hold because he was still drunk and off balance. Somehow we
pushed into the kitchen where I kept looking at this big knife.
But I didn't pick it up. Somehow, no matter how much I hated
him at that moment, I still couldn't imagine putting the knife in
his flesh, and then I was afraid he would grab it and stick it into
me. Then he was hitting me again and somehow we pushed
through the back door of the kitchen and onto the porch steps.
We fell down the steps and that's when he started to strangle
me. He was on top of me. He just went on and on until finally I
lost consciousness. I did scream, though my screams sounded
like whispers to me. But what happened was that a cab driver
happened by and frightened him away. The cab driver revived
me—I was out only a minute at the most. And then I ran across
the street and I grabbed the woman who was our neighbor and
screamed at her, 'Am I alive? Am I still alive?' "

Rape is an act of aggression in which the victim is denied her
self-determination. It is an act of violence which, if not actually
followed by beatings or murder, nevertheless always carries
with it the threat of death. And finally, rape is a form of mass
terrorism, for the victims of rape are chosen indiscriminately,
but the propagandists for male supremacy broadcast that it is
women who cause rape by being unchaste or in the wrong place
at the wrong time—in essence, by behaving as though they were
free.

The threat of rape is used to deny women employment. (In
California, the Berkeley Public Library, until pushed by the
Federal Employment Practices Commission, refused to hire
female shelvers because of perverted men in the stacks.) The
fear of rape keeps women off the streets at night. Keeps women
at home. Keeps women passive and modest for fear that they be
thought provocative.

It is part of human dignity to be able to defend oneself, and women are learning. Some women have learned karate; some to shoot guns. And yet we will not be free until the threat of rape and the atmosphere of violence is ended, and to end that, the nature of male behavior must change.

But rape is not an isolated act that can be rooted out from patriarchy without ending patriarchy itself. The same men and power structure who victimize women are engaged in the act of raping Vietnam, raping black people and the very earth we live upon. Rape is a classic act of domination where, in the words of Kate Millett, "the emotions of hatred, contempt, and the desire to break or violate personality" take place. This breaking of the personality characterizes modern life itself. No simple reforms can eliminate rape. As the symbolic expression of the white male hierarchy, rape is the quintessential act of our civilization, one which, Valerie Solanis warns, is in danger of "humping itself to death."

Carolyn M. Shafer
Marilyn Frye

# Rape and Respect

It is part of public piety to hold rape in low regard. Rape is, in fact, generally counted among the crimes of great moral moment. At the same time, there is a certain warm solicitude for the accused rapist, more than for the accused murderer, for instance. This seems to be due to the prevalence of a belief that a hugely disproportionate number of accused rapists are falsely accused, innocent, and in need of unusual legal and moral protection, and that real rape—real, culpable criminal rape—is in fact very rare. It might have been supposed that such an attitude was justified because the very heinousness of the crime deflated the enthusiasm of all but the most hardened aspiring rapists. Quite recently, however, this belief has been discredited by the public discovery of the actual and frequent occurrence of rape. This discovery was a significant moral advance, one for which we are indebted to the feminists.

The present state of affairs presents at least two significant problems. First, what exactly is so bad about rape? Traditional mutterings about loss of purity, chastity, and honor, and about the diminution of the woman's value as the property of her father, husband, or other male keeper will hardly account for

This paper was presented as an invited paper at the meetings of the Western Division of the American Philosophical Association in Chicago, April 1975. I note my indebtedness to conversations with R. H. Kotzin and D. Sachs, which affected parts of my thinking on these subjects. M. F.

the rage and horror feminists express about the matter. Nor, to be fair, do they seem to capture fully the professed public sentiments about rape. Second, the existence of a general public stance of unqualified moral condemnation of rape, in tandem with a general public pretense that rape almost never happens and an attitude of skepticism and reproach toward purported victims of rape, intimates the presence of some ulterior motivation in the public psyche. This raises the question: what unsavory social purposes could this piece of hypocrisy be serving? We will offer answers to both these questions.

What we shall here refer to as "rape" is sexual intercourse performed without the consent of the woman involved. As conservatives on the matter tirelessly remind us, rape is not done only by males or suffered only by females. So long as one is speaking strictly in terms of the anatomical characteristics of the participants, we certainly have no quarrel with this. But using the terms "man" and "woman" and invoking their associations with social and political roles rather than their associations with anatomical characteristics, one may nonetheless sensibly claim that rape is a man's act, whether it is a male or a female man and whether it is a man relatively permanently or relatively temporarily; and being raped is a woman's experience, whether it is a female or a male woman and whether it is a woman relatively permanently or relatively temporarily. We will speak of women and men as though all women were female and all men male, bearing in mind that what we say must be capable of extension to instances where this is not the case and also to instances where the sexual acts in question would not comfortably fit under the rubric "sexual intercourse." With these caveats, we shall proceed to presume that rape is sexual intercourse performed without the consent of the woman. Since we share the public view that rape is morally wrong and gravely so, and since we would not want to say that there is anything morally wrong with sexual intercourse per se, we conclude that the wrongness of rape rests with the matter of the woman's consent.[1]

# I

Giving consent is a conventional, institutional speech act and shares the general characteristics of such acts. There is an explicit verbal formula, "I (hereby) consent," by which it may be

performed, though other phrases or gestures may be employed
more frequently and colloquially and though consent is often
tacitly given. The act of consenting is a formal one and is
sharply to be distinguished from the emotional states which
ideally accompany it and which it is often presumed to express,
most notably a feeling of willingness.

To consent is to reverse a prima facie presumption about
what may and may not be done. For example, there is a prima
facie presumption that one person should not use another's
books; after the owner gives consent, however, it is prima facie
all right for the person to whom it is given to use those books on
a particular occasion or occasions. In the case where a person
grants general consent, a general prima facie presumption is
reversed. Without general consent, one may not use a person's
library unless she says one may; with general consent, one may
use her books unless she says one may not. The person who
gives a general consent does not yield up the right to alter,
qualify, or revoke that consent. If one day the owner of the
library tells you to leave a particular book on the shelf and you
spirit it away even so, you have taken it without her consent,
and this is theft—regardless of the fact that you had and still
have general consent to use the library. At any time and without
explanation she may revoke her consent, and this act will constitute the immediate reversal once again of the presumption
about your use of her library: you may no longer remove a
book unless she says you may.

(It becomes clear, now, that a married woman cannot correctly be said to have granted general consent to intercourse
with her husband, since she does not retain the right to revoke
or modify this so-called consent at will.)

As in the case of other speech acts, there are preconditions
for a felicitous act of consenting. There is the usual requirement
that performance of the act not be secured by coercion or fraud,
but there are conditions more peculiar to consent as well. In the
first place, one can have power of consent only over something
that could in principle be effected or affected by human agency.
One cannot consent to the occurrence of a thunderstorm or to
the laws of physics. Within the range where one might have
power of consent there are further limitations. Because of the
conventional nature of the act of consent, one can effectively
consent or withhold consent only where others are prone to
consider one's wishes—that is, where one's act of giving consent

can secure uptake. In another dimension, one can properly consent or withhold consent only where one has a right to exercise control. Obviously, the range of one's actual, effective power of consent may or may not coincide with the range within which, morally, one ought to have power of consent, for one's effective power of consent depends upon the acknowledgment of others.

## II

The proper scope of one's power of consent depends on one's *domain*, and the notion of domain is inextricably linked with that of personhood, for it is as a person that one has a domain. The concept of personhood is a peculiarly behavioral one: a certain respect is accorded to a creature because it has certain traits and capabilities which normally result in, and are exercised in, certain behaviors. What is held in high regard is not the behaviors but the properties and capacities assumed to reside inside the black box. (This is confirmed by expressed moral intuitions about the personhood of fetuses, small children, once competent paralyzed adults, robots and so on.) But the only way we know a creature has those traits and capacities is that they are manifest in its behavior. It is recognized that temporary or explicable absence of the characteristic behavior does not necessarily indicate the absence of the privileged properties, especially if impediments to the behavior are readily discernible, but complete absence of the behaviors (as with someone in a lengthy coma) or constitutional inability to manifest recognizable behaviors of the appropriate sort (as with porpoises or machines) tend to disqualify a creature as a person.

The list of traits and capacities regarded as characteristic of persons is much debated, and the question of the number of these properties a creature must possess, and in what degree, in order to satisfy personhood criteria is usually answered by consulting the intestines rather than the brain. Nevertheless, it seems fairly safe to list among the more popular traits intelligence, self-awareness, linguistic ability, emotional sensibility, moral sense, and the ability to choose and make decisions. Perhaps another way to put this point is to say that to qualify as a person, a candidate must be the sort of creature that is capable of identifying its own interests, choosing a fairly wide range of more or less complex goals for itself, and engaging in com

munication about and pursuit of those interests and goals. And
the behavior by which it manifests these abilities is the evident
exercise of them.

(There are numerous indications that personhood can come
in degrees—as our perception of small children, idiots, and the
senile will testify. But in order to reveal the fundamental moral
situation, we shall carry on here as though all persons were
paradigm cases of full personhood.)

Now we can say quite simply what a domain is. A domain is
where this sort of creature, a person, lives. The very center of
the domain is the highly touted person-properties themselves
and their physical locus, the body. In this context, theories on
whether or how the properties and the body are related are
irrelevant. In dealing with persons, one is dealing with behaving
bodies, and it is these that have domains. It is to be noted that
the body is not the property of a person who possesses it along
with the rest of the domain. Rather, the behaving body *is* a
person, the sort of thing which acts and owns and consents, and
cannot be owned or consented over, even by itself.[2] The disposition of the body, because in one aspect it directly affects
and in another it is that body's behavior, is also central to the
person's domain. Since biological life and health are prerequisites for the pursuit of any other interests and goals whatever,
everything necessary for their maintenance and sustenance evidently will fall very close to the center of the domain. Anything
which exerts an influence on the person-properties themselves—
which, for example, bends a person's will or dulls its intelligence
or affects its own sense of its identity—also comes very near the
center of the domain. Whatever has a relatively permanent
effect on the person, whatever affects its relatively constant
surroundings, whatever causes it discomfort or distress—in
short, whatever a person has to live with—is likely to fall
squarely within its domain. A person's domain includes the
activities, the tools and materials, and the physical spaces used
in the pursuit of that person's goals and the carrying out of its
projects; its domain includes the resources of its work, play,
recreation, exercise, solace, and amusement. This domain becomes attenuated as the items in question are removed from
physical, temporal, or emotional proximity to the person—that
is, from the center of the domain.

## III

What makes a person's domain the delimiter of the morall*
proper scope of that person's power of consent is that intruding
into a person's domain comes dangerously (sometimes indistin
guishably) close to treading upon the person itself. It seems
obvious that a person, which is a person precisely in virtue of
traits that give it among other things a capacity for and a ten
dency toward self-determination, ought to have power of consen
over anything that seriously affects it, and that violation of a
person's domain can be justified only by reference to som
higher principle. Upon examination, most if not all higher prin
ciples commonly suggested seem reducible to rules for settling
conflicts among domains. This does introduce a problem. A
lone person in the world would seem to have a right to power of
consent over any and every thing it could (and cared to
control—except that it makes no sense to talk of consent in th
absence of other persons. The fact is that there are a multitud
of persons in the world, and their domains can and frequentl
do overlap; this is just what makes the convention of consen
necessary. It also necessitates some principle for resolving con
flicts between scopes of powers of consent resulting from th
overlap of domains. Each person qua person has as much righ
to power of consent within its own domain as any other ha
within its domain. When domains overlap, it seems only rea
sonable to concede the power of consent in a conflict over
given item to the person to whose domain it is more central—
that is, to the one more profoundly affected by it. If an item i
of equal centrality to the domains of the opponents, they shoul
negotiate the matter. If and only if that fails, direct confronta
tion and struggle may be permissible, so long as each recognize
the prima facie equal right of the other. *Possibly* if an item i
equally central to several persons the decision of the majorit
should carry, though those outnumbered should not be expecte
to relinquish their claims. *Possibly* a lesser effect on a grea
many persons can outweigh a greater effect on just one. An
so on. The conceivable configurations are endless and endlessl
complex, but the appropriate general principle and attitude seer
clear enough. A person's domain is the physical, emotiona
psychological, and intellectual space it lives in. The spac
diminished only by overlap with the domains of others, define

the rightful scope of the person's power of consent. It should be noticed that one person, being itself the center of a domain and a sort of thing which cannot be *in* a domain, can never properly fall under another's power of consent.

## IV

The morally appropriate attitude upon encountering another person is one of respect: recognition of its domain, and deference to its rightful power of consent. Ideally, the range of a person's effective power of consent should coincide with that of its rightful power of consent, but the conventionality of consent allows for considerable slippage. It is quite possible honestly to misperceive or misjudge the extent of a person's domain and consequently to accord it a greater or lesser effective power of consent than that to which it is entitled. Such an error is probably not morally reprehensible, so long as one has taken seriously the moral requirement of deferring to the other within the range of its rightful power of consent. This, of course, involves taking seriously the business of discerning the boundaries of the other's domain. It is also quite possible disingenuously and self-deceptively to misperceive or misjudge the extent of another's domain, usually because there appears to be some advantage to (or survival value in) doing so. This also can result in the concession to another of a greater or lesser effective power of consent than is proper; such attitudes we label obsequious or overbearing. A common example of such attitudes flourishing in symbiosis can be observed in the relationship of many an enterprising junior executive with his boss. It is furthermore quite possible for a person to have a clear and accurate perception of the domain of another and to disregard it deliberately nonetheless. While it is possible thus to aggrandize the domain of another, it seems likely that the rightful scope of a person's power of consent is more often blatantly flouted by diminishing than by expanding its effective power of consent.

Because of the conventional, linguistic nature of the act of consent, the corresponding uptake has a communicative function as well. Whatever the moral status of the processes from which it results, the concession of a particular range of effective power of consent to a person constitutes a statement about the domain of that person and, in the light of the intimate connection between a person and its domain, about the person itself. It is prima facie far more culpable to refuse to grant a person its rights than to grant it unwarranted privileges; and on the other hand, the expansion of one person's effective power of consent is almost inevitably correlated with the diminution of someone else's. Therefore we shall concentrate here on the significance of conceding to someone an effective power of consent narrower than its rightful one. Failure to defer to someone's expressed wishes is in effect either a formal denial that the person is within its domain or a formal assertion that the item in question is more central to your domain than it is to the other person's. Now, on our view, the extent of a person's domain is determined by the person-qualities themselves, while the shape (or, so to speak, the intensity) of the domain is determined by the person's personal identity (its ordering of things according to their centrality to itself). So to fail to defer to a person's rightful power of consent is to deny either the actual extent of its personhood or its actual personal identity. Either is flagrantly disrespectful, and thus grievously wrong. The closer the item is to the center of the domain of the person whose rightful power of consent over it is not recognized, the more violent is the attack upon that creature's personhood itself. To presume to wield an effective power of consent over the personal properties and/or the body of that creature, the center of its domain, is ipso facto to deny that there is a person there at all. The ultimate in disrespect is to exercise the power of consent over those properties and the body in action (that is, over the creature's behavior), for it is precisely as a behaving body that the creature is a person and is the person that it is. The ultimate disrespect is, then, the exercise of the power of consent over another *person*. And this is exactly what rape is.

# V

As we mentioned at the beginning, there is a standing public pretense that rape is rare. And it would be rare if women were in general creatures viewed with respect. When among people whose acts are motivated, guided, and restricted by respect, no one has to attend with any great vigilance to threats of assault, either physical or emotional. When one is among friends, one need not worry that someone is going suddenly to get a notion to pursue steadfastly an end which requires as a means one's murder or one's humiliation. But a woman, in the world we live in, is not among friends. A woman does not have this sort of security. There are people around her who will suddenly take it into their heads to rape her—to coerce her submission to sexual intercourse. This naturally raises the question, why would anyone take it into his head to do this?

One answer given by conventional wisdom is that men do this out of sexual need or desire. That a man would rape with such motivation reveals his unwillingness to exercise a certain kind and degree of control where he should be deferring to the wishes of another. In fact, it is a rather extreme case. He is controlling not just the disposition of things which are within the range of the woman's rightful power of consent, but the woman herself, through the manipulation of her body. He is not merely diverting her resources or using her property to further ends other than hers, he is using *her* in furtherance of ends other than hers. Moreover, the ends for which he is using her body are ends which are *contrary* to hers, given that her ends include the maintenance of her bodily integrity and health. The use of a person in the advancement of interests contrary to its own is a limiting case of disrespect. It reveals the perception of the person simply as an object which can serve some purpose, a tool or a bit of material, and one which furthermore is dispensable or replaceable and thus of little value even as an object with a function.

But the phenomena of rape present us with a maze of humiliations more complex yet than this. The victim of this sort of rape is not, of course, an insensate object, and this event is not without meaning to her. It conveys to her that she is seen as an object with a sexual function. The person raping her sees her through a perceptual schema which presents her and anything she does as something associated or connected with sexual intercourse—with his penetration and ejaculation. The rape reveals to her his sexual perception of her; it gives her a picture of herself as a being within someone's domain and not as a being which has domain. The rape means that she is not seen as a person; and she is the observer *to whom* it means this.

The plot thickens when we shift from rape as a sort of simple, selfish act of appropriation and look at rape in the boudoir, between friends, lovers, or spouses. When a person with whom a woman has a friendly or personal or intimate relationship rapes her, it is typically with some intention more complicated than merely the satisfaction of his sexual desires. The act of rape itself has the same meaning in such cases, perhaps, but it is done with the intention that it have this meaning. The boudoir rapist acts with the intention of informing, reminding, or telling the woman of his sexual perception of her. This intention is involved in or subserves other more specific communication intentions which vary with the sort of situation the pair are in and the sorts of things he may have to say to her.

Many of the relationships women and men enter into within our society are more or less close analogues of those in which the two people implicitly strike a sort of bargain. Facing the world alone, the woman discovers or rediscovers that she is chronically liable to exploitation and victimization so long as she is without male support and protection. The man, facing the world alone, discovers or senses that his happiness and peace of mind are precarious at best if he does not have a wife or mistress. The woman and the man form an alliance: he provides her with male sponsorship and she provides him with sexual and other services. In such a situation, if she shows unwillingness or lack of inclination to engage with him in sexual intercourse, he may wish to remind her of the nature of the bargain they struck. The act of rape may serve conveniently as a communicative vehicle for reminding her of the situation from which she negotiated this arrangement, in such a way as to threaten to return her to that situation if she withholds sexual services. The situation from which she started was that of a being without respect; and treating her as such in the act of rape, he may communicate his message with considerable clarity and directness.

Rape is an act which belies respect, and it is often an act actually intended to communicate the fact of disrespect. Whether it is the rapist's intention or not, being raped conveys for the woman the message that she is a being without respect, that she is not a person. And it is in part because of this that the institution of rape can play the role it does in the structure of intersexual relations in general.

## VI

Women in this society live generally under the threat of rape. The threat of sexual assault limits the movements of women about their communities, restricts their access to various services and amusements, restricts their pursuit both of comfort and of self-expression in their clothes and personal styles, portends penalty and punishment for various assertions of their interests and claims to domain, and greatly restricts the range of possible exploration of sexual experience and expression. Even if the threat were simple and direct and open, it would have these effects to a considerable degree. But it is not generally posed as an open threat.

The public denial that rape is common, or even that it happens at all, is effectively also a public denial that there is any significant threat of rape. This denial is at best an insult to women's common sense; at worst it is the sort of public denial of the veracity of a person's perceptions that, if sustained, can simply drive a person mad. The woman is subjected not only to the controlling influence of the threat, but at the same time to the maddening influence of the denial that the threat exists.

Although the threat of physical assault of any sort could no doubt be fairly effective as a means of social control of a large population, one would expect such a threat to have to be made plausible through considerable open advertisement and vivid examples. But the threat of rape is very effective even though its existence is publicly denied, and no great amount of resource is expended in publicity and enforcement. This remarkable efficiency is attained by there being another twist in the mechanism.

What is threatened when rape is threatened is not just physical assault, but the vigorous revelation of the simple fact that rape happens. Rape is the exposure of the public lie that women are respected persons. It reveals to the woman that she is viewed in such a way that men do not have prohibitive moral compunctions about using her as an object whose function is their sexual gratification and expression—as an object, like a sheep in the field, with regard to which no question of its consent or the lack of it arises. The threat of rape operates like a form of blackmail. It is the threat of exposure of the woman as a being without respect, or, as some women experience it, exposure of the woman as a being unworthy of respect.

A woman knows her status in this society—her status as a being generally not respected. It is taught her from the crib. But it is an ugly and painful fact, and she is likely to be all too willing to be persuaded that it isn't really so. It is also of value in a society such as ours that populations being controlled and used should in general be self-deceived about it, for then they will be less prone to railing and rebellion. There is here a perfect role for the gentleman and the pedestal.

Many women in many aspects of their lives are treated relatively gently and with a fair amount of generosity by the males around them. They live in the house of some male, like a child living under a broad blanket of general consents in its parents' home. Generous and open-minded parents grant their children the privilege of acting to a fair extent as though they had domains of their own, like frequent and welcome visitors enjoying a broad hospitality. And women often enjoy such privileges as well—often as comfortably as their menfolk can financially manage. It is easy to mistake the privilege of freedom of movement and choice within another's domain for the right of power of consent within one's own domain. And the kindly granting of the privilege can be mistaken for the recognition of the right; the condescending deference to a cherished object in a man's domain mistaken for the deference given a person in its own domain.[3]

Taking kindness and humane treatment for respect, the woman can convince herself, or be convinced, that she is a respected being, while living in a society where in general she is not and where she constantly receives hints and reminders of this fact. While rueing the fact of her willingness to be deceived or to deceive herself, we may see that this may be absolutely necessary to her survival. The clear-eyed perception that one is not in general respected (when others say one is) is, other things being equal, a challenging threat to one's maintenance of self-respect. To maintain one's sense of being a person and respectable, it is surely in some situations essential to avoid the influence of the public perception to the contrary. The position a woman has by birth in this sexist society makes it valuable, in some cases essential, for her to exercise some self-deception and to cooperate in some trickery in order to view herself as a creature viewed with respect. This can coerce her into collaboration with her oppressors in their disrespectful behavior. And once again we see the woman herself being used in furtherance of ends inimical to her own well-being.

The woman's (coerced) collusion in the myth of her respectability would make her doubly susceptible to the blackmail involved in the threat of rape. The thing threatened (in addition to mere assault) is the disclosure of the evil fact of her real status, a fact in whose cover-up the woman herself is implicated by her willingness to collaborate in the deception. Welcoming neither the disclosure of the fact of her status nor the disclosure of her betrayal of herself, she will go to great lengths to accommodate the blackmailer.[4]

## VII

Looked at microscopically, an individual rape on the street, as it were, done by a stranger simply in pursuit of sexual gratification (if there are such cases—the motivation is usually more complex) is bad in the way assault in general is, but its wickedness is compounded by the fact that it is a use of a person, not just the injury of a person, and a use of a person in pursuit of ends not its own and/or contrary to its own. That is profoundly disrespectful and a clear case of failing to treat a person *as* a person. It is also a use of a person which involves tampering with parts of its self which are for most people centrally rather than peripherally involved in their personal identity.

Looked at macroscopically, rape is the point of application of a monstrous device of social control in which insult and injury are heaped upon one another in such complex abundance that one can scarcely keep the accounts, much less stomach the contemplation of it.

The public discovery of rape and women's boldly facing the terrible fact of their status in society can disarm the machine. One who knows and acknowledges the grim fact cannot be tricked into the treachery of self-deception or frightened by the threat or the actuality of the fact's disclosure. One has then to deal merely with the widespread threat of intentional violation of one's domain, and the out-and-out disregard of one's power of consent by persons who see one as an object with a purely sexual function—persons who are therefore unlikely to be moved to desist by the mere withholding of one's consent to sexual intercourse.

## NOTES

1. Some of Pamela Foa's observations move in a different direction from ours at this point. She notes that though an enlightened view may reveal that sexual intercourse per se is morally neutral,

there is in our culture a strong tradition of classifying it as taboo, forbidden, or sinful, and this, whether misguided or not, complicates the politics of rape. (See Pamela Foa, "What's Wrong with Rape," this volume.) Our account is intended to explore the intuition that rape has peculiar moral features even *apart* from the odd moral sentiments about sex which pervade this culture. Sexual intercourse, even if not felt to be sinful or taboo in itself, has a peculiar role in the moral and political intercourse between the sexes in a sexist culture.

2. In much of the debate about abortion, the conflicting positions seem to share the presupposition that a human body is a piece of property; once the rhetorical smokescreens dissipate, the disputants seem to be disagreeing merely about who owns which body —that is, who has property rights over what.

3. Conversations I have had with women who are either not middle class or not white, or not either, suggest that not only are they less accustomed to being treated so gently and granted such privileges, they are also less intimidated by the fear of rape than are those who are white and middle class. M. F.

4. The assault on the woman's personhood is exacerbated by the fact that in this culture the act by which it is accomplished is taboo. According to some of the prevailing mores, she is defiled and made into a transgressor, and to the extent that she is susceptible to their influence, she feels herself to be such. The "assertion" that she is not a person is made in such a way as to be self-verifying, for the act through which it is asserted itself *casts* her outside the taboo-defined community of persons.

Pamela Foa

# What's Wrong with
# Rape

It is clear that rape is wrong. It is equally clear that the wrongness of rape is not completely explained by its status as a criminal assault. Dispute begins, however, when we attempt to account for the special features of rape, the ways in which its
wrongness goes beyond its criminal character. I shall argue
against those who maintain that the special wrongness of rape
arises from and is completely explained by a societal refusal to
recognize women as *people*. I shall offer a different explanation:
The special wrongness of rape is due to, and is only an exaggeration of, the wrongness of our sexual interactions in general.
Thus, a clear analysis of the special wrongness of rape will help
indicate some of the essential features of healthy, non-rapine
sexual interactions.

## I. THE WRONGNESS OF RAPE GOES
## BEYOND ITS CRIMINALITY

It is to be expected during this period of resurgent feminism that
rape will be seen primarily as a manifestation of how women

An earlier version of this paper was presented to the Society of Women
in Philosophy, Midwestern Division, October 1975, and to the American
Philosophical Association, Pacific Division, March 1976. Research for
this paper was supported by a generous grant from the University of
Pittsburgh. Thanks are due to many colleagues who helped me clarify
my views: especially John Cooper, Paul Guyer, Jonathan Himmelhoch,
Alexander Nehamas, and, of course, Marilyn Frye and Carolyn Shafer.

are mistreated in our society. For example, consider these remarks of Simone de Beauvoir:

> All men are drawn to B[rigitte] B[ardot]'s seductiveness, but that does not mean that they are kindly disposed towards her. . . . They are unwilling to give up their role of lord and master. . . . Freedom and full consciousness remain their [the men's] right and privilege. . . . In the game of love BB is as much a hunter as she is a prey. The male is an object to her, just as she is to him. And that is precisely what wounds the masculine pride. In the Latin countries where men cling to the myth of "the woman as object," BB's naturalness seems to them more perverse than any possible sophistication. It is to assert that one is man's fellow and equal, to recognize that between the woman and him there is a mutual desire and pleasure. . . .
>
> But the male feels uncomfortable if, instead of a doll of flesh and blood, he holds in his arms a conscious being who is sizing him up. "You realize," an average Frenchman once said to me, "that when a man finds a woman attractive, he wants to be able to pinch her behind." A ribald gesture reduces a woman to a thing that a man can do with as he pleases without worrying about what goes on in her mind and heart and body.[1]

And rape is apparently the quintessential instance of women being viewed as objects, of women being treated as entities other than, and morally inferior to, men. It is implicit in this object-view that if men, and therefore society, viewed women as full moral equals, rape would be an assault no different in kind than any other. Thus, it is a consequence of this view that the special wrongness of rape is to be found in the nonsexual aspects of the act.

To this end, Marilyn Frye and Carolyn Shafer suggest in their paper "Rape and Respect" that the wrongness of rape is twofold: first, it is the use of a person without her consent in the performance of an act or event which is against her own best interests; and second, it is a social means of reinforcing the status of women as kinds of entities who lack and ought to lack the full privileges of personhood—importantly, the freedom to move as they will through what is rightfully their domain.[2] What is good about this account is that it provides one way of understanding the sense of essential violation of one's *person* (and not mere sexual abuse), which seems to be the natural concomitant of rape.

This account, further, gives one explanation for the continuous social denial of the common fact of criminal rape. On this view, to recognize rape as a criminal act, one must recognize the domains of women. But if domains are inextricably connected with personhood—if personhood, in fact, is to be analyzed in terms of domains—then it ought to be obvious that where there is no domain there can be no criminal trespass of domain; there can only be misperceptions or misunderstandings. To recognize domains of consent is to recognize the existence of people at their centers. Without such centers, there can be no rape.

Unfortunately, I do not believe that this kind of account can serve as an adequate explanation of what's wrong with rape. I find irrelevant its emphasis on the ontological status of women as persons of the first rank. It is granted that in any act of rape a person is used without proper regard to her personhood, but this is true of every kind of assault. If there is an additional wrongness to rape, it must be that more is wrong than the mere treatment of a person by another person without proper regard for her personhood. Later in this paper, I shall show that there is no need to differentiate ontologically between victim and assailant in order to explain the special wrongness of rape. However, it is important to recognize that rape is profoundly wrong even if it is not an act between ontological equals.

The special wrongness of rape cannot be traced to the fact that in this act men are not recognizing the full array of moral and legal rights and privileges which accrue to someone of equal status. Rape of children is at least as heinous as rape of adults, though few actually believe that children have or ought to have the same large domain of consent adults (male and female) ought to have. In part, this is what is so disturbing about a recent English decision I shall discuss in a moment: it seems to confuse the ontological with the moral. Men's wishes, intentions, and beliefs are given a different (and more important) weight, just because they are (wrongly in this case, perhaps rightly in the case of children) viewed as different kinds of entities than women.

But even if one thinks that women are not people, or that all people (for example, children) do not have the same rights or, prima facie, the same domains of consent, it seems that rape is still especially horrible, awful in a way that other assaults are not. There is, for example, something deeply distressing, though not necessarily criminal, about raping one's pet dog. It is disturbing in ways no ordinary assault, even upon a person, seems to be disturbing. It may here be objected that what accounts for the moral outrage in these two cases is that the first is an instance of pedophilia, and the second of bestiality. That is, the special wrongness of these acts is due to the "unnatural" direction of the sexual impulse, rather than to the abusive circumstances of the fulfillment of a "natural" sexual impulse.

I would argue in response that outrage at "unnatural" acts is misdirected and inappropriate. The notion that acting "against" nature is immoral stems from the false belief that how things are in the majority of cases is, morally speaking, how things always ought to be. Acting unnaturally is not acting immorally unless there is a moral design to the natural order—and there is no such structure to it. This means, then, that if it is reasonable to feel that something very wrong has occurred in the above two cases, then it must be because they are rapes and not because they are "unnatural acts." However, even if this argument is not conclusive, it must be agreed that the random raping of a mentally retarded adult is clearly wrong even though such an individual does not, in our society, have all the legal and moral rights of normal people.[3]

Of course, another very reasonable point to make here may well be that it is not just people who have domains, and that what's wrong with rape is the invasion by one being into another's domain without consent or right. But if something like this is true, then rape would be wrong because it was an "incursion" into a domain. This would make it wrong in the same way that other assaults are wrong. The closer the incursion comes to the center of a person's identity, the worse the act.

The problem here is that such an argument suggests that rape is wrong the same way, and only the same way, that other assaults are wrong. And yet the evidence contradicts this. There is an emotional concomitant to this assault, one that is lacking in nonsexual criminal assaults. What must be realized is that when it comes to sexual matters, people—in full recognition of the equal ontological status of their partners—treat each other abominably. Contrary to the Frye/Shafer theory, I believe that liberated men and women—people who have no doubts about the moral or ontological equality of the sexes—can and do have essentially rape-like sexual lives.

The following case is sufficient to establish that it is not just the assault upon one's person, or the intrusion into one's domain, that makes for the special features of rape. In New York twenty or so years ago, there was a man who went around

Manhattan slashing people with a very sharp knife. He did not do this as part of any robbery or other further bodily assault. His end was simply to stab people. Although he was using people against their own best interests, and without their consent—that is, although he is broadly violating domains—to be the victim of the Mad Slasher was not to have been demeaned or dirtied as a person in the way that the victim of rape is demeaned or dirtied. It was not to be wronged or devalued in the same way that to be raped is to be wronged or devalued. No one ever accused any of the victims of provoking, initiating, or enjoying the attack.

Yet the public morality about rape suggests that unless one is somehow mutilated, broken, or killed in addition to being raped, one is suspected of having provoked, initiated, complied in, consented to, or even enjoyed the act. It is this public response, the fear of such a response and the belief (often) in the rationality of such a response (even from those who do unequivocally view you as a person) that seems to make rape especially horrible.

Thus, what is especially bad about rape is a function of its place in our society's sexual views, not in our ontological views. There is, of course, nothing necessary about these views, but until they change, no matter what progress is made in the fight for equality between the sexes, rape will remain an especially awful act.

## II. SEX, INTIMACY, AND PLEASURE

Our response to rape brings into focus our inner feelings about the nature, purpose, and morality of all sexual encounters and of ourselves as sexual beings. Two areas which seem immediately problematic are the relation between sex and intimacy and the relation between sex and pleasure.

Our Victorian ancestors believed that sex in the absence of (at least marital) intimacy was morally wrong and that the only women who experienced sexual pleasure were nymphomaniacs.[4] Freud's work was revolutionary in part just because he challenged the view of "good" women and children as asexual creatures.[5] Only with Masters and Johnson's work, however, has there been a full scientific recognition of the capacity of ordinary women for sexual pleasure.[6] But though it is now recognized that sexual pleasure exists for all people at all stages of life and is, in its own right, a morally permissible goal, this contemporary attitude is still dominated by a Victorian atmosphere. It remains the common feeling that it is a kind of pleasure which should be experienced only in private and only between people who are and intend to be otherwise intimate. Genital pleasure is private not only in our description of its physical location, but also in our conception of its occurrence or occasion.

For the rape victim, the special problem created by the discovery of pleasure in sex is that now some people believe that *every* sex act must be pleasurable to some extent, including rape.[7] Thus, it is believed by some that the victim in a rape must at some level be enjoying herself—and that this enjoyment in a non-intimate, non-private environment is shameful. What is especially wrong about rape, therefore, is that it makes evident the essentially sexual nature of women, and this has been viewed, from the time of Eve through the time of Victoria, as cause for their humiliation. Note that on this view the special evil of rape is due to the feminine character and not to that of her attacker.[8]

The additional societal attitude that sex is moral only between intimates creates a further dilemma in assessing the situation of the rape victim. On the one hand, if it is believed that the sex act itself creates an intimate relationship between two people, then, by necessity, the rape victim experiences intimacy with her assailant. This may incline one to deny the fact of the rape by pointing to the fact of the intimacy. If one does not believe that sex itself creates intimacy between the actors, but nonetheless believes that sex is immoral in the absence of intimacy, then the event of sex in the absence of an intimate relationship, even though involuntary, is cause for public scorn and humiliation. For the rape victim, to acknowledge the rape is to acknowledge one's immorality. Either way, the victim has violated the social sexual taboos and she must therefore be ostracized.

*What is important is no longer that one is the victim of an assault, but rather that one is the survivor of a social transgression.* This is the special burden that the victim carries.

There is support for my view in Gary Wills' review of Tom Wicker's book about the Attica prisoners' revolt.[9] What needs to be explained is the apparently peculiar way in which the safety of the prisoners' hostages was ignored in the preparations for the assault on the prison and in the assault itself. What strikes me as especially important in this event is that those outside the prison walls treated the *guards* exactly like the *prisoners*. The critical similarity is the alleged participation in taboo sexual activity, where such activity is seen as a paradigm of humiliating behavior. In his review Wills says,

Sexual fantasy played around Attica's walls like invisible lightning. Guards told their families that all the inmates were animals. . . .

When the assault finally came, and officers mowed down the hostages along with the inmates, an almost religious faith kept faked stories alive against all the evidence—that the hostages were found castrated; that those still living had been raped. . . . None of it was true, but the guards knew what degradation the prisoners had been submitted to, and the kind of response that might call for. . . .

One has to go very far down into the human psyche to understand what went on in that placid town. . . . The bloodthirsty hate of the local community was so obvious by the time of the assault that even Rockefeller . . . ordered that no correction personnel join the attack. . . . [Nonetheless] eleven men managed to go in. . . . Did they come to save the hostages, showing more care for them than outsiders could? Far from it. They fired as early and indiscriminately as the rest. Why? I am afraid Mr. Wicker is a bit too decent to understand what was happening, though his own cultural background gives us a clue. Whenever a white girl was caught with a black in the old South, myth demanded that a charge of rape be brought and the "boy" be lynched. But a shadowy ostracism was inflicted on the girl. Did she fight back? Might she undermine the myth with a blurted tale or a repeated episode? At any rate, she was tainted. She had, willed she or nilled she, touched the untouchable and acquired her own evil halo of contamination. Taboos take little account of "intention." In the same way, guards caught in that yard were tainted goods. . . . They were an embarrassment. The white girl may sincerely have struggled with her black assailant; but even to imagine that resistance was defiling—and her presence made people imagine it. She was a public pollution—to be purged. Is this [comparison] fanciful? Even Wicker . . . cannot understand the attitude of those in charge who brought no special medical units to Attica before the attack began. . . . The lynch mob may kill the girl in its urgency to get at the boy—and it will regret this less than it admits.[10]

Accounts like the one offered by Frye and Shafer might explain why the *prisoners* were treated so callously by the assaulting troops, but they cannot explain the brutal treatment of the hostages. Surely they cannot say that the guards who were hostages were not and had never been viewed as people, as ontological equals, by the general society. And yet there was the same special horror in being a hostage at Attica as there is for a woman who has been raped. In both cases the *victim* has acquired a "halo of contamination" which permanently taints. And this cannot be explained by claiming that in both cases society is denying personhood or domains of consent to the victim.

The victim in sexual assault cases is as much a victim of our confused beliefs about sex as of the assault itself. The tremendous strains we put on such victims are a cruel result of our deep confusion about the place of, and need for, sexual relationships and the role of pleasure and intimacy in those relationships.

In spite of the fact, I believe, that as a society we share the *belief* that sex is only justified in intimate relationships, we act to avoid real intimacy at almost any cost. We seem to be as baffled as our predecessors were about the place of intimacy in our sexual and social lives. And this is, I think, because we are afraid that real intimacy creates or unleashes sexually wanton relationships, licentious lives—and this we view as morally repugnant. At the same time, we believe that sex in the absence of an intimate relationship is whoring and is therefore also morally repugnant. It is this impossible conflict which I think shows us that we will be able to make sense of our response to rape only if we look at rape as the model of all our sexual interactions, not as its antithesis.

## III. THE MODEL OF SEX: RAPE

Though we may sometimes speak as though sexual activity is most pleasurable between friends, we do not teach each other to treat our sexual partners as friends. Middle-class children, whom I take to be our cultural models, are instructed from the earliest possible time to ignore their sexual feelings. Long before intercourse can be a central issue, when children are prepubescent, boys are instructed to lunge for a kiss and girls are instructed to permit nothing more than a peck on the cheek. This encouragement of miniature adult sexual behavior is instructive on several levels.

It teaches the child that courting behavior is rarely spontaneous and rarely something which gives pleasure to the people involved—that is, it is not like typical playing with friends. It gives the child a glimpse of how adults do behave, or are expected to behave, and therefore of what is expected in future life and social interactions. Importantly, boys are instructed *not* to be attentive to the claims of girls with respect to their desires and needs. And girls are instructed *not* to consult their feelings as a means of or at least a check on what behavior they should engage in.

Every American girl, be she philosopher-to-be or not, is well acquainted with the slippery-slope argument by the time she is ten. She is told that if she permits herself to become involved in anything more than a peck on the cheek, anything but the most innocent type of sexual behavior, she will inevitably become involved in behavior that will result in intercourse and pregnancy. And such behavior is wrong. That is, she is told that if she acquiesces to any degree to her feelings, then she will be doing something immoral.

Meanwhile, every American boy is instructed, whether explicitly or not, that the girls have been given this argument (as a weapon) and that therefore, since everything that a girl says will be a reflection of this argument (and not of her feelings), they are to ignore everything that she says.

Girls are told never to consult their feelings (they can only induce them to the edge of the slippery slope); they are always to say "no." Boys are told that it is a sign of their growing manhood to be able to get a girl way beyond the edge of the slope, and that it is standard procedure for girls to say "no" independently of their feelings. Thus, reasonably enough, boys act as far as one can tell independently of the explicit information they are currently receiving from the girl.

For women, it is very disconcerting to find that from the age of eight or nine or ten, one's reports of one's feelings are no longer viewed as accurate, truthful, important, or interesting. R. D. Laing, the English psychiatrist and theorist, claims that it is this type of adult behavior which creates the environment in which insanity best finds its roots.[11] It is clear, at least, that such behavior is not a model of rationality or health. In any event, rape is a case where only the pretense of listening has been stripped away. It is the essence of what we have all been trained to expect.

In a sexually healthier society, men and women might be told to engage in that behavior which gives them pleasure as long as that pleasure is not (does not involve actions) against anyone's will (including coerced actions) and does not involve them with responsibilities they cannot or will not meet (emotional, physical, or financial).

But as things are now, boys and girls have no way to tell each other what gives them pleasure and what not, what frightens them and what not; there are only violence, threats of violence, and appeals to informing on one or the other to some dreaded peer or parental group. This is a very high-risk, high-stake game, which women and girls, at least, often feel may easily become rape (even though it is usually played for little more than a quick feel in the back seat of the car or corner of the family sofa). But the ultimate consequences of this type of instruction are not so petty. Consider, for example, the effects of a recent English high-court decision:

Now, according to the new interpretation, no matter how much a woman screams and fights, the accused rapist can be cleared by claiming he believed the victim consented, even though his belief may be considered unreasonable or irrational.

On a rainy night seven months ago, a London housewife and mother of three claims she was dragged into this dilapidated shed. Annie Baker says she screamed for help and she fought but she was raped. Mrs. Baker lost her case in court because the man claimed he thought when she said no, she meant yes.

One member of Parliament [predicts juries will] "now have the rapist saying that the woman asked for what she got and she wanted what they [sic] gave her."

However, the Head of the British Law Society maintains, "Today juries are prepared to accept that the relationship between the sexes has become much more promiscuous, and they have to look much more carefully to see whether the woman has consented under modern conditions. . . . One mustn't readily assume that a woman did not consent, because all indications are that there is a greater willingness to consent today than there was thirty years ago."[12]

"The question to be answered in this case," said Lord Cross of Chelsea, "as I see it, is whether, according to the ordinary use of the English language, a man can be said to have committed rape if he believed that the woman was consenting to the intercourse. I do not think he can."[13]

This is the most macabre extension imaginable of our early instruction. It is one which makes initially implausible and bizarre any suggestion that the recent philosophical analyses of sexuality as the product of a mutual desire for communication

—or even for orgasm or sexual satisfaction—bear any but the most tangential relation to reality.[14]

As we are taught, sexual desires are desires women ought not to have and men must have. This is the model which makes necessary an eternal battle of the sexes. It is the model which explains why rape is the prevalent model of sexuality. It has the further virtue of explaining the otherwise puzzling attitude of many that women will cry "rape" falsely at the slightest provocation. It explains, too, why men believe that no woman can be raped. It is as though what was mildly unsatisfactory at first (a girl's saying "no") becomes, over time, increasingly erotic, until the ultimate turn-on becomes a woman's cry of "rape!"

## IV. AN ALTERNATIVE: SEX BETWEEN FRIENDS

Understanding what's wrong with rape is difficult just because it is a member of the most common species of social encounter. To establish how rape is wrong is to establish that we have *all* been stepping to the wrong beat. Rape is only different in degree from the quintessential sexual relationship: marriage.

As Janice Moulton has noted, recent philosophical attention to theories of sexuality seem primarily concerned with sex between strangers.[15] On my view, we can explain this primary interest by noticing that our courting procedures are structured so that the couple must remain essentially estranged from each other. They do not ever talk or listen to each other with the respect and charity of friends. Instead, what is taken as the height of the erotic is sex without intimacy.

As long as we remain uncertain of the legitimacy of sexual pleasure, it will be impossible to give up our rape model of sexuality. For it can only be given up when we are willing to talk openly to each other without shame, embarrassment, or coyness about sex. Because only then will we not be too afraid to listen to each other.

Fortunately, to give this up requires us to make friends of our lovers.[16] Once we understand that intimacy enlarges the field of friendship, we can use some of the essential features of friendship as part of the model for sexual interaction, and we can present the pleasures of friendship as a real alternative to predatory pleasures.

I am not here committing myself to the view that the correct model for lovers is that of friends. Though I believe lovers involved in a healthy relationship have a fairly complex friendship, and though I am at a loss to find any important feature of a relationship between lovers which is not also one between friends, it may well be that the two relationships are merely closely related and not, in the end, explainable with the identical model.

It remains an enormously difficult task to throw over our anachronistic beliefs, and to resolve the conflict we feel about the sexual aspects of ourselves. But once this is done, not only will there be the obvious benefits of being able to exchange ignorance and denial of ourselves and others for knowledge, and fear for friendship, but we will also be able to remove the taboo from sex—even from rape. There will be no revelation, no reminder in the act of rape which we will need so badly to repress or deny that we must transform the victim into a guilt-bearing survivor. An act of rape will no longer remind us of the "true" nature of sex or our sexual desires.

Where there is nothing essentially forbidden about the fact of our sexual desires, the victim of rape will no longer be subject to a taboo or be regarded as dirty and in need of societal estrangement. The victim can then be regarded as having been grievously insulted, without simultaneously and necessarily having been permanently injured.

Further, if the model of sexual encounters is altered, there will no longer be any motivation for blaming the victim of rape. Since sex and rape will no longer be equated, there will be no motive for covering our own guilt or shame about the rapine nature of sex in general by transferring our guilt to the victim and ostracizing her. Rape will become an unfortunate aberration, the act of a criminal individual, rather than a symbol of our systematic ill-treatment and denial of each other.

# NOTES

1. Simone de Beauvoir, *Brigitte Bardot and the Lolita Syndrome* (London: New English Library, 1962), pp. 28, 30, 32.
2. Frye and Shafer characterize a domain as "where . . . a person . . . lives. . . . Since biological life and health are prerequisites for the pursuit of any other interests and goals, . . . everything necessary for their maintenance and sustenance evidently will fall very close to the center of the domain. Anything

which exerts an influence on . . . a person's will or dulls its intelligence or affects its own sense of its identity . . . also comes very near the center of the domain. Whatever has a relatively permanent effect on the person, whatever affects its relatively constant surroundings, whatever causes it discomfort or distress—in short, whatever a person has to live with—is likely to fall squarely within its domain" ("Rape and Respect," this volume, p. 337).

3. This societal attitude, however, that the mentally retarded are not the equals of normal people is not one with which I associate myself.

4. Francoise Basch, *Relative Creatures: Victorian Women in Society and the Novel* (New York: Schocken Books, 1974), pp. 8–9, 270–71.

5. See *The Basic Writings of Sigmund Freud*, ed. A. A. Brill (New York: Random House, 1948), pp. 553–633.

6. William H. Masters and Virginia E. Johnson, *Human Sexual Response* (Boston: Little, Brown, 1966).

7. It may well be that Freud's theory of human sexuality is mistakenly taken to support this view. See Sigmund Freud, *A General Introduction to Psychoanalysis* (New York: Washington Square Press, 1962), pp. 329–47.

8. What is a complete non sequitur, of course, is that the presence of such pleasure is sufficient to establish that no criminal assault has occurred. The two events are completely independent.

9. Tom Wicker, *A Time to Die* (New York: Quadrangle Books, 1975).

10. Gary Wills, "The Human Sewer," *New York Review of Books*, 3 April 1975, p. 4.

11. See, for example, R. D. Laing and A. Esterson, *Sanity, Madness and the Family* (Baltimore: Penguin, Pelican Books, 1970).

12. CBS Evening News with Walter Cronkite, 22 May 1975.

13. *New American Movement Newspaper*, May 1975, p. 8.

14. See R. C. Solomon, "Sex and Perversion," Tom Nagel, "Sexual Perversion," and Janice Moulton, "Sex and Reference," in *Philosophy and Sex*, ed. Robert Baker and Frederick Elliston (Buffalo, N.Y.: Prometheus Books, 1975).

15. Janice Moulton, "Sex and Sex," unpublished manuscript.

16. See Lyla O'Driscoll, "On the Nature and Value of Marriage," this volume. She argues that marriage and the sexual relations it entails should be based on friendship rather than romantic love.

Susan Rae Peterson

# Coercion and Rape: The State As a Male Protection Racket

Recent papers on rape have dealt with the disturbing problem of ferreting out precisely what is wrong with rape. That there is something very much wrong with rape is clear, but many feel that as yet the worst feature of rape has gone unnoticed. In this vein, what is wrong with rape is variously seen as its treatment of women as non-persons,[1] as its being an extreme case of the wrongness of our sexual interactions generally,[2] or the fact that laws about rape show women to be property.[3] It seems to *me* that what is wrong with rape is primarily its restriction of the freedom of bodily movement for women.

Now I do not mean that an individual act of rape restricts freedom of movement for women, although it certainly does at least that for the individual rape victim. The increasing frequency of rape, together with the pervasive threat of becoming a victim, amount to *social* coercion. The reason for this is that rape is not merely an accidental series of individual events, but is institutionalized. It is a Rawlsian kind of "practice": a "form of activity specified by a system of rules which define offices, roles, moves, penalties, defences, and so on, and which give the

This paper was originally read at the University of Toronto on 19 April 1976; I am especially indebted to L. Wayne Sumner, whose detailed prepared critique of my paper occasioned serious and necessary revisions.

activity its structure."[4] The implications of rape as a practice will be drawn out shortly; the important point here is that rape is not natural and inevitable, but social and alterable. Practices which are socially coercive are ultimately the responsibility of the political system. It is up to the state to provide personal protection for each of its members, until they lose or forfeit that right to protection by misbehaving in socially significant ways (that is, by breaking the law). Because of the practice of rape, women are denied not only their personal rights and liberties, but their political ones as well. I will show that (a) the practice of rape constitutes social coercion; (b) that this coercion is applied solely to women through sexually differentiated risks; and (c) that this effectively precludes women from membership in civil society, lacking as they do fundamental protection by the state.

# I. RAPE AS SOCIAL COERCION

### The Practice of Rape

Rape is not a matter of isolated, individual events, but is a Rawlsian practice, as stated above. An action can be repeated with statistical frequency and regularity and still not be a "practice." Rape, however, is a form of activity specified by a system of rules, in this case by rules formulating desirable and undesirable (or moral and immoral) sexual behavior. These rules are steeped in our prevailing attitudes and beliefs about sex, which in turn are largely informed by the dominant ideology of patriarchal, male-dominated society. The psychological theories that serve this ideology explain why women are or ought to be socially and sexually passive, less biologically inclined to want sexual intercourse—in short, primarily sexual creatures for the satisfaction of powerful male drives. (That these beliefs are inconsistent does not hinder their acceptance and promulgation.) Popular sexist morality holds the central belief that men are men, but there are two kinds of women, good and bad ones. Good women deserve not only protection, but honor and good position. Bad women deserve punishment and disrepute; if they get raped, they only "get what is coming to them." Thus the offices, roles, and moves of this practice are set out by widely believed notions about appropriate behavior for males and females.

## Keeping Women in Their Place

According to the prevailing behavioral codes, what is appropriate for one sex is rarely also appropriate for the other. This dimorphic morality is reflected in the law and in the structure of the practice, where defenses are stipulated for both parties. The law is revealing in this respect, for it is true by legal definition that only men can rape, and raping another man is not rape but buggery or indecent assault. Moreover, a man cannot rape his wife. Rape in the law is treated primarily as an assault upon the social mechanism designed to control reproduction and property arrangements related to the family. This accounts for the seriousness of the crime, and for the severity of sentences in rape laws. Morally, however, there is a widespread reluctance to consider a woman as the real victim of a rape, rather than society or her husband or her father. When a woman is acknowledged as a victim, many people are reluctant to consider her morally blameless. The penalties and defenses of the practice of rape, therefore, presuppose a normative ideological perspective, as well as explanations about the causes of rape. Within our ideology, women are not held to have the right to freedom of bodily movement at all. Moving about freely is rather a male privilege, which only immoral women seek to exercise.

If women had the same kind of freedom of bodily movement as men, it would be difficult for the current social mechanisms (like marriage, divorce, and parental custody of children) to control reproduction, the most fundamental of property relations. By one means or another, women must not be allowed to roam about like vagrants, walk anywhere they want at any hour they want, drink in bars alone, or travel without a companion. Only a certain kind of woman, supposedly, would do these things. But when we look at these things, they are things that men can do at any time, and indeed, things that men believe they have a right to do, without interference from others. To control the behavior of women, coercive devices are needed, so they do not "act like men." This does not mean that these devices are repressive *because* coercive. Society can quite justifiably control the behavior of social groups by coercive devices such as taxes and prohibitive laws. The question here is whether the behavioral control of women so that they cannot move about freely alone is justified. The practice of rape effectively "keeps women in their places"; indeed, because many women fear being raped, they remain much more stationary and sedentary than men.

## Coercion

Feinberg describes coercion as "the deliberate forceful interference in the affairs of human beings by other human beings."[5] The state needs to justify interference which is both deliberate and forceful, and does so usually in two basic ways: according to desert or paternalism. The individual may deserve to have his affairs interfered with (because he has forfeited a right); or though he may not deserve it, it may be in his own interest for the state to interfere. Rape is seen as justified interference if the woman "deserves" it for exercising her freedom, when, for instance, she drinks in a bar. Police frequently will not prosecute a case of rape because it occurred just after a woman was in a bar drinking, since it is hard to get a conviction in such cases. They ask, "What did you expect? You took an undue risk by behaving in that way." But surely women do not expect to get raped when they go out for a drink, any more than a man expects to get assaulted when doing the same thing. The victim's foresight is not an issue: if an attack takes place, the fault is on the side of the offender, not the victim.

Less plausibly, it is maintained by some that rape is justified because it is in the woman's best interest: hence the myth that all women secretly want to be raped. One result of this view is that the state is thought to be justified in interfering in the affairs of a rapist (by punishing him) only if the rapist was *not* justified in interfering in the affairs of his victim. This is what the victim must prove. Because an accused person is presumed innocent, the rapist is presumed to have been justified, and the victim guilty. On this view, rape is prima facie justified sexual interference by men with women.

## Prohibition and Prevention

A useful feature of our notion of coercion is the distinction between direct and indirect coercion: direct coercion involves force, and indirect coercion, the threat of force. Feinberg says:

For this intermediate range, threats are like burdens on a man's back, rather than shackles, or bonds, or bayonets. They make one of his alternatives more difficult but not impossible. This is the way in which taxes on socially undesirable conduct can be said to be coercive. *Although they discourage without actually prohibiting, they can quite effectively prevent.*[6]

Rape is a practice which effectively prevents women from the alternative of walking freely in public places. The net result of sexually dimorphic behavior laws is a curfew upon women. And yet formal curfews are only justified by extreme or extenuating circumstances. How is it that no one complains of the injustice of women not being able to go where they will, when they will, as men do? Women must secure protection for themselves to do the most necessary and elementary things, such as shop for food. What these laws are actually discouraging (though not prohibiting) is not rape by the offender, but the mobility of women. Laws prohibiting women to go out or to go drinking might as well exist. It is legally permissible for women to exercise their freedom of bodily movement, but only so long as they accept the resulting constraint: that any act of rape committed against them cannot be prosecuted. A freely-moving woman forfeits her right to protection by the state, even where there is elaborate machinery set up for the purpose.

## Rape: Sex or Assault?

A complicating factor is that rape is both a sex crime and a crime of assault. The gravity of the crime depends on which feature is taken to be the primary one. I submit that rape is first and foremost a crime of violence against the body, and only secondarily (although importantly) a sex crime. Presuming rape to be primarily sexual misplaces much attention on such things as the victim's past sexual history, on establishing whether she is the "kind" of woman who can get raped. However, all women can get raped: victims include mothers, daughters, grandmothers, and infants. There is no analogy for men, for no one would maintain, for instance, that generous men cannot get robbed. Unlike women, property owners are not divided into good and bad character types.[7]

## Rape and "Normal" Sex

There is no convincing evidence to show that sexual intercourse *with* consent is the norm. Typical sexual involvement includes some resistance on the part of women (because they have been taught to do so, or they do not want to appear "easy" or "cheap"); this fact clouds the difference between rape sex and non-rape sex. If we consider rape as assault, it is more obviously a curtailment of one's freedom of bodily movement. People often make out rape to be less of an assault because it is sexual, as if violence in sex were more permissible than violence without sex.

Indeed, the paradigm of sexual interaction is closer to rape than to "happy" sexual intercourse. This is because, according to the predominant ideology, aggressiveness is acceptable in males but not in females. One psychologist says:

A sexual offense is not necessarily a sexual aberration. Sexual offenses are acts that offend a particular society in a particular culture. . . . Thus a sex offender is a person who breaks the law. . . . Most sex offenders are not deviates; only a small percentage of sexually aberrant individuals become sexual offenders. . . . *By law, rape and adultery are sexual offenses and not usually signs of sexual aberration.*[8]

That this authority does not consider rape aberrant at all shows that there is a real problem differentiating rape sex from non-rape sex. A criminologist, discussing sex and aggression, says:

aggressive sexual behavior is considered by psychoanalysis as a negative form of behavior, as a sign of some personality disturbances. However, sexual aggression was found to be the case among those [men] presumably normal.[9]

If we look at rape purely behaviorally, as would a visitor from Mars witnessing various instances of sexual intercourse, the problem becomes even clearer. Karpman does this, saying:

Some psychiatrists attach primary importance to the trauma of the boy who witnesses his parents engaging in the sexual act, which to him seems to be an assault made by an aggressive man upon a passive woman. There is a tendency for such a boy to generalize and see all sexual relations as relations between an aggressive man and a passive or resisting woman.[10]

Since healthy sex is so valuable, and violent sex so repugnant, one would hope that it would be far more difficult than it is to generalize male-female relationships as coercive.

## Rape vs. Seduction

Some confusion is cleared up by distinguishing between rape and seduction: rape occurs when the woman never consents to an act of sexual intercourse; seduction occurs when consent is finally given. We could say that in rape a woman does not consent, or consents by coercion; whereas in seduction a woman consents after persuasion. This problem is recognized by Rogers in *Sex and Law in Canada*:

> The borderline between rape and criminal seduction is not entirely distinct because the definition of seduction is somewhat similar to the terms of [the rape law].[11]

If the prevailing ideology made it permissible for women to be sexually aggressive, rape would probably be far less frequent.

## Unequal Treatment before the Law

The dimorphic nature of our moral beliefs is also apparent in the law, where drinking women are far less tolerable than drinking men. If drinking is wrong, it should be no more wrong for women. Should anyone doubt the ultimate effect of the law, consider the following from the criminologist Menachem Amir:

> In criminal law the presence of alcohol in the offender is considered one of the extenuating circumstances of nonculpability insofar as the drinking person temporarily does not know the nature of what he is doing and cannot distinguish between right and wrong. While the law may sometimes allow being under the influence of alcohol to offset the assessment of specific intent, it does not free persons from responsibility when they voluntarily engage in behavior which has a foreseeable dangerous consequence. Thus, the Model Penal Code expresses recognition of the elements of the victim's drinking in suggesting that when a woman loses capacity to control her own behavior by voluntary use of intoxicants or drugs, any resulting intercourse cannot be charged as rape.[12]

Clearly, a woman is not free to drink if by so doing she leaves herself open to what is clearly justifiable rape in the eyes of the law. A woman cannot be free to go where she pleases if a rapist is free to rape her. What is wrong with rape, then, is that it is really not wrong at all.

## II. SEX-DIFFERENTIATED RISKS

Clearly, the type of social coercion so far described applies only to women. Some persons (men) are more free than others (women) to go where they will. Although the constraints on men are also suffered by women, there is at least one additional constraint suffered only by women: the threat of being raped. What men do not suffer from is a sexually differentiated risk. Admittedly, men are subject with alarming frequency today to assault, robbery, burglary, or even sexual molestation. But admitting this does my case no harm, for women bear these risks plus one more. A woman may be robbed and then raped.

For any woman who may object that she does not alter her behavior pattern because of the threat of rape, my reply would be similar to Hobbes': Does she frequently walk out on the street at night alone? If she does take precautions, she is accusing men by her actions, as I do by my words. Unlike Hobbes, however, I am not trying to persuade the reader that men are habitually apt to invade and destroy *one another*, but rather *women*. That some women feel no fear is readily granted since there are few, if any, of those who feel no fear and who also exercise no caution. It is enough for my case that women, even if they believe they are free, *behave* as if they were coerced. When a woman's walking on the street after dark constitutes "taking an undue risk," the question becomes "How much caution and prudence on the part of citizens can a state justify before losing its legitimacy?"

There could be a possible objection that other social groups besides women are denied the protection of the state, and that men are included in these groups. My reply to this is that these groups definitely have a claim against the state because of the lack of protection afforded them, but this claim is not on the basis of their sex. (Of course it may be on the basis of an equally irrelevant feature.) The women in these groups bear all the risks of the men, with the addition of one more risk that is on the basis of their sex alone.

## III. STATE PROTECTION IN
## STATE-OF-NATURE THEORY

Political society is one in which each person's body and property are secured through the protective monopoly of the state. A state in which a significant number of persons are left unprotected in their freedom of bodily movement is one which denies that group its political freedom.

If someone objects to this, saying that the denial of political freedom necessarily involves the prohibition of participation in political procedures such as the vote, let me offer a counterexample. Animals and children could be granted the vote, on the basis of their right to be treated with minimal care as sentient beings. Would they then be politically free? Surely no one would want to insist that in order to be doing something properly called "voting" a voter would have to vote intelligently. If some were to charge that society would alter beyond recognition if pets and children got the vote, I would submit that this is not true. Pets would probably vote as their masters, and children their parents, in the same way that studies show that wives vote as their husbands. Would such sentient beings have political freedom? I think it is clear that they would not. This is at least partially because as pets or wards they lack freedom of bodily movement. Securing freedom of bodily well-being is the *first political action* in natural-rights theory. If a state does not protect individual members against coercion, those members have little reason to acknowledge its legitimacy.[13]

Since the state fails them in its protective function, to whom can women turn for protection? Generally, women make agreements with husbands or fathers (in return for fidelity or chastity, respectively) to secure protection. From whom do these men protect women? From other men, it turns out. The state itself is little more than a group of men in political offices, like district attorney, judge, legislator.

There is a striking parallel between this situation and tactics used by crime syndicates who sell protection as a racket. The buyer who refuses to buy the protective services of an agency because he needs no protection finds out soon that *because* he refuses to buy it, he very definitely needs protection. Women are in the same position. They are victimized, unwilling clients of an organized protection racket, because they cannot turn to each other, being unorganized themselves.

The crime-syndicate analogy bears fruit if carried further, for the client of the protective criminal agency finds that he is not at all protected if attacked by a member of another agency, or of no agency whatsoever. He has, it turns out, only paid for protection from his agent's aggression. And so a woman finds out that when she is attacked by a man other than her protector, the matter is out of her protector's hands.

Following Nozick's state-of-nature reasoning,[14] women operate as *independents* in civil society, in much the way he imagines Indians would have operated had they not been forced off their land and refused to affiliate with settlers' society. (Locke pointed out that people cannot be compelled to join civil society. In the present case, however, it seems that people *can* be compelled to remain outside civil society.) As independents, women are effectively left in a state of nature with respect to the state. Nozick describes his Indian-and-settler society as a "swiss cheese" society, with internal as well as external boundaries, resulting in acute problems of protective relations. On my view, society is more like a fine-grained sieve, since women are not banded together into tribes; the problems of protective relations are even more acute in such a case.

On a Lockean view of natural rights, women turn out not to be members of civil society at all. At best, they are members only in a sense similar to that in which all sentient beings are members. They lack political freedom, since there is neither protection against bodily attack nor guarantee of just recourse through the state.

A state must show itself capable of protecting, but this does not mean it cannot still be merely a protection racket (as anarchists would claim). What makes the state's protective powers different from the racketeers' is its coercive monopoly: when a state denies its protective function to a significant social group, it risks degenerating into racketeering. Clients of the state protection agency are not merely bargaining for protection *from* it, but also *by* it, from coercive acts of others. Since it fails effectively to protect one significant group in society—namely, women—the state has turned out to be no more than a male protection racket. A woman who refuses to reach an agreement with the state finds out quickly that because she wishes to exercise her right to freedom of bodily movement, she definitely does need protection. And there is no competing agency to which she can turn. For the state, a woman deserves protection only if she never needs it. For women, as for victims of racketeers, it becomes clear that they only need protection if they refuse to pay for it.

## NOTES

1. Carolyn Shafer and Marilyn Frye, "Rape and Respect," this volume.
2. Pamela Foa, "What's Wrong with Rape," this volume.
3. Lorenne Clark, "The Politics of Rape," read at the University of Toronto.
4. John Rawls, "Two Concepts of Rules," *Philosophical Review* 64 (1955): 3.
5. Joel Feinberg, *Social Philosophy* (Englewood Cliffs, N.J.: Prentice-Hall, 1973), p. 7.
6. Ibid., p. 8. Italics added.
7. An analogous case for property owners would be the thief who was robbed; in such a case, his being a thief very well may influence the decision as to whether he was "robbed," for a person who doesn't own something cannot be robbed of it.
8. R. Thorpe, *The Psychology of Abnormal Behavior: A Dynamic Approach* (New York: Ronald Press, 1961), p. 314. Italics added.
9. Menachem Amir, *Patterns in Forcible Rape* (Chicago: University of Chicago Press, 1971), p. 297. Amir cites as his source here E. J. Kanin, "Male Aggressions in Dating Relations," *American Journal of Sociology* 63 (1957): 197–204.
10. Amir, op. cit., p. 305; reference is to Karpman, *The Sexual Offender*.
11. R. S. Rogers, *Sex and Law in Canada* (Toronto: Policy Press, 1962), p. 57.
12. Amir, op. cit., p. 97.
13. Locke says in the Second Treatise that man "hath by nature a power not only to preserve his property—that is, his life, liberty, and estate—against the injuries and attempts of other men, but to judge of and punish the breaches of that law. . . . Whenever, therefore, any number of men are so united into one society as to quit everyone his executive power of the law of nature and to resign it to the public, there and there only is a political or civil society" (John Locke, *Two Treatises of Government* [1685; New York: Hafner Publishing Company, 1965], pp. 163–

64). Hobbes says that "the final Cause, End, or Designe of men (who naturally love liberty, and dominion over others), in the introduction of that restraint upon themselves in which we see them live in Commonwealths, is the foresight of their own preservation" (Thomas Hobbes, *Leviathan* [1651; Baltimore: Penguin Books, 1968], p. 223).

14. Robert Nozick, *Anarchy, State and Utopia* (New York: Basic Books, 1974).

# Rape

## *Further References*

Starred items are those of philosophical interest.

*Amir, Menachem. *Patterns in Forcible Rape*. Chicago: University of Chicago Press, 1971.

*Aquinas, Thomas. *Summa Theologica*. New York: Blackfriars–McGraw-Hill, 1968. Vol. 43, p. 249 (2:2, question 154, article 12).

Astor, Gerald M. *A Question of Rape*. New York: Pinnacle Books, 1974.

———. *The Charge Is Rape*. Chicago: Playboy, 1975.

Blackstone, William. *Of Public Wrongs*. Vol. 4 in *Commentaries on the Laws of England*. Boston: Beacon Press, 1972. Chap. 15.

Blanchard, W. H. "The Group Process in Gang Rape." *Journal of Social Psychology* 49 (1959): 259–66.

Bromberg, Walker. *Crime and the Mind*. New York: Macmillan, 1965.

*Brownmiller, Susan. *Against Our Will*. New York: Simon & Schuster, 1974.

Bullins, Ed. *The Reluctant Rapist*. New York: Harper & Row, 1973.

*Burgess, Ann W., and Holmstrom, Lynda L. *Rape: Victims of Crisis*. Bowie, Md.: R. J. Brady, 1974.

Cleaver, Eldridge. *Soul on Ice*. New York: Dell, 1968. Pp. 14–17.

"Code R for Rape." *Newsweek*, 13 November 1972, p. 75.

Csida, June B., and Csida, Joseph. *Rape: How to Avoid It and What to Do about It*. Chatsworth, Calif.: Books for Better Living, 1974.

*Curley, E. M. "Excusing Rape." *Philosophy and Public Affairs* 5:4 (Summer 1976): 325–60.

Czinner, R. "The Many Kinds of Rape." *Sexology*, January 1970, pp. 12–15.

"Defending Yourself against Rape: Excerpts from *Our Bodies, Our Selves*." *Ladies Home Journal*, July 1973, p. 62.

De Gramont, S., and de Gramont, N. R. "Couple—Speak Rape, True and False." *Vogue*, June 1971, pp. 108–9.

DeRiver, J. Paul. *Crime and the Sexual Psychopath*. Springfield, Ill.: Charles C. Thomas, 1958.

*De Sade, Marquis. *The Complete Justine, Philosophy in the Bedroom, and Other Writings*. Translated by Richard Seaver and Austin Wainhouse. New York: Grove Press, 1965. Pp. 318–26.

*Deutsch, Helene. *The Psychology of Women*. New York: Grune & Stratton, 1944, 1945. Vol. 1, pp. 219–78.

Drzazga, John. *Sex Crimes*. Springfield, Ill.: Charles C. Thomas, 1960.

Duffy, C., and Hirschberg, A. *Sex and Crime*. New York: Pocket Books, 1967.

Edwards, Chilperic. *The Hammurabi Code*. London: Watts, 1921. Pp. 27–31.

Ellis, A., and Brancale, R. *The Psychology of Sex Offenders*. Springfield, Ill.: Charles C. Thomas, 1956.

*Encyclopaedia Britannica*. 1969 ed. S.v. "Rape."

"Forcible and Statutory Rape: An Exploration of the Operation and Objectives of the Consent Standard." *Yale Law Journal* 62 (December 1952): 55–83.

Gager, Nancy, ed. *Women's Rights Almanac*. New York: Harper & Row, 1974. Pp. 488–94.

*Gebhard, Paul H.; Gagnon, John H.; Pomeroy, Wardell B.; and Christenson, Cornelia V. *Sex Offenders: An Analysis of Types*. New York: Harper & Row, 1965.

Genet, Jean. *Miracle of the Rose*. Translated by Bernard Frechtman. London: Anthony Blond, 1965.

Gill, Raj. *Rape*. Thompson, Conn.: Interculture Associates, 1974.

Glueck, Bernard. *Final Report: Research Project for the Study and Treatment of Crimes Involving Sexual Aberrations*. Minnesota, 1952–55.

*Goldberg, Jacob A., and Rosamund, W. *Girls on City Streets: A Study of 1400 Cases of Rape*. New York: Foundation Books, 1935.

Grimstad, K., and Rennie, S., eds. *The New Woman's Survival Catalog*. New York: Coward, McCann & Geohegan, 1973. Chap. 4.

Haskell, Molly. *From Reverence to Rape*. Baltimore: Penguin Books, 1975.

Hayman, Charles R., and Lanza, Charlene. "Victimology of Sexual Assault." *Medical Aspects of Human Sexuality* 5 (October 1971): 152, 157–58, 160–61.

"Healthy Rise in Rape." *Newsweek*, 31 July 1972, p. 72.

Herschberger, Ruth. *Adam's Rib*. New York: Pellegrini & Cudahy, 1948. Pp. 15–27.

Horos, Carol V. *Rape*. New Canaan, Conn.: Tobey Publishing Co., 1976.

Kanowitz, Leo. *Women and the Law*. Albuquerque: University of New Mexico Press, 1969. Pp. 18–25.

*Karpman, Benjamin. *The Sexual Offender and His Offense*. New York: Julian Press, 1954.

Katchadourian, Herant A., and Lunde, Donald T. *The Fundamentals of Human Sexuality*. New York: Holt, Rinehart & Winston, 1972. Pp. 482–85, 514–16.

Lake, A. "Rape: The Unmentionable Crime." *Good Housekeeping*, November 1971, pp. 104–5.

Lear, M. W. "Q. If You Rape a Woman and Steal Her T.V., What Can They Get You For in N.Y.? A. Stealing Her T.V." *New York Times Magazine*, 30 January 1972. Discussion, 27 February 1972.

"Least-Punished Crime." *Newsweek*, 18 December 1972, p. 33.

Le Grand, C. E. "Rape and Rape Laws: Sexism in Society and Law." *California Law Review* 61 (1973): 919–41.

LeVine, Robert A. "Gusii Sex Offenses: A Study in Social Control." *American Anthropologist* 61 (December 1959): 965–90.

Lipton, M. A. "Violence Is a Part of the Times." *U.S. News and World Report*, 25 January 1971, pp. 73–74.

Lindsey, Karen, et al. "Aspects of Rape." *Second Wave* 2 (1972): 20–28.

Livneh, Ernst. "On Rape and the Sanctity of Matrimony." *Israel Law Review* 2 (July 1967): 415–22.

Loenig, R. "Rape: Most Rapidly Increasing Crime." *McCall's*, July 1973, p. 25.

Lynch, W. Ware. *Rape: One Victim's Story*. New York: Berkley Publishing Corp., 1975.

McCaldon, R. J. "Rape." *Canadian Journal of Corrections* 9 (January 1967): 37–59.

*McDonald, John Marshall. *Rape: Offenders and Their Victims*. Springfield, Ill.: Charles C. Thomas, 1971.

*Medea, Andrea, and Thompson, Kathleen. *Against Rape*. New York: Noonday, 1974.

*Mehrhof, Barbara, and Kearon, Pamela. "Rape: An Act of Terror." In *Radical Feminism*, edited by Anne Koedt, Ellen Levine, and Anita Rapone. New York: Quadrangle Books, 1973.

Menen, A. "Rapes of Bangla Desh." *New York Times Magazine*, 23 July 1972, p. 10.

Mohr, J. W. "Rape and Attempted Rape." *Sexual Behavior and the Criminal Law: Preliminary Report*. Toronto, 1965.

*Mulvihill, Donald J., et al. *Crimes of Violence: A Staff Report to* *the National Commission on the Causes and Prevention of Violence.* Washington, D.C.: U.S. Government Printing Office, 1969. Vol. 11.

Norman, Eve. *Rape.* Los Angeles: Wollstonecraft, Inc., 1973.

Oliver, B. J., Jr. "What the Rapist Is Like." *Sexology*, July 1965, pp. 849–51.

Pittman, David J. "Rape Cases Decrease in Detroit, Other Cities." *Detroit Free Press*, 9 February 1971, section C, pp. 1–2.

Ploscowe, Morris. "Rape." In *Problems of Sex Behavior*, edited by Edward Sagarin and Donald E. J. MacNamara. New York: Thomas Y. Crowell, 1968.

"Police Discretion and the Judgment That a Crime Has Been Committed: Rape in Philadelphia." *University of Pennsylvania Law Review* 117 (December 1968): 277–322.

"Portrait of a Rapist." *Newsweek*, 20 August 1973, p. 67.

Prevost, Earle G. "Statutory Rape: A Growing Liberalization." *Southern Carolina Law Review* 18 (1966): 254–66.

"Rape." In *Sex Code of California*, edited by Elizabeth R. Gatou. Los Altos, Calif.: William Kaufmann, 1973. Pp. 153–58.

*Rape and Its Victims.* Washington, D.C.: U.S. Department of Justice, 1976.

*Rape and the Treatment of Rape Victims in Georgia.* Atlanta: Governor's Office, 1975.

"The Rape Corroboration Requirement." *Yale Law Journal* 81 (June 1972): 1365–91.

"Rape Wave: Creation of Rape Investigation and Analysis Section." *Newsweek*, 29 January 1973, p. 59.

Reynolds, J. "Rape As Social Control." Unpublished paper read at Michigan Sociological Association meetings, Detroit, 1971.

Ross, Susan, C. *The Rights of Women: The Basic ACLU Guide to a Woman's Rights.* New York: Avon Books, 1973. Chap. 5.

*Russell, Diana. *The Politics of Rape.* New York: Stein & Day, 1975.

Schultz, Gladys. "Society and the Sex Criminal." *Reader's Digest*, November 1966, pp. 141–46.

Schultz, Terri. "Rape, Fear and the Law." *Chicago Guide*, November 1972, pp. 56–62.

"Sex Offenses and Sex Offenders." *Annals of the American Academy* (March 1969), pp. 151–52.

Slovenko, R. "Statutory Rape." *Medical Aspects of Human Sexuality* 5 (March 1971): pp. 155–67.

Storaska, Frederick. *How to Say No to a Rapist—and Survive.* New York: Warner Books, 1976.

Sutherland, Sandra, and Scherl, Donald J. "Patterns of Response among Victims of Rape." *Journal of Orthopsychiatry* 40:3 (April 1970): 503–11.

Svalastoga, K. "Rape and the Social Structure." *Pacific Sociological Review* 5 (1962): 48–53.

Trevor, Leslie. *Rape.* Hauppage, N.Y.: Universal Publishing & Distributing Corp., 1975.

*Wilson, Cassandra, and Connell, Noreen. *Rape: The First Sourcebook for Women.* New York: New American Library, 1974.

"Women against Rape." *Time*, 23 April 1973, p. 104.

Woods, G. D. "Some Aspects of Pack Rape in Sydney." *Australian and New Zealand Journal of Criminology* 2 (1969): 105–19.

# Part VII
# Abortion

# Part VII

# Abortion

## *Introduction*

While reproductive freedom is of concern to both sexes, women have always shouldered more of the burdens of reproduction than have men. In addition to the physical pain and inconvenience of pregnancy and childbirth, women have usually raised, fed, clothed, and educated the children. So the consequences of contraceptive failure, premarital sex, and so forth have fallen more heavily on women than on men. For a girl, an unwanted teenage pregnancy may mean a lifelong commitment to a child, ostracism and social disapproval, or dropping out of school, in addition to the medical dangers and burdens of pregnancy. Since these are unequal burdens which limit women's freedom and sometimes deny them equal opportunity, contraception and abortion are of special concern to feminists.

Contraception has received wide acceptance in recent years, but the heated dispute about abortion continues, and philosophers have entered it. They have been primarily concerned with the moral question, "Is abortion wrong?" and only secondarily with the legal question, "Should abortion be prohibited by law?"[1] On the moral question, philosophers have examined the two most popular positions and found them to have serious problems. Then they have gone on to develop and defend positions intermediate between the extreme liberal and conservative ones.

The "conservative" view is that abortion is wrong because it is the murder of a human being with a right to life. Conservatives reason:

> A fetus is a human being.
> All human beings have a right to life.
> It is wrong to kill anything with a right to life.
>
> ---
>
> Therefore, abortion is wrong.

Two major objections have been raised to this position. First, though both sides agree that a fetus will *become* a human being if the pregnancy is continued, they disagree as to whether it is a moral person already. It is not clear just what it takes to qualify as a person. Some conservatives have proposed "having a unique set of genes,"[2] others "being conceived of humans"[3] as the criterion. Second, even if a fetus is a person, not all killings of persons are wrong. For example, killing in self-defense, in war, as punishment, or to save many lives may be morally permissible.

In response to these objections, the thinkers in the Catholic tradition have improved on the popular conservative argument by developing a sophisticated theory to distinguish which killings of human beings are wrong and which are permissible. Susan T. Nicholson examines their ideas in detail. One position they have held is that while it is wrong actively to do something which leads to a death, it is not wrong to refrain from doing something else which would prevent a death. In abortion situations where the woman's life is threatened, this principle advocates "allowing" the woman to die rather than actively killing the fetus in order to save her life.

However, this distinction between "doing" and "refraining" is open to serious objections. For example, even refraining is doing something. Although it does seem to be true that most malicious "doings" are worse than a "refraining" with the same consequences, this is usually because the positive action (such as pushing a non-swimmer into the lake) requires a more evil character or worse intentions than a refraining (not jumping in to save the non-swimmer). But then it seems we should have looked directly at the intentions involved, and not at whether the action was a doing or a refraining. Someone who sits calmly by and withholds the antidote from a poison victim certainly seems as evil as one who administers the poison.

Another central idea in the Catholic tradition which Nicholson discusses is that direct killing is wrong where indirect killing may be all right. If killing the fetus is the result of a hysterectomy or some other medical procedure sometimes used on nonpregnant women, the killing is thought to be all right because it is an indirect consequence of a procedure done for some other reason. Nicholson argues that this distinction does not result in any reasonable or defensible position on abortion. For instance, it permits killing a fetus to save a woman from cervical cancer, but prohibits killing the fetus to save her from a heart attack that pregnancy or childbirth would cause.

At the other extreme, the "liberal" position is that abortion is not wrong, because a fetus is not a person yet, but simply part of the woman's body. Their argument runs:

> A fetus is not a person but merely part of the woman's body.
> You have a right to do whatever you want in and to your own body.
> _____
> Therefore, you have a right to have an abortion.

This view also has some serious problems, however. For one thing, it is not true that you can do whatever you want to your own body. It is not a private matter whether or not to swallow gelignite and explode yourself in a crowded airport. How others are affected matters, even if it is your body. For another thing, just because a fetus isn't a person does not mean you can do whatever you want to it. For instance, you cannot wantonly destroy streams or kill birds for no reason, even though they are not persons with human rights. Like animals, a fetus may have some rights even if it is not a person.

Judith Jarvis Thomson developed a more sophisticated "liberal" position in her 1971 article, "A Defense of Abortion."[4] Thomson attempted to explain to what extent you can and cannot do whatever you want to your body by describing a parallel example about a "famous violinist." Suppose you are kidnaped by the Society of Music Lovers, the story goes, and wake up to find yourself in a hospital bed with your kidneys attached by tubes to those of a famous violinist. He has a rare kidney disease, they inform you, and needs nine months of dependence on your kidneys to survive. You are the only one with the right blood type. Must you lie there for nine months, Thomson asks, or may you unplug yourself and walk away? After all, violinists are persons, too, and persons have a right to life.

Her answer is interesting: it depends. If the sacrifice being asked of you is small—say, only nine minutes in bed—only a morally indecent person would refuse. If the sacrifice would be great, such as dropping out of school or losing your sanity or your life, even a Good Samaritan would refuse. In either case, she claims, the violinist has no *right* to the use of your kidneys. His right to life is not a right to demand from others whatever it takes to keep him alive. The parallel with pregnancy is obvious. In this way, Thomson argues that even if a fetus is a person with a right to life, this does not imply that a woman has to undergo heavy sacrifices to support its life. However, she would be morally indecent to refuse to undergo a small sacrifice to support its life.

More radical "liberal" positions are defended by Mary Anne Warren and Michael Tooley.[5] They hold that the central element in our concept of a person is the possession of a certain kind of consciousness and rationality. But these characteristics are not acquired at birth, only some time afterward. Therefore, they hold that both abortion and infanticide, at least during the first few months of life, are permissible. To draw this conclusion, however, one must assume that it is always permissible to kill beings who lack these rationality characteristics, regardless of whether they would develop them. Central to this position, then, is a rejection of the conservatives' "potentiality principle": that if having $X$ gives you a right to $Y$, then having the potential to develop $X$ also gives you a right to $Y$.

ELIZABETH RAPAPORT and PAUL SAGAL criticize these liberal approaches. They conclude that since no one knows whether a fetus is a person or not, we do not know whether abortion is wrong. In the absence of a solution to this moral question, they argue that laws should not prohibit abortions. After all, freedom is important to us, too. Only if abortion were known to be wrong, and if this were a greater evil than depriving women of full control over their bodies, would it be right to have laws prohibiting abortion.

The question of whether a fetus is a person or not has been a central point in the abortion debate. Liberals typically say you become a person at birth (or later), while conservatives choose the moment of conception. Since the biological development between these points is gradual, it has been argued that it is a "slippery slope": if you pick 12 weeks as the time before which abortions are permitted, it goes, you have no *reason* to prohibit them at 12½ weeks, at 13 weeks, etc., so that only the two endpoints, conception and birth, are rational candidates for a stopping point. But it is interesting to note that many times in-between have nonetheless been used. Some philosophers have suggested the acquisition of a heartbeat (3 weeks), some the onset of brain waves (8 weeks), others viability (about 28 weeks), the time when the fetus becomes able to survive on its own. Historically, "quickening," the time when the fetus begins to move, was a popular legal dividing point. The Supreme Court has similarly picked the three trimesters to mark important differences.[6] This opens the door for abortion positions which are intermediate between the liberal and conservative extremes.

JANE ENGLISH examines the concept of a person and argues that it is not clear-cut enough to support any solution to the abortion debate. Instead, she proposes an intermediate solution which can be reached without settling the personhood question. Her argument is in the form of what is called a "constructive dilemma":

> Either $X$ or not-$X$.
> If $X$, then $Y$.
> If not-$X$, then $Y$.
>
> ———————————
>
> Therefore, $Y$.

If a fetus is a person, she argues, then abortions early in pregnancy to save a woman from serious consequences are justified by self-defense, but late abortions for trivial reasons are not justifiable. Similarly, even if a fetus is not a person, late abortions for trivial reasons are wrong but early ones to avoid serious harms are all right. Here she relies on a parallel with the rights of other non-persons such as animals. In short, this view results whether a fetus is a person or not. The most controversial issue here is how serious a harm must be before killing a person to avoid it can be justified.

HOWARD COHEN takes yet a different approach, without appealing either to personhood or to self-defense. He discusses the impact it has on our quality of life to have the right to make responsible and mature reproductive decisions. He argues that abortion must be available along with contraception to make such responsible control of our lives possible. For example, if responsibility is our model, then a woman pregnant due to rape and a teenager pregnant due to ignorance will be viewed as entitled to abortions, since they did not have a chance to make responsible decisions to enter into pregnancy. Similarly, unforeseen circumstances will make abortion justifiable. If a couple intentionally conceives, but then the husband is killed in a car crash, for instance, this changes the family situation seriously enough that the wife is entitled to re-evaluate the decision to bear a child and to terminate the pregnancy if that is the best outcome for her life. But usually, on this model, abortion will not be needed beyond the early weeks of pregnancy. If we believe that responsible family planning is a right or even a duty, we ought to include abortion as one option, Cohen reasons, since even responsible planners cannot always avoid contraceptive failure or foresee all the consequences of their actions.

Thus Cohen and English both present positions which are intermediate between the popular view that all abortions are wrong because they are murder and the view that abortion is simply an operation on part of a woman's body, on a par with tonsillectomy. The stage of the pregnancy and the responsible decision to avoid undesirable consequences are the two main factors to be considered.

J. E.

## NOTES

1. It is helpful to keep these two questions separate, since not all wrong actions are or should be prohibited by law. Nor are all illegal actions wrong. For example, it may be wrong but not illegal to be ungrateful to your parents or to break a promise to meet a friend for lunch. One possible position on abortion is that some (or all) abortions are wrong, but that none (or not all) should be illegal. By the same token, however, it would be possible to hold that although abortion is morally all right, it should be prohibited or restricted by law if it would lead to undesirable consequences such as increased promiscuity, infanticide, or the extinction of the species.
2. Paul Ramsey, "The Morality of Abortion," in *Moral Problems*, ed. James Rachels (New York: Harper & Row, 1975).
3. John T. Noonan, Jr., "Abortion and the Catholic Church: A Summary History," *Natural Law Forum* 12 (1967): 125–31.

4. Judith Thomson, "A Defense of Abortion," *Philosophy and Public Affairs* 1 (1971): 47–66.
5. Mary Anne Warren, "On the Moral and Legal Status of Abortion," *Monist* 57 (1973): 43–61; and Michael Tooley, "Abortion and Infanticide," *Philosophy and Public Affairs* 2 (1972): 37–65.
6. *Roe* v. *Wade*, 410 U.S. 113 (1973). In the first three months of pregnancy, abortion is solely a decision between a woman and her doctor; in the second three months, the state may impose regulations relating to health such as requiring all abortions to take place in accredited hospitals; only in the third trimester may the states restrict or prohibit abortion.

Susan T. Nicholson

# The Roman Catholic Doctrine of Therapeutic Abortion

Life-threatening pregnancies present a conflict between the life of the pregnant woman and the life of the fetus. What is the moral thing to do in situations of mortal conflict between two innocent human beings? Roman Catholic moral theology has evolved a detailed response to this question in the context of abortion.

It should be acknowledged that with advances in medical technology, such situations infrequently arise in the United States. Ectopic pregnancy, where the embryo implants and develops outside its normal uterine site, is the exception to this statement. Such pregnancies occur frequently—according to one study, at the rate of one to every seventy-eight uterine pregnancies.[1] With regard to uterine pregnancies, however, even medical proponents of abortion-law liberalization acknowledge that there are few diseases or complications of pregnancy which call for termination of pregnancy in order to save the woman's life. Nevertheless, considerable criticism has been leveled against the traditional Roman Catholic view of what should be done were such situations to arise.

On the basis of the following authoritative statements, one

This paper is reprinted by permission of the *Journal of Religious Ethics*.

might assume that Roman Catholic doctrine opposes therapeutic abortion. The first statement is from "Casti Connubi," an
address by Pope Pius XI, and the second is from the more
recent "Declaration on Abortion" issued by the Sacred Congre-
gation for the Doctrine of the Faith and confirmed by Pope Paul
VI:

As to the *medical and therapeutic "indication"* to which, using their
own words, We may have made reference, Venerable Brethren,
however much We may pity the mother whose health and even *life*
is gravely imperiled in the performance of the duty allotted to her by
nature, nevertheless what could ever be a sufficient reason for excusing in any way the direct murder of the innocent? This is precisely what we are dealing with here. Whether inflicted upon the
mother or upon the child, it is against the precept of God and the
law of nature: "Thou shalt not kill." The life of each is equally
sacred, and no one has the power, not even the public authority, to
destroy it. It is of no use to appeal to the right of taking away life,
for here it is a question of the innocent, whereas that right has regard
only to the guilty; nor is there here question of defense by blood-
shed against an unjust aggressor (for who would call an innocent
child an unjust aggressor?); again there is no question here of what
is called the "law of extreme necessity" which could never extend to
the direct killing of the innocent. *Upright and skillful doctors strive
most praiseworthily to guard and preserve the lives of both mother
and child; on the contrary, those show themselves most unworthy
of the noble medical profession who encompass the death of one
or the other, through a pretense at practicing medicine or through
motives of misguided pity.*[2]

We must face up to these very serious difficulties: for example, the
mother's health, or *even her life*, may be endangered [by preg-
nancy]. . . .
    Nonetheless we must assert without qualification that *none* of
these reasons justifies disposing of the life of another human being,
even in its earliest stages.[3]

This assumption, however, is mistaken. While Roman Catholic
doctrine does not permit all therapeutic abortions, it does permit *some*. This intriguing distinction among abortions, all of
which are aimed at preserving the life of the pregnant woman, is
the subject of the present paper. Four obstetrics cases are presented for the purpose of assessing the consistency of the
Roman Catholic doctrine of therapeutic abortion. Two of the

cases involve situations in which Catholic doctrine permits therapeutic abortion; the other two involve situations in which therapeutic abortion is forbidden. The problem is to determine the difference between the licit and illicit abortions, and whether or not that difference is morally relevant.

Clarification of terminology employed here is in order at this point. The term "fetus" is used to refer to the conceptus from fertilization through all subsequent stages of pregnancy. Although the standard medical definition of abortion is the interruption of pregnancy before the fetus is viable,[4] it is useful in this study to extend usage of the term to include both the removal of a non-viable fetus and destructive operations in which the death of a viable fetus is a foreseen result.

The term "therapeutic abortion" is used here to refer only to those abortions believed necessary to prevent the "natural" (non-suicidal) death of the woman during pregnancy or shortly thereafter. This is admittedly a departure from common usage, as abortions performed to preserve health and even psychological well-being are frequently called therapeutic. Adoption of this restricted usage is simply for convenience. Since the task is to determine how it is possible to discriminate morally among abortions all of which are undertaken to preserve the woman's life, it is useful to have a term which refers strictly to life-saving abortions.

## FOUR CASES OF CONFLICT BETWEEN MATERNAL AND FETAL LIFE

The following four cases are intended to be medically accurate. However, the reader should be alerted to the fact that there are aspects of the cases concerning which medical authorities themselves disagree.

*Case A.* A woman in early pregnancy has invasive cancer of the cervix. If removal of her uterus (hysterectomy) is promptly performed, she has a good chance of survival. The operation will, of course, result in the death of the fetus, whose development would otherwise be normal.[5]

*Case B.* A woman has a pre-viable pregnancy which is developing in one of her fallopian tubes instead of in her uterus. If an operation is not performed to excise the fetus or remove the tube containing the fetus, she may die from a spontaneous tubal abortion or rupture. Although this operation will result in the death of the fetus, it is extremely unlikely that the fetus could survive in any event.[6]

*Case C.* A woman in early pregnancy is suffering from chronic hypertensive heart disease associated with severe renal insufficiency. If her pregnancy is not terminated, she may die as a result of the increased demands the pregnancy places on her cardiovascular and renal functions. Although termination of the pregnancy will result in the death of the fetus, its chances for survival are slight in any event.[7]

*Case D.* A woman in prolonged obstructed labor will die unless an operation is performed in which the head of her unborn fetus is crushed (craniotomy). If craniotomy is not performed and the woman dies from uterine rupture or exhaustion, the fetus will in all likelihood die also.[8]

According to standard Roman Catholic doctrine, the physician in case A is permitted to remove the cancerous uterus, even though he/she foresees the death of the non-viable fetus as a certain result. Similarly, in the event of a tubal pregnancy, case B, the fallopian tube may be removed, even though the death of the non-viable fetus is foreseen as an inevitable result. In cases C and D, however, the physician may not operate. He/she may not abort the woman with chronic hypertension, and may not perform a craniotomy on a living fetus.[9]

Roman Catholic moralists do not justify their judgments on the basis of the probabilities of maternal/fetal survival. It should be observed that it would not be possible to do so. Consider fetal survival, for instance. It might be supposed that abortion of a tubal pregnancy, case B, is permissible because of the extremely slight chance that the fetus could be delivered alive in any event. However, the same may be said of case C, where therapeutic abortion is not permissible.

Nor can it be supposed that maternal mortality is the critical factor. Many women survive tubal pregnancy without the surgical intervention which is licit according to Catholic moral theology.[10] On the other hand, a woman will certainly die if her obstructed labor is not relieved, yet craniotomy—in past times the only way of relieving certain abnormalities of labor—is forbidden by Roman Catholic doctrine.[11] In order to justify the moral discriminations made among these cases, it is evident that appeal must be made to factors other than the chances of maternal/fetal survival.

To account for the moral discriminations among these cases, Roman Catholic moralists invoke the important principle of Catholic moral theology called the Principle of Double Effect. We turn now to an examination of that principle.

## THE PRINCIPLE OF DOUBLE EFFECT

The Principle of Double Effect is used by Roman Catholic moralists to identify those situations in which it is morally permissible to aim at a good effect, even though evil is also a foreseen consequence of one's actions. The principle is aptly termed "Double Effect," as two effects, one good and one bad, are involved. This principle is applied frequently in contemporary Roman Catholic treatment of such topics as abortion, sterilization, prolongation of life, suicide, and conduct in war.[12]

The following statement of the Principle of Double Effect, paraphrased from Farraher and given equivalent formulations by Callahan and Granfield, is typical:

> An act having the double effect of a good and an evil consequence is permissible where:
>
> (1) the immediate action performed be good or indifferent;
> (2) the foreseen evil effect be not intended in itself;
> (3) the good which is intended be not an effect of the evil; and
> (4) the good intended be commensurate with the evil foreseen.[13]

Roman Catholic moralists maintain that abortion in cases A and B satisfies the Principle of Double Effect, and hence is licit. By contrast, abortion in cases C and D is said to violate the conditions of that principle, and hence to be illicit.[14]

In a therapeutic abortion, the foreseen *evil* effect is of course the death of the fetus, and the *good* effect is the preservation of the pregnant woman's life. Condition (4) of the Principle of Double Effect requires that the good and bad effects be commensurate or proportional. Since the good effect and the bad effect are the same for every therapeutic abortion, it is evident that condition (4) cannot be used to make moral discriminations among therapeutic abortions. Roman Catholic moralists regard preservation of the woman's life as commensurate with fetal death, and hence regard condition (4) as satisfied by all therapeutic abortions. (An example of an operation which would clearly violate this condition is the removal of a small ovarian cyst in a pregnant woman. Roman Catholic moralists would not consider the slight benefit to the woman's health to be commensurate with the risk of loss of fetal life.)

Associated with the Principle of Double Effect is a distinction between evil effects brought about *directly* and those brought about *indirectly*. The Principle of Double Effect is said to forbid direct killing, for example, but to permit some instances of indirect killing. With regard to therapeutic abortion, licit therapeutic abortions are said to involve indirect killing of the fetus, whereas in the illicit ones the fetus is said to be killed directly. Pius XI alludes to this distinction in the passage quoted earlier from "Casti Connubi," which had at first sight appeared to condemn all therapeutic abortions:

As to the medical and therapeutic "indication" to which, using their own words, We have made reference, Venerable Brethren, however much We may pity the mother whose health and even life is gravely imperiled in the performance of the duty allotted to her by nature, nevertheless what could ever be a sufficient reason for excusing in any way the *direct* murder of the innocent?[15]

Similarly, it is stated in the recent "Declaration on Abortion"[16] that nothing could ever justify the *direct* killing of the innocent. These remarks, while leaving open the possibility that indirect killing could be excused, emphasize that direct killing is always forbidden even for the commensurately serious reason of saving the life of the pregnant woman. We may infer that the characterization of fetal killing as direct or indirect is independent of condition (4), and depends upon conditions (1), (2), or (3), or some combination of these.

But condition (2) of the Principle of Double Effect cannot be used to distinguish among therapeutic abortions, for in no case is the foreseen evil effect, fetal death, intended in itself. It is manifest that the end for which therapeutic abortion is undertaken is not fetal death but preservation of the life of the pregnant woman. That leaves conditions (1) and (3) as possible bases for the moral discriminations among therapeutic abortions.

Papal pronouncements may be cited to suggest that it is condition (3) which serves to distinguish licit from illicit therapeutic abortions. Pius XII, for example, in "The Apostolate of the Midwife," defines a *direct* attack upon human life as an action which "aims at its [life's] destruction either as an end in itself or as the means of attaining another end that is perhaps in no way illicit in itself."[17] This passage suggests that killing is *indirect* where death is neither an end nor a means to an end. Thus, according to Pius XII, an indirect killing satisfies conditions (2) and (3) of the Principle of Double Effect, whereas a direct killing violates one or the other of these conditions. It will be recalled that all therapeutic abortions satisfy condition (2). It follows that on the formulation of direct and indirect killing provided by Pius XII, licit therapeutic abortions are distinguishable from illicit ones with reference to condition (3) of the Principle of Double Effect. Reflection upon the four obstetrics cases will show, however, that condition (3) cannot be the key to understanding the application of the Double Effect Principle to therapeutic abortion.

Consider an instance in which therapeutic abortion is licit—case A, for example. This is the case of the pregnant woman with the cancerous cervix. Since removal of her uterus is licit, one would expect that in this instance the operating surgeon does not aim at fetal death either as an end or as a means to the desired end. And indeed this would appear to be true. As stated previously, the end aimed at is manifestly preservation of the woman's life. And the means to this end is not fetal death, but rather removal of the woman's uterus. Death of the non-viable fetus is a by-product of this means. Should the fetus, contrary to expectation, be removed alive, there would be no point in killing it. This may be contrasted with an instance where a person's death is truly aimed at as a means. Imagine a gunman hired to kill a person in order to prevent that person from revealing certain information. Should the victim, contrary to expectation, survive the first attempt upon his/her life, another attempt would be made.

But the same may be said of case C, where therapeutic abortion is *il*licit. This is the case of the pregnant woman suffering from chronic hypertension. Here it is removal of the fetus, not its death, which is the means to the end of saving the woman's life. Again, there would be no point in killing the fetus should it, contrary to expectation, be removed alive. That the fetus be removed dead rather than alive serves no end of the doctor, or of the woman.

Even in the forbidden case of craniotomy, case D, fetal death is not a means to the desired end. Some Catholic writers have claimed otherwise. For instance, Kenny states in reference to craniotomy that "The person who performs the operation necessarily *wills* the death of the child either as a *means* of saving the mother's life or because he judges it to be the lesser of two evils."[18]

It is not, however, the death of the fetus that is required for the woman's survival, but the narrowing of the fetus' head sufficiently to prevent the hemorrhaging and exhaustion which will bring about her death. That the narrowing of the head and not the death of the fetus is the means to this end is demonstrated by the fact that the fetus would not be killed should it somehow survive the force applied to its skull and be removed alive from the birth canal. Paul Ramsey expresses this point by saying that "the intention of this action is not the killing, not the death of the fetus," but rather the "*incapacitation* of the fetus from doing what it is doing to the life of the mother."[19]

It would appear then that in any abortion undertaken strictly to prevent the "natural" (non-suicidal) death of the woman during pregnancy or shortly thereafter, the death of the fetus is a foreseen consequence of the means chosen, but is not itself a means to an end. If this conclusion is correct, then all therapeutic abortions satisfy condition (3) of the Principle of Double Effect.

It may be noted that this point is obscured by the failure of some Catholic authors to distinguish in a consistent way between the removal of the fetus from the woman's body and its subsequent death. For instance, Gerald Kelly writes that therapeutic abortion in the case of a woman with a cancerous cervix is licit, for "it is the removal of the cancer, *not the death of the fetus*, that saves the woman's life." In other words, Kelly disapproves only of those procedures in which the death of the fetus is the means to the desired end. On the other hand, he writes that the removal of a non-viable fetus as a last resort in a case of hyperemesis gravidarum (severe vomiting) is not licit, because the vomiting "is stopped only by the *emptying of the uterus*."[20] This suggests the alternative interpretation that Kelly disapproves of those procedures in which the *removal of the fetus* occurs as a means to the end.

In fact, neither view is satisfactory. As I have just argued, the view that a therapeutic abortion is immoral only where *fetal death* is a means to an end is incompatible with making moral distinctions among the four obstetrics cases presented above, distinctions which Kelly himself makes. The second view, that therapeutic abortions are immoral only where *removal of the fetus* is a means to an end, also runs into difficulty. This view presupposes that removal of the fetus is evil, otherwise there would be no reason to condemn its employment as a means to a good end. What makes removal of a non-viable fetus evil, however, is precisely that it results in fetal death. Roman Catholic moralists do not disapprove of removal of a viable fetus for therapeutic reasons. To be consistent, then, any surgical procedure which inevitably results in fetal death should be forbidden as a means. But removal of a cancerous pregnant uterus prior to viability of the fetus is as inevitably associated with fetal death as removal of a non-viable fetus by itself. Consequently, adoption of the second view is again incompatible with the distinctions Kelly and traditional Roman Catholic moralists draw among therapeutic abortions.

On the basis of the discussion thus far, we may criticize an interpretation of the Principle of Double Effect provided by Leonard Geddes. Geddes claims that the essence of the Principle of Double Effect is to distinguish between the *intended* and the *merely foreseen* consequences of a voluntary action.[21] Death is an *intended* consequence of an action, Geddes says, where the action aims at death either as an end in itself, or as a means to an end. A killing is *intentional* where death is intended. In voluntary but *non-intentional* killing, on the other hand, death is a foreseen (though not intended) consequence.

There is a broader sense of "intended" which may be more in accord with ordinary usage than this narrow sense provided by Geddes. Hart suggests that in ordinary usage one does intentionally what one sets out to achieve, either as a means or an end, as well as what is "so immediately and invariably connected with the action done that the suggestion that the action might not have had that outcome would by ordinary standards be regarded as absurd."[22]

Let us examine the possibility that the Principle of Double Effect is meant to distinguish between the intended and merely foreseen consequences of a voluntary action, in one or the other of these two senses of "intended." If Hart's broad sense of "intended" be adopted, it follows that any and all cases of therapeutic abortion would count as intentional killing. That is, the connection between the removal of a cancerous uterus containing a non-viable fetus and the death of the fetus is as close as the connection between crushing the head of the unborn child and the resultant death of that child. To suggest that a six-week fetus might have survived removal of the uterus would by ordinary standards be regarded as absurd.

But a parallel difficulty is encountered if Geddes' narrow sense of "intended" be adopted. If the preceding discussion is correct, it follows that no cases of therapeutic abortion would count as intentional killing, for in no case is fetal death sought as either means or end. Geddes himself acknowledges this with regard to craniotomy, the single instance of therapeutic abortion considered by him.

Thus, whichever sense of "intended" be adopted, we have the problem of accounting for the fact that the Principle of Double Effect has traditionally been used to distinguish permissible from forbidden cases of therapeutic abortion.

In the same year that Pius XII characterized a killing as indirect in which death is the aim neither as means nor end, he offered in another address a quite different criterion of indirect killing. In "Morality in Marriage" he said:

On purpose We have always used the expression "direct attempt on the life of an innocent person," "direct killing." Because if, for example, the saving of the life of the future mother, *independently of her pregnant state*, should urgently require a surgical act or other therapeutic treatment which would have as an accessory consequence, in no way desired or intended but inevitable, the death of the fetus, such act could no longer be called a direct attempt on an innocent life.[23]

This criterion of indirect killing also appears in the writings of Charles Curran. According to Curran, some theologians have proposed as a rule of thumb that abortion is indirect "if the action could be done without killing the fetus or if the procedure would be done if the fetus is present or not."[24] The rule of thumb proposed in the first half of the sentence may be set aside as it fails to discriminate between the licit and illicit cases of therapeutic abortion, all of which usually result in fetal death. Contained in the second half of the sentence, however, is another rule of thumb according to which the procedures involved in licit abortions would be done *regardless* of the presence of the fetus. It is plausible to regard such procedures as required independently of pregnancy, thus connecting Curran's second rule of thumb with the papal criterion above.

According to that papal criterion, what types of therapeutic abortion count as direct killing? It is plausible to regard craniotomy and abortion in the case of a woman suffering from chronic hypertension as direct killing since each involves a threat to the woman's life clearly related to, rather than independent of, her pregnancy or its circumstances. Removal of the cancerous uterus of a pregnant woman, on the other hand, would count as indirect destruction of innocent life since its removal would be medically indicated whether or not the woman was pregnant. Thus far, application of the criterion provides results consistent with the doctrine on therapeutic abortion found in the manuals of medical ethics.

Application of the criterion in the case of ectopic pregnancy, however, proves to be more troublesome. It would seem evident that the threat to a woman's life caused by an ectopic pregnancy is *not* independent of that pregnancy, and consequently that removal of a fallopian tube cannot be justified under this criterion of indirect killing. Nevertheless, in his study of abortion in canon law, Huser says that "almost every ectopic pregnancy will, sooner or later, engender a pathological condition which then, *independently of the pregnancy itself*, constitutes a serious danger to the mother's life."[25]

In order to understand this surprising claim it is necessary to refer to an influential study by T. Lincoln Bouscaren on the morality of ectopic operations.[26] Prior to Bouscaren's study, no consensus existed concerning the morality of surgical intervention in a tubal pregnancy before the tube had actually ruptured. Once rupture had occurred, the physician was permitted to treat the acute medical emergency by removing the tube and its contents.

Bouscaren points out that the objection to removal of the tube prior to rupture was based on the mistaken assumption that the tube remained sound until the moment of its actual rupture. Bouscaren introduces medical evidence showing that, on the contrary, the tube begins to deteriorate well before it actually bursts. Placental cells which would normally penetrate the thick mucous lining of the uterus instead penetrate the thin wall of the fallopian tube. This "burrowing in" action of the fetus, even in early pregnancy, results in perforation of blood vessels and dissection of muscles in the tube wall. When rupture occurs, the major cause is not the mechanical inability of the wall to stretch sufficiently to accommodate the growing fetus, but rather the erosion of the tubal wall.[27]

Thus, Bouscaren is able to claim that from the early stages of pregnancy the tube itself is weakened and dangerous, quite apart from any further development of the pregnancy. On this basis Bouscaren concludes that removal of an unruptured pregnant tube constitutes *indirect* killing since the *direct* object of the operation is removal of a pathological organ of the woman's body. This conclusion was inconsistent with a 1902 decree of the Holy Office which explicitly forbade removal of immature ectopic fetuses.[28] Theologians following Bouscaren maintain, however, that the 1902 decree was correctly based upon the medical facts as then known, but is no longer applicable in the light of subsequent medical research.[29]

We may now return to the criterion of indirect killing proposed by Pius XII in "Morality in Marriage."[30] It will be recalled that in this address he characterizes fetal killing as indirect if the treatment killing the fetus is required independently of the woman's pregnant condition. Now it would clearly be a mistake to conclude from Bouscaren's study that removal of a pregnant fallopian tube is medically indicated independently of pregnancy. Although it is true that at some point prior to rupture the tube becomes dangerous in itself, it is the pregnancy which *causes* the pathological alterations of the tube. Nevertheless, it is possible to see how such a conclusion might be drawn. Bouscaren shows that after a certain point in a tubal pregnancy the tube would have to be removed even if the fetus were no longer present. That the tube would have to be removed even if the fetus *were no longer present* might mistakenly be thought to imply that the tube would have to be removed even if the fetus *had not been present*.

To put the point another way, Bouscaren showed that if the fallopian tube of a non-pregnant woman were to undergo pathological changes similar to those occurring in a tubal pregnancy, it would have to be removed. Just as any other part of the body, the fallopian tube is subject to infection and tumors, either of which can cause deterioration similar to that occurring in a tubal pregnancy.[31] Consequently there are reasons for removing the fallopian tube of a woman who is not pregnant, just as there are reasons for removing the uterus of a woman who is not pregnant. But the fact that a fallopian tube could deteriorate and require excision as a result of factors other than a tubal pregnancy does not mean that the deterioration is independent of the pregnancy when there *is* one. The fundamental reason for removing a pregnant tube is manifestly *that the tube contains a misplaced fetus.* That particular tube would not be removed at that particular time if the fetus were not present. By contrast, the reason for removing a pregnant cancerous uterus is *that the uterus is cancerous, not that it contains a fetus.*

When these confusions have been removed, however, one is left with the following facts. Both pregnant and non-pregnant women may have cancer of the cervix, and the fallopian tubes of either may deteriorate. When such pathological conditions arise, the medical remedy is the same for the non-pregnant women as it is for the pregnant women: remove the diseased organ. The situation is quite different with regard to a pregnant woman suffering from chronic hypertension or an obstructed labor. Although a non-pregnant woman may have chronic hypertension, the medical remedy indicated for her cannot be removal of her fetus, for she doesn't have one. And a non-pregnant woman cannot be in obstructed labor at all.

One may hazard a guess that these facts are exploited in the application of the Principle of Double Effect to therapeutic abortion. According to that principle, four conditions establish an act as an instance of permissible killing:

(1) that the immediate action performed be good or indifferent;
(2) that the foreseen evil (fetal death) be not intended in itself;
(3) that the good (preservation of the woman's life) which is intended be not an effect of the evil (fetal death); and
(4) that the good (preservation of the woman's life) be commensurate with the evil (fetal death) foreseen.

It should be clear from the previous discussion that conditions (2) through (4) fail to distinguish permissible from non-permissible cases of therapeutic abortion. That leaves condition (1') as a possible basis for distinguishing among therapeutic abortions. It has been argued that it is impossible to distinguish

among therapeutic abortions in terms of the temporal priority of
their good and bad effects. Adoption of another sense of "immediate," however, may provide a solution to the problem.

Observe that removal of a diseased organ from a *non*-preg-
nant woman cannot result in fetal death. Instead, removal is
unambiguously life-preserving, and thus has positive moral
value. Suppose, now, that one were to describe "the immediate
action performed" in removal of a pregnant cancerous uterus or
pregnant fallopian tube as *the removal of a diseased organ of
the woman's body*. Suppose further that one were to transfer the
positive moral value such operations acquire in ordinary contexts to the special context of pregnancy. If this were done,
some therapeutic abortions would satisfy condition (1) of the
Principle of Double Effect whereas others wouldn't. Specifically,
therapeutic abortion in cases A and B would satisfy this condition, while therapeutic abortion in cases C and D would not.
"Crushing the head of a fetus" or "removal of a non-viable
fetus" are comparable descriptions of immediate actions whose
consequences always include the bad effect of loss of life. Consequently, the distinction comes to this: In the case of permissible therapeutic abortion there exists a description of what the
surgeon does such that, considered under this description, the
surgeon's action in *other* contexts is solely life-preserving. In the
case of illicit therapeutic abortion no comparable description is
available.

Consideration of the following case suggests a more precise
formulation of this conclusion. Suppose a woman in early pregnancy suffering from chronic hypertension (case C) also has
benign uterine tumors. According to the preceding analysis,
removal of her non-viable fetus is illicit. However, the presence
of uterine tumors in non-pregnant women is an indication for
hysterectomy. Consequently, it might appear licit to terminate
her pregnancy by hysterectomy.

In analyzing this case, however, it must be observed that
uterine tumors are usually a threat to health but not to life.
Consequently, while Roman Catholic moralists would describe
fetal killing as indirect if a hysterectomy were performed to rid
the woman of uterine tumors, they would probably not consider
the gain to health from ridding her body of tumors to be commensurate with the loss of fetal life. Certainly this would be true
where the benefit to her health was small.

We may now formulate more precisely the difference between

licit and illicit therapeutic abortions. Licit abortions meet the following conditions:

(1′) Fetal death occurs as a result of medical procedures employed to modify *life-threatening* conditions which can occur apart from pregnancy and which, if they did occur apart from pregnancy, would necessitate employment of similar procedures. (For brevity of exposition, procedures which satisfy this description will hereafter be referred to as *standard procedures*.)

(2) The foreseen evil effect is not intended in itself.

(3) The good which is intended is not an effect of the evil.

(4) The good intended is commensurate with the evil foreseen.

On this interpretation, the only difference between licit and illicit therapeutic abortions is that the licit ones involve *standard procedures* whereas the illicit ones do not. That is, in a licit therapeutic abortion fetal death occurs as a result of a standard medical procedure, as defined above; in an illicit therapeutic abortion, it does not. We may refer to the distinction embodied in (1′) as the *standard/nonstandard procedures* distinction. Our investigation suggests, then, that it is not the means/foresight distinction but the standard/nonstandard procedures distinction which accounts for the orthodox Roman Catholic doctrine of therapeutic abortion.

That the standard/nonstandard procedures distinction has no moral relevance should be evident. Therapeutic abortions satisfying condition (1′) involve medical procedures which are exclusively life-preserving in ordinary contexts but which in the context of pregnancy have both life-preserving and life-destroying consequences. Removal of a cancerous uterus, for instance, has a positive value in ordinary contexts *because* its foreseen consequences are exclusively life-preserving. Thus in appraising its moral value in the context of pregnancy, it cannot be considered *apart from* its foreseen consequences, which in this case include fetal death. That is, it is morally irrelevant that removal of a cancerous uterus has purely beneficial effects in *other* contexts when in the context in question it has the same foreseen effects as any procedure of therapeutic abortion. However, on the assumption that Roman Catholic moralists *do* employ the

Double Effect Principle to make such spurious distinctions, sense can be made of the application of the principle to a number of cases.

Consider, for example, the striking illustration of the doctrine presented in Häring's discussion of abortion. Häring describes an incident recounted to him by a gynecologist who removed a benign uterine tumor from a woman four months pregnant. On the womb the doctor encountered numerous very thin and fragile varicose veins which bled profusely, and whose bleeding was only aggravated by suturing. Two means of preventing the woman's death from loss of blood were available: (1) removal of the bleeding uterus with the fetus inside; (2) removal of the fetus from the uterus, whereupon the bleeding would be stopped by contraction of the uterus. Death of the fetus would result in either case. Thinking that the fetus could not be saved in any event and that preservation of the woman's fertility was desirable, the gynecologist chose the latter course. He was later told by "a noted Catholic moral theologian" (unidentified by Häring) that the course he chose was objectively wrong. According to the gynecologist, "I would have been allowed to remove the bleeding uterus with the fetus itself, he said, but was not permitted to interrupt the pregnancy while leaving the womb intact. This latter, he said, constituted an immoral termination of pregnancy, though done for the purpose of saving the mother, while the other would have been a lawful direct intention and action to save life."[32]

It is instructive to note the similarity between the sanctioned removal of the uterus containing the fetus and the forbidden removal of the fetus from the uterus. Both procedures have the negative and undesired effect of fetal death; both have the positive and desired effect of preservation of maternal life. In neither case is the negative effect the means to the positive one. The procedures are similar in their physical aspects except that the first involves the removal of an additional piece of tissue. That variation in physical detail, however, allows description of what the surgeon does in terms of a standard medical procedure which in other contexts lacks the negative effect of fetal death (although it does of course have the negative effect of loss of fertility). That is, in the second case the surgeon removes a nonviable fetus, whereas in the first case he removes a dangerously hemorrhaging uterus.

Still another striking application of the Principle of Double

Effect confirms this interpretation and illustrates the extraordinary detail of which the Catholic analysis is capable. In an extremely rare type of ectopic pregnancy a fetus which has been growing in the fallopian tube will, after spontaneous abortion or rupture of the tube, pass into the abdominal cavity. The fetus may reimplant on the external surface of the bowel, ovary, uterus, or liver, or in the lining of the body wall, and continue to grow. This condition is known as secondary abdominal pregnancy, and as in tubal pregnancy, the chances of fetal survival are slight.[33]

The morality of intervention in such cases is also considered in Bouscaren's study. As mentioned earlier, Bouscaren concludes that it is licit under the Principle of Double Effect to remove an unruptured fallopian tube containing a non-viable fetus. This conclusion rests upon the medical finding that the tube undergoes deterioration prior to rupture. On the other hand, a fetus growing in the abdominal cavity presents a rather different problem. As Bouscaren queries, "Where, in this case, is the dangerous organ which must be the *direct object of the operation*?"[34] In his view, to remove the fetus while leaving intact the tissues or organs to which the fetus is attached would be a direct attack upon the fetus. Yet an abdominal pregnancy is dangerous not so much because of changes in the tissues but because it will probably terminate in a spontaneous abortion involving severe hemorrhage. Hence it is not possible to describe the tissues as themselves diseased. Bouscaren is thus led to conclude that although it would have been permissible to operate while the fetus was growing in the fallopian tube, once the fetus has moved into the abdominal cavity an attempt to remove it cannot be justified.[35]

It seems peculiar that the morality of killing a misplaced fetus depends solely upon the fetus' location in the woman's body, when this factor is not significantly related either to its life-chances or to the threat that it poses to the woman's life. Nevertheless this is to be expected in an approach which fixes on whether or not the fetus is killed by a standard medical procedure.

Summarizing then: Abortionists who follow Roman Catholic manuals of medical ethics control hemorrhaging or remove cancerous uteruses and diseased fallopian tubes: the gynecologist of Häring's account should have removed a hemorrhaging uterus. Ignored in this accounting of what the physician does is the fact

that in each case he deliberately kills what is, on Catholic doctrine, one of his patients and an innocent human being. At this
point it is difficult to suppress the suspicion that a necessary
condition of licit killing in Roman Catholic moral theology is
that it be possible to represent the fatal act as something other
than killing. By requiring that therapeutic abortions satisfy condition (1'), Catholic doctrine ensures that what the surgeon
does be describable as a completely innocuous procedure neces-
sitated by conditions unrelated to pregnancy. Such moralizing
exploits the variety of descriptions by which it is always possible to refer to one and the same set of events, and ignores the
fact that any and all therapeutic abortions could equally well be
described as an attempt to save life or as a destruction of innocent human life.

In conclusion: We have described the orthodox Roman
Catholic doctrine which forbids some therapeutic abortions
while permitting others, and have examined the important Principle of Double Effect with reference to which this doctrine is
justified. It was shown that all therapeutic abortions satisfy
conditions (2) and (4) of the Double Effect Principle. Condition (3), which distinguishes among acts according to whether
their evil effects are a means to the good end or are only foreseen consequences, is the key to many applications of the Double Effect Principle. It was argued, however, that the doctrine of
therapeutic abortion cannot be accounted for by reference to
the means/foresight distinction. In no therapeutic abortion is
fetal death aimed at as a means. Additional formulations of the
distinction between licit and illicit killing found in papal documents and the writings of moral theologians were rejected as
irreconcilable with the doctrine of therapeutic abortion.

Our investigation revealed, however, that the moral judgments made concerning therapeutic abortion may be understood
in terms of the standard/nonstandard procedures distinction.
That is, licit therapeutic abortions involve the use of medical
procedures indicated by life-threatening conditions whose occurrence in non-pregnant women requires similar treatment; illicit therapeutic abortions do not. Moreover, therapeutic abortions involving standard procedures may be construed as
satisfying condition (1) of the Double Effect Principle, while
those involving nonstandard procedures may be construed as
violating that condition.

Finally, it was suggested that the standard/nonstandard procedures distinction is without moral relevance. Consequently, it would appear that the orthodox Roman Catholic doctrine of therapeutic abortion is internally inconsistent.

## NOTES

1. J. Robert Willson et al., *Obstetrics and Gynecology*, 5th ed. (St. Louis: C.V. Mosby, 1975), p. 202.

2. Pius XI, "Casti Connubi" (1930), reprinted in *Ethics and Metaethics*, ed. Raziel Abelson (New York: St. Martin's Press, 1963), pp. 134–35. Italics added.

3. "Declaration on Abortion," *The Pope Speaks* 19 (1974): 257. Italics added.

4. See J. P. Greenhill and Emanuel A. Friedman, *Biological Principles and Modern Practice of Obstetrics* (Philadelphia: W.B. Saunders, 1974), p. 185.

5. Treatment of invasive cancer of the cervix complicated by pregnancy is discussed in Louis S. Lapid et al., "Carcinoma of the Cervix," in *Medical, Surgical and Gynecologic Complications of Pregnancy*, 2d ed., ed. Joseph H. Rovinsky et al. (Baltimore: Williams & Wilkins, 1965), pp. 349–58. Three alternative therapies—hysterectomy, irradiation, and irradiation combined with hysterotomy—are outlined for women in the first or second trimester of pregnancy, and each is described as fatal to the fetus. The authors state that in most cases the cancer does not disturb the course of gestation. The opinion that it is very unlikely that the cancer would have adverse effects upon the fetus was confirmed in conversation with Dr. John Josimovich, Professor of Obstetrics and Gynecology at the University of Pittsburgh. Dr. Josimovich also remarked that death of the woman prior to viability of the fetus is unlikely with this variety of slow-growing cancer.

6. Tubal pregnancy accounts for the vast majority of ectopic pregnancies (see Willson et al. [above, n. 1], p. 202). Fetal mortality is nearly 100 percent (see Claude Gompel and S. G. Silverberg, *Pathology in Gynecology and Obstetrics* [Philadelphia: Lippincott, 1969], p. 388; and J. Donald Woodruff and Carl J. Pauerstein, *The Fallopian Tube: Structure, Function, Pathology, and Management* [Baltimore: Williams & Wilkins, 1969], p. 196). The profuse hemorrhage and shock associated especially with tubal rupture is a life-threatening situation for the woman, requiring emergency care given with the utmost dispatch (see Greenhill and Friedman [above, n. 4], p. 359).

7. Because of placental dysfunction and increased incidence of preeclampsia (hypertensive disorder peculiar to pregnancy),

the fetal mortality rate is close to 100 percent, according to Simon Dack et al., "Heart Disease," in Rovinsky et al. (above, n. 5), p. 52. See also Willson et al. (above, n. 1), p. 198.

8. The extremely slight chance of salvaging a live fetus from a woman who dies in an obstructed labor is confirmed by Dr. John Josimovich (see above, n. 5) and Dr. Thomas Allen, Director of Women's Health Services, Pittsburgh, Pennsylvania. It should be noted that craniotomy has been superseded by cesarean section. With the exception of the presence of hydrocephalus (enlargement of the fetal head caused by excessive cerebrospinal fluid), craniotomy on a living fetus is virtually obsolete (see Louis M. Hellman et al., *Williams Obstetrics*, 14th ed. [New York: Appleton-Century-Crofts, 1971], pp. 1140–41). That such operations were performed in the past, however, is indicated by pronouncements concerning craniotomy issued by the Holy Office in 1884 and 1889 (see Gerald Kelly, *Medico-Moral Problems* [St. Louis: Catholic Hospital Association, 1958], pp. 69–70). In previous centuries when the maternal mortality rate from cesarean section approached 100 percent (see David N. Danforth, ed., *Textbook of Obstetrics and Gynecology* [New York: Harper & Row, 1966], p. 672), cutting up the fetus was the only means of saving the life of a woman unable to deliver vaginally.

9. The following Roman Catholic texts of medical ethics were consulted: Bernard Häring, *Medical Ethics* (Notre Dame, Ind.: Fides, 1973); Edwin F. Healy, *Medical Ethics* (Chicago: Loyola University Press, 1956); Gerald Kelly (above, n. 8); John P. Kenny, *Principles of Medical Ethics*, 2d ed. (Westminster, Md.: Newman Press, 1962); Charles J. McFadden, *Medical Ethics*, 6th ed. (Philadelphia: F.A. Davis, 1967); Albert Niedermeyer, *Compendium of Pastoral Medicine*, trans. Fulgence Buonanno (New York: Joseph F. Wagner, 1961); Thomas J. O'Donnell, *Morals in Medicine* (Westminster, Md.: Newman Press, 1959). Except for Häring, who explicitly acknowledged his departure from orthodox doctrine, there was unanimity of opinion concerning the four obstetrics cases described above.

10. A tubal pregnancy may spontaneously abort rather than rupture the fallopian tube. While some spontaneous tubal abortions require emergency care, others (at early stages of pregnancy) occur without symptoms, and the products of conception are absorbed (see Woodruff and Pauerstein [above, n. 6], pp. 192–94).

11. Craniotomy should be distinguished from the less drastic procedure of tapping the skull of a hydrocephalic fetus to drain off the excess fluid. Since an intraventricular tap is the same operation that would be performed if the child were born and gave

hope of survival, Roman Catholic moralists approve this procedure on a hydrocephalic fetus (see McFadden [above, n. 9],
p. 192).

12. One can acquaint oneself with application of the Principle of
Double Effect to a variety of moral problems by scanning "Notes
on Moral Theology" which have appeared in the Roman Catholic journal *Theological Studies* over the past 20 years, and the
texts of medical ethics cited in note 9 above.

13. Joseph J. Farraher, "Notes on Moral Theology," *Theological
Studies* 24 (1963): 71; Daniel Callahan, *Abortion: Law, Choice
and Morality* (New York: Macmillan, 1970), p. 423; David
Granfield, *The Abortion Decision*, rev. ed. (Garden City, N.Y.:
Doubleday, 1971), pp. 127–28.

14. While these are the judgments required by standard Roman
Catholic doctrine and imposed upon Catholic hospitals by the
*Ethical and Religious Directives for Catholic Health Facilities*
(Washington, D.C.: U.S. Catholic Conference, Department of
Health Affairs, 1971), it should be acknowledged that in the last
decade some Catholic moralists have expressed dissatisfaction
with them (see, for example, Charles E. Curran, *A New Look
at Christian Morality* [Notre Dame, Ind.: Fides, 1970]; and Bernard Häring [above, n. 9]). Several writers have undertaken to
reexamine the Double Effect Principle, proposing reinterpreta-
tions which have the effect of liberalizing traditional judgments
concerning therapeutic abortion (see Joseph Fuchs, "The Abso-
luteness of Moral Terms," *Gregorianum* 52 [1971]: 415–58;
Germain G. Grisez, *Abortion: The Myths, the Realities and the
Arguments* [New York: Corpus Books, 1970]; idem, "Toward
a Consistent Natural-Law Ethics of Killing," *American Journal
of Jurisprudence* 15 [1970]: 64–96; Peter Knauer, "The Herme-
neutic Function of the Principle of Double Effect," *Natural Law
Forum* 12 [1967]: 132–62; William Van der Marck, *Toward a
Christian Ethic: A Renewal of Moral Theology* [Westminster,
Md.: Newman Press, 1967]; Cornelius Van der Poel, "The Principle of Double Effect," in *Absolutes in Moral Theology*, ed.
Charles Curran [Washington, D.C.: Corpus Books, 1968], pp.
186–210). With the exception of Grisez, these critics suggest
abandonment of condition (3) and the adoption of an underlying ethical theory which is thoroughly teleological. These recent developments in Roman Catholic moral theology will not
be considered here because, first, a teleological ethical theory is
not, in my opinion, acceptable; and, second, the criticism
offered in this study of the application of the Double Effect
Principle to therapeutic abortion is quite independent of the
more general criticism of Double Effect found in recent Roman
Catholic literature. For a comprehensive review of that lit-

erature, see Richard A. McCormick, "Ambiguity in Moral Choice," the 1973 Pere Marquette Theology Lecture. McCormick is Professor of Christian Ethics at the Kennedy Institute, Georgetown University.

15. See above, n. 2. Italics added.
16. See above, n. 3, p. 257.
17. Pius XII, "The Apostolate of the Midwife" (1951), reprinted in *The Major Addresses of Pope Pius XII*, vol. 1 (St. Paul, Minn.: North Central Publishing Co., 1961), p. 163. This account of the direct/indirect distinction is also invoked in "Declaration on Abortion" (above, n. 3), p. 254.
18. Kenny (above, n. 9), p. 192.
19. Paul Ramsey, "The Morality of Abortion," in *Moral Problems*, ed. James Rachels (New York: Harper & Row, 1971), p. 21.
20. Gerald Kelly, *Medico-Moral Problems*, part 1 (St. Louis: Catholic Hospital Association, 1955), p. 12. Italics added.
21. Leonard Geddes, "On the Intrinsic Wrongfulness of Killing Innocent People," *Analysis* 33 (1973): 93–97. Geddes bases his interpretation of the Principle of Double Effect on a reading of the principle by G. E. M. Anscombe (see Anscombe, "War and Murder," in *Nuclear Weapons: A Catholic Response*, ed. Walter Stein [New York: Sheed & Ward, 1961], pp. 45–62).
22. H. L. A. Hart, "Intention and Punishment," in *Punishment and Responsibility: Essays in the Philosophy of Law* (New York: Oxford University Press, 1968), p. 120.
23. Pius XII, "Morality in Marriage" (1951), reprinted in *The Unwearied Advocate: Public Addresses of Pope Pius XII*, vol. 3 (St. Cloud, Minn.: Vincent A. Yzermans, 1954), p. 189. Italics added. Grisez refers to this formulation as "what is probably the clearest statement of the concept of *indirect* abortion to be found in the entire Catholic tradition" (Grisez, *Abortion* [above, n. 14], p. 182).
24. Curran (above, n. 14), p. 240.
25. R. J. Huser, *The Crime of Abortion in Canon Law* (Washington, D.C.: Catholic University of America Press, 1942), p. 136. Italics added.
26. T. Lincoln Bouscaren, *Ethics of Ectopic Operations*, 2d ed. (Milwaukee: Bruce Publishing Co., 1944).
27. See Woodruff and Pauerstein (above, n. 6), p. 199.
28. The Holy Office is the division of pontifical government entrusted with the doctrine of faith and morals.
29. See Grisez, *Abortion* (above, n. 14), p. 180; Kelly (above, n. 8), pp. 108–9; Healy (above, n. 9), pp. 221–26.
30. Pius XII (above, n. 23), p. 189.
31. A number of such conditions are described in Woodruff and Pauerstein (above, n. 6).

32. Bernard Häring, "A Theological Evaluation," in *The Morality of Abortion*, ed. John T. Noonan, Jr. (Cambridge: Harvard University Press, 1970), p. 136.

33. See Greenhill and Friedman (above, n. 4), p. 359.

34. Bouscaren (above, n. 26), p. 164.

35. A fact not mentioned by Bouscaren is that the placenta may attach to a vital organ such as the liver. Removal of the woman's liver (with the fetus attached) is obviously not a standard medical procedure; it would be fatal to the woman. On the other hand, removal of the fetus while leaving the liver intact is not a standard medical procedure, either; it could not be performed on a non-pregnant woman.

Elizabeth Rapaport
Paul Sagal

# One Step Forward, Two Steps Backward: Abortion and Ethical Theory

The question is: What is the most extensive moral and legal right of women to have abortions? The answer is: It depends. It depends largely upon the answer to another question: What theories or explicit conceptions of moral and legal rights and of the moral franchise can be sustained? Simply to employ the language of moral and legal rights at the outset, without facing the last-mentioned question, is to inherit all the ambiguities associated with this language. The alternative is to present and defend a theoretical account of rights. This then would provide the theory on which our answer to the original question would depend.

Unfortunately, most discussion of the abortion problem proceeds as if there is some stable, agreed-upon, and presumably defensible moral theory which can provide the necessary basis for satisfactory resolution. Sometimes this theory seems to be little more than moral common sense, sometimes it is a full-blown philosophical theory like Thomism. And of course there are combinations of the two approaches. Still, philosophers who, when doing systematic ethics and meta-ethics, are sensitive to problems, differences, and doubts seem quite willing to confront a complex substantive question like abortion as if theory had merely marginal significance, and could somehow safely be ignored. We can call this approach the "short-cut" approach. On our view, this approach is not viable.[1]

In what follows, we will illustrate our contentions with a critique of an influential contemporary defense of the extreme liberal position: the Tooley/Warren argument.[2] This argument rests on strong claims about the notion of a person. We will raise some meta-ethical questions fundamental to the abortion issue in general and conclude that no quick solutions to substantive moral problems like abortion are available. But this skepticism has important consequences for practical moral decisions. For certain positions on the abortion question are incompatible with skepticism and, if we are right, they will therefore have to be rejected.

The argumentative line introduced independently by Tooley and Warren holds that if two crucial questions can be answered negatively, an unrestricted right to abortion can be sustained. These questions are: (1) Is the fetus a person? and (2) Does a potential person have a right to life? We will be concerned here only with the claim that, if these two questions are answered negatively, then the extreme liberal position on abortion can be sustained. Unfortunately, even if we grant that the case for the two negative answers has been successfully made, the extreme liberal position is vulnerable. The problem is that if one accepts this claim and a certain kind of argument which supports it, one must also endorse a right to infanticide. For it looks as though there will be no morally relevant difference between killing a fetus and killing a newborn infant.

Both Tooley and Warren argue persuasively that we must distinguish between a human being in the genetic or specific sense and a human being in the moral sense—a person. A human fetus is most certainly a human being in the specific sense. Biologically it belongs to the human species. But it is not thereby a person, if personhood and the moral rights that attach to being a person require self-consciousness as Tooley claims,[3] or the presence of consciousness and reasoning as Warren claims.[4] Let us suppose for the sake of argument that a newborn infant would be unable to qualify as a person. If an infant has no rights in virtue of its potentiality to become a person (which we will assume has been established), then infanticide at parental discretion is apparently justifiable for Tooley, Warren, and any extreme liberal who argues along the same lines. An infant must be properly regarded both morally and legally as the property of its parents and nothing more.

Warren does not comment upon the apparent necessity for treating infanticide as wholly discretionary in the absence of some morally significant difference between abortion and infanticide. Tooley does comment, but with a curious lack of appreciation of the problematic nature of his stand: determining the age at which an infant becomes a person "is not troubling because there is no serious need to know the exact point at which a human infant acquires a right to life. For in the vast majority of cases in which infanticide is desirable, its desirability will be apparent within a short time after birth."[5] Many would deny that all eugenically undesirable infants may be destroyed at parental discretion. But Tooley's position further permits unrestricted infanticide whether it is eugenically desirable or not. What he apparently fails to appreciate is that while he is prepared to treat infanticide as wholly a matter for parental discretion because it follows from his position on the moral status of the fetus, many would consider the necessity of treating infanticide as wholly discretionary a reductio ad absurdum of his position on the moral status of the fetus. If so, the right to abortion in all but those situations where the pregnant woman's life is imperiled is left without adequate defense in the eyes of those who cannot countenance a blanket right of infanticide.

Writers on abortion often assume, as does Tooley,[6] that if a pregnant woman has an obligation to carry to term, it must be in virtue of a right the fetus has: namely, a right to life. This assumption, common to many advocates and opponents of abortion, is in our view doubly mistaken. We will contend that the right to abortion is not secured if we grant that a fetus has no right to life, and that a pregnant woman may have no right to abortion even if the fetus has no rights of any kind. This phase of our argument is aimed at easy *liberal* solutions to the abortion problem. The reader should bear in mind that our more embracing goals are to articulate grounds for rejecting *all easy* solutions, pro and contra, and to provide a more sound basis for the liberal position.

Let us begin by considering a possible line of defense against the charge that the liberal Tooley/Warren argumentative line leads to sanctioning infanticide. The liberal may argue that what distinguishes the abortion case from the infanticide case is that while the pregnant woman is the unique individual who can take responsibility for the survival of the fetus, the care of an infant can be assumed by others. While the infant has no right to life, it has great value to other persons in virtue of its potential to become a person, and these other persons—potential adoptive parents or society—may not be deprived of the infant by its biological parents if the parents do not themselves want it. This argument will not serve because it fails to establish a crucial moral difference between the fetus *in utero* and the infant. Why may a pregnant woman destroy this valuable potential during pregnancy but not after? The only difference here cited is that in pregnancy the responsibility is not transferable to another. But being the sole individual who can assume a responsibility is not in itself a morally adequate reason to assume a responsibility or refuse it. We can see that this is so if we consider a moral situation which is like pregnancy in that only one individual can assume responsibility for the life of another.

Consider the following not very fictional case. During the Nazi occupation, a Pole offers to hide a Jew on his property until such time as arrangements can be made to get the Jew safely out of the country. Let us suppose that the Pole knows no one who would share or take over responsibility for hiding the Jew. The Pole has by making a promise assumed a responsibility that is uniquely his, not transferable in the circumstances. In our example, the Pole's obligation arises not because the Jew has a right to life (although the Jew does have a right to life), but because he has promised to hide the Jew. By promising, the Pole acquires an obligation to undergo peril and sacrifice (although probably not death should the likelihood of discovery become very great) to save the Jew's life. Our obligation to save life does not extend to putting our own in grave peril. No one has the right to expect this of us simply because he has a right to life.[7] Such actions are morally heroic; they go beyond the requirements of duty. But if we make such a promise with knowledge of the risk we incur, we create a right in the person to whom we make the promise. It is the promise and not his right to life which entitles him to our aid. Not all rights of persons to help in sustaining their life arise out of their right to life. Some arise out of special moral relationships, as in our case of a promise. Before the Pole promised, he had no such obligation simply in virtue of the Jew's right to life, even though he alone could save the Jew. After he promised, he could not with moral title refuse to accept the responsibility—simply because he had taken on an untransferable burden. We may ask, does pregnancy constitute or occasion another special moral relationship which can create an obligation to assume an untransferable responsibility?

We may be led to answer this question in the negative because of an important respect in which our fictional example and the pregnancy case differ. While the Jew's right to life may not entitle him to the Pole's aid, he nevertheless has a right to life. We have conceded, at least for the space of the present argument, that the fetus does not. It may be said that although the Pole was not obligated to save the Jew because he is a person, it is nevertheless because he is a person that the Pole promised to save him. It is his being a person that made the Jew worth taking a grave risk to save and made him eligible for having a right conferred on him by a promise made to him.

To this we reply, even if the fetus is ineligible to have rights of any kind, either so-called natural rights (rights held simply in virtue of being a person), or acquired rights (rights conferred by society or individuals through implicit or explicit promises or agreements), a woman may still not have a right to an abortion. Women (and men) may be under obligations to treat objects (whatever they may be—persons, potential persons, or nonpersons) in a certain manner, not because of any rights, natural or acquired, of the objects, but because of the rights of *other* people, natural or acquired. Here, we may get arguments involving obligations to one's family, to one's class, to one's generation, to future generations, or even to humankind. Such obligations may well be involved in the question of how the fetus should be treated. And, of course, all this raises deep and controversial issues of morals and social policy, especially the social function of women in light of their unique capacity to bear children. The value of children, of human life in general, may be importantly involved.

To make matters worse, even if no rights of any kind appear to be involved, it would not follow that a fetus ought not to be treated in certain ways. All this depends upon one's ethical theory—particularly the way "ought" and "obligation" are construed. For instance, prima facie, duties of "imperfect obligation" (for example, charity) are such that no one, no class of persons, nor the class of all persons, has a right which entitles them to our charity. More generally, some utilitarian theories construe "ought" and "obligation" exclusively in terms of the quantity of happiness produced. No mention of human rights is made at all.

Thus, even if a fetus has no original right to life (by virtue of its personhood or potential personhood) it still might be the case that the life of the fetus ought to be protected. But the argument for this will be an arduous one. There will be no short cuts.

It is important to ask why abortion has become a moral, legal, and political issue in the last several years. Whatever the law has been, abortion was a widely used option of pregnant women long prior to the changes in the law. It is the reemergence of the woman question that has made abortion a contemporary public issue, whether or not the social context is always explicit in philosophical and other debates about abortion. The "traditional" role of women within and outside of the "traditional" family—that is, the nuclear family characteristic of advanced industrial societies—is rapidly changing. This context of deeply significant social change renders the short-cut method particularly inappropriate and disappointing. Profound change carries an unavoidable challenge to reexamine our value systems, to make explicit and question the continuing validity of their deepest theoretical assumptions. We must add that our society patently lacks moral consensus.[8] There are not one but several more or less coherent value systems in our heterodox culture. In light of these considerations, the program of ignoring systematic normative ethics and the epistemological justification of these ethics while attempting to settle substantive issues in social ethics cannot be sustained.

Much of the recent philosophical literature on abortion seems to proceed as if we face a choice between what we shall call naive religious ethics and naive secular ethics. We call each "naive" because each fails to recognize the necessity of explicating and defending the normative framework it employs, and yet at the same time it argues that this framework should provide the decisive basis for social policy to a wider community for whom its crucial theoretical premises are controversial rather than consensual.

The basis for the religious solution to the abortion problem rests on the unique value of created human life and the moral obligations that God has ordained to preserve and nurture human life. Such arguments are obviously not persuasive to those without the requisite religious beliefs. Secular theorists prefer to base social ethics on *some* theory of the rights of persons qua persons, some theory which provides the legitimate critical standard to challenge any legal or other social institution which violates these rights. Personhood is understood, as by Warren and Tooley, not as an essential characteristic of any member of the human species but as developmentally emergent for biologically normal human beings in normal social conditions. Admittedly this is an advance over treating personhood as a primitive notion accessible directly to the natural light of reason. But this view will of course lack persuasiveness to anyone who holds the life of all members of the human species at any stage of development to be sacred. Further, secular theorists focus almost exclusively on individual persons and their rights and obligations. They neglect relationships involving family, class, race, and humankind—relationships which might prove crucial to the resolution of a problem like abortion.[9] Even if the extreme liberals could make good their claim for the non-personhood of the fetus, obligations involving other social relations would still require careful attention, for these factors might yield restrictions on the extreme liberal position.

So where are we? Square in the lap of skepticism, it would appear. But this is neither a general skepticism about ethical knowledge nor necessarily a long-term skepticism concerning the abortion question. We would like to call our skepticism *Socratic*: On our view no one *now* knows (since no one has presented and defended an adequate conceptual framework) what the answer to our original question is. We, like Socrates, claim to know at least that we (and others) do not know. But this absence of knowledge is itself not without consequences. If no one knows what the moral status of abortion is, then no one has the right to coerce others into having or not having an abortion. Each woman must ultimately make her decision and take responsibility for it. Knowledge involves at least the explicit statement of a position along with its rational defense. The rational defense would be one which could stand up to criticism, and ultimately result in some kind of consensus. When knowledge is lacking, the appeal to conscience has point. No one thus far has the moral authority to employ coercive measures, because no one has the requisite moral knowledge.[10]

# NOTES

1. It is frequently said that principles of law follow upon the resolution of specific cases, or at least that there has to be an interplay between theory and practice, principle and cases. There is another maxim that has more point here. And that is that *hard cases make bad law*. The abortion issue is just such a hard case in the sense of being complex, difficult, even unusual. A methodological justification of the short-cut approach, of common-sense morality, could perhaps appeal to ordinary language. But as the late J. L. Austin, the leading practitioner of ordinary-language philosophy, put it in *A Plea for Excuses*, "Ordinary language is only a *first* word." First words don't take us very far with an issue like abortion, since it is in this case the first words, especially the moral and legal first words, which cause so much of the trouble.

2. Michael Tooley, "Abortion and Infanticide," *Philosophy and Public Affairs* 2 (Fall 1972): 37–65; Mary Anne Warren, "On the Moral and Legal Status of Abortion," *Monist* 57 (January 1973): 43–61.

3. Tooley's claim is: "An organism possesses a serious right to life only if it possesses the concept of a self as a continuing subject of experiences and other mental states, and believes that it is itself such a continuing entity" (op. cit., p. 45).

4. Warren lists five traits as central to our concept of personhood: (1) consciousness (of objects and events external and/or internal to the being), and in particular the capacity to feel pain; (2) reasoning (the *developed* capacity to solve new and relatively complex problems); (3) self-motivated activity (activity which is relatively independent of either genetic or direct external control); (4) the capacity to communicate, by whatever means, messages of an indefinite variety of types, that is, not just with an indefinite number of possible contents, but on indefinitely many possible topics; (5) the presence of self-concepts, and self-awareness, either individual or racial, or both.

   Traits (1) through (3) are probably sufficient. (1) and (2) may well be sufficient, and (1) through (3) are probably necessary, she claims.

5. Tooley, p. 65.

6. Ibid., p. 41.

7. See Judith Thomson, "A Defense of Abortion," *Philosophy and Public Affairs* 1 (1971): 47–66. Thomson argues that the right to life does not in itself entitle someone to everything he may need to sustain his life from anyone who may be in a position to provide such aid.

8. See Alasdair MacIntyre, "How Virtues Become Vices," in *Evaluation and Explanation in the Biomedical Sciences*, ed. H. Tristram Engelhardt, Jr., and Stuart F. Spicker (Dordrecht, Holland: D. Reidel, 1974).

9. We emphatically do not associate ourselves with the position sometimes taken by American black militants or third-world revolutionaries that birth control and abortion are forms of genocide; nor, for example, do we agree with the vacillating course of Soviet policy on population which has seen both permissive and restrictive use of birth control and abortion. But it cannot be assumed *without* argument that claims involving the future of a family, a race, a class, a nation, or humankind are entirely without moral weight, or are without sufficient moral weight to affect the rights of women seeking abortion.

10. For a somewhat similar line of argument, see Roger Wertheimer, "Understanding the Abortion Argument," *Philosophy and Public Affairs* 1 (Fall 1971): 67–95.

Jane English

# Abortion and the
# Concept of a Person

The abortion debate rages on. Yet the two most popular positions seem to be clearly mistaken. Conservatives maintain that a
human life begins at conception and that therefore abortion
must be wrong because it is murder. But not all killings of
humans are murders. Most notably, self-defense may justify
even the killing of an innocent person.

Liberals, on the other hand, are just as mistaken in their
argument that since a fetus does not become a person until
birth, a woman may do whatever she pleases in and to her own
body. First, you cannot do as you please with your own body if
it affects other people adversely.[1] Second, if a fetus is not a
person, that does not imply that you can do to it anything you
wish. Animals, for example, are not persons, yet to kill or torture them for no reason at all is wrong.

At the center of the storm has been the issue of just when it is
between ovulation and adulthood that a person appears on the
scene. Conservatives draw the line at conception, liberals at
birth. In this paper I first examine our concept of a person and
conclude that no single criterion can capture the concept of a
person and no sharp line can be drawn. Next I argue that if a
fetus is a person, abortion is still justifiable in many cases; and

Reprinted from *Canadian Journal of Philosophy* 5 (October 1975):
233–43, by permission of the Canadian Association for Publishing in
Philosophy.

if a fetus is not a person, killing it is still wrong in many cases. To a large extent, these two solutions are in agreement. I conclude that our concept of a person cannot and need not bear the weight that the abortion controversy has thrust upon it.

# I

The several factions in the abortion argument have drawn battle lines around various proposed criteria for determining what is and what is not a person. For example, Mary Anne Warren[2] lists five features (capacities for reasoning, self-awareness, complex communication, etc.) as her criteria for personhood and argues for the permissibility of abortion because a fetus falls outside this concept. Baruch Brody[3] uses brain waves. Michael Tooley[4] picks having-a-concept-of-self as his criterion and concludes that infanticide and abortion are justifiable, while the killing of adult animals is not. On the other side, Paul Ramsey[5] claims a certain gene structure is the defining characteristic. John Noonan[6] prefers conceived-of-humans and presents counter-examples to various other candidate criteria. For instance, he argues against viability as the criterion because the newborn and infirm would then be non-persons, since they cannot live without the aid of others. He rejects any criterion that calls upon the sorts of sentiments a being can evoke in adults on the grounds that this would allow us to exclude other races as non-persons if we could just view them sufficiently unsentimentally.

These approaches are typical: foes of abortion propose sufficient conditions for personhood which fetuses satisfy, while friends of abortion counter with necessary conditions for personhood which fetuses lack. But these both presuppose that the concept of a person can be captured in a straitjacket of necessary and/or sufficient conditions.[7] Rather, "person" is a cluster of features, of which rationality, having a self-concept, and being conceived of humans are only part.

What is typical of persons? Within our concept of a person we include, first, certain biological factors: being descended from humans; having a certain genetic makeup; having a head, hands, arms, eyes; being capable of locomotion, breathing, eating, sleeping. There are psychological factors: sentience, perception, having a concept of self and of one's own interests and desires, the ability to use tools, the ability to use language or symbol systems, the ability to joke, to be angry, to doubt. There are rationality factors: the ability to reason and draw conclusions, the ability to generalize and to learn from past experience, the ability to sacrifice present interests for greater gains in the future. There are social factors: the ability to work in groups and respond to peer pressures; the ability to recognize and consider as valuable the interests of others; seeing oneself as one among "other minds"; the ability to sympathize, encourage, love; the ability to evoke from others the responses of sympathy, encouragement, love; the ability to work with others for mutual advantage. Then there are legal factors: being subject to the law and protected by it; having the ability to sue and enter contracts; being counted in the census; having a name and citizenship; having the ability to own property, inherit, and so forth.

Now the point is not that this list is incomplete, or that you can find counter-instances to each of its points. People typically exhibit rationality, for instance, but someone who was irrational would not thereby fail to qualify as a person. On the other hand, something could exhibit the majority of these features and still fail to be a person, as an advanced robot might. There is no single core of necessary and sufficient features which we can draw upon with the assurance that they constitute what really makes a person; there are only features that are more or less typical.

This is not to say that no necessary or sufficient conditions can be given. Being alive is a necessary condition for being a person, and being a U.S. Senator is sufficient. But rather than falling inside a sufficient condition or outside a necessary one, a fetus lies in the penumbra region where our concept of a person is not so simple. For this reason, I think it impossible to attain a conclusive answer to the question of whether a fetus is a person.

Here we might note a family of simple fallacies that proceed by stating a necessary condition for personhood and showing that a fetus has that characteristic. This is a form of the fallacy of affirming the consequent. For example, some have mistakenly reasoned from the premise that a fetus is human (after all, it is a human fetus rather than, say, a canine fetus), to the conclusion that it is *a* human. Adding an equivocation on "being," we get the fallacious argument that since a fetus is something both living and human, it is a human being.

Nonetheless, it does seem clear that a fetus has very few of the above family of characteristics, whereas a newborn baby exhibits a much larger proportion of them—and a two-year-old has even more. One traditional anti-abortion argument has centered on pointing out the many ways in which a fetus resembles a baby. They emphasize its development ("It already has ten fingers . . .") without mentioning its dissimilarities to adults (it still has gills and a tail). They also try to evoke the sort of sympathy on our part that we only feel toward other persons ("Never to laugh . . . or feel the sunshine?"). This all seems to be a relevant way to argue, since its purpose is to persuade us that a fetus satisfies so many of the important features on the list that it ought to be treated as a person. Also note that a fetus near the time of birth satisfies many more of these factors than a fetus in the early months of development. This could provide reason for making distinctions among the different stages of pregnancy, as the U.S. Supreme Court has done.[8]

Historically, the time at which a person has been said to come into existence has varied widely. Muslims date personhood from fourteen days after conception. Some Medieval scholars followed Aristotle in placing ensoulment at forty days after conception for a male fetus and eighty days for a female fetus.[9] In European common law since the 17th century, abortion was considered the killing of a person only after quickening, the time when a pregnant woman first feels the fetus move on its own. Nor is this variety of opinions surprising. Biologically, a human being develops gradually. We shouldn't expect there to be any specific time or sharp dividing point when a person appears on the scene.

For these reasons I believe our concept of a person is not sharp or decisive enough to bear the weight of a solution to the abortion controversy. To use it to solve that problem is to clarify *obscurum per obscurius*.

## II

Next let us consider what follows if a fetus is a person after all. Judith Jarvis Thomson's landmark article, "A Defense of Abortion,"[10] correctly points out that some additional argumentation is needed at this point in the conservative argument in order to bridge the gap between the premise that a fetus is an innocent person and the conclusion that killing it is always wrong. To arrive at this conclusion, we would need the additional premise that killing an innocent person is always wrong. But killing an innocent person is sometimes permissible, most notably in self-defense. Some examples may help draw out our intuitions or ordinary judgments about self-defense.

Suppose a mad scientist, for instance, hypnotized innocent people to jump out of the bushes and attack innocent passers-by with knives. If you are so attacked, we agree you have a right to kill the attacker in self-defense, if killing him is the only way to protect your life or to save yourself from serious injury. It does not seem to matter here that the attacker is not malicious but himself an innocent pawn, for your killing of him is not done in a spirit of retribution but only in self-defense.

How severe an injury may you inflict in self-defense? In part this depends upon the severity of the injury to be avoided: you may not shoot someone merely to avoid having your clothes torn. This might lead one to the mistaken conclusion that the defense may equal but not exceed the threatened injury in severity; that to avoid death you may kill, but to avoid a black eye you may only inflict a black eye or the equivalent. Rather, our laws and customs seem to say that you may create an injury somewhat, but not enormously, greater than the injury to be avoided. To fend off an attack whose outcome would be as serious as rape, a severe beating, or the loss of a finger, you may shoot; to avoid having your clothes torn, you may blacken an eye.

Aside from this, the injury you may inflict should only be the minimum necessary to deter or incapacitate the attacker. Even if you know he intends to kill you, you are not justified in shooting him if you could equally well save yourself by the simple expedient of running away. Self-defense is for the purpose of avoiding harms rather than equalizing harms.

Some cases of pregnancy present a parallel situation. Though the fetus is itself innocent, it may pose a threat to the pregnant woman's well-being, life prospects, or health—mental or physical. If the pregnancy presents only a slight threat to her interests, it seems that self-defense cannot justify abortion. But if the threat is on a par with a serious beating or the loss of a finger, she may kill the fetus that poses such a threat, even if it is an innocent person. If a lesser harm to the fetus could have the same defensive effect, killing it would not be justified. It is unfortunate that the only known way to free the woman from the pregnancy entails the death of the fetus (except in the very late stages of pregnancy). Thus a self-defense model supports Thomson's point that the woman has a right only to be freed from the fetus, not a right to demand its death.[11]

The self-defense model is most helpful when we take the pregnant woman's point of view. In the pre-Thomson literature, abortion was often framed as a question for a third party: do you, a doctor, have a right to choose between the life of the woman and that of the fetus? Some have claimed that if you were a passer-by who witnessed a struggle between the innocent hypnotized attacker and his equally innocent victim, you would have no reason to kill either in defense of the other. They have concluded that the self-defense model implies that a woman may attempt to abort herself, but that a doctor should not assist her. I think the position of the third party is somewhat more complex. We do feel some inclination to intervene on behalf of the victim rather than the attacker, other things equal. But if both parties are innocent, other factors come into consideration. You would rush to the aid of your husband whether he was attacker or attackee. If a hypnotized famous violinist were attacking a skid-row bum, we would try to save the individual who is of more value to society. These considerations would tend to support abortion in some cases.

But suppose you are a frail senior citizen who wishes to avoid being knifed by one of these innocent hypnotics, so you have hired a bodyguard to accompany you. If you are attacked, it is clear we believe that the bodyguard, acting as your agent, has a right to kill the attacker to save you from a serious beating. Your rights of self-defense are transferred to your agent. I suggest that we should similarly view the doctor as the pregnant woman's agent in carrying out a defense she is physically incapable of accomplishing herself.

Thanks to modern technology, the cases are rare in which a pregnancy poses as clear a threat to a woman's bodily health as an attacker brandishing a switchblade. How does self-defense fare when more subtle, complex, and long-range harms are involved?

To consider a somewhat fanciful example, suppose you are a highly trained surgeon when you are kidnapped by the hypnotic attacker. He says he does not intend to harm you but to take you back to the mad scientist who, it turns out, plans to hypnotize you to have a permanent mental block against all your knowledge of medicine. Suppose this would automatically destroy your career and have a serious adverse impact on your family, your personal relationships, and your happiness. It seems to me that if the only way you can avoid this outcome is to shoot the innocent attacker, you are justified in so doing. You are defending yourself from a drastic injury to your life prospects. I think it is no exaggeration to claim that unwanted pregnancies (most obviously among teenagers) often have such adverse lifelong consequences as the surgeon's loss of livelihood.

Several parallels arise between various views on abortion and the self-defense model. Let's suppose further that these hypnotized attackers only operate at night, so that it is well known that they can be avoided completely by the considerable inconvenience of never leaving your house after dark. One view is that since you could stay home at night, therefore if you go out and are selected by one of these hypnotized people, you have no right to defend yourself. This parallels the view that abstinence is the only acceptable way to avoid pregnancy. Others might hold that you ought to take along some defense such as Mace, which will deter the hypnotized person without killing him, but that if this defense fails, you are obliged to submit to the resulting injury, no matter how severe it is. This parallels the view that contraception is all right but abortion is always wrong, even in cases of contraceptive failure.

A third view is that you may kill the hypnotized person only if he will actually kill you, but not if he will only injure you. This is like the position that abortion is permissible only if it is required to save a woman's life. Finally, we have the view that it is all right to kill the attacker, even if only to avoid a very slight inconvenience to yourself, and even if you knowingly walked down the very street where all these incidents have been taking place without taking along any Mace or protective escort. If we assume that a fetus is a person, this is the analogue of the view that abortion is always justifiable, "on demand."

The self-defense model allows us to see an important difference that exists between abortion and infanticide, even if a fetus is a person from the time of conception. Many have argued that the only way to justify abortion without justifying infanticide would be to find some characteristic of personhood that is acquired at birth. Michael Tooley, for one, claims infanticide is justifiable because the really significant characteristics of a person are acquired some time after birth. But all such approaches look to characteristics of the developing human and ignore the relation between the fetus and the woman. What if, after birth, the presence of an infant or the need to support it posed a grave threat to the woman's sanity or life prospects? She could escape this threat by the simple expedient of running away. So a solution that does not entail the death of the infant is available. Before birth, such solutions are not available because of the biological dependence of the fetus on the woman. Birth is the crucial point not because of any characteristics the fetus gains, but because after birth the woman can defend herself by a means less drastic than killing the infant. Hence self-defense can be used to justify abortion without necessarily thereby justifying infanticide.

## III

On the other hand, supposing a fetus is not, after all, a person, would abortion always be morally permissible? Some opponents of abortion seem worried that if a fetus is not a full-fledged person, then we are justified in treating it in any way we wish. However, this does not follow. Non-persons do get some consideration in our moral code, though of course they do not have the same rights as persons have (and in general they do not have moral responsibilities), and though their interests may be overridden by the interests of persons. Still, we cannot just treat them in any way at all.

Treatment of animals is a case in point. It is wrong to torture dogs for fun or to kill wild birds for no reason at all. It is wrong, period, even though dogs and birds do not have the same rights persons do. However, few people think it is wrong to use dogs as experimental animals, causing them considerable suffering in some cases, provided that the resulting research will probably bring discoveries of great benefit to people. And most of us think it all right to kill birds for food or to protect our crops. People's rights are different from the consideration we give to animals, then, for it is wrong to experiment on people, even if others might later benefit a great deal as a result of their suffering. (You might volunteer to be a subject, but this would be supererogatory; you certainly have a right to refuse to be a medical guinea pig.)

But how do we decide what you may or may not do to non-persons? This is a difficult problem, one for which I believe no adequate account exists. You do not want to say, for instance, that torturing dogs is all right whenever the sum of its effects on people is good—when it doesn't warp the sensibilities of the torturer so much that he mistreats people. If that were the case, it would be all right to torture dogs if you did it in private, or if the torturer lived on a desert island or died soon afterward, so that his actions had no effect on people. This is an inadequate account, because whatever moral consideration animals get, it has to be indefeasible, too. It will have to be a general proscription of certain actions, not merely a weighing of the impact on people on a case-by-case basis.

Rather, we need to distinguish two levels on which the consequences of actions can be taken into account in moral reasoning. The traditional objections to Utilitarianism focus on the fact that it operates solely on the first level, taking all the consequences into account in particular cases only. Thus Utilitarianism is open to "desert island" and "lifeboat" counterexamples because these cases are rigged to make the consequences of actions severely limited.

Rawls' theory could be described as a teleological sort of theory in some sense, but with teleology operating on a higher level.[12] In choosing the principles to regulate society from the original position, his hypothetical choosers make their decision on the basis of the total consequences of various systems. Furthermore, they are constrained to choose a general set of rules which people can readily learn and apply. An ethical theory must operate by generating a set of sympathies and attitudes toward others which reinforce the functioning of that set of moral principles. Our prohibition against killing people operates by means of certain moral sentiments including sympathy, compassion, and guilt. But if these attitudes are to form a coherent set, they carry us further: we tend to perform supererogatory actions, and we tend to feel similar compassion toward person-like non-persons.

It is crucial that psychological facts play a role here. Our psychological constitution makes it the case that for our ethical theory to work, it must prohibit certain treatment of non-persons which are significantly person-like. If our moral rules allowed people to treat some person-like non-persons in ways we do not want people to be treated, this would undermine the system of sympathies and attitudes that makes the ethical system work. For this reason, we would choose in Rawls' original position to make mistreatment of some sorts of animals wrong in general (not just wrong in the cases with public impact), even though animals are not themselves parties in the original position. Thus it makes sense that it is those animals whose appearance and behavior are most like those of people that get the most consideration in our moral scheme.

It is because of "coherence of attitudes," I think, that the similarity of a fetus to a baby is very significant. A fetus one week before birth is so much like a newborn baby in our psychological space that we cannot allow any cavalier treatment of the former while expecting full sympathy and nurturative support for the latter. Thus, I think that anti-abortion forces are indeed giving their strongest arguments when they point to the similarities between a fetus and a baby, and when they try to evoke our emotional attachment to and sympathy for the fetus. An early horror story from New York about nurses who were expected to alternate between caring for six-week premature infants and disposing of viable twenty-four-week aborted fetuses is just that—a horror story. These beings are so much alike that no one can be asked to draw a distinction and treat them so very differently.

Remember, however, that in the early weeks after conception, a fetus is very much unlike a person. It is hard to develop these feelings for a set of genes which doesn't yet have a head, hands, beating heart, response to touch, or the ability to move by itself. Thus it seems to me that the alleged "slippery slope" between conception and birth is not so very slippery. In the early stages of pregnancy, abortion can hardly be compared to murder psychologically, but in the latest stages it is psychologically akin to murder.

Another source of similarity is the bodily continuity between fetus and adult. Bodies play a surprisingly central role in our attitudes toward persons. One has only to think of the philosophical literature on how far physical identity suffices for personal identity, or Wittgenstein's remark that the best picture of the human soul is the human body. Even after death, when all agree the body is no longer a person, we still observe elaborate customs of respect for the human body; like people who torture dogs, necrophiliacs are not to be trusted with people.[13] So it is appropriate that we show respect toward a fetus as the body continuous with the body of a person. This is a degree of resemblance to persons that animals cannot rival.

Michael Tooley also utilizes a parallel with animals. He claims that it is always permissible to drown newborn kittens and draws conclusions about infanticide.[14] But it is only permissible to drown kittens when their survival would cause some hardship. Perhaps it would be a burden to feed and house six more cats or to find other homes for them. The alternative of letting them starve produces even more suffering than the drowning. Since the kittens get their rights second-hand, so to speak, via the need for coherence in our attitudes, their interests are often overridden by the interests of full-fledged persons. But if their survival would be no inconvenience to people at all, then it is wrong to drown them, contra Tooley.

Tooley's conclusions about abortion are wrong for the same reason. Even if a fetus is not a person, abortion is not always permissible, because of the resemblance of a fetus to a person. I agree with Thomson that it would be wrong for a woman who is seven months pregnant to have an abortion just to avoid having to postpone a trip to Europe. In the early months of pregnancy, when the fetus hardly resembles a baby at all, then, abortion is permissible whenever it is in the interests of the pregnant woman or her family. The reasons would only need to outweigh the pain and inconvenience of the abortion itself. In the middle months, when the fetus comes to resemble a person, abortion would be justifiable only when the continuation of the pregnancy or the birth of the child would cause harms—physical, psychological, economic, or social—to the woman. In the late months of pregnancy, even on our current assumption that a fetus is not a person, abortion seems to be wrong except to save a woman from significant injury or death.

The Supreme Court has recognized similar gradations in the alleged slippery slope stretching between conception and birth. To this point, the present paper has been a discussion of the moral status of abortion only, not its legal status. In view of the great physical, financial, and sometimes psychological costs of abortion, perhaps the legal arrangement most compatible with the proposed moral solution would be the absence of restrictions, that is, so-called abortion "on demand."

So I conclude, first, that application of our concept of a person will not suffice to settle the abortion issue. After all, the biological development of a human being is gradual. Second, whether a fetus is a person or not, abortion is justifiable early in pregnancy to avoid modest harms and seldom justifiable late in pregnancy except to avoid significant injury or death.

## NOTES

1. We also have paternalistic laws which keep us from harming our own bodies even when no one else is affected. Ironically, anti-abortion laws were originally designed to protect pregnant women from a dangerous but tempting procedure.
2. Mary Anne Warren, "On the Moral and Legal Status of Abortion," *Monist* 57 (January 1973): 43–61, p. 55.
3. Baruch Brody, "Fetal Humanity and the Theory of Essentialism," in *Philosophy and Sex*, ed. Robert Baker and Frederick Elliston (Buffalo, N.Y.: Prometheus Books, 1975).
4. Michael Tooley, "Abortion and Infanticide," *Philosophy and Public Affairs* 2 (Fall 1972): 37–65.
5. Paul Ramsey, "The Morality of Abortion," in *Moral Problems*, ed. James Rachels (New York: Harper & Row, 1971).
6. John T. Noonan, Jr., "Abortion and the Catholic Church: A Summary History," *Natural Law Forum* 12 (1967): 125–31.
7. Wittgenstein has argued against the possibility of so capturing the concept of a game. See *Philosophical Investigations* (Oxford: Basil Blackwell, 1953), sections 66–71.
8. Not because the fetus is partly a person and so has some of the rights of persons, but rather because of the rights of person-like non-persons. This I discuss in section III below.
9. Aristotle himself was concerned, however, with the different question of when the soul takes form. For historical data, see Jimmye Kimmey, "How the Abortion Laws Happened," *Ms.*, April 1973, pp. 48f.; and Noonan (above, n. 6).
10. Judith Thomson, "A Defense of Abortion," *Philosophy and Public Affairs* 1 (1971): 47–66.
11. Ibid., p. 52.
12. John Rawls, *A Theory of Justice* (Cambridge, Mass.: Harvard University Press, 1971), sections 3–4.
13. On the other hand, if they can be trusted with people, then our moral customs are mistaken. It all depends on the facts of psychology.
14. Tooley (above, n. 4), pp. 40, 60–61.

Howard Cohen

# Abortion and the Quality of Life

Very little in the current philosophical literature on abortion addresses the concerns of women who must decide whether or not to bring a fetus to term. By and large, philosophers have not tried to identify, analyze, or assess the kinds of reasons which typically support such decisions. Instead, they have focused almost exclusively on the questions of whether the fetus is a person and whether it has the right to life.[1] While no discussion of abortion can ultimately afford to ignore these questions, none of the attempts to deal with them have provided much moral guidance.

There are several reasons why this is so. In the first place, the dispute over the personhood of the fetus has gone on interminably without any sign that the issue will be settled. If anything, the attempts to analyze the concept of a person seem to suggest that the prospects for settlement are dismal. Another reason why these discussions are not helpful is that the links between the proposed answers to these questions and the reasons women give for their decisions are never made very clear. Philosophical discussions of abortion are rarely cast in the context of practical reasoning. Finally, philosophical discussion typically centers on examples which are representative of only a tiny fraction of the situations in which abortion decisions are made. Judging from the literature, one might suppose that only women in mortal danger, women carrying deformed fetuses, and women who have been raped would seek abortions. Reasons less grave—but more prevalent—are hardly considered.

The explanation of the concentration on crisis cases is not hard to fathom. Anti-abortionists do not want to be accused of taking a cheap shot. They want to show that even in the gravest of circumstances abortion is impermissible. Pro-abortionists want to discuss the cases in which the woman's moral position is clearest—where the purity of her motives cannot be questioned. Unfortunately, however, this restricted range of examples encourages us to forget the fact that the vast majority of abortion decisions are made in light of other problems. One effect of this sin of omission is that pro-abortionists are perceived as defending abortion only in special cases. Their silence is either a concession that abortion is mostly wrong or a failure to address the heart of the issue.

A cursory look at the statistics is sufficient to show that abortions are primarily sought for psychological, social, and economic reasons:

> About half the women having induced abortions, if questioned concerning their reasons, say they already have as many or more children than they feel able to cope with; between ten and twenty per cent mention limitations imposed by financial reasons, about 15 per cent report they are unmarried; and amongst the remainder a wide variety of reasons such as death or invalidism of the husband, rape, carnal knowledge, alcoholism, etc. . . . is offered.[2]

None of these reasons are frivolous. They all speak to substantial sacrifices which women may have to make in bearing and raising a child. When these sacrifices are expected to lead to serious disruption in the lives of people close to abortion decisions, the reasons concern what is sometimes called "quality of life".[3] In certain circumstances, life with a(nother) child would deteriorate markedly, and many women feel that this is relevant when they consider abortion.

In spite of the importance of these reasons to women, philosophical defenses of abortion do not accommodate them very well. The main pro-abortion strategies tend to argue either that the fetus has no moral status whatever or that the fetus has rights, but they are sometimes superseded by those of the pregnant woman. For the first sort of argument, any reason—or none at all—will suffice for an abortion; for the second, only very weighty reasons will overcome the presumptive rights of the fetus. Neither of these argument strategies, however, provides a satisfactory account of how reasons concerning the quality of life should figure into the decision-making process on abortion. In the first case, such reasons are superfluous; in the second, they are probably insufficient.

To argue in defense of abortion on the grounds that the fetus has no moral status is to ignore the relevance of the fact that it would have that status if it continued to develop in the expected way. So although it may be true that a fetus, as such, is not deserving of moral consideration, to say this—and no more—is to evade the look into the future which makes this argument seem overly technical and self-serving. Furthermore, even if no particular fetus has any moral claim on us, if we are willing to acknowledge that the continuation of the human species is (in some sense) good, then the decision to abort cannot be torn completely free of moral arguments. Of course, this sort of consideration cannot, by itself, be used to deduce that the continuation of any particular pregnancy is good. Still, one ought to be prepared to say why, in light of this, it would be better to terminate. Pro-abortion arguments which try to remove the issue from all moral grounds will simply not be helpful to most women who presently have decisions to make.

The other sort of pro-abortion argument which stresses limitations on the fetus' right to life generally stops short of finding a place for considerations of quality of life. Consider, for example, one of the essays of this type which is most sympathetic to women seeking abortions: Judith Thomson's "A Defense of Abortion."[4] One of the strong points of her discussion is that she does draw connections between the larger philosophical questions and the concern women have that to deny them abortions is to violate their right to control over their own bodies. In spite of this, Thomson's arguments leave the impression that considerations of an economic, social, or psychological nature have a status somewhat beneath moral worth. For the purposes of her argument, she concedes that a fetus may well be a person with a right to life. Nevertheless, she goes on to show that "having a right to life does not guarantee having either a right to be given the use of or a right to be allowed the continued use of another person's body—even if one needs it for life itself."[5] Thomson's argument exposes the deficiencies of the standard right-to-life objections to abortion, but she stops short of defending women who, although within their rights, would choose to end the life of a fetus. While a woman is not "morally *required* to make large sacrifices, of health, of all other interests and concerns, of all other duties and commitments,"[6] there are standards of decency to be considered. Although Thomson never explicitly classifies carrying a fetus to term as either minimally decent or extraordinarily virtuous, in at least one case where she applies her principle she suggests that the woman who exercises this right may well be indecent:

And similarly, that even supposing a case in which a woman pregnant due to rape ought to allow the unborn to use her body for the hour he needs, we should not conclude that he has a right to do so; we should conclude that she is self-centered, callous, indecent, but not unjust, if she refuses. The complaints are no less grave; they are just different.[7]

If this is the best that can be said for an abortion under such circumstances, the difference is hardly worth insisting upon.

I do not cite these passages to suggest that Thomson actually opposes abortion. She is, after all, arguing within the confines of some fairly stringent assumptions. Yet I do think she has slighted the importance of women's sacrifices of health, interests, concerns, duties, and commitments by misrepresenting the role they play in decision-making on abortion. For surely pregnancy is not *so* great an inconvenience in most cases (though it is in some). There is, to be sure, some sickness and some restriction on activity, but the portrait of nine months of pain and isolation is highly exaggerated. Furthermore, with the possibility of putting a child up for adoption, the burden of child-rearing also seems less serious. Under such conditions we are left with the distinct impression that Thomson would have any "decent" woman go through with the pregnancy. Such pregnancies may be burdens—even hardships—but we are being asked to balance these burdens against the killing of a person. How much pain and misery is a human life worth? And who is willing to say? In fact, we will not say. Both questions are avoided, for there is no figure in any moral calculus which is assigned as the value of human life independently of all contexts.[8] Those who use this argument strategy without giving guidance about how much hardship outweighs aborting a fetus can only encourage thoughtful women to martyr themselves to the bearing of unwanted children. For what, in the end, is even substantial personal sacrifice, economic or social loss, or the inability to cope in the face of so grave an act as killing a person?

With all due respect for the service Thomson has done by exposing the weakness of the right-to-life argument, her "defense" is restricted to a very small range of abortion decisions. If the standard kinds of reasons women who seek abortions appeal to have any moral weight, we must try to see them in another light.

I want now to suggest how reasons having to do with quality of life are relevant to principled action on abortion, and why they are morally sufficient to justify abortion in cases in which bearing a child would result in a deterioration of that quality. At the same time, we need to find a framework which places psychological, social, and economic reasons for abortion in the context of familiar and reasonably non-controversial moral principles. A usable defense of abortion should show how the reasons women actually give for abortion decisions fit into a moral outlook which those women might be expected to have. The notion of family planning seems to me to be best suited for this task. Abortion decisions should be thought of as a variety of family planning after conception. In the development of this argument I shall leave aside the philosopher's worries about the personhood of the fetus. They will be taken up where they more properly belong: as a possible objection to this way of proceeding.

Quality-of-life considerations have a clearly acknowledged place in decision-making about family composition and the use of birth-control methods when this planning occurs prior to conception. Women (or couples) who take their present and future psychological, social, and economic circumstances into account before having children are generally thought to exemplify an awareness of their world, of the consequences of their actions on it, and of their own responsibility for those actions. When those who are responsible for the welfare of a family deliberately determine its composition in accordance with some conception of what is best for those affected[9] rather than leaving its composition to chance, they are widely recognized as exhibiting maturity. Maturity, in this sense, does not come with age. It is based on the dignity and respect from others that the attempt to gain control over one's own life commands. Seen in this light, the principle of family planning becomes a kind of moral maxim and its adoption a moral virtue.

This, then, is the line of argument that underlies the moral value of family planning prior to conception. Its virtues are widely enough acknowledged to provide a useful starting point in a defense of abortion, although, to be sure, they are denied by the Roman Catholic Church and some writers on population policy.[10] The former objects to planning, per se; the latter object to the presumed ineffectiveness of controlling population levels through uncoordinated individual decisions. A full defense of the family-planning maxim would have to take both sorts of objections into account, but that task can perhaps be avoided for present purposes. The important thing is that people who hold this maxim are presently counted as acting in a morally responsible way—and people who act on well-accepted moral principles need not go around justifying the fact that they do so or defending themselves to those who may disapprove. One need not be dogmatic about holding to this maxim. Circumstances might change sufficiently to require its adherents to reconsider it. But for the present it is as solid a starting point as one could hope for. It is not particularly in need of a more secure grounding in some theoretical system, since no ethical theory is more generally acceptable and free from objection than it is.

I want to argue that the maxim can be extended to cover family planning beyond the time of conception. If this is so, then considerations of quality of life will have a clear-cut place in abortion decisions.

The main aim of family planning is to improve the quality of life for individuals and (it is hoped) thereby for societies.[11] With advancement in knowledge of human reproductive biology and the development of a contraception technology, it has become possible for people to gain a measure of control over their lives. Of course, the quality of one's life does not depend solely or even primarily on the composition of one's family. The availability of material goods and services, the opportunity to develop and exercise one's capacities, and the ability to establish satisfying personal relationships are all conditions which affect the quality of life. Individuals have control over these conditions to varying degrees; for the most part such control is lamentably slight. But the one condition that is well within the reach of most people is the number of family members who share wealth and work. Present scarcity of resources, population growth, and unjust distribution of wealth makes family planning in accordance with the psychological, economic, and social needs of those affected an act of responsible, rational living.

For the creation of human life under any conditions and without limit is not itself of moral value. Rather, it is the creation of life in particular circumstances that may produce happiness, pleasure, satisfaction, or some other human good. But although the creation of a child may and often does do this, it may also produce hardship, pain, oppression, or a host of other evils. So there are no guarantees that childbearing will be of value, even though the potential impact of that event on the quality of human lives may be very great. In light of this, it would seem that those whose lives are most affected by such an event should have all reasonable powers of decision over their occurrence. Prior to pregnancy, should people decide that life would be poorer—in any sense—with (more) children, their decision is counted as justifiable and responsible.

Implicit in the claim that the quality of life is relevant to the decision to have children or not is the assumption that this decision is within the bounds of human prerogative. In our present society this means that the decision rests with the prospective parents. Here, too, the maxim rests on social arrangement and human knowledge. When reproduction and contraception are not understood, it is plausible for people to believe that having children is something that just happens to them. Also, in societies where children are a valuable social asset or where child-rearing is not primarily the responsibility of child-bearers, the decision-making power may be variously distributed. As things stand now, though, those who are able to bear children and are not certified mental incompetents have the exclusive right of decision. This is as it should be, since the responsibilities of child-rearing—and the costs—are borne by those who bear the child.[12]

It may be worth emphasizing here that the family-planning maxim incorporates both the right to create children and the right to refuse to do so. This causes no special problems even for those who oppose contraception. So long as opponents of contraception permit sexual abstinence, they leave the decision and the right of refusal with the potential parents. Childbearing and child-rearing are often a pleasure, perhaps even a virtue, but they are certainly no duty.

So far, I have been discussing the right to create a person—or refuse to—when it is exercised prior to conception. If there is good reason to leave this right with the potential parents after conception, considerations having to do with the quality of life will be morally sufficient to justify abortion in most cases. A woman who learns she is carrying an unplanned child may then make the same sort of mature decision concerning family planning as the woman who is not pregnant. The same sorts of psychological, social, and economic considerations can figure into her decision in the same ways. The question, then, is whether and to what extent this right should belong *after* conception to those responsible for the welfare of the family. In other words: why should it be reasonable to extend the time of decision-making beyond conception? The answer, I would suggest, is that it extends the control that people have over their lives in a significant way by affording them the opportunity to make deliberate and possibly better decisions concerning the welfare of those involved.

Abortion only becomes an issue for people in the face of unwanted (and usually accidental) pregnancy, often due to the unavailability of simple, safe, and effective contraception or the proper instruction in its use. Typically, people in these circumstances have either not yet given much thought to childbearing (perhaps putting the decision off for some future time) or they have made an explicit decision not to reproduce. Some of these pregnancies were originally intended, but changes in circumstances make them hardships. For example, the death of a husband or financial ruin can turn a good decision into a bad one unless it is revised. In all of these situations, unforeseen or undesired circumstances become barriers to the control that people have over their lives—they stand in the way of mature family planning. Abortion is an available remedy to such situations. It allows the return of morally significant decision-making to those who wish to exercise it.

Second, it is also reasonble that the right to decide whether or not to have a child should continue into pregnancy because people are sometimes not in the best position to decide until then. Life with children is not easily conceptualized. This, in turn, can make it quite difficult for people to assess their own attitudes, fears, and desires about child-rearing. Sometimes people are capable of such self-reflectiveness only when decision-making is imminent. In this case, that may mean after conception. If people can make better (not easier) decisions in these circumstances, they ought to retain the right to do so. The option of abortion is consistent with our sense that morality requires the exercise of choice over significant aspects of our lives.

While these arguments do suggest that the family-planning maxim should be applicable after conception, they do not countenance putting off decision-making indefinitely. Indecision is no virtue, and there is little reason to extend areas of human control if control is not to be exercised. Once a woman learns of her pregnancy, a few weeks may be needed to come to some decision. For people with very complicated lives, it may take longer. But we need not set a time limit. Cautious decision-making shades into indecisiveness. Allowing for some benefit of the doubt, we can tell the difference—and make our moral judgments accordingly.

It also happens sometimes that circumstances change suffi-ciently after such decisions are made to warrant remaking them. As we have noted, financial ruin or the death of a husband shortly after the conception of a desired pregnancy might lead to a change in the decision to have a child. People tend to be critical of reconsideration, for it may be a sign of previous hasty thought or continuing indecision. Thus, questions about which changes of circumstance are "sufficient" to reopen the decision-making process become more sensitive. Where the changes seem trivial—the chance to take a trip, for example—re-evalua-tion may appear morally indefensible. But it is important to see that what is indefensible here is not the decision to have an abortion but the cavalier attitude with which such a serious decision is being treated.[13] In general, we do not insist that moral decisions, once made, must stand come what may, and there is no reason to make an exception in the case of abortion.

One consequence of arguing for abortion in this way is that the defense of abortion does not become a defense of infanti-cide. It is almost impossible to think of real-life cases in which one could justify putting off a family-planning decision until after birth. But even if such a case could be constructed, the family-planning maxim could, at most, be used to justify placing the baby for adoption. The moral value of the decision to abort does not depend in any way on some property that a fetus either has or lacks—so nothing is to be gained by showing that small babies have or lack similar properties.

This, I suppose, is what opponents of abortion will find most objectionable about presenting the issue in the way that I have. For most anti-abortionists, it is precisely that property which fetuses are said to share with small babies (and large adults)— namely, personhood—which makes abortion morally wrong. They will insist that the personhood of the fetus is the morally significant fact which differentiates family planning prior to conception from family planning afterwards. Presumably, they also believe that the personhood of the fetus is of greater importance than the measure of control people might gain over their lives through the practice of abortion.

It is worth remembering, though, that the claim that a fetus is a person is highly problematic. In the first place, there is substantial disagreement about the definition of a person. Various commentators have fixed on quite different criteria, and virtually every proposed definition has been criticized as not in accordance with someone's intuitions. Repeated failures to arrive at a satisfactory analysis have led other commentators to suggest that "person" is a cluster concept which cannot be precisely specified.[14] Furthermore, within the cluster, the relative importance of the specified features cannot be settled as a matter of empirical fact. The dispute is not about which features fetuses possess, but rather about which features are sufficiently significant to call beings which possess them persons. Questions of importance are questions of perception and values.

If, as Jane English suggests, "foes of abortion propose sufficient conditions for personhood which fetuses satisfy, while friends of abortion counter with necessary conditions for personhood which fetuses lack,"[15] then this whole line of objection to the family-planning approach to abortion becomes blatantly question-begging. The anti-abortionist may simply be selecting as important those features of personhood that fetuses are known to possess. But even if the source of the anti-abortionist's belief in the personhood of the fetus lies elsewhere— say, in religious doctrine—we are no more required to accept the assertion that the fetus is a person than we are required to accept the doctrine.

For those who do not hold the belief that a fetus is a person, family planning after conception is a viable way to exercise control over their lives. From the time a woman learns of her pregnancy—and for enough time thereafter as it takes to come to a thoughtful decision—abortion is justifiable for any reason which would justify deciding not to have children prior to con-

ception. Since these reasons are generally those which we think
of as having to do with the quality of life, it is now possible to
understand the role that such considerations may play in abortion decisions.

## NOTES

1. See, for example, the recent anthology edited by Joel Feinberg,
   *The Problem of Abortion* (Belmont, Calif.: Wadsworth, 1973),
   or the articles from *Philosophy and Public Affairs* collected in
   *The Rights and Wrongs of Abortion*, ed. Marshall Cohen,
   T. Nagel, and T. Scanlon (Princeton, N.J.: Princeton University
   Press, 1974). One recent exception is R. M. Hare, "Abortion
   and the Golden Rule," *Philosophy and Public Affairs* 4 (1975):
   201–22. Hare expores the application of the golden rule to
   abortion decisions.
2. John Peel and Malcom Potts, *Textbook of Contraceptive Practice* (London: Cambridge University Press, 1969), p. 176.
3. Some examples of situations in which the quality of life is said
   to deterioriate include: the substantial reduction of family income which occurs when a woman leaves a job to bear a child,
   the overcrowding which results from additional people inhabit-
   ing a limited space, the loss of a stimulating home environment
   due to the depression of a woman who does not want to raise
   another child, and the inability of a woman to pursue a career
   which is incompatible with the duties of motherhood.
4. Judith Thomson, "A Defense of Abortion," reprinted in Feinberg (above, n. 1), pp. 121–39.
5. Ibid., p. 130.
6. Ibid., p. 135.
7. Ibid., p. 134.
8. There are numerous ways to illustrate this point. For one, many
   opponents of abortion approve of capital punishment—and vice
   versa—and assess the value of the life in question differently in
   each case. For another, all but the most absolute pacifists approve of at least some killing in wars, self-defense and the like.
   Presumably some of these people disapprove of abortion.
9. The phrase is deliberately vague, since who is affected depends
   so much upon the relationship of the family to society at large.
   There will be substantial differences in figuring the effects of
   such decisions for isolated nuclear families on the one hand
   and for socially integrated extended families on the other.
10. For example, see *Readings in Human Population Ecology*, ed.
    Wayne H. Davis (Englewood Cliffs, N.J.: Prentice-Hall, 1971).

11. Whatever might be said in criticism of the policy of trying to achieve population control through family planning (and there is a lot to say), one must not lose sight of the fact that burdens on particular families can be alleviated in this way.

12. This is basically correct, but not precisely. Through public welfare, the state bears some of the costs in some cases. However, the poor in turn bear the costs which make public welfare a social necessity. At any rate, the fact that this right of decision does rest with potential parents in our society may be seen in the strong opposition to involuntary sterilization.

13. It seems to me that this—rather than the age of the fetus—may account for Judith Thomson's intuition that it would be indecent for a woman to request an abortion in her seventh month to avoid postponing a trip abroad (Thomson, p. 138).

14. Jane English holds this view in "Abortion and the Concept of a Person," this volume, p. 418. She also surveys the current state of the personhood-of-the-fetus problem in that paper.

15. Ibid.

# Abortion

# *Further References*

Starred items are those of philosophical interest.

Annis, David. "Self-Consciousness and the Right to Life." *Southwestern Journal of Philosophy* 6 (1975): 123–28.

Baker, Robert, and Elliston, Frederick, eds. *Philosophy and Sex*. Buffalo, N.Y.: Prometheus Books, 1975.

*Benn, S. I. "Abortion, Infanticide and Respect for Persons." In Feinberg, ed., *The Problem of Abortion*.

Bennett, John. "Avoid Oppressive Laws." *Christianity and Crisis* 32 (1973): 287–88.

*Bennett, Jonathan. "Whatever the Consequences." *Analysis* 26 (1966): 83–102. Reprinted in Feinberg, ed., *The Problem of Abortion*.

*Bok, Sissela. "Ethical Problems of Abortion." *Hastings Center Study* 2 (1974): 33–52.

———. "Who Shall Count As a Human Being?" In Perkins, ed., *Abortion: Pro and Con*.

Boston Women's Health Book Collective. *Our Bodies, Ourselves*. 2d ed. New York: Simon & Schuster, 1976.

*Brandt, Richard. "The Morality of Abortion." *Monist* 56 (1972): 504–26.

*Brody, Baruch. "Abortion and the Law." *Journal of Philosophy* 68 (1971): 357–69.

———. "Abortion and the Sanctity of Human Life." *American Philosophical Quarterly* 10 (1973): 133–40.

———. "Fetal Humanity and the Theory of Essentialism." In Baker and Elliston, eds., *Philosophy and Sex*.

———. "Thomson on Abortion." *Philosophy and Public Affairs* 1 (1972): 335–40. [See Thomson.]

Byrne, F. "Abortion: A Legal View." *Commonweal* 85 (1967): 679–80.

Callahan, Daniel. "Abortion Decisions: Personal Morality." In Feinberg, ed., *The Problem of Abortion.*

———. *Abortion: Law, Choice and Morality.* London: Macmillan, 1970.

———. "Abortion: Thinking and Experiencing." *Christianity and Crisis* 32 (1973): 295–98.

Casey, John. "Killing and Letting Die: A Reply to Bennett." In *Ethics and Public Policy*, edited by Tom Beauchamp. Englewood Cliffs, N.J.: Prentice-Hall, 1975. [See Jonathan Bennett.]

Char, W., and McDermott, J. "Abortions and Acute Identity Crises in Nurses." *American Journal of Psychiatry* 128 (1972): 952–57.

Childress, James. "A Response to 'Conferred Rights and the Fetus.' " *Journal of Religious Ethics* 2 (1974): 77–83. [See Green.]

*Clark, Lorenne. "Reply to Sumner on Abortion." *Canadian Journal of Philosophy* 4 (1974): 183–90. [See Sumner.]

Cohen, Marshall; Nagel, T.; and Scanlon, T.; eds. *The Rights and Wrongs of Abortion.* Princeton, N.J.: Princeton University Press, 1974.

Dinello, Daniel. "On Killing and Letting Die." *Analysis* 31 (1971): 84–86. Reprinted in *Ethics and Public Policy*, edited by Tom Beauchamp. Englewood Cliffs, N.J.: Prentice-Hall, 1975.

Donceel, J. F. "A Liberal Catholic's View." In *Abortion in a Changing World*, vol. 1, edited by R. E. Hall. New York: Columbia University Press, 1970.

Drinan, Robert. "The Jurisprudential Options on Abortion." *Theological Studies* 31 (1970): 149–69.

———. "The Morality of Abortion Laws." *Catholic Lawyer* 14 (1968).

Duff, R. "Intentionally Killing the Innocent." *Analysis* 34 (1973): 16–19.

*Engelhardt, H. Tristram, Jr. "The Ontology of Abortion." *Ethics* 84 (1974): 217–34. [See Newton.]

———. "Viability, Abortion and the Difference between a Fetus and an Infant." *American Journal of Obstetrics and Gynecology* 116 (1973): 429–34.

*Feinberg, Joel, ed. *The Problem of Abortion.* Belmont, Calif.: Wadsworth Publishing Co., 1973.

*———. "What Kinds of Beings Can Have Rights?" In *Social and Political Philosophy*, edited by David Sidorsky. New York: Harper & Row, 1974.

*Finnis, John. "The Rights and Wrongs of Abortion." *Philosophy and Public Affairs* 2 (1973): 117–45. [See Thomson.]

*Foot, Philippa. "The Problem of Abortion and the Doctrine of Double Effect." In Rachels, ed., *Moral Problems*.

Forssman, H., and Thuwe, I. "120 Children Born after Application for Abortion Refused." In *Abortion and the Unwanted Child*, edited by C. Reiterman. New York: Springer Publishing Co., 1971.

Fost, Norman. "Our Curious Attitude toward the Fetus." *Hastings Center Study Report* 4 (1974): 4–5.

Geddes, L. "On the Intrinsic Wrongness of Killing Innocent People." *Analysis* 33 (1972): 93–97.

Gerber, D. "The Uptake Argument." *Ethics* 83 (1972): 80–83.

Gerber, R. J. "Abortion: Parameters for Decision." *Ethics* 82 (1972): 137–54.

Gianella, Donald. "The Difficult Quest for a Truly Humane Abortion Law." *Villanova Law Review* 13 (1968): 257–302.

Green, Ronald. "Conferred Rights and the Fetus." *Journal of Religious Ethics* 2 (1974): 55–75. [See Childress.]

Grisez, Germain. *Abortion: The Myths, the Realities and the Arguments*. New York: Corpus Books, 1970.

———. "Toward a Consistent Natural-Law Ethics of Killing." *American Journal of Jurisprudence* 15 (1970): 64–96.

Guttmacher, Alan, and Pilpel, H. "Abortion and the Unwanted Child." *Family Planning Perspectives* 2 (1970): 16–24.

Hall, R. E., ed. *Abortion in a Changing World*. New York: Columbia University Press, 1970.

Hardin, Garrett. "Abortion—or Compulsory Pregnancy?" *Journal of Marriage and the Family* 30 (1968): 246–51.

*Hare, R. M. "Abortion and the Golden Rule." *Philosophy and Public Affairs* 4 (1975): 201–22. Reprinted in Baker and Elliston, eds., *Philosophy and Sex*.

*Hastings Center Report* 3 (April 1973).

Humber, James. "The Case against Abortion." *Thomist* 39 (1975): 65–84.

*Jaggar, Alison. "Abortion and a Woman's Right to Decide." *Philosophical Forum* 5 (1973–74): 347–60. Reprinted in Baker and Elliston, eds., *Philosophy and Sex*.

Kimmey, Jimmye. "How the Abortion Laws Happened." *Ms.*, April 1973.

*Kohl, Marvin. "Abortion and the Argument from Innocence." *Inquiry* 14 (1971): 147–50. Reprinted in Feinberg, ed., *The Problem of Abortion*.

Lader, Lawrence. *Abortion*. Indianapolis, Ind.: Bobbs-Merrill, 1966.

———. *Abortion II: Making the Revolution*. Boston: Beacon Press, 1973.

Lederberg, J. "A Geneticist Looks at Contraception and Abortion." *Annals of Internal Medicine* 67, suppl. 7 (1967): 25–27.

Leebensohn, Zigmond. "Abortion, Psychiatry and the Quality of Life." *American Journal of Psychiatry* 128 (1971): 946–54.

*Lindsay, Anne. "On the Slippery Slope Again." *Analysis* 35 (1974): 32. [See Rudinow.]

Maginnis, P., and Phelan, L. *The Abortion Handbook*. North Hollywood, Calif.: Contact Books, 1969.

Mead, Margaret. "Rights to Life." *Christianity and Crisis* 32 (1973): 288–92.

Moody, Howard. "Church, State and the Rights of Conscience." *Christianity and Crisis* 32 (1973): 292–94.

*Moore, Emily. "Abortion and Public Policy." *New York Law Forum* 17 (1971): 411–36.

———. *Induced Abortion: An Inventory of Information*. New York: International Institute for the Study of Human Reproduction, 1973.

*Newton, Lisa. "Humans and Persons: A Reply to Tristram Engelhardt." *Ethics* 85 (1975): 332–36. [See Engelhardt.]

Noonan, John T., Jr. "Abortion and the Catholic Church: A Summary History." *Natural Law Forum* 12 (1967): 85–131.

*———. "An Almost Absolute Value in History." In Feinberg, ed., *The Problem of Abortion*.

———. *The Morality of Abortion*. Cambridge, Mass.: Harvard University Press, 1970.

Notman, M. T. "Pregnancy and Abortion: Implications for Career Dropout of Professional Women." *Annals of the New York Academy of Sciences* 208 (1973): 205–10.

O'Connor, J. "On Humanity and Abortion." *Natural Law Forum* 13 (1968): 127–33.

O'Donnell, Thomas. "Abortion Is a Case of Moral Malice." In *Readings for an Introduction to Philosophy*, edited by James Hamilton, C. Regan, and B. R. Tilghman. New York: Macmillan, 1976.

Perkins, Robert, ed. *Abortion: Pro and Con*. Cambridge, Mass.: Schenkman Publishing Co., 1974.

Pole, Nelson. "To Respect Human Life." *Philosophical Context* 2 (1973): 16–22.

Prescott, James. "Abortion or the Unwanted Child." *Humanist*, March-April 1975, pp. 11–15.

*Purdy, Laura, and Tooley, Michael. "Is Abortion Murder?" In Perkins, ed., *Abortion: Pro and Con*.

Rachels, James, ed. *Moral Problems*. 2d ed. New York: Harper & Row, 1975.

Ramsey, Paul. "Abortion: A Review Article." *Thomist* 37 (1973): 174–226.

*———. "The Morality of Abortion." In Rachels, ed., *Moral Problems*.

———. "Reference Points in Deciding about Abortion." In Noonan, ed., *The Morality of Abortion.*

Richardson, Herbert. "What Is the Value of Life?" In *Updating Life and Death*, edited by Donald Cutler. Boston: Beacon Press, 1969.

*Rudinow, Joel. "On 'The Slippery Slope.'" *Analysis* 34 (1974): 173–76. [See Lindsay.]

Schulder, Diane, and Kennedy, Florynce. *Abortion Rap.* New York: McGraw-Hill, 1971.

Sloane, R. B., ed. *Abortion: Changing Views and Practices.* New York: Grune & Stratton, 1970.

Sloane, R. B., and Horvitz, D. *A General Guide to Abortion.* Chicago: Nelson Hall Publishers, 1973.

Smith, D. T., ed. *Abortion and the Law.* Cleveland: Case Western Reserve University Press, 1967.

*Sumner, L. W. "Toward a Credible View of Abortion." *Canadian Journal of Philosophy* 4 (1974): 163–81. [See Clark.]

Supreme Court, U.S. *Roe* v. *Wade*, 410 U.S. 113 (1973).

———. *Doe* v. *Bolton*, 410 U.S. 179 (1973).

———. *Griswold* v. *Connecticut*, 381 U.S. 479 (1965).

Teo, Wesley. "Abortion: The Husband's Constitutional Rights." *Ethics* 85 (1975): 337–42.

*Thomson, Judith. "A Defense of Abortion." *Philosophy and Public Affairs* 1 (1971): 47–66.

*———. "Rights and Deaths." *Philosophy and Public Affairs* 2 (1973): 146–59. [See Finnis.]

*Tooley, Michael. "Abortion and Infanticide." *Philosophy and Public Affairs* 2 (1972): 37–65. Revised version printed in Feinberg, ed., *The Problem of Abortion.*

Walbert, D., and Butler, J., eds. *Abortion, Society and the Law.* Cleveland: Case Western Reserve University Press, 1973.

*Warren, Mary Anne. "On the Moral and Legal Status of Abortion." *Monist* 57 (1973): 43–61.

Wellman, Carl. *Morals and Ethics.* Glenview, Ill.: Scott, Foresman, 1975. Chap. 7.

Werner, Richard. "Abortion: The Moral Status of the Unborn." *Social Theory and Practice* 3 (1974): 201–22.

*Wertheimer, Roger. "Understanding the Abortion Argument." *Philosophy and Public Affairs* 1 (1971): 67–95.

Williams, Glanville. "Euthanasia and Abortion." *University of Colorado Law Review* 38 (1966): 178–201.

———. *The Sanctity of Life and the Criminal Law.* New York: Knopf, 1957.

Zalba, M. "The Catholic Church's Viewpoint on Abortion." *World Medical Journal* 13 (1966): 87–93.

# Notes on Contributors

Joseph E. Barnhart is a professor of philosophy at North Texas· State University. He is the author of *Religion and the Challenge of Philosophy* (Littlefield, Adams, 1975), *The Billy Graham Religion* (Pilgrim Press, 1972), *The Study of Religion and Its Meaning: A Reappraisal after Positivism* (Mouton, forthcoming), and numerous articles in philosophy and religious journals. Dr. Barnhart co-edits the *Southwestern Journal for Social Education*.

Mary Ann Barnhart is currently doing research for a book on marriage and divorce. She has co-authored "Marital Faithfulness and Unfaithfulness," which appeared in *Morality in the Modern World* (Dickenson, 1976), and is a member of the Society for the Scientific Study of Religion.

Sandra Lee Bartky is a professor of philosophy at the University of Illinois, Chicago Circle, and chairs the women's studies program there. Her philosophical interests include Màrxism, existentialism, phenomenology, and the philosophy of feminism. She is also active in the Society for Women in Philosophy and the Chicago Women's Liberation Union.

Elizabeth L. Beardsley has taught philosophy at the University of Delaware and at Lincoln University. She is currently a professor of philosophy at Temple University, doing work on ethical theory, moral psychology, and the philosophy of law.

She has published a number of essays on ethics and the philosophy of language and is a past vice-president of the American Society for Political and Legal Philosophy.

CAROLINE BIRD is the author of numerous articles and books on feminist issues, including *Born Female* (1968), *Everything a Woman Needs to Know to Get Paid What She's Worth* (1973), and *Enterprising Women* (1976). Ms. Bird is also an active lecturer.

HOWARD COHEN teaches in the philosophy department and in the Law and Justice Program at the University of Massachusetts, Harbor Campus. His areas of interest include social philosophy, historiography, and the philosophy of history.

LAWRENCE CROCKER is an assistant professor of philosophy at the University of Washington in Seattle. He has published papers on moral theory and on Marx and Marxism.

ANNE DICKASON has taught philosophy at Colorado State University and Wake Forest University, and is currently completing her dissertation, "Sophia Denied: Philosophers' Views of Women and the Myth of Human Nature," at the University of Colorado. She has published articles on Aristotle's sea fight and on the role of biology in Plato's view of women.

FREDERICK A. ELLISTON has taught philosophy at Trinity College and York University in Canada and now teaches at Union College in Schenectady, New York. He has co-edited the collections *Philosophy and Sex* and *Husserl: Expositions and Appraisals* and is co-editor and co-translator of *Husserl: Shorter Works* (forthcoming).

JANE ENGLISH is an assistant professor of philosophy at the University of North Carolina in Chapel Hill. She has taught courses about women's rights there and at the University of Washington. The editor of the book *Sex Equality*, she has also published articles in ethics and the philosophy of science.

ANN FERGUSON received her doctorate from Brown University and is currently teaching philosophy at the University of Massachusetts in Amherst. She helped organize the first Eastern regional meeting of the Society for Women in Philosophy and is active in the Marxist Activist Philosophers group. Her interests include social thought, ethics, aesthetics, and feminist studies.

PAMELA FOA received her B.A. from Sarah Lawrence College and her Ph.D. from Stanford University. Her recent work has dealt with the intersection of metaphysics and ethics, leading to the present paper on rape, as well as to work on human rights. Dr. Foa has taught at the University of Pittsburgh and at the University of California, San Diego.

MARILYN FRYE is a feminist philosopher working primarily on the development of feminist views in moral philosophy, broadly construed. She is an assistant professor of philosophy at Michigan State University and author of several articles in the areas of philosophy of language and feminist topics.

ROBERT K. FULLINWIDER is an assistant professor of philosophy at the State University of New York at Albany. He has written on a variety of topics in ethics.

ALAN H. GOLDMAN, an assistant professor of philosophy at the University of Idaho, has published articles on social philosophy, theory of knowledge, and philosophy of mind. Since receiving his Ph.D. degree from Columbia University in 1972, he has held fellowships from the National Endowment for the Humanities at Tufts and Princeton universities. The article included in this text was written while he was at Tufts.

SUSAN GRIFFIN is a poet and an instructor in women's studies at the University of California Extension, Berkeley. Her first book of poetry, *Dear Sky*, and a collection of her short stories, *The Sink*, have been published by the Shameless Hussy Press, and her second book of poetry, *Let Them Be Said*, was published by Mama Press. Her play *Voices*, written with funds from the National Endowment for the Arts, went into production at radio station KPFA in San Francisco early in 1974.

PATRICK GRIM, who holds a Ph.D. in philosophy from Boston University, presently teaches at the State University of New York at Stonybrook. He has taught at Boston University as well as in the Cambridge Adult Education Program, and his current interests include ethics, philosophy of science, and philosophy of religion.

ALISON JAGGAR currently teaches philosophy at the University of Cincinnati. Her early training and research were in the fields of philosophical methodology, philosophy of language, and analytic philosophy. More recently, however, her interest has turned toward moral and political philosophy, especially the application of systematic political philosophies to contemporary normative issues such as those raised by feminists.

SARA ANN KETCHUM is an assistant professor of philosophy at the State University of New York at Oswego. She has published on feminism and philosophy and is currently working on the development of a systematic feminist social and political philosophy.

CAROLYN KORSMEYER received her Ph.D. from Brown University in 1972 and is now an assistant professor of philosophy at the State University of New York at Buffalo. In addition to her interest in issues of feminist philosophy, her major area of research is in the fields of aesthetics and philosophy of art.

CLORINDA MARGOLIS is head of the Consultation and Education Service, Jefferson Community Mental Health Center, and an associate professor in the department of psychiatry at Thomas Jefferson University. She has published on such issues as drugs, homosexuality, women's roles, and the Karen Ann Quinlan case. She is currently working on a book on power.

JOSEPH MARGOLIS is a professor of philosophy at Temple University and editor of *Philosophical Monographs*. His most recently published books include *Negativities: The Limits of Life* (1975) and *Art and Philosophy* (1976). His latest book, *Persons and Minds*, is forthcoming.

JANICE MOULTON, who received her doctorate degree at the University of Chicago, has taught at the University of North Carolina, Temple University, and the University of Maryland. She has served as the executive secretary for the Society for Women in Philosophy and is on the Committee on Research as well as the Executive Committee of the American Philosophical

Association. She is the author of *Guidebook for Publishing Philosophy*, and has contributed to *Signs, Journal of Philosophy*, and *International Journal of Man-Machine Studies*. She is currently in the department of psychology at Duke University.

SUSAN T. NICHOLSON received a Ph.D. in philosophy at the University of Pittsburgh and has taught for several years at Chatham College in Pittsburgh. Her most recent work is *Abortion and the Roman Catholic Church* (forthcoming), published under the auspices of the American Academy of Religion.

LYLA H. O'DRISCOLL, whose research concentrates on issues in ethics as well as political and social philosophy, is a visiting assistant professor of philosophy at Iowa State University.

ONORA O'NEILL teaches philosophy at Barnard College, Columbia University. She has written in the fields of ethics and social philosophy, and on the philosophy of Immanuel Kant.

SUSAN RAE PETERSON received her B.A. from the New School in New York City, her M.A. from San Francisco State College, and is currently completing her Ph.D. dissertation at the University of Toronto. Her philosophic interests range from political philosophy, philosophy of law, and meta-ethics to fields such as criminology and feminist theory. She is currently researching a book on propaganda.

ELIZABETH RAPAPORT is an assistant professor of philosophy at Boston University. She has written articles on ethics, politics, and feminist issues. Her current interests lie primarily in the field of political theory.

PAUL SAGAL is presently a visiting associate professor at New Mexico State University. His articles have appeared in many philosophy journals, and he has completed a number of book-length manuscripts which are being reviewed for publication. His current interests include meta-philosophy, philosophy of economics, and moral and political philosophy.

CAROLYN M. SHAFER studied philosophy at the University of Georgia and the University of Pittsburgh. She is a lesbian femin-

*73*

ist activist and theoretician and is manager of a branch of the Feminist Federal Credit Union.

JOYCE TREBILCOT teaches feminist philosophy at Washington University in St. Louis, where she helped found a women's studies program. She has also taught at the University of California at Santa Barbara, Bryn Mawr College, and the University of Wisconsin in Milwaukee. "Two Forms of Androgynism" was written as part of a study of sex and values supported by a National Endowment for the Humanities Younger Humanist Fellowship.

VIRGINIA VALIAN received her Ph.D. in psychology from Northeastern University, with psycholinguistics as her field of specialization. She is presently an assistant professor at the Graduate Center of the City University of New York, and her research interests include sentence production, theories of performance, and the nature of mental representation.

MARY VETTERLING-BRAGGIN received her doctorate degree in the philosophy of science from Boston University. She has taught philosophy at Union College in Schenectady, New York, and now works in the microscope division of E. Leitz, Inc. Her major fields of interest include the philosophy of natural and social science, as well as feminist theory, particularly theories of preferential hiring and sexism in ordinary language.

FT 39 287